A Computational Model
of Natural Language Communication

Roland Hausser

A Computational Model of Natural Language Communication

Interpretation, Inference, and Production
in Database Semantics

 Springer

Author

Roland Hausser

Friedrich Alexander University Erlangen Nürnberg
Department of Computational Linguistics
Bismarckstr. 6
91054 Erlangen, Germany
rrh@linguistik.uni-erlangen.de

Cover picture: Japanese, katabori netsuke, foo dog (temple lion),
Meiji period, ivory, 3.9 x 2.8 x 3.8 cm, private collection

ACM Computing Classification (1998): I.2, H.1.2, H.3.1, H.5.2, D.2.11, J.5

ISBN 978-3-642-07130-0   e-ISBN 978-3-540-35477-2

Springer is a part of Springer Science+Business Media

springer.com

© Springer-Verlag Berlin Heidelberg 2010
Printed in Germany

Cover design: KünkelLopka Werbeagentur, Heidelberg

Preface

In the preface to the first edition of *The Principia*,[1] Sir Isaac Newton distinguished two aspects of mechanics: theoretical and practical. The theoretical aspect, called rational by Newton, consists in accurate demonstration. The practical aspect includes all the manual arts. What would be the result of applying a corresponding distinction to the current state of linguistics?

Instead of first praising the importance of our field – as Newton would – let us go straight to the questions at hand: What is theoretical linguistics and what is practical linguistics? Practical linguistics is instantiated by such tasks as speech recognition, desktop publishing, word processing, machine translation, content extraction, classification, querying the Internet, automatic tutoring, dialogue systems, and all the other applications involving natural language. They have generated a huge demand for practical linguistic methods.

Compared to the users' needs and expectations, however, the results leave much to be desired. Today, the most successful applications in practical linguistics are based on the methods of statistics and metadata mark-up. These are *smart solutions*,[2] which try to get by without a general theory of how communicating with natural language works. Instead they aim to maximally exploit the special properties and natural limitations of each application or kind of application.

Now consider practical mechanics: It is instantiated by tasks ranging from accurately predicting the tides, to predicting the future positions of the planets, to aiming cannon balls, to landing on the moon. These applications have created an equally large demand for applied methods as in linguistics.

In contrast to linguistics, however, the field of mechanics was able to satisfy any such demands far beyond the users' imagination. This was possible because Newton's general theory can be translated into the specific applications while maintaining compatibility with traditional craft skills. Each translation is hard work and requires theoretical knowledge as well as practical experience, but the results are nothing but spectacular.

The example of Newton's mechanics leads naturally to the question: Can we do the same in linguistics? Can we conceive a new framework suitable to fulfill all the

---

[1] Orginal Latin title: *Philosophiæ Naturalis Principia Mathematica* (1687), complete English title *The Principia: Mathematical Principles of Natural Philosophy*.

[2] Cf. FoCL, Section 2.3. The alternative is a solid solution.

wide-ranging demands of the users by simply translating the linguistic theory into the limited and specialized contexts of various practical applications? This question may be taken as a worthy challenge to our basic research.

As a first step towards a complete, general linguistic framework, let us reconstruct the cognitive 'mechanics' of natural language communication between humans. The theory, called *Database Semantics*[3] (DBS) is presented here as the declarative specification of a talking robot. It is in the nature of our project that its potential to improve practical applications correlates directly with its relative success in adequately modeling human cognition.[4]

The declarative specification of a talking robot must be designed as a *functional* model, which effectively realizes the mechanism of natural language communication. To ensure *completeness*, the model must take the language-based interaction between humans as its prototype. The model's functionality and data coverage must be *verified* automatically by an efficient implementation as a running computer program. This combination of functionality, completeness, and verifiability constitutes the best scientific basis for the long-term success of *upscaling* the model.

The resulting system is able to serve in all the practical applications involving natural language communication. In most cases it is sufficient to simply reduce the functionality and the data coverage of the model to fit the demands of the application at hand. For example, when using the cognition of the talking robot for building an automatic dialogue system used over the phone, there is no need for artificial vision, manipulation, or locomotion.[5]

Other applications, notably machine translation, not only allow a reduction, but also require an extension of the theory. For such extensions, however, Database Semantics provides a solid basis, given that it models monolingual communication, including monolingual language understanding.

Furthermore, any application-independent (theoretical) improvements regarding the data coverage of the lexicon, of automatic word form recognition, of syntactic–semantic parsing, of absolute and episodic world knowledge, of inferencing, etc., may directly benefit existing practical applications simply by routinely replacing their components with improved versions. This is possible because the theory provides functionally motivated modules with clearly defined interfaces.

The following pages aim at presenting Database Semantics as directly and simply as possible. Intended audiences are graduate students, researchers, and software engi-

---

[3] As the name of a specific scientific theory, the term Database Semantics is written with initial capital letters. This use is distinct from referrring to generic issues, for example semantic constraints on databases (cf. Bertossi, Katona, Schewe, and Thalheim (eds.) 2003).

[4] Like any basic science with practical ramifications, a computational reconstruction of natural language communcation raises the threat of possible misuse. This must be curtailed by developing responsible guidelines for clearly defined laws to protect privacy and intellectual property while maintaining academic liberty, access to information, and freedom of discourse.

[5] Similar reductions apply to such applications as automatic grammar checking, content extraction, indexing to improve recall and precision of Internet querying, or supporting automatic speech recognition.

neers in linguistics and natural language processing. The text may also be of interest to scholars in philosophy of language, cognitive psychology, and artificial intelligence.

As background literature for readers who are new to computational linguistics in general and Database Semantics in particular, *Foundations of Computational Linguistics* (1999, 2nd ed. 2001) is recommended. FoCL'99 is a textbook that systematically describes the traditional components of grammar, compares a wide range of different linguistic approaches in their historical settings, and develops the SLIM theory of language, which is also used here.

A complementary effort in cognitive psychology is the ACT-R theory by Anderson (cf. Anderson and Lebiere 1998). Like Database Semantics, ACT-R is essentially symbol-based rather than statistical, and uses computational modeling as the method of verification. However, ACT-R focusses on memory, learning, and problem solving, while Database Semantics concentrates on modeling the speaker and the hearer mode in natural language communication.

ACKNOWLEDGEMENTS

This book evolved in the context of the laboratory of Computational Linguistics of the University Erlangen–Nürnberg (CLUE). I am grateful to the members of my team (in alphabetical order), Matthias Bethke, Johannes Handl, Besim Kabashi, and Jörg Kapfer, who discussed the technical and conceptual issues of the theory and the implementation at great length and in great depth, and contributed many ideas. I am also grateful to my students, especially Arkadius Kycia, who programmed the first Java^{TM} implementation of DBS.1 and DBS.2 in the speaker, the think, and the hearer mode. I would like to thank Brian MacWhinney (Carnegie Mellon University, Pittsburgh) and Haitao Liu (Communications University of China, Bejing) for providing detailed comments on an earlier stage of the manuscript. Mike Daly (Dallas) proofread the manuscript and made many valuable suggestions. I am indebted to Marie Hučinova (Charles University, Prague), Vladimir Petroff (Northeastern University, Boston), Kiyong Lee (Korea University, Seoul), and a team of copy editors at Springer for numerous improvements in the final phase of the manuscript. All remaining mistakes are mine.

February 2006   Roland Hausser
Erlangen–Nürnberg

ABBREVIATIONS REFERRING TO PREVIOUS WORK

SCG'84   = Hausser, R. (1984) *Surface Compositional Grammar*, pp. 274,
            München: Wilhelm Fink Verlag

NEWCAT'86   = Hausser, R. (1986) *NEWCAT: Parsing Natural Language Using
            Left-Associative Grammar*, Lecture Notes in Computer Science 231,
            pp. 540, Berlin Heidelberg New York: Springer

CoL'89   = Hausser, R. (1989) *Computation of Language, An Essay on Syntax,
            Semantics, and Pragmatics in Natural Man-Machine Communication*,
            Symbolic Computation: Artificial Intelligence, pp. 425, Berlin
            Heidelberg New York: Springer

TCS'92   = Hausser, R. (1992) "Complexity in Left-Associative Grammar,"
            Theoretical Computer Science, 106.2:283-308, Amsterdam: Elsevier

FoCL'99   = Hausser, R. (1999/2001) *Foundations of Computational Linguistics,
            Human–Computer Communication in Natural Language, 2nd ed.*,
            pp. 578, Berlin Heidelberg New York: Springer

AIJ'01   = Hausser, R. (2001) "Database Semantics for natural language."
            Artificial Intelligence, 130.1:27–74, Amsterdam: Elsevier

L&I'05   = Hausser, R. (2005) "Memory-Based pattern completion in Database
            Semantics," *Language and Information*, 9.1:69–92, Seoul: Korean
            Society for Language and Information

Contents

Part II. The Major Constructions of Natural Language

Part III. The Declarative Specification of Formal Fragments

Appendices

Introduction

I. BASIC ASSUMPTIONS

A computational model of natural language communication cannot be limited to the grammatical analysis of the language signs. Instead it must start with the general recognition and action procedures of the cognitive agents, treating language interpretation and production as special cases.

Recognition and action are based on the external interfaces of the cognitive agent's body, which contains a database for storing content. Agents without language have only one level of cognition, called the context level. Agents with language have two levels of cognition: the context level and the language level. The connection between language and the world, i.e., reference, is established solely by the cognitive procedures of the agent. Reference is based (i) on the external interfaces, and (ii) on relating the cognitive levels of language and context using pattern matching.[1]

Database Semantics (DBS) models the behavior of natural agents, including language communication, by automatically (a) reading propositional content resulting from recognition into the agent's database and (b) reading content out of the agent's database resulting in action. Recognition and action are (c) related by a control structure based on reasoning which results in sensible (meaningful, rational, successful) conduct.

II. COMPONENTS OF A COGNITIVE AGENT

At the most abstract level, cognitive agents consist of three basic components. These are (i) the external interfaces, (ii) the database, and (iii) the algorithm.[2] They use a common format, called the data structure,[3] for representing and processing content.

---

[1] Autonomy from the metalanguage. See FoCL'99, pp. 382–383.

[2] These components correspond roughly to those of a von Neumann machine (vNm): The external interfaces represent the vNm input-output device, the database corresponds to the vNm memory, and the algorithm performs the functions of the vNm arithmetic-logic unit. For a comparison of standard computers, robots, and virtual reality machines see FoCL'99, p. 16.

[3] The term "data structure" is closely related in meaning to the term "data type." Even though there has been some argument that the format in question should be called an abstract data type rather than a data structure, the latter term is preferred here to avoid confusion with the classic type/token distinction (cf. Sect. 4.2). It is for the same reason that we use the term "kind of sign" rather than "sign type" (cf. Sect. 2.6), "kind of sentence" rather than "sentence type," "kind of word" rather than "word type," "kind of coordination" rather than "coordination type," etc.

The external interfaces are needed by the agent for recognition and action. Recognition is based, for example, on eyes to see, and ears to hear. Action is based, for example, on a mouth to talk, hands to manipulate, and legs to walk. Without them the agent would not be able to tell us what it perceives and to do what we tell it to do.

The agent's database is needed for the storage and retrieval of content provided by the interfaces. Without it, the agent would not be able to determine whether or not it has seen an object before, it could not remember the words of language and their meaning, and it would be limited to reflexes connecting input and output directly.

The algorithm is needed to connect the interfaces and the database (i) for reading content provided by recognition into the database, and (ii) for reading content out of the database into action. Also, the algorithm must (iii) process the content in the database for determining goals, planning actions, and deriving generalizations.

In the cognition of natural agents, the external interfaces, the data structure, and the algorithm interact very closely. Therefore, in a computational model of natural cognition they must be codesigned within a joint functional cycle. The three basic components may be simple initially, but they must be *general* and *functionally integrated* into a coherent framework from the outset.

III. TREATING NATURAL LANGUAGE

A model of natural language communication requires the traditional components of grammar, i.e., the language-specific *lexicon* and the language-specific rules of *morphology*, *syntax*, and *semantics*. During communication, these components must cooperate in (i) the hearer mode, (ii) the think mode, and (iii) the speaker mode.

In the hearer mode, the external interfaces provide the input, consisting of language signs. The algorithm parses the signs into a representation of content which is stored in the database. The parsing of the signs is based on a system of automatic word form recognition and a system of automatic syntactic–semantic analysis.

In the think mode, the algorithm is used for autonomously navigating through the database, thus selectively activating content. This general method of navigation is also used for deriving inferences which relate the current input and the content stored in the database to derive action.

In the speaker mode, the activation of content and the derivation of inferences is used for the conceptualization of language production, i.e., choosing what to say. The production of language from activated content requires the selection of language-dependent word form surfaces, and the handling of word order and agreement.

IV. DIFFERENT DEGREES OF DETAIL

In the following chapters, some components of DBS are worked out in great detail, while others are only sketched in terms of their input, their function, and their output. This is unavoidable because of the magnitude of the task, its interdisciplinary nature, and the fact that some technologies are more easily available than others.

For example, realizing Database Semantics as the prototype of an actual robot with external interfaces for recognition and action, i.e., artificial vision, speech recognition, robotic manipulation, and robotic locomotion, was practically out of reach. This is regrettable because the content in the database is built from concepts which are "perceptually grounded" in the agents' recognition and action procedures (Roy 2003).

While the external interfaces of the artificial agent are described here at a high level of abstraction, the algorithm and the data structure are worked out not only in principle, but are developed as "fragments," that model the hearer, the think, and the speaker mode using concrete examples. These fragments are defined as explicit rule systems and are verified by means of a concomitant implementation in Java^{TM}.

V. AVAILABLE SYSTEMS AND APPROACHES

Today many kinds of parsers are available. Some are based on statistical methods, such as the Chunk Parser (Abney 1991; Déjean 1998; Vergne and Giguet 1998), the Brill Tagger and Parser (Brill 1993, 1994), and the Head-Driven Parser (Collins 1999; Charniak 2001). Others are based on the rules of a Phrase Structure Grammar such as the Earley Algorithm (Earley 1970), the Chart Parser (Kay 1980; Pereira and Shieber 1987), the CYK Parser (Cocke and Schwartz 1970; Younger 1967; Kasami 1965), and the Tomita Parser (Tomita 1986).

Also, there are many theories of syntax. Some are based on Categorial Grammar (Leśniewski 1929; Ajdukiewicz 1935; Bar-Hillel 1964). Related to Categorial Grammar is the approach of Valency Theory (Tesnière 1959; Herbst 1999; Ágel 2000; Herbst et al. 2004) and Dependency Grammar (Mel'čuk 1988; Hudson 1991; Hellwig 2003). Others are based on Phrase Structure Grammar (Post 1936; Chomsky 1957), for example Generalized Phrase Structure Grammar (GPSG, Gazdar et al. 1985), Lexical Functional Grammar (LFG, Bresnan 1982, 2001), Head-Driven Phrase Structure Grammar (HPSG, Pollard and Sag 1987, 1994), and Construction Grammar (Östman and Fried 2004; Fillmore et al. forthcoming).

Similarly, there are many approaches to semantic analysis. Some are based on Model Theory (Tarski 1935, 1944; Montague 1974), others on Speech Act Theory (Austin 1962; Grice 1957, 1965; Searle 1969), or Semantic Networks (Quillian 1968; Sowa 1984, 2000). In addition, there is Rhetorical Structure Theory (RST, Mann and Thompson 1993), Text Linguistics (Halliday and Hasan 1976; Beaugrande and Dressler 1981) as well as different approaches to the definition of concepts in cognitive psychology, such as the schema, the template, the prototype, and the geon approach (cf. Sect. 4.2).

This list of partial systems may be continued by pointing to efforts at providing a more general theory of machine translation (Dorr 1993), finding a universal set of semantic primitives (Schank and Abelson 1977; Wierzbicka 1991), application-oriented systems of language production (Reiter and Dale 1997), as well as efforts to improve indexing and retrieval on the Internet by means of metadata mark-up based on XML,

RDF, and OWL (Berners-Lee, Hendler, and Lassila 2001). This raises the question: Which of the partial systems should be chosen to serve as components of a general, complete, coherent, computational model of natural language communication?

On the one hand, there is little interest in reinventing a component that is already available. On the other hand, reusing partial theories by integrating them into a general system of natural language communication comes at a considerable cost: Given that the available theories have originated in different traditions and for different purposes, much time and effort would have to be spent on making them compatible.

Apart from the time-consuming labor of integrating partial theories there is the more general question of which of them could be suitable in principle to be part of a coherent, functional theory of how natural language communication works. This question has been investigated in FoCL'99 for the majority of the systems listed above.[4]

As a result, Database Semantics was developed from scratch. Thereby many of the ideas and methods of the above systems have been absorbed. The most basic ideas are the notions of a proposition, as formulated by Aristotle, and of the time-linear structure of language, as emphasized by de Saussure.

While our grammatical analysis is very traditional in many respects, it does not adopt the commonly practiced separation between syntax (combinatorics) and semantics (interpretation). Instead, syntactic and semantic composition are derived simultaneously (cf. Tugwell 1998) in a time-linear order. Thus, the only difference between a purely syntactic and a syntactic–semantic grammar is that the former defines (i) fewer lexical properties of the parts, and (ii) fewer relations between the parts, than the latter.

VI. FORMAL FOUNDATIONS

Database Semantics is the first and so far the only rule system in which natural language interpretation and production are reconstructed as *turn-taking*, i.e., the cognitive agent's ability to switch between the speaker and the hearer mode. The reconstruction of the communication cycle in Database Semantics is founded on two innovations:

The *algorithm* of Left-Associative Grammar (LA-grammar, TCS'92):
LA-grammar is based on the principle of possible continuations. This is in contrast to the algorithms commonly used in today's linguistics, namely Phrase Structure Grammar (PSG) and Categorial Grammar (CG), which are based on the principle of possible substitutions. Computing possible continuations models the time-linear structure of natural language and permits us to handle turn-taking as the interaction of three kinds of LA-grammar, namely LA-hear, LA-think, and LA-speak.

---

[4] These analyses are conducted at a high level of abstraction. For example, rather than discussing in detail how Situation Semantics might differ from Discourse Semantics, FoCL'99 concentrates on the more basic question of whether or not a metalanguage-based truth-conditional approach could in principle be suitable for a computational model. Similarly, rather than comparing GPSG, LFG, HPSG, and GB, FoCL'99 concentrates on the question of whether or not the algorithm of substitution-based Phrase Structure Grammar could in principle be suitable for modeling the speaker and the hearer mode.

The *data structure* of a Word Bank (AIJ'01):
A Word Bank stores propositional content in the form of flat (nonrecursive) feature structures called *proplets*. While the substitution-based approaches embed, for example, the feature structure of the subject into the feature structure of the verb (unification, cf. 3.4.5), no such embedding is allowed in Database Semantics. Instead, the individual proplets code the grammatical relations between them in terms of features (i.e., attribute-value pairs) only. As a consequence, content represented as a set of proplets is well-suited for (i) storage and retrieval in a database, and for (ii) pattern matching, as needed to relate (iia) the levels of grammar rules and language (cf. 3.4.3 and 3.5.1) and (iib) the levels of context and language (cf. 3.3.1).

The algorithm of LA-grammar and the data structure of a Word Bank together provide the basis for an autonomous navigation through propositional content, utilizing the grammatical relations between proplets as a kind of railroad system and LA-grammar as a kind of locomotive which moves a unique focus point along the rails. This new way of combining a data structure and an algorithm serves as our basic model of thought. It may be used for merely activating content selectively in the Word Bank (free association), but may also be extended into a control structure which relates the agent's recognition and action using stored knowledge and inferences.

VII. SCOPE OF THE LINGUISTIC ANALYSIS

Our linguistic analysis aims at a systematic development of the major constructions of natural language. These are (i) functor–argument structure, (ii) coordination, and (iii) coreference. They occur intra- and extrapropositionally, and may be freely mixed.

The major constructions are analyzed in a strictly time-linear derivation order, in the hearer mode and in the speaker mode. It is shown that the much greater functional completeness of Database Semantics as compared to the sign-oriented approaches is no obstacle to a straightforward, linguistically well-motivated, homogeneous analysis, which provides for a highly efficient computational implementation.

The analyses include constructions which have eluded a generally accepted treatment within Nativism.[5] These are the gapping constructions (cf. Chaps. 8 and 9), especially "right-node-raising", and coreference (cf. Chap. 10) in the "donkey" and the "Bach–Peters" sentence.

VIII. STRUCTURE OF THE BOOK

The content of this book is presented in three parts. Part I presents the general framework of the SLIM Theory of Language (FoCL'99) in terms of the cognitive agent's external interfaces, data structure, and algorithm. This part addresses many questions

---

[5] Nativism (Chomsky 1957 et seq.) is a sign-oriented theory of language using substitution-based Phrase Structure Grammar. Nativism aims at characterizing the speaker hearer's innate knowledge of language (competence) – excluding the use of language in communication (performance).

which are crucial for the overall system, but cannot be pursued in further detail. Examples are the nature of concepts and their role in recognition and action, the reference mechanisms of the different sign kinds, and the formal structure of the context level.

Part II systematically analyzes the major constructions of natural language, presented as schematic derivations of English examples in the hearer and the speaker mode. The hearer mode analyses show the strictly time-linear coding of functor–argument structure and coordination into sets of proplets, treating coreference as a secondary relation based on inferencing. The speaker mode analyses show the retrieval-based navigation through a Word Bank (conceptualization), as well as the language-dependent sequencing of word forms and the precipitation of function words.

Part III presents fragments of English. Expanding on Montague's use of this term, a "fragment" refers to a system of natural language communication which is functionally complete but has limited coverage. The fragments show the interpretation and the production of small sample texts in complete detail, explicitly defining the lexicon and the LA-hear, LA-think, and LA-speak grammars required.

The different scope and the different degrees of abstraction characterizing the three parts may be summarized schematically as follows:

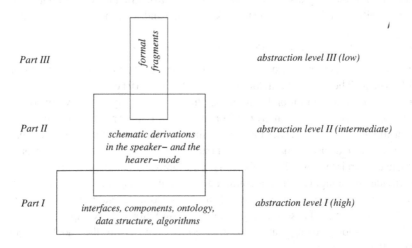

A high degree of abstraction corresponds to a low degree of linguistic and technical detail, and vice versa.

The general framework outlined in Part I is built upon in Part II. The methods of analysis presented in Part II are built upon in Part III. The analyses and definitions of Part II and III have served as the declarative specification of an implementation called JSLIM (Kycia 2004), which is currently being reimplemented by Jörg Kapfer and Johannes Handl using Java^{TM} version 5 (1. 5).

The Communication Mechanism of Cognition

1. Matters of Method

In science, the method of verification is the outermost line of defense against error. It may be crude as long as it can be made objective. Designed for a particular theory (or kind of theories), the verification method should interact with its theory in such a way that there constantly arise new questions of a kind (i) which can be decided more or less conclusively by the method of verification, and (ii) the answers to which are relevant to the theory's further development.

In natural science, verification consists in experiments which are (i) specified exactly in quantitative terms and (ii) which can be repeated by anybody anywhere. This requires that the notions and structures of the theory are so precise that they are suitable for the scientific setup of experiments. For the grammatical analysis of language, however, the quantitative verification method happens to be unsuitable.

The method we propose instead consists in building a functional model of natural language communication. This requires (i) a declarative specification in combination with an efficiently running implementation (prototype of a talking robot), (ii) establishing objective channels of observation, and (iii) equating the adequacy of the robot's behavior with the correctness of the theory – which means that the robot must have (iv) the same kinds of external interfaces as humans, and process language in a way which is (v) input/output-equivalent with the language processing of humans.

1.1 Sign- or Agent-Oriented Analysis of Language?

A natural language manifests itself in the form of signs, the structures of which have evolved as conventions within a language community. Produced by cognitive agents in the speaker mode and interpreted by agents in the hearer mode, these signs are used for the transfer of content from the speaker to the hearer. Depending on whether the scientific analysis concentrates on the isolated signs or on the communicating agents, we may distinguish between *sign-oriented* and *agent-oriented* approaches.[1]

Sign-oriented approaches like Generative Grammar, Truth-Conditional Semantics, and Text Linguistics analyze expressions of natural language as objects, fixed on paper, magnetic tape, or by electronic means. They abstract away from the aspect of communication and are therefore neither intended nor suitable to model the speaker

---

[1] Clark (1996) distinguishes between the *language-as-product* and *language-as-action* traditions.

and the hearer mode. Instead, linguistic examples, isolated from the communicating agents, are analyzed as hierarchical structures which are formally based on the principle of *possible substitutions*.

The agent-oriented approach of Database Semantics (DBS), in contrast, analyzes signs as the result of the speaker's language production and as the starting point of the hearer's language interpretation. Inclusion of the agents' production and interpretation procedures requires a time-linear analysis which is formally based on the principle of *possible continuations*.

The goal of Database Semantics is a theory of natural language communication which is complete with respect to function and data coverage, of low mathematical complexity, and is suitable for an efficient implementation on the computer. The central question of Database Semantics is:

How does communicating with natural language work?

In the most simple form, this question is answered as follows.

Natural language communication takes place between cognitive agents. They have real bodies "out there" in the world with external interfaces for nonverbal recognition and action at the context level, and verbal recognition and action at the language level. Each agent contains a database in which contents are stored. These contents consist of the agent's knowledge, its memories, current recognition, intentions, plans, etc.

The cognitive agents can switch between the speaker and the hearer mode (turn-taking).[2] In a communication procedure, an agent in the speaker mode codes content from its database into signs of language which are realized externally via the language output interface. These signs are recognized by another agent in the hearer mode via the language input interface, their content is decoded, and is then stored in the second agent's database. This procedure is successful if the content coded by the speaker is decoded and stored equivalently by the hearer.

In Database Semantics, the modeling of turn-taking is based on a special data structure in combination with the time-linear algorithm of Left-Associative Grammar (LA-grammar).[3] The algorithm is used in three variants, called LA-hear, LA-think, and LA-speak. In communication, these three LA-grammars cooperate as follows:

1.1.1 THE BASIC MODEL OF TURN-TAKING

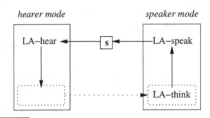

---

[2] For a study of turn-taking see Thórisson (2002).

[3] For the formal definition and complexity analysis of LA-grammar as well as a detailed comparison with Phrase Structure Grammar and Categorial Grammar see FoCL'99, Part II.

In the agent shown on the right (speaker mode), LA-think selectively activates content stored in the agent's database. The activated content is mapped into surfaces of a natural language by LA-speak, which are realized as external signs (represented by the small box containing **s**). In the agent shown on the left (hearer mode), LA-hear interprets the signs, which are stored in the agent's database.

The representation of turn-taking shown in 1.1.1 may be interpreted in two ways:

1.1.2 TWO VIEWS OF TURN-TAKING

1. *Viewed from the outside:*
   Two communicating agents are observed as they are taking turns. This is represented by 1.1.1 when the two boxes are taken to be two different agents, one in the hearer and the other in the speaker mode.

2. *Viewed from the inside:*
   One communicating agent is observed as it switches between being the speaker and the hearer. This is represented by 1.1.1 when the two boxes are taken to be the same agent switching between the speaker and the hearer mode (with the dotted right-hand arrow indicating the switch).

In DBS, turn-taking is regarded as a well-defined, well-motivated computational problem, which is central to the linguistic analysis of natural language: all syntactic and semantic analysis must be integrated into turn-taking as the most basic mechanism of communication. Without it, there is only one-sided monologue as the limiting case.

1.2 Verification Principle

Our theory of natural language communication is developed as a functional model, presented as a *declarative specification* for an efficient computer program with associated hardware. A declarative specification describes the necessary properties of a software, such as the external interfaces, the data structure, and the algorithm. Thereby, the accidental[4] properties of an implementation, such as the choice of programming language or the stylistic idiosyncrasies of the programmer, are abstracted away from.

In contrast to an algebraic definition[5] in logic, a declarative specification is not based purely on set theory. Instead, it takes a procedural point of view, specifying the general architecture in terms of components with input and output conditions as well as the functional flow through the system. A declarative specification must be general enough to provide a solid mathematical foundation and structure, and detailed enough to permit easy programming in different environments.

A declarative specification is needed because machine code is not easily read by humans. Even programs written in a higher level programming language such as Lisp

---

[4] The term accidental is used here in the philosophical tradition of Aristotle, who distinguishes between the necessary and the accidental (or incidental – kata sumbebêkos).

[5] The algebraic definition of LA-grammar in CoL'89 benefited greatly from help by Dana Scott.

are meaningful only to experts. What one would like to see in a piece of software is the *abstract functional solution* to the task it was designed to perform.

The declarative specification for a certain application consists of two levels: (i) a general theoretical framework (e.g., a functional system of natural language communication) and (ii) a specialization of the general framework to a specific application (e.g., English, German, Korean, or any other natural language). The theoretical framework in combination with a specialized application may in turn be realized (iii) in various different implementations, written in Lisp, C, or Java, for example.

1.2.1 CORRELATION OF DECLARATIVE SPECIFICATION AND IMPLEMENTATIONS

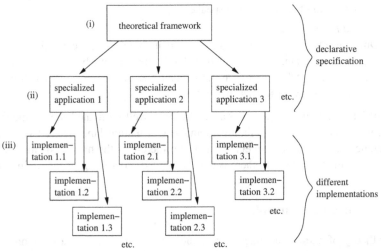

A declarative specification may have many different implementations which are equivalent with respect to the necessary properties. In Database Semantics, the evolving declarative specification must always be accompanied by at least one up-to-date implementation in order to automatically demonstrate the functioning of the theory in its current stage, and to test it with respect to an ever-widening range of various tasks. In this way, errors, incompletenesses, and other weaknesses of the current stage may be determined (explicit hypothesis formation, cf. FoCL'99, 7.2.3), which is a precondition for developing the next improved stage of the declarative specification.

The cycle of theory development and automatic testing is the *verification method* of Database Semantics. It differs from the quantitative methods of the natural sciences (repeatability of experiments) as well as the logical-axiomatic methods of mathematics (proof of consistency), though it is compatible with them.

The verification method[6] of Database Semantics is important for the following reasons. First, the signs of natural language are based on conventions which are not sus-

---

[6] See also FoCL'99, Introduction VIII–X.

ceptible to the quantitative methods of the natural sciences. Second, the analysis of the natural languages in linguistics and neighboring fields such as the philosophy of language is fragmented into a very large number of different schools and subschools, which raises the question of their comparative evaluation.

1.3 Equation Principle

Database Semantics aims at modeling the language communication of artificial agents as naturally as possible for two reasons. First, maximal *user-friendliness* should be provided in practical applications. User-friendliness in man–machine communication means that the human and the robot can understand each other (i) correctly and (ii) without the human having to adapt to the machine.[7]

Second, long-term *upscalability* in theory development should be ensured. Upscaling in the construction of a talking robot means that one can proceed without difficulty from the current prototype to one of greater functional completeness and/or data coverage.[8] In the history of science, difficulties in upscaling have practically always indicated a fundamental problem with the theory in question.[9]

To ensure user-friendliness and upscalability in the long run, Database Semantics must strive to approximate at the various levels of abstraction what has been called "psychological reality." For this purpose, we propose the following principle, which equates the correctness of the theoretical description with the behavioral adequacy of the electronic model (prototype of a talking robot).

1.3.1 THE EQUATION PRINCIPLE OF DATABASE SEMANTICS

1. The more realistic the reconstruction of cognition, the better the functioning of the model.

---

[7] For this, the robot must be designed to have procedural counterparts of human notions. For example, in order to understand the word red, the robot must be capable of physically selecting the red objects from a set; in order to understand the notion of being happily surprised, the robot must be capable of experiencing this emotion itself; etc.

Given that the technical preconditions for this kind of user-friendliness will not become available for some time, Liu (2001) proposes to integrate current robotic capabilities with practical tasks guided by humans. This is a positive example of a smart solution, like the use of restricted language in machine translation (cf. FoCL'99, p. 47).

[8] For example, functional completeness requires the ability of automatic word form recognition in principle. Extending the data coverage means that more and more word forms of the language can be recognized; similarly, functional completeness requires the ability of contextual action in principle. Extending the data coverage means that more and more contextual action types such as different kinds of locomotion, manipulation, etc., become available.

[9] Problems with upscaling in Truth-Conditional Semantics arise in the attempts to handle the Epimenides Paradox (cf. FoCL'99, Sect. 19.5), propositional attitudes (cf. ibid, Sect. 20.3), and vagueness (ibid, Sect. 20.5). Problems with upscaling in Generative Grammar arise in the attempts to handle the constituent structure paradox (ibid, Sect. 8.5) and gapping constructions (cf. Chaps. 8 and 9 below).

2. The better the functioning of the model, the more realistic the reconstruction of cognition.

The first part of the Equation Principle looks for support from and convergence with the neighboring sciences in order to improve the performance of the prototype. This means, for example, that we avoid conflicts with established facts or strong conjectures regarding the phylogenetical and the ontogenetical development as provided by ethology and developmental psychology, include the functional explanations of anatomy and physiology, and take seriously the results of mathematical complexity theory (no undecidable or exponential algorithms).

The second part of the equation principle provides a heuristic strategy in light of the fact that the "real" software structures of cognition (at their various levels of abstraction) are not accessible to direct observation.[10] Our strategy tries to achieve a realistic reconstruction indirectly by aiming for functional completeness and completeness of data coverage in the incremental upscaling of an artificial cognitive agent.

1.4 Objectivation Principle

For a functional reconstruction of cognition in general and natural language communication in particular, different kinds of data are available. The differences stem in part from alternative constellations in which the data originate, and in part from alternative channels which are used in the respective constellations.

The constellations regard the interaction between (i) the user, (ii) the scientist, and (iii) the electronic model (robot). They are distinguished as follows:

1.4.1 CONSTELLATIONS PROVIDING DIFFERENT KINDS OF DATA

1. Interaction between (i) the user and (iii) the robot

2. Interaction between (i) the user and (ii) the scientist

3. Interaction between (ii) the scientist and (iii) the robot

Depending on the constellation, data can be transmitted via the following channels:

1.4.2 DATA CHANNELS OF COMMUNICATIVE INTERACTION

1. The *auto-channel* processes input automatically and produces output autonomously, at the context as well as the language level. In natural cognitive agents, i.e., the user and the scientist, the auto-channel is present from the very beginning in its

---

[10] A notable exception is the direct study of central cognition in neurology, especially fMRI or functional magnetic resonance imaging (cf. Matthews et al. 2003; Jezzard et al. 2001). Currently, however, these data leave room for widely differing interpretations, and are used to support conflicting theories.

full functionality. In artificial agents, in contrast, the auto-channel must be reconstructed – and it is the goal of Database Semantics to reconstruct it as realistically
as possible.

2. The *extrapolation of introspection* is a specialization of the auto-channel and results from the scientists' effort to improve man–machine communication by taking the view of the human user. This is possible because the scientist and the user
are natural agents.

3. The *service channel* is designed by the scientist for the observation and control
of the artificial agent. It allows direct access to the robot's cognition because its
cognitive architecture and functioning is a construct which in principle may be
understood completely by the scientist.

The three constellations and the role of the three data channels in the interaction between user, scientist, and robot may be summarized graphically as follows:

1.4.3 INTERACTION BETWEEN USER, ROBOT, AND SCIENTIST

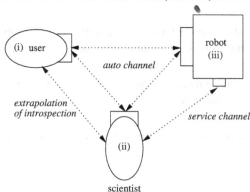

The scientist observes the external behavior of the user and the robot via the auto-
channel, i.e., the scientist sees what they do and can also interview them about it.
In addition, the scientist observes the cognitive states of (a) the user indirectly via a
scientifically founded extrapolation of introspection and (b) the robot directly via the
service channel. For the scientist, the user and the robot are equally real agents "out
there" in the world, and their cognitive states have the same ontological status.

Of the three channels, the auto-channel is available to the user, the robot, and the
scientist. It is the channel used most, but it is also most prone to error: At the level of
context there are the visual illusions, for example, and at the level of language there are
the misunderstandings. In addition, one has to take into account the possibility that the
partner of discourse might deviate from the truth, either consciously or unconsciously.

As long as everyday access to the partner of discourse is restricted to the auto-
channel, we can never be completely certain whether what we said was really understood as intended by us, or whether we really understood what was intended by

the other, or whether what was said was really true. In philosophy, this is the much discussed problem known as *solipsism* (Wittgenstein 1921).

For a scientific analysis of natural language communication, however, there are the priviledged accesses of (i) the extrapolation of introspection and (ii) the service channel. In the extrapolation of introspection, the discourse between the scientist and the user is restricted to the domain of user–robot interaction. Therefore, misunderstandings between the scientist and the user are much less likely than in free communication, though they are still possible. The direct access to the robot via the service channel, furthermore, allows the scientist to determine objectively whether or not the cognition of the artificial agent is functioning properly. Thus, artificial cognitive agents are special insofar as they are not subject to the problem of solipsism.

1.5 Equivalence Principles for Interfaces and for Input/Output

The methodological principles of Database Semantics presented so far, namely

1. the *Verification Principle*
   i.e., the development of the theory in the form of a declarative specification which is continuously verified by means of an implemented prototype (cf. Sect. 1.2),

2. the *Equation Principle*
   i.e., the equating of theoretical correctness with the behavioral adequacy of the prototype during long-term upscaling (cf. Sect. 1.3), and

3. the *Objectivation Principle*
   i.e., the establishing of objective channels for observing language communication between natural and artificial agents (cf. Sect. 1.4),

are constrained by

4. the *Interface Equivalence Principle*, and

5. the *Input/Output Equivalence Principle*.

According to the Principle of Interface Equivalence (4), the artificial surrogate must be equipped with the same interfaces to the external world as the natural original. At the highest level of abstraction, this requires the external interfaces of recognition and action at the context and the language level (cf. 2.1.3). At lower levels of abstraction, the interfaces in question split up into the different modalities (cf. Sect. 2.2) of vision, audio, tactile, etc., for recognition, and locomotion, manipulation, etc., for action.

The Interface Equivalence between the model and the natural original is crucial for the automatic reconstruction of reference, i.e., the relation between language and the world. For example, if the robot cannot perceive, it cannot understand the human's reference to a new object in their joint task environment. The Interface Equivalence

Principle has fundamental consequences on the theory of semantics for natural language, especially the ontological foundations (cf. 2.3.1).

The Principle of Input/Output Equivalence (5) presupposes Interface Equivalence (4). Input/Output Equivalence requires that the artificial agent (i) takes the same input and produces the same output as the natural original, (ii) disassembles input and output in the same way into parts, and (iii) orders the parts in the same way during intake and discharge. The input and output data, like the external interfaces, are concretely given and therefore are susceptible to an objective structural analysis.

The Input/Output Equivalence between the model and the natural original is especially relevant for the automatic interpretation and production of the signs used in natural language communication. Therefore, this principle has fundamental consequences on the theory of grammar for natural language.

The two Equivalence Principles constitute a *minimal requirement* for any scientific reconstruction of cognition in general and the mechanism of natural language communication in particular. The reason is as follows: If we had direct access to the architecture and the functioning of cognition, comparable to the investigation of the physical structures and functions of the bodily organs in the natural sciences (anatomy, physiology, chemistry, physics), the resulting model would certainly have to satisfy the Principles of Interface Equivalence and Input/Output Equivalence.

If, due to the absence of direct access, the nature of the cognitive system must be inferred indirectly, namely in an incremental process of upscaling the functional completeness and the data coverage of an artificial surrogate, this does not diminish the importance of the external interfaces and the input/output data. On the contrary, as concretely given, directly observable structures they constitute the external fixpoints for any reconstruction of the internal cognition procedures which is scientifically well-founded.

1.6 Surface Compositionality and Time-Linearity

The general principles of Interface Equivalence and Input/Output Equivalence require a careful analysis and reconstruction (i) of the natural agent's recognition and action components and (ii) of the data being passed through these components. One important kind of data are the expressions of natural language produced in the speaker mode and interpreted in the hearer mode.

Externally, these data are objects in a certain medium, represented by sounds, handwritten or printed letters, or gestures of a sign language, which can be recorded on film, tape, or disc, and measured and described with the methods of the natural sciences. Given that these objects are concretely given, they constitute the empirical basis which linguistic analysis should neither add to nor subtract from. This elementary methodological principle is known as Surface Compositionality (SCG'84):

1.6.1 SURFACE COMPOSITIONALITY

A grammatical analysis is surface compositional if it uses only the concrete word forms as the building blocks of composition, such that all syntactic and semantic properties of a complex expression derive systematically from the syntactic category and the literal meaning of the lexical items.

Surface Compositionality is best illustrated by examples which violate it, such as the following grammatical analysis:

1.6.2 ANALYSIS VIOLATING SURFACE COMPOSITIONALITY

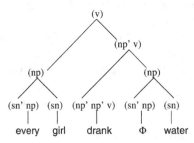

In order to treat the noun phrases every girl and water alike, this analysis postulates the zero element Φ. The presumed "linguistic generalization" is illegitimate, however, because the postulated determiner Φ of water is not concretely given in the surface.

Nevertheless, the categories of 1.6.2 are well-motivated and defined as follows:

1.6.3 THE CATEGORIES OF 1.6.2

(sn' np)   = *determiner*, takes a singular noun sn' and makes a noun phrase np.
(sn)   = *singular noun*, fills a valency position sn' in the determiner.
(np' np' v)= *transitive verb*, takes a noun phrase np and makes an intransitive verb (np' v).
(np)   = *noun phrase*, fills a valency position np' in the verb.
(np' v)   = *intransitive verb*, takes a noun phrase np and makes a (v).
(v)   = *verb* with no open valency positions (sentence).

The rules generating Example 1.6.2 are based on the principle of possible substitutions, and are defined as follows:

1.6.4 RULES COMPUTING POSSIBLE SUBSTITUTIONS FOR DERIVING 1.6.2

(v)   → (np) (np' v)
(np)   → (sn' np) (sn)
(np' v)   → (np' np' v) (np)
(sn' np)   → every, Φ
(sn)   → girl, water
(np' np' v) → drank

Each rule replaces the category on the left-hand side of the arrow by the categories on the right-hand side (top-down derivation). It is also conceivable to replace the categories on the right-hand side by the one on the left-hand side (bottom-up derivation).

Without the zero determiner postulated in 1.6.2, at least one additional rule would have to be defined. However, according to the Principle of Surface Compositionality, it is methodologically unsound to simply postulate the existence of something that is absent, but considered necessary or desirable.[11] Failure to maintain Surface Compositionality leads directly to high mathematical complexity and computational intractability.

Having determined the basic elements of linguistic analysis, i.e., the surfaces in the concretely given sign and their standard lexical analysis, let us turn to the proper grammatical relations between these basic items. The most elementary relation between the words in a sentence is their time-linear order. Time-linear means linear like time and in the direction of time (cf. Sect. 3.4).

The time-linear structure of natural language is so fundamental that a speaker cannot but utter a text sentence by sentence, and a sentence word form by word form. Thereby the time-linear principle suffuses the process of utterance to such a degree that the speaker may decide in the middle of a sentence on how to continue.

Correspondingly, the hearer need not wait until the utterance of a text or sentence has been finished before his or her interpretation can begin. Instead the hearer will interpret the beginning of the sentence without having to know how it will be continued.

Example 1.6.2 violates not only Surface Compositionality, but also Time-Linearity. The grammatical analysis is not time-linear because it fails to combine every girl with drank directly. Instead, based on the principle of possible substitutions, the complex expression drank water must be derived first.

A time-linear analysis, in contrast, is based on the principle of possible continuations. As an example, consider the following time-linear derivation, which uses the same categories (cf. 1.6.3) as the non-time-linear derivation 1.6.2:

1.6.5 SATISFYING SURFACE COMPOSITIONALITY AND TIME-LINEARITY

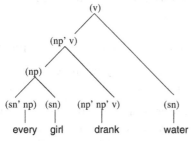

This bottom-up derivation always combines a sentence start with a next word into a new sentence start, using the following (simplified) rules of Left-Associative Grammar:

---

[11] The inverse kind of violating Surface Compositionality consists in treating words which are concretely given in the surface as if they weren't there, simply because they are considered unnecessary or undesirable for one's "linguistic generalization." For a more detailed discussion see SCG'84 and FoCL'99, Sects. 4.5, 17.2, 18.2, and 21.3.

1.6.6 RULES COMPUTING THE POSSIBLE CONTINUATIONS FOR DERIVING 1.6.5

$$(VAR' \; X) \; (VAR) \Rightarrow (X)$$
$$(VAR) \; (VAR' \; X) \Rightarrow (X)$$

Each rule consists of three patterns. The patterns are built from the variables VAR, VAR', and X.[12]

The first pattern of a rule, e.g., (VAR' X), represents the sentence start *ss*, the second pattern, e.g., (VAR), the next word *nw*, and the third pattern, e.g., (X) the resulting sentence start *ss'*. The variables VAR and VAR' are restricted to a single category segment, while X is a variable for a sequence of category segments consisting of zero or more elements.

Rules computing possible continuations are based on matching their patterns with the input expressions, thereby binding their variables:

1.6.7 APPLICATION OF A RULE COMPUTING A POSSIBLE CONTINUATION

	ss	*nw*		*ss'*	
rule patterns	(VAR' X)	(VAR)	⇒	(X)	
	| |	|		|	*matching and binding*
categories	(sn' np)	(sn)		(np)	
surfaces	every	girl		every girl	

During matching, the variable VAR' is "vertically" bound to sn', the variable X to np, and the variable VAR to sn. In the result, the valency position sn' of the determiner category (sn' np) has been filled (or canceled), producing the *ss'* category (np), and the input surfaces every and girl are concatenated into every girl.

To handle the combination between a verb and object nouns with or without a determiner, e.g., ...drank + a coke versus ...drank + water, in a surface compositional manner, the possible values of the variables VAR and VAR' are restricted[13] and correlated as follows:

1.6.8 VARIABLE DEFINITION OF THE TIME-LINEAR RULES FOR DERIVING 1.6.5

If VAR' is sn', then VAR is sn.   (*identity-based agreement*)
If VAR' is np', then VAR is np, sn, or pn.   (*definition-based agreement*)

The formalism of a time-linear derivation sketched in 1.6.5–1.6.8 is of a preliminary kind. It was used in NEWCAT'86 for the automatic time-linear analysis of 221 syntactic constructions of German and 114 of English, complete with LISP source code. It was also used in CoL'89 for 421 syntactic–semantic constructions of English with a sign-oriented, hierarchical semantic analysis.

---

[12] There is a convention in Database Semantics that constants are written in lowercase Roman letters, while variables are written in uppercase Roman letters or in lowercase Greek letters. Cf. Appendix C, Sect. C.3.

[13] The variable restrictions for handling agreement in English are summarized in the Appendix C, C.3.4.

2. Interfaces and Components

That cognitive agents have bodies[1] with interfaces for transporting cognitive content from the external world into the agent (recognition) and out of the agent into the external world (action) is hardly controversial. The properties of the interfaces may be established externally by observing the interaction of other agents with their environment and with each other, and internally by observing the functioning of one's own interfaces through introspection (cf. 1.4.3). In addition, there is the analysis of the external interface organs involved, provided by the natural sciences such as physiology and anatomy, as well as the modeling of these organs in robotics.

Yet starting the reconstruction of cognition with the agents' external interfaces determines the ontological foundations of Database Semantics (DBS) in a way which makes it incompatible with the traditional sign-oriented theories. The reason is that the sign-oriented theories abstract the cognitive agent away, defining semantics as a direct relation between "language and the world." This may have advantages, yet without an agent there cannot be external interfaces, and a cognitive theory without external interfaces is unsuitable as the control unit of a talking robot

There remains the possibility of extending the sign-oriented theories without external interfaces into ones which have them. This is not a promising option, however, as shown by the analogy with software development: A piece of running software can practically never be extended to an interface which was forgotten in the initial design – except for ad hoc emergency measures cleverly adapting some accidental feature of the program. For a clean solution, the program has to be rewritten from scratch.

2.1 Cognitive Agents with and without Language

There are cognitive agents without language which have external interfaces very similar to those of cognitive agents with language. A squirrel, for example, has two eyes, two ears, a nose, etc., for recognition, and hands, hind-legs, a mouth, etc., for action. It can bury a nut, when needed retrieve it even after a long time, and eat it.

In our terminology, the squirrel has a very good context component, but no language component.[2] If we could use the cognition of an artificial squirrel as our context, we

---

[1] The role of the body has recently been reemphasized by Emergentism, cf. MacWhinney (1999).

[2] Though this may be debated. See Hauser (1996).

would adapt the ears to hearing language, add synthesizers for speaking, provide ample computing power, and design a theory to use it for natural language communication. Such a theory is the topic of this book.

As no artificial squirrels are available at present, let us briefly outline the basic structure of the context component required. That we begin our model of natural language communication with the context level may be motivated as follows:

2.1.1 SUPPORT FOR BUILDING THE CONTEXT COMPONENT FIRST

1. Constructs from the context-level may be reused at the language level. This holds for (i) the concepts, as types and as token, (ii) the external interfaces for input and output, (iii) the data structure, (iv) the algorithm, and (v) the inferences.

2. The context is universal – in the sense of being independent of a particular language, yet all the different languages may be interpreted relative to the same kind of context component.

3. In phylogeny (evolution) and ontogeny (child development) the context component comes first.

The external interfaces of the context component correspond to those of a cognitive agent without language, and may be shown schematically as follows:

2.1.2 EXTERNAL INTERFACES OF A COGNITIVE AGENT WITHOUT LANGUAGE

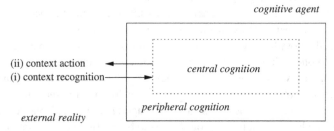

For present purposes we deal with the interfaces at a very high level of abstraction, such that the distinction between recognition and action in general is sufficient.

The differentiation of the external interfaces into different modalities such as vision, audio, variants of locomotion, manipulation, etc., will be the topic of the following Sect. 2.2. It is relevant here only insofar as peripheral cognition during recognition translates the heterogeneous modality-dependent data of the different interfaces into the homogenous coding of central cognition. During action, peripheral cognition translates the homogeneously coded commands of central cognition into the heterogeneous modality-dependent kinds of different external action procedures.[3]

---

[3] We know of two kinds of homogeneous coding: neurological in natural agents and electronic in computers. Functionally, the task of central cognition is the analysis and storage of modality-independent (homogenous) content, inferencing on the content, and turning the result of these inferences into action schemata.

The step from agents without language to agents with language can be visualized as a doubling of the context, whereby the newly gained component is reutilized for the purposes of language.[4] For example, the existing interfaces for (i) context recognition and (ii) context action can be reused by the new language component for (iii) sign recognition and (iv) sign synthesis, respectively.

2.1.3 EXTERNAL INTERFACES OF A COGNITIVE AGENT WITH LANGUAGE

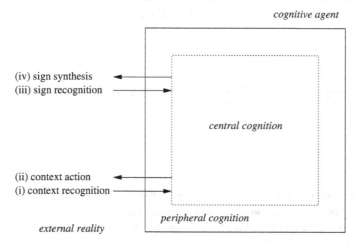

The distinction between the external interfaces of language (upper level) and context (lower level) may be motivated by differences in their interpretation. For example, when we observe some vague pattern on the bark of a tree we may not be sure whether it is accidentally provided by nature or produced on purpose by another human as a sequence of letters, e.g., Caution, Tiger! When we suddenly realize that the pattern is a sign intended for communication, the raw visual input is still the same, but the significance of its interpretation becomes completely different: We switch from the context to the language level.[5]

2.2 Modalities and Media

For natural language communication, different input and output devices may be used. Sign recognition may be based on the input interfaces of the ears (spoken language), the eyes (written, signed language), and the skin (Braille). Sign production may be based on the output interfaces of the vocal tracts in combination with the mouth (spoken language), the hand (written language, including Braille), and hand–arm–face gestures (signed language).

---

[4] This is in line with the Emergentist view (MacWhinney 1999) of evolution reusing older forms for newer functions.

[5] On the functioning of written language see FoCL'99, Sect. 6.5.

The different input and output interfaces are called the *modalities*, at the language as well as the context level. Translating between the modality-dependent data of the different interfaces and the homogenous coding of central cognition is the task of peripheral cognition. The following example shows the switching between modality-independent and modality-dependent coding in the transfer of a language sign from the speaker to the hearer:

2.2.1 MODALITY-INDEPENDENT AND MODALITY-DEPENDENT CODING

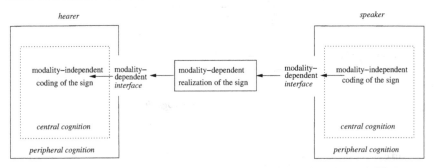

The peripheral cognition of the speaker translates the sign from a modality-independent (homogeneous) coding into a modality-dependent coding which is realized externally. The peripheral cognition of the hearer translates the modality-dependent coding of the sign back into a modality-independent coding.[6]

The modalities of action differ from the modalities of recognition. For example, spoken language is produced with the mouth, but recognized with the ears. Similarly, written and signed language is produced with the hands, but recognized with the eyes. Furthermore, there are monomodal and multimodal recognition and action. An example of a multimodal contextual recognition is simultaneously seeing, touching, smelling, and hearing another agent. An example of multimodal contextual action is holding and biting a fruit. Recognition and action may also combine, as when seeing (recognition) and reaching for (action) an object.

Even more diverse than the different modalities are the forms of existence in the external world, such as different materials, physical states, motions, natural laws, social conventions, etc., which can all be recognized, processed, and acted upon. Due to the translation of peripheral cognition, however, these diverse forms of existence are rep-

---

[6] Let us assume, for example, that language in central cognition is coded homogeneously in ASCII (American Standard Code for Information Interchange). Externally the signs of language may be represented acoustically as spoken language, or visually as hand-written, printed, or signed language. In sign production (speaker mode), the agent must select a modality in which to realize a word; thus the single ASCII coding of the word is translated by peripheral cognition into one of practically infinitely many different modality-dependent realizations based on visual, acoustic, or tactile representations. In sign recognition (hearer mode), the many possible modality-dependent representations of the word as bitmap outlines, sound waves, or raised dots (Braille) are translated by peripheral cognition back into an equivalent single ASCII coding.

resented in the form of a homogenous coding inside the cognitive agent – inasmuch as they have been perceived at all.

In any modality, we must distinguish between *immediate* recognition and action and *mediated* recognition and action. The latter is related to the frequently used notion of the *medium* or the *media*, for example, print or television. Basically, different media are different substances for the mediated storing and reactivating of content. For example, we can see and hear an oncoming train immediately in reality, or we can see and hear a mediated image in a cinema, whereby the event has been stored and reactivated in the medium of film. In both cases the recognition is here multimodal.

While the notion of modality refers to the input/output devices of the cognitive agent, the choice of a medium refers to a means of agent-external storage (cf. Meyer-Wegener 2003). The notions of medium and modality are related, however, because each medium, e.g., print, is designed for a certain modality, e.g., vision, or modalities.

2.3 Alternative Ontologies for Referring with Language

Relating language expressions to the intended objects or events in the world is called reference. The agent-oriented approach of Database Semantics reconstructs reference as a cognitive procedure in the agent's head. In addition to the external interfaces at the levels of language and context, this requires the definition of (i) a data structure for representing content inside the agent and (ii) an algorithm for reading content into and out of the agent's database.

The sign-oriented approach of Truth-Conditional Semantics, in contrast, treats reference as an external relation between "language and the world," whereby the latter is defined as a set-theoretical model. The reference relation is established by means of definitions formulated in a *metalanguage*. The metalanguage, the definitions relating language to the model, and the model itself are all constructed by the logicians.

The different ontologies underlying the sign-oriented approach of Truth-Conditional Semantics and the agent-oriented approach of Database Semantics may be compared schematically as follows:

2.3.1 REFERENCE IN ALTERNATIVE ONTOLOGIES

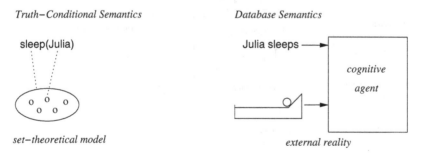

In Truth-Conditional Semantics, the sentence at the language level is formalized as sleep(Julia), indicating that sleep is a functor denoting a set while Julia is an argument denoting an element. The metalanguage-defined relation between the language expressions and their set-theoretic denotations is indicated by the dotted lines. The approach is sign-oriented insofar as there is no agent and consequently there are no external interfaces. Thus there is neither a need nor a place for an agent-internal database, or an algorithm for reading content into and out of the agent's database. Also, there is no distinction between the speaker and the hearer mode.

In Database Semantics, the example shows an agent in the hearer mode.[7] The agent relates the sentence Julia sleeps to the referent provided by contextual recognition. The agent, the language expression, and the referent with its property of sleeping are all part of the real world. The real world is treated as given and there is no attempt to model it set-theoretically or in any other way. Instead, the goal of Database Semantics is to model the *agent*. This includes the agent's recognition of the real world at the language and the context level, as well as the agent's actions – externally relative to the real world, but also internally in the form of such procedures as free association, inference, derivation of plans, wishes, etc.

2.4 Theory of Language and Theory of Grammar

Database Semantics establishes the relation of reference between the language expressions and the referents *procedurally* rather than metalanguage-based.[8] As a first step towards a procedural reconstruction of reference, let us transfer the distinction between the levels of language and world, familiar from Truth-Conditional Semantics, into the head of the cognitive agent. Thereby, the "world" changes into an agent-internal representation of episodic and absolute knowledge, called the *context*.

2.4.1 STRUCTURING CENTRAL COGNITION IN AGENTS WITH LANGUAGE

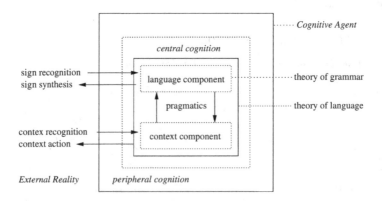

Compared with 2.1.3, central cognition has a more differentiated structure: There is a distinction between the language and the context component, and the connection between the two is provided by the operations of language pragmatics.[9]

Pragmatics in general is defined as the theory of use. Examples of pragmatic tasks are the use of a screwdriver to fasten a screw, the use of one's legs to go from *a* to *b*, the nightly scavenging of food from the refrigerator to fix a sandwich and satisfy one's hunger, or the request that someone else fix and serve the sandwich.

Depending on whether or not an act is performed by means of language signs, we speak of language or of context pragmatics. Language pragmatics must be analyzed as a phylogenetical and ontogenetical specialization of context pragmatics, just as language recognition and synthesis are analyzed as phylogenetical and ontogenetical specializations of contextual recognition and action, respectively.

The context component has long been neglected in linguistics, even though it is functionally essential for modeling natural language communication. Without a context component, the artificial cognitive agent cannot report to us what it perceives (contextual recognition), and cannot do what we tell it to do (contextual action).

The language component is traditionally described by the *theory of grammar*, and includes the subcomponents of the morphology, the lexicon, the syntax, and the semantics. For the purposes of Database Semantics, the language component must not merely analyze the signs as isolated objects, but must provide declarative specifications of the computational procedures which map meanings into surfaces (speaker mode) and surfaces into meanings (hearer mode).

The language component, the context component, and the language pragmatics combine into the *theory of language*. For the purposes of Database Semantics, the theory of language must model reference with language to external objects, in the speaker as well as the hearer mode. Furthermore, it must provide a natural method of *conceptualization*, i.e., the speaker's choice of *what to say* and *how to say it*, as well as for handling nonliteral language use in the speaker and the hearer mode (cf. Sects. 5.4 and 5.5).

2.5 Immediate Reference and Mediated Reference

From an ontogenetical and phylogentical point of view, the most basic form of reference is *immediate reference*. It consists in referring with language to objects in the immediate task environment of the communicating agents, for example, to the book

---

[7] The different constellations of recognition and action at the language and the context level are categorized as the 10 SLIM states of cognition (cf. FoCL'99, Sect. 23.5).

[8] In order to utilize metalanguage definitions computationally, they must be reconstructed procedurally. Most existing metalanguage-based systems, for example, modal logic, are unsuitable for a procedural reconstruction. See FoCL'99, Sect. 19.4.

[9] Thus, one of the functions of pragmatics in Database Semantics is to perform the role of the metalanguage in Truth-Conditional Semantics, namely to establish the connection between "language and the world," here the agent-internal levels of language and context.

in front of them. Thereby, the agents' external interfaces are involved at the language as well as the context level (as in 2.4.1).

In addition, there is also the referring with language to referents which are not in the immediate task environment, but that exist solely in the databases of the communicating agents, for example, the historical figure of Aristotle. In this *mediated reference*, only the external interfaces of the language level, but not of the context level, are involved:[10]

2.5.1 USE OF EXTERNAL INTERFACES IN MEDIATED REFERENCE

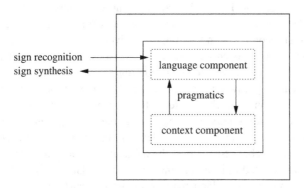

Even though immediate reference is phylogenetically and ontogenetically primary, it is a special case of mediated reference from a theoretical point of view. This is because the cognitive procedures of mediated reference are used also by immediate reference. In other words, the functional difference between immediate and mediated reference consists in that immediate reference requires the additional external interfaces of the context level.

Cognitive agents without contextual interfaces but with language (and thus limited to mediated reference) are interesting for the following reasons. First, the contextual recognition and action capabilities of today's robots are still far removed from those of a squirrel, for example. Recognition and action at the language level, in contrast, can always be managed without principled loss of function by using the keyboard and the screen of today's standard computers. Thus, if we want to model natural language communication with today's technologies, i.e., without suitable robots, we must make due with cognitive agents which lack contextual interfaces and are therefore incapable of immediate reference.

Second, there are many tasks for which agents without contextual interfaces but with language are sufficient. In research, this applies to the modeling of cognitive operations which are based on stored data alone. In practice, it applies to such applications as the natural language interaction with databases and the Internet, involving the reading in of new content and the answering of queries.

---

[10] For further discussion of immediate and mediated reference see FoCL'99, Sect. 4.3.

In the long run, however, an absence of external interfaces at the context level (with the associated capabilities of recognition and action) has the following disadvantages:

2.5.2 DISADVANTAGES OF NOT HAVING CONTEXTUAL INTERFACES

1. *The conceptual core of language meanings remains undefined.*
   Most basic concepts originate in agents without language as recognition and action procedures of their contextual interfaces, and are reused as the core of language meanings in agents with language.[11] Therefore, agents with language but without contextual interfaces use meanings which are void of a conceptual core – though the relations between the concepts, represented by placeholder words, may still be defined, both absolutely (for example, in the *is-a* or *is-part-of* hierarchies) and episodically.

2. *The coherence or incoherence of content cannot be judged autonomously.*
   The coherence of stored content originates in the coherence of the external world.[12] Therefore, only agents with contextual interfaces are able to relate content "imported" by means of language to the data of their own experience. An agent without contextual interfaces, in contrast, has nothing but imported data – which is why the responsibility for their coherence lies solely with the users who store the data in the agent.

Due to the absence of suitable robots, the software development of Database Semantics is currently limited to standard computers. As soon the technologies needed for contextual interfaces become available, however, the theoretical framework of Database Semantics will be ready for the extension. The reason for this is – roughly speaking – that immediate reference is a special case of mediated reference.

Thus, all the components developed for the version without contextual interfaces will be suitable to serve in the extended system as well. This holds, for example, for the components of the lexicon, the automatic word-form recognition and production, the syntactic–semantic and semantic–syntactic parsers, and the pragmatic inferences in the speaker and the hearer mode.

2.6 The SLIM Theory of Language

The theory of language which Database Semantics is based on is called SLIM. In contrast to other theories of language such as Structuralism, Behaviorism, Nativism, Model Theory, or Speech Act Theory, SLIM has been designed from the outset to explain the understanding and purposeful production of signs in terms of completely explicit, mechanical (i.e., logically electronic) procedures.

---

[11] Cf. FoCL'99, Sect. 22.1.

[12] Ibid, Sect. 24.1.

The letters of the acronym SLIM have the following interpretation:

S = **S**urface Compositionality (methodological principle, cf. 1.6.1):
Syntactic–semantic composition assembles only concrete word forms, excluding the use of zero-elements, identity mappings, or transformations.

L = time-**L**inearity (empirical principle, cf. 1.6.5):
Interpretation and production of utterances are based on a strictly time-linear derivation order.

I = **I**nternal (ontological principle, cf. 2.3.1):
Interpretation and production of utterances are analyzed as cognitive procedures located inside the speaker–hearer.

M = **M**atching (functional principle, cf. 3.2.3):
Referring with language to past, current, or future objects and events is modeled in terms of pattern matching between language meanings and a context.

SLIM models communication based on the Seven Principles of Pragmatics.

2.6.1 FIRST PRINCIPLE OF PRAGMATICS (POP-1)

The speaker's utterance meaning$_2$ is the use of the sign's literal meaning$_1$ relative to an internal context.

Meaning$_1$ is the *literal meaning* of the sign; meaning$_2$ is the *speaker meaning* of an utterance in which the sign's meaning$_1$ is used. Even in the hearer mode, meaning$_2$ is called the "speaker meaning" because communication is successful only if the hearer uses the sign's meaning$_1$ to refer to the same objects or events as the speaker.

A sign can only be used successfully if the context of interpretation has been determined (and delimited) correctly. Finding the context is based on the sign's STAR:

S = space (location where the sign has been uttered)
T = time (time when the sign has been uttered)
A = author (agent who produced the sign)
R = recipient (agent intended to receive the sign)

The role of the STAR is described by the Second Principle of Pragmatics:

2.6.2 SECOND PRINCIPLE OF PRAGMATICS (POP-2)

A sign's STAR determines the *entry context* of production and interpretation in the contextual databases of the speaker and the hearer.

Once the initial context of interpretation has been found, based on the STAR, other contexts may be accessed according to the Third Principle of Pragmatics:

2.6.3 THIRD PRINCIPLE OF PRAGMATICS (POP-3)

> The matching of signs with their respective subcontexts is incremental, whereby in production the elementary signs follow the time-linear order of the underlying thought path, while in interpretation the thought path follows the time-linear order of the incoming elementary signs.

In natural language communication, PoP-3 presupposes PoP-2. The first step in the production or interpretation of a natural language sign is to determine the entry context as precisely as possible (PoP-2). Then the complex sign is matched word form by word form with a sequence of referents at the level of context (PoP-3).[13]

Next, the meaning$_1$ and the associated reference mechanisms of the three basic kinds of signs, namely symbol, indexical, and name, are defined. The literal meaning$_1$ of a symbol is a concept type (as illustrated by the analysis of the word square in Sect. 4.2).

2.6.4 FOURTH PRINCIPLE OF PRAGMATICS (POP-4)

> The reference mechanism of a *symbol* is based on a meaning$_1$ which is defined as a concept type. Symbols refer from their place in a positioned sentence by matching their meaning$_1$ with corresponding concept tokens at the context level.

The reference mechanism of symbols is called iconic because the functioning of symbols and icons is similar: Both can be used to refer spontaneously to new objects of a known kind. The difference resides in the relation between the meaning$_1$ and the surface, which is arbitrary in the case of symbols, but motivated in the case of icons.

The literal meaning$_1$ of an indexical is defined as a pointer. Examples of indexicals are the words here, now, I, you, and this.

2.6.5 FIFTH PRINCIPLE OF PRAGMATICS (POP-5)

> The reference mechanism of an *indexical* is based on a meaning$_1$ which is defined as one of two characteristic pointers. The first points into the agent's context and is called the context pointer or C. The second points at the agent and is called the agent pointer or A.

The two kinds of pointers are illustrated by the following examples:

---

[13] The time-linear derivation order in the speaker and the hearer mode is strongly supported by experimental results in cognitive psychology, especially regarding the interpretation of spoken language. For example, Sedivy, Tanenhaus, et al., (1999, p. 127) present "compelling evidence for a processing model in which linguistic expressions are undergoing continuous, moment-by-moment semantic interpretation, with immediate mapping onto the a referential model." Similarly, Eberhard, et al., (1995, p. 422) report that subjects incrementally "interpreted each word of the spoken input with respect to the visual discourse model and established reference as soon as distinguishing information was received." See also Spivey et al. (2002) in a similar vein.

2.6.6 INDEXICALS AS NOUNS AND ADJECTIVES WITH A AND C POINTERS

noun A	noun C	adj A	adj C
I, we	you	here	there
	he, she, it	now	then
	this, they		

Indexicals sharing the same pointer may differ in terms of additional symbolic-grammatical distinctions. For example, the context pointer of the word this is restricted to single, nonanimate referential objects, while the word they is restricted to a plurality of referential objects which may be animate or inanimate. Similarly, you is restricted to referential objects of any number and gender which are potential partners of communication, while he is restricted to a single referential object of male gender which currently is not regarded as a partner of communication.

In names like John or R2D2, the role of the literal meaning$_1$ is taken up by private identity markers. They originate at the level of context in order to indicate that different appearances of a referential object are recognized as being the same individual.

In cognitive agents with language, (copies of) the private markers are reused by attaching them to public surfaces in an act of naming. Thereafter, reference with a name uses the public surface to call up each agent's private marker to match the corresponding marker in each agent's cognitive representation of the referential object.

2.6.7 SIXTH PRINCIPLE OF PRAGMATICS (POP-6)

> The reference mechanism of a *name* is based on a private marker which matches a corresponding marker contained in the cognitive representation of the object referred to.

Acts of naming may be explicit, as in a ceremony of baptism, or implicit, as in the following example: Agent A observes an unfamiliar dog running around, appearing and disappearing in the bushes. For continuity, the private identity marker $#%& is inserted into the cognitive structures representing the different appearances of the dog in A's context, indicating that they represent the same individual. Later, the owner calls the dog by its name Fido. Agent A adopts the name by attaching $#%& to the public surface Fido. Henceforth, the name Fido refers for A to the dog in question by matching the private marker attached to the name with the corresponding marker inserted into (the cognitive representations of) the referent.

The distinction between the different *kinds of signs*, i.e., symbol, indexical, and name, is orthogonal to the distinction between the main *parts of speech*, i.e., verb, adjective, and noun. For example, an adjective (part of speech) can occur as a symbol or an indexical (kind of sign) – but not as a name.

This independence is functionally motivated: The part of speech controls the combinatorics of a word in a sentence (horizontal relations), while the kind of sign determines the reference mechanism which relates the word meanings to the context (vertical relations, cf. 3.2.4). The correlation between the kinds of signs and the parts of speech is described by the Seventh Principle of Pragmatics:

2.6.8 SEVENTH PRINCIPLE OF PRAGMATICS (POP-7)

Symbols occur as verbs, adjectives, and nouns. *Indexicals* occur as adjectives and nouns. *Names* occur only as nouns.

This means conversely that *nouns* occur as symbols, indexicals, and names; *adjectives* occur as symbols and indexicals; and *verbs* occur only as symbols.[14]

As an illustration, consider the following example:

2.6.9 RELATION BETWEEN THE KINDS OF SIGN AND THE PARTS OF SPEECH

name	Fido		
indexical	this	here	
symbol	dog	black	see
	noun	*adj.*	*verb*

The kind of sign that is the most general with respect to the parts of speech is the symbol, while the name is the most restricted. Conversely, the part of speech that is the most general with respect to different kinds of sign is the noun (object, argument), while the verb (relation, functor) is the most restricted.

The different parts of speech combine into propositions, regardless of the kind of sign used. For example, the following two sentences combine the same parts of speech, but use different kinds of signs:

2.6.10 CORRELATION OF PART OF SPEECH AND KIND OF SIGN IN SENTENCES

	noun	verb	adjective
name	John		
symbol		slept	
symbol			in the kitchen
indexical	he		
symbol		slept	
indexical			there

The Seven Principles of Pragmatics are not merely of academic interest, but have far-reaching implications for the practical implementation and the basic functioning

---

[14] This applies to the semantic core, and is not in conflict with the fact that verbs in English, German, and other European languages integrate a strongly indexical component, namely the tense system – which is absent in Chinese, for example.

of the system in communication. PoP-1 allows to separate the literal meaning$_1$ of the sign type from the meaning$_2$ aspects of using tokens of the sign in an utterance – which is a precondition for a systematic syntactic–semantic analysis in accordance with surface compositionality. PoP-2 provides the point of reference for the spatio-temporal interpretation of indexicals, and is thus a precondition for finding the correct context of use. PoP-3 establishes a uniform mechanism of interpretation which works in the speaker and the hearer mode. PoP-4, PoP-5, and PoP-6 explain for each kind of sign how it relates to the intended referent in the context of interpretation. PoP-7 specifies which of the three mechanisms of reference must be implemented for which of the three parts of speech.

Based on the Seven Principles of Pragmatics, the SLIM theory of language models the natural communication mechanism at a level of abstraction where the meaningful use of language (i) between a human and a human, and (ii) between a human and a suitably constructed cognitive machine function in the same way – just as a sparrow and a jumbo jet are based on the same aerodynamic principles for being airborne (cf. FoCL'99, pp. 4 ff.).

Database Semantics was developed as the technical realization of SLIM in the form of a running software program. The construction of the intuitive SLIM theory evolved in parallel with the technical means required for Database Semantics, in particular the algorithm of LA-grammar in CoL'89 and the data structure of a Word Bank in FoCL'99 (see also TCS'92 and AIJ'01).

3. Data Structure and Algorithm

While the external interfaces of an agent as well as their input and output can be observed directly (cf. 1.4.3), the data structure and the algorithm must be inferred from their functions in natural cognition. In the case of natural language communication, the algorithm must (i) map the input provided by the sign recognition component into a format suitable for storage in the agent's database (hearer mode), (ii) selectively activate and modify content in the database (think mode), and (iii) provide the sign synthesis component with suitably formatted content to be read out of the database in the form of natural language surfaces (speaker mode).

In Database Semantics, these functions are performed by the algorithm of time-linear LA-grammar, used in three variants called *LA-hear*, *LA-think*, and *LA-speak*. The data structure supporting the algorithm is a classic network database (cf. Elmasri and Navathe 1989), called *Word Bank*; it stores flat (nonrecursive) feature structures, called *proplets*, which are structurally equivalent to the records of classic databases.

3.1 Proplets for Coding Propositional Content

A feature structure is defined as a set of features. The features are defined as attribute–value pairs (avp).[1] In proplets, the attributes are displayed in a predefined standard order (for better readability and improved computational efficiency). The values of proplet attributes are restricted to lists which consist of one or more atomic items; the embedding of feature structures as attribute values is not allowed.[2]

For example, the propositional content of an agent perceiving a barking dog (recognition) and running away (action) is represented as the following set of proplets:

3.1.1 CONTEXT PROPLETS REPRESENTING *dog barks. (I) run.*

$$
\begin{bmatrix} \text{sur:} \\ \text{noun: } dog \\ \text{fnc: bark} \\ \text{prn: 22} \end{bmatrix}
\begin{bmatrix} \text{sur:} \\ \text{verb: } bark \\ \text{arg: dog} \\ \text{nc: 23 run} \\ \text{prn: 22} \end{bmatrix}
\begin{bmatrix} \text{sur:} \\ \text{verb: } run \\ \text{arg: moi} \\ \text{pc: 22 bark} \\ \text{prn: 23} \end{bmatrix}
$$

---

[1] This terminology follows general practice in computer science (e.g., Carpenter 1992). The ISO standard CD 2460-1 defines a feature structure as a set of feature–value pairs.

[2] This is in contradistinction to the use of recursive feature structures within Nativism, for example, in LFG (Bresnan 1982) , GPSG (Gazdar et al. 1985), or HPSG (Pollard and Sag 1994). See 3.4.5.

The semantic relations between these proplets are coded solely by means of nonrecursive features, i.e., attribute–value pairs which do not contain feature structures as values. For example, the functor–argument relation between the argument *dog* and the functor *bark* is coded by the attribute fnc (functor) of the *dog* proplet having the value bark, and the attribute arg (argument) of the *bark* proplet having the value dog.

The proplets of a proposition are held together by a common proposition number. For example, the first two proplets in 3.1.1, representing the proposition *dog bark*, have the same prn value, namely 22. Different propositions may be concatenated by means of the attributes nc (next conjunct) and pc (previous conjunct) contained in the verb proplets (see *bark* and *run*). For unique identification of successor or predecessor proplets, the nc and pc values are preceded by their prn value, for example, [nc: 23 run] or [pc: 22 bark].

The noncombinatorial semantic content of a proplet is coded as the value of its *core attribute*. Possible core attributes are noun, verb, and adj. In accordance with PoP-7 (cf. 2.6.8), core attributes may take a concept (PoP-4, 2.6.4), a pointer (PoP-5, 2.6.5), or a marker (PoP-6, 2.6.7) as their values. For example, the first proplet in 3.1.1 has the core attribute noun with the concept *dog* as its core value.

Concepts originate as patterns for recognition and action in the agent's peripheral cognition. As values of the core attribute of proplets, concepts also provide the main key for the storage and retrieval of context proplets in central cognition.

By embedding concepts as core values into proplets, the semantic relations between concepts (i.e., their combinatorial aspects) are defined not directly on the concepts, but in terms of the proplets containing them, as visualized by the dotted lines in the following example:

3.1.2 CODING OF RELATIONS BETWEEN CONCEPTS VIA PROPLETS

This method of coding grammatical relations between proplets solely by means of nonrecursive features (i.e., flat attribute–value pairs) is called bidirectional pointering.

3.2 Internal Matching between Language and Context Proplets

In order to ensure a proper functional interaction between the language and the context level, the two levels must be structurally compatible. This is achieved by representing content at the language level with proplets which resemble the context proplets except that their sur (for surface) attribute must have a non-NIL value.

The sur value of a language proplet is a specialized, language-dependent concept pattern for a word surface, for example, the German sound form Hund. A sequence of concatenated propositions coded with language proplets is illustrated in the following variant of Example 3.1.1 using German surfaces:

3.2.1 LANGUAGE PROPLETS REPRESENTING *dog barks. (I) run.*

$$
\begin{bmatrix} \text{sur: Hund} \\ \text{noun: } dog \\ \text{fnc: bark} \\ \text{prn: 122} \end{bmatrix}
\begin{bmatrix} \text{sur: bellt} \\ \text{verb: } bark \\ \text{arg: dog} \\ \text{nc: 123 run} \\ \text{prn: 122} \end{bmatrix}
\begin{bmatrix} \text{sur: fliehe} \\ \text{verb: } run \\ \text{arg: moi} \\ \text{pc: 122 bark} \\ \text{prn: 123} \end{bmatrix}
$$

While a context proplet has only one main key, namely the core value, a language proplet has two, the surface and the core value. The sur value is used in the lexical lookup of the hearer mode for retrieving a language proplet corresponding to a given surface. The value of the core attribute is used in the lexical lookup of the speaker mode for retrieving a language proplet corresponding to the value, e.g., a certain concept.

3.2.2 KEYS FOR LEXICAL LOOKUP IN THE SPEAKER AND THE HEARER MODE

$$
\begin{bmatrix} \text{sur: Hund} \\ \text{noun: } dog \\ \text{fnc:} \\ \text{prn} \end{bmatrix}
\begin{array}{l} \leftarrow \textit{key for lexical lookup in the hearer mode} \\ \leftarrow \textit{key for lexical lookup in the speaker mode} \end{array}
$$

The relation between the language and the context level, needed for reference, is formally based on a matching between language proplets and context proplets. Such a match is successful if the proplets involved fulfill the following conditions:[3]

3.2.3 CONDITIONS ON SUCCESSFUL MATCHING

1. *Attribute condition*
   The matching between two proplets A and B requires that the intersection of their attributes contains a predefined list of attributes regarded as relevant:

   {list} ⊆ {{proplet A attributes} ∩ {proplet B attributes}}

2. *Value condition*
   The matching between two proplets requires that the variables (and a fortiori the constants) of their common attributes are compatible.[4]

These conditions apply also in the application of LA-grammar rules, which is based on matching the proplet patterns of a rule with the proplet tokens of its input (cf. 3.4.3).

---

[3] The matching condition 3.2.3 may be used for a computational realization of Frege's relation between the sense and the referent (cf. 4.5.2), though in an ontologically different setting (cf. FoCL'99, Sect. 20.4).

[4] In order for language and context proplets to match, their prn values need not agree. Their purpose is to hold the proplets of a proposition "horizontally" together by means of a common proposition number. For example, in 3.2.4 the prn values at the language level are 122/123, but 22/23 at the context level.

For simplicity, matching language and context proplets in the following examples have the same set of attributes.

In the matching between the language and the context component, the speaker mode and the hearer mode must be distinguished. In the speaker mode (mapping contextual content into language), context proplets are matched by compatible language proplets and their language-specific surfaces are uttered. In the hearer mode (embedding language-coded content into the context), language proplets are matched with compatible context proplets, which are then stored in the context.

Even though the (vertical) matching takes place between individual proplets, the (horizontal) semantic relations holding between the proplets at each of the two levels are taken into account as well. As an example, consider the matching between the context proplets of 3.1.1 and the language proplets of 3.2.1:

3.2.4 IMPACT OF INTERPROPLET RELATIONS ON MATCHING

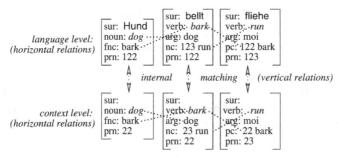

The automatic extension of vertical matching between individual proplets (reference) to their horizontal grammatical relations is best illustrated by a matching failure. Assume, for example, that the noun proplet *dog* at the language level has the fnc value bark, while the corresponding proplet at the context level had the fnc value sleep. In this case, the two proplets would be vertically incompatible – due to their horizontal relations to different verbs, coded as different values of their respective fnc attributes.

3.3 Storage of Proplets in a Word Bank

By coding the relations within propositions (intrapropositional relations) and between propositions (extrapropositional relations) solely by means of features, the proplets of the language and the context level are autonomous items which can be represented and stored independently of any restrictions imposed by two-dimensional space (as in trees). In other words, the constellation of proplets is completely free, and the principle for their storage can be chosen according to the needs of one's database.

In Database Semantics, proplets are stored in *token lines*. A token line is a sequence of proplets with the same core value. A collection of token lines is called a *Word Bank*.

A Word Bank has the structure of a classical network databank: Each token line begins with an "owner record," followed by an arbitrary number of "member records."

Consider the Word Bank of a cognitive agent with language which contains the context and language proplets defined in the previous examples 3.1.1 and 3.2.1:

3.3.1 DATA STRUCTURE OF A WORD BANK

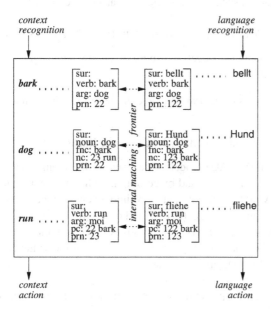

For easier presentation of the token lines, the context and language "levels" have been rotated by 90 degrees such that the internal matching frontier between context and language proplets is vertical rather than horizontal (cf. double arrows). Thus, the area on the left of the Word Bank contains the context proplets, while the area on the right contains the language proplets. (Note that the notions of "horizontal" and "vertical" relations continue to be used in the sense of the intuitive representation of 3.2.4.)

In the Word Bank example 3.3.1, three token lines are shown. When viewed from the left, each token line begins with a concept, here *bark, dog,* and *run,* followed by an arbitrary number of context proplets (indicated by dots). When viewed from the right, each token line begins with a language-dependent surface, here bellt, Hund and fliehe, followed by an arbitrary number of language proplets (also indicated by dots).

A Word Bank is connected to the world via the agent's recognition and action interfaces at the language and the context side. Therefore, artificial cognitive agents containing a Word Bank satisfy the Interface Equivalence Principle (cf. Sect. 1.5, 4) at the highest level of abstraction (i.e., independently of the different modalities). By folding the schema 3.3.1 along its horizontal middle, the input and the output devices are oriented in the same direction, enabling hand–eye coordination, for example.

3.4 Time-Linear Algorithm of LA-Grammar

Next we return to the Principle of Input/Output Equivalence (cf. Sect. 1.5, 5). It applies to the *algorithm* operating on the data structure. What it means for an artificial agent to (i) take the same input and produce the same output as the natural original, (ii) disassemble input and output in the same way into parts, and (iii) order the parts in the same way during intake and discharge is especially clear in the case of language:

3.4.1 APPLYING THE INPUT/OUTPUT EQUIVALENCE PRINCIPLE TO LANGUAGE

1. Input and output at the language level are signs of natural language, such as phrases, sentences, or texts.

2. The parts into which the signs of natural language disassemble during intake and discharge are word forms.

3. The order of the parts during intake and discharge is time-linear.

The algorithm of LA-grammar (LAG) models time-linearity by taking a sequence of word forms, e.g., a b c d e ..., as input, and by combining what has been analyzed so far, called sentence start, with the current next word into a new sentence start, i.e., a and b into (a b), (a b) and c into ((a b) c), ((a b) c) and d into (((a b) c) d), etc. This kind of combination is called *left-associative* – which gives LAG its name.

The following example shows the LA-grammatical derivation of the sentence Julia knows John in the hearer mode of Database Semantics:

3.4.2 TIME-LINEAR DERIVATION (PRINCIPLE OF POSSIBLE CONTINUATIONS)

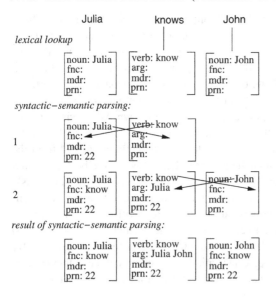

Incremental *lexical lookup* replaces the incoming surfaces Julia, knows, and John with "isolated" proplets, most attributes of which have no value yet. Incremental *syntactic–semantic parsing* turns these proplets into "connected" proplets by means of copying values between the proplets (indicated by the arrows). The final *result* is a set of autonomous proplets, held together by a common proposition number (here [prn: 22]). They are ready to be sorted automatically into the Word Bank.

This analysis is input-equivalent with a natural hearer insofar as it takes a time-linear sequence of unanalyzed surfaces as input and reconstructs the functor–argument structure by means of lexical lookup and syntactic–semantic parsing. The derivation is based on the rules of an LA-grammar which is called LA-hear. The following example shows the rule application of the first composition (explanations in italics). Complete LA-hear grammars are defined in 3.6.2, 11.4.1, 13.2.4, and 15.6.2:

3.4.3 EXAMPLE OF AN **LA-hear** RULE APPLICATION

	rule name	*ss-pattern*	*nw-pattern*	*operations*	*rule package*
rule level	NOM+FV:	$\begin{bmatrix} \text{noun: } \alpha \\ \text{fnc:} \end{bmatrix}$	$\begin{bmatrix} \text{verb: } \beta \\ \text{arg:} \end{bmatrix}$	copy α nw.arg copy β ss.fnc	{FV+OBJ, ...}
proplet level		$\begin{bmatrix} \text{noun: Julia} \\ \text{fnc:} \\ \text{mdr:} \\ \text{prn: 22} \end{bmatrix}$	$\begin{bmatrix} \text{verb: know} \\ \text{arg:} \\ \text{mdr:} \\ \text{prn:} \end{bmatrix}$		

The *rule level* consists of (i) a rule name, (ii) a pattern for the sentence start, (iii) a pattern for the next word, (iv) a set of operations, and (v) a rule package. The rule patterns are matched with the proplets at the *proplet level*, whereby the conditions[5] of 3.2.3 apply. During matching, the variables of the rule level are vertically[6] bound to corresponding values at the proplet level. This is the basis for executing the rule level operations at the proplet level. The output is as follows:

3.4.4 RESULT OF THE **LA-hear** RULE APPLICATION

$$\begin{bmatrix} \text{noun: Julia} \\ \text{fnc: know} \\ \text{mdr:} \\ \text{prn: 22} \end{bmatrix} \quad \begin{bmatrix} \text{verb: know} \\ \text{arg: Julia} \\ \text{mdr:} \\ \text{prn: 22} \end{bmatrix}$$

In the next time-linear combination, the current result serves as the sentence start, while lexical lookup provides the proplet *John* as the next word (cf. 3.4.2, line 2).

The substitution-based algorithm of Phrase Structure Grammar (PSG), in contrast, is not time-linear, as illustrated by the following derivation of the same example:

---

[5] In rule applications, the attribute condition is simplified and merely requires that the attributes of the pattern must be a *subset* of the attributes of the matching proplet.

[6] The *vertical* variable binding of Database Semantics is based on matching between the grammar and the proplet level, in contrast to the *horizontal* variable binding based on quantifiers, as in Predicate Calculus (cf. Sects. 5.3 and 6.2).

3.4.5 NON-TIME-LINEAR DERIVATION (PRINCIPLE OF POSS. SUBSTITUTIONS)

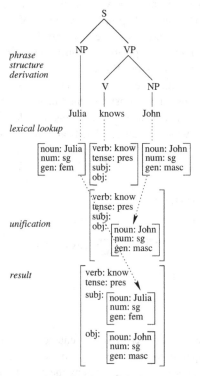

This PSG analysis begins with the start symbol S, from which the phrase structure tree is derived by substituting NP and VP for S, etc., until the terminal nodes Julia, knows, and John are reached (*phrase structure derivation*). Next the terminal nodes are replaced by feature structures via *lexical lookup*. Finally, the lexical feature structures are unified (indicated by the dotted arrows), resulting in one big recursive feature structure (*result*). The order of unification mirrors the derivation of the PS tree.[7] Because the PSG derivation does not analyze the sentence word by word starting at the beginning, it violates the Principle of Input/Output Equivalence (cf. Sect. 1.5, 4).

As a sign-oriented approach, PSG also violates the Principle of Interface Equivalence (cf. Sect. 1.5, 5) in that the declarative specification of its rules and derivations does not provide any relation to the recognition and action components of the cognitive agent: All PS trees are derived from the same start symbol S via different substitutions.[8] Because the feature structure resulting from unification directly mirrors the

---

[7] The sample derivation is generalized insofar as it emphasizes what is common to the different variants of Nativism, such as GPSG, HPSG, LFG, and (somewhat more obscurely) GB.

[8] Because of the principle of possible substitution in combination with missing external interfaces, PSG-based parsers require a sizeable work-around based on often huge intermediate structures, called charts, tables, or state-sets. Accordingly, in comparison with LA-parsers, PSG-parsers are inefficient.

structure of the PS tree, the recursive embedding of subfeature structures is essential. For the same reason, only isolated sentences can be represented in PSG.

In LAG, in contrast, each rule has an interface to the external data. It consists in the rule *patterns* which input proplets are matched with (cf. 3.4.3). Furthermore, representing a sentence analysis as a set of autonomous proplets is the precondition for the storage in, and retrieval from, a Word Bank. This storage and retrieval, in turn, is the precondition for the time-linear functioning of the hearer mode and the speaker mode. Proplets permit not only intrapropositional concatenation for representing functor–argument structure, coordination, and coreference, but also the corresponding extrapropositional concatenation between propositions, as in a text of arbitrary length.

3.5 Cycle of Natural Language Communication

In a normal conversation between two agents A and B, A talks and B listens, then B talks and A listens, and so on. This cycle of natural language communication requires that A and B are capable of switching between the speaker and the hearer mode (turn-taking, cf. 1.1.1). Database Semantics models the cycle of natural language communication by realizing the external interfaces of language recognition (hearer mode) and language action (speaker mode) as variants of LA-grammar. These external interfaces, called *LA-hear* and *LA-speak*, are firmly attached to the agent's Word Bank.

A third variant of LA-grammar, called *LA-think*, is located in the context section of the agent's Word Bank and has the task of moving a unique focus point through the data in order to selectively activate content. Thereby, the semantic relations between proplets are used as a kind of railroad system and LA-think as a kind of locomotive which moves the focus point along the rails (autonomous navigation).

The rules of LA-think resemble those of LA-hear (cf. 3.4.3). The function of the LA-think rules, however, is to power the navigation by retrieving a *successor proplet* for any given proplet in the Word Bank. The following example shows the application of an LA-think rule to the *know* proplet of the proposition derived in 3.4.2 (explanations in italics). Complete LA-think grammars are defined in 3.6.7, 10.6.1, 12.1.1, and 14.1.1:

3.5.1 EXAMPLE OF AN **LA-think** RULE APPLICATION

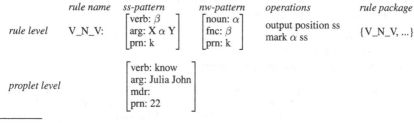

	rule name	*ss-pattern*	*nw-pattern*	*operations*	*rule package*
rule level	V_N_V:	$\begin{bmatrix} \text{verb: } \beta \\ \text{arg: X } \alpha \text{ Y} \\ \text{prn: k} \end{bmatrix}$	$\begin{bmatrix} \text{noun: } \alpha \\ \text{fnc: } \beta \\ \text{prn: k} \end{bmatrix}$	output position ss mark α ss	{V_N_V, ...}
proplet level		$\begin{bmatrix} \text{verb: know} \\ \text{arg: Julia John} \\ \text{mdr:} \\ \text{prn: 22} \end{bmatrix}$			

Cf. FoCL, Part II.

The *ss*-pattern of the rule matches an activated proplet in the Word Bank, vertically binding the variable β to the value know, α to Julia or John, and k to 22. Assuming that α has been bound to Julia, the rule retrieves (activates) the *Julia* proplet using the prn value 22, and returns to the verb proplet (operation output position ss). In order to prevent repeated traversal of the same proplet (relapse, see *tracking principles*, FoCL'99, p. 454), the arg value currently retrieved is marked with "!":

3.5.2 RESULT OF THE **LA-think** RULE APPLICATION

$$
\begin{bmatrix} \text{verb: know} \\ \text{arg: !Julia John} \\ \text{mdr:} \\ \text{prn: 22} \end{bmatrix}
\begin{bmatrix} \text{noun: Julia} \\ \text{fnc: know} \\ \text{mdr:} \\ \text{prn: 22} \end{bmatrix}
$$

Next, the rule V_N_V can apply again (see rule package in 3.5.1), this time activating the proplet *John*.

Given that any proplet in the Word Bank usually provides more than one possible successor,[9] LA-think must make choices. The most basic solutions are either random selection or fixed selection according to some predefined schema. For rational behavior, including meaningful natural language communication, however, the LA-think grammar must be refined into a control structure which *intelligently* chooses between continuation alternatives based on the evaluation of external and internal stimuli, the frequency of previous traversals, learned procedures, theme/rheme structure, etc.[10]

For present purposes we assume the fixed schemata of a standard navigation, starting with the verb (functor, relation) and continuing with the nouns (arguments, objects) in the order given in the arg slot of the verb. Such a navigation may be represented schematically as VNN, with V representing the verb proplet, the first N the subject, and the second N the object (cf. Appendix A).

In principle, any such navigation through the Word Bank is independent of language. However, in agents with language, the navigation serves as the speaker's conceptualization, i.e., as the speaker's choice of what to say and how to say it.

A conceptualization defined as a time-linear navigation through content makes language production relatively straightforward: If the speaker decides to communicate a navigation to the hearer, the core values of the proplets traversed by the navigation are translated into their language-dependent counterparts and realized as external signs. In addition to this language-dependent lexicalization of the universal navigation, the system must provide language-dependent

1. word order,
2. function word precipitation,[11] and
3. word form selection for proper agreement.

---

[9] For example, the *know* proplet provides two successors, namely *Julia* and *John*. If *John* were chosen first (backward navigation), the resulting surface in English would be a passive (cf. Sect. 6.5).

[10] To what degree such a control structure can eventually match human intelligence is another, controversial question. For a combination of historical and recent discussions, see Shieber (2004).

This process is handled by language-dependent LA-speak grammars in combination with language-dependent word form production. For example, the word form ate is produced from an *eat* proplet, the sem attribute of which contains the value past. Complete LA-speak grammars are defined in 12.4.1 and 14.2.1.

Language production based on LA-think and LA-speak may be presented in a simplified format, illustrated below with the realization of Julia knows John. from a VNN navigation. The derivation characterizes the incremental handling of word order and function word precipitation, while morpho-syntactic details are omitted:

3.5.3 SCHEMATIC PRODUCTION OF Julia knows John.

activated sequence				realization			
i							
	V						
i.1		n		n			
	V	N					
i.2	fv	n		n	fv		
	V	N					
i.3	fv	n	n	n	fv	n	
	V	N	N				
i.4	fv p	n	n	n	fv	n	p
	V	N	N				

The letter "i" stands for the sentence number. The letters n, fv, and p are abstract surfaces for *name, finite verb*, and *punctuation* (here full stop), respectively.

In line i.1, the derivation begins with a navigation from V to N, based on LA-think. Also, the N proplet is realized as the n Julia by LA-speak. In line i.2, the V proplet is realized as the fv knows by LA-speak. In line i.3, LA-think continues the navigation to the second N proplet, which is realized as the n John by LA-speak. Finally, LA-speak realizes the p . from the V proplet (line i.4). Thus, a VNN navigation is realized here as a surface with the word order n fv n p.

This method of production can be used to realize not only a subject–verb–object surface (SVO)[12] as in the above example, but also an SOV and (trivially) a VSO surface (cf. Appendix A). The word order and lexicalization of different natural languages are handled by the rules of language-specific LA-speak grammars, whereby their design is supported conceptually by abstract derivations like 3.5.3.

The operations of the three LA-grammars partially[13] determine the possible states of the artificial agent: When LA-hear is active, the agent is in the hearer mode; when LA-think is active, the agent is in the think mode; when LA-think and LA-speak are active, the agent is in the speaker mode.

---

[11] Function word precipitation during production (e.g., 6.2.2) is the counterpart to function word absorption during interpretation (e.g., 6.2.1).

[12] The SVO, SOV, VSO terminology follows Greenberg (1963).

[13] Additional factors are possible input/output activities at the context level.

The interaction of the three variants of LA-grammar in the cycle of natural language communication is summarized in the following schema:

3.5.4 THE CYCLE OF NATURAL LANGUAGE COMMUNICATION

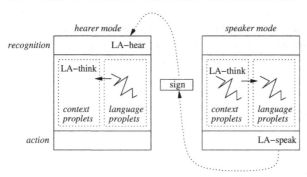

The schema shows two agents, one in the hearer mode and the other in the speaker mode. Each agent contains its own Word Bank with a context and a language section as well as external interfaces for recognition and action.

The agent in the speaker mode happens to use only the interface for language action, i.e., LA-speak, while the agent in the hearer mode happens to use only the interface for language recognition, i.e., LA-hear. In other words, the interaction between the two agents happens to be an instance of mediated reference (no external interface activity at the context level), corresponding to 2.5.1.

The sequencing of word forms during production originates in the time-linear navigation through the set of context proplets in the speaker's Word Bank, powered by LA-think and indicated as a zig-zag line in the agent on the right. The context proplets traversed are matched by corresponding language proplets, which serve as input to LA-speak. The output of LA-speak is the external sign, i.e., a sequence of unanalyzed surfaces, which serves as input to LA-hear. The proplets derived by LA-hear reconstruct the speaker's navigation, whereby the external order of the incoming proplets is lost during their sorting into appropriate token lines. Communication is successful if the content coded by the speaker is reconstructed equivalently by the hearer.

3.6 Bare Bone Example of Database Semantics: DBS-letter

The basic functioning of Database Semantics in a simple, but complete system is illustrated below with the formal definition of DBS-letter. Having no linguistic motivation, this example uses a suitable LA-hear grammar for the time-linear parsing of letter sequences into sets of connected proplets, sorts them into a Word Bank, and uses a suitable LA-think/LA-speak grammar for reading the sequences out again.

The input to DBS-letter are letters defined as proplets. Below, the letters of the sample words LOVE, LOSS, and ALSO are lexically defined, in alphabetical order:

3.6.1 ISOLATED PROPLETS REPRESENTING THE LETTERS A, E, L, O, S, V

$$
\begin{bmatrix} \text{lett: A} \\ \text{prev:} \\ \text{next:} \\ \text{wrd:} \end{bmatrix}
\begin{bmatrix} \text{lett: E} \\ \text{prev:} \\ \text{next:} \\ \text{wrd:} \end{bmatrix}
\begin{bmatrix} \text{lett: L} \\ \text{prev:} \\ \text{next:} \\ \text{wrd:} \end{bmatrix}
\begin{bmatrix} \text{lett: O} \\ \text{prev:} \\ \text{next:} \\ \text{wrd:} \end{bmatrix}
\begin{bmatrix} \text{lett: S} \\ \text{prev:} \\ \text{next:} \\ \text{wrd:} \end{bmatrix}
\begin{bmatrix} \text{lett:} \qquad\text{V} \\ \text{prev:} \\ \text{next:} \\ \text{wrd:} \end{bmatrix}
$$

The core attribute of these proplets is lett, the continuation attributes are previous and next, and the bookkeeping attribute is wrd (cf. 4.1.2).

The LA-hear grammar of DBS-letter is called LA-letter-IN. It copies the value of the lett attribute of the current proplet into the prev slot of the next proplet, and the value of the lett attribute of the next proplet into the next slot of the current proplet.

3.6.2 DEFINITION OF **LA-letter-in** FOR CONNECTING ISOLATED PROPLETS

$\text{ST\_}S = \{(\text{lett: } \alpha, \{\text{r-in}\})\}$

$$
\text{r-in:} \begin{bmatrix} \text{lett: } \alpha \\ \text{prev:} \\ \text{next:} \end{bmatrix}
\begin{bmatrix} \text{lett: } \beta \\ \text{prev:} \\ \text{next:} \end{bmatrix}
\begin{array}{l} \text{copy } \alpha \text{ nw.prev} \\ \text{copy } \beta \text{ ss.next} \end{array}
\qquad \{\text{r-in}\}
$$

$\text{ST\_}F = \{(\text{lett: } \beta, \text{rp}_{r-in})\}$

Like any LA-grammar, LA-letter-IN has a start state ST_S, a set of rules (here containing only one), and a set of final states ST_F. The values α and β are unrestricted variables which may be (vertically) bound to any value at the level of input proplets. An application of the rule r-in is illustrated below:

3.6.3 EXAMPLE OF AN **LA-letter-in** RULE APPLICATION

	rule name	*ss-pattern*	*nw-pattern*	*operations*	*rule package*
rule level	r-in:	$\begin{bmatrix} \text{lett: } \alpha \\ \text{prev:} \\ \text{next:} \end{bmatrix}$	$\begin{bmatrix} \text{lett: } \beta \\ \text{prev:} \\ \text{next:} \end{bmatrix}$	copy α nw.prev copy β ss.next	{r-in}
proplet level		$\begin{bmatrix} \text{lett: L} \\ \text{prev:} \\ \text{next:} \\ \text{wrd:} \end{bmatrix}$	$\begin{bmatrix} \text{lett: O} \\ \text{prev:} \\ \text{next:} \\ \text{wrd:} \end{bmatrix}$		

After binding α to the value L and β to the value O, the operations copy these values into their opposite slots, resulting in the following output:

3.6.4 RESULT OF THE RULE APPLICATION 3.6.3

$$
\begin{bmatrix} \text{lett: L} \\ \text{prev:} \\ \text{next: O} \\ \text{wrd: 1} \end{bmatrix}
\begin{bmatrix} \text{lett: O} \\ \text{prev: L} \\ \text{next:} \\ \text{wrd: 1} \end{bmatrix}
$$

In addition to the cross-copying of continuation values based on the grammar rules, the control structure of the parser provides the wrd value "1," indicating that the proplets L and O belong to the same word.

The derivation of a letter sequence is shown schematically below (similar to 3.4.2):

3.6.5 TIME-LINEAR DERIVATION CONNECTING THE LETTERS OF love

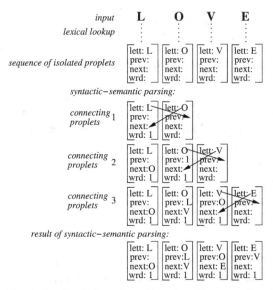

The derivation is based on three time-linear applications of the rule r-in. In the result, the beginning of the word is indicated formally by a proplet the prev attribute of which has the value NIL (represented by space). Similarly, the end of the word is represented by a proplet the next attribute of which has the value NIL. The derivation of the words LOSS and ALSO is analogous to 3.6.5.

The Word Bank of DBS-letter stores the resulting connected proplets as follows:

3.6.6 PROPLETS FOR love, loss, and also IN A WORD BANK

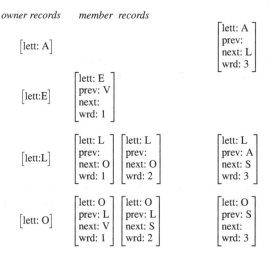

owner records   *member records*

$$
[\text{lett: S}] \qquad
\begin{bmatrix} \text{lett: S} \\ \text{prev: O} \\ \text{next: S} \\ \text{wrd: 2} \end{bmatrix}
\begin{bmatrix} \text{lett: S} \\ \text{prev: S} \\ \text{next:} \\ \text{wrd: 2} \end{bmatrix}
\begin{bmatrix} \text{lett: S} \\ \text{prev: L} \\ \text{next: O} \\ \text{wrd: 3} \end{bmatrix}
$$

$$
[\text{lett: V}] \qquad
\begin{bmatrix} \text{lett: V} \\ \text{prev: O} \\ \text{next: E} \\ \text{wrd: 1} \end{bmatrix}
$$

Compared to 3.3.1, this Word Bank is simplified in that there is no distinction between the context and the language area/level.

Next let us turn to production. It begins with the autonomous navigation through the Word Bank 3.6.6. The LA-think grammar of DBS-letter is called LA-letter-OUT. It is defined to navigate from any letter proplet to the continuation proplet specified in terms of the values of the next and wrd attributes.

3.6.7 DEFINITION OF **LA-letter-out** FOR TRAVERSING CONNECTED PROPLETS

$$
\text{ST\_}S = \{(\text{lett: } \alpha, \{\ \text{r-out}\})\}
$$

$$
\text{r-out:} \begin{bmatrix} \text{lett: } \alpha \\ \text{next: } \beta \\ \text{wrd: k} \end{bmatrix}
\begin{bmatrix} \text{lett: } \beta \\ \text{prev: } \alpha \\ \text{wrd: k} \end{bmatrix} \qquad \text{output position nw} \qquad \{\text{r-out}\}
$$

$$
\text{ST\_}F = \{(\text{lett: } \beta, \text{rp}_{r-out})\ \}
$$

The rule application navigating from L to O of word 1 is illustrated below:

3.6.8 EXAMPLE OF AN **LA-letter-out** RULE APPLICATION

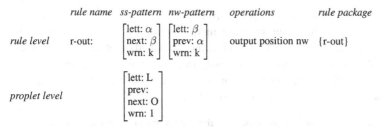

Based on the value assignment to the variables α, β, and k, the rule r-out activates the successor proplet O, using the retrieval mechanism of the database:

3.6.9 RESULT OF THE **LA-letter-out** RULE APPLICATION

$$
\begin{bmatrix} \text{lett: L} \\ \text{prev:} \\ \text{next: O} \\ \text{wrn: 1} \end{bmatrix}
\begin{bmatrix} \text{lett: O} \\ \text{next: V} \\ \text{prev: L} \\ \text{wrn: 1} \end{bmatrix}
$$

The derivation continues by navigating from O to V, and from V to E, using the same rule (see rule package of r-out as defined in 3.6.7).[14]

The proplets traversed are the input to an LA-speak grammar. In our example, this LA-speak grammar is trivial in that it simply realizes the core values of the proplets activated by the navigation, in the order of their traversal and without change.

Extending the purposely simple system of DBS-letter into a full-fledged system for natural language communication requires the following steps:

3.6.10 EXTENSIONS NEEDED FOR NATURAL LANGUAGE COMMUNICATION

1. *Automatic word form recognition and production:*
   Instead of LA-letter-IN recognizing only elementary letters like L or O, a full system must recognize complex word forms in different languages, and similarly for LA-letter-OUT and word form production.

2. *Separation of navigation and language realization:*
   Instead of LA-letter-OUT treating the core values of proplets in the database and the surface items of the output as the same, a full system must handle the functions of navigation and language realization separately by means LA-think and LA-speak, respectively (cf. 3.5.4). This requires a distinction between the core and the surface attributes of proplets (cf. 3.2.2).

3. *Distinction between language and context data:*
   The distinction between language and context requires a division of the Word Bank into a context and a language area (compare 3.6.6 and 3.3.1). Reference to the external world requires that the input-output component of the language level is complemented with an input-output component at the context level (compare 2.5.1 and 2.4.1).

4. *Extending the navigation into a control structure:*
   Instead of LA-letter-OUT merely following the continuations coded into the proplets, a full system must extend the navigation into a method of inferencing. This requires a distinction between absolute propositions[15] and episodic propositions (cf. Sect. 5.2). After complementing the agent with a value structure, the inferencing must be extended into a control structure.

Of these extensions, the first two are mainly in the area of natural language processing, while the latter two require contextual interfaces provided by robotics. The extensions 1 and 2 will be realized in Parts II and III.

---

[14] Given the continuation attributes prev and next and the definition of the rule r-out in 3.6.7, LA-letter-OUT is limited to forward navigation. An extension to backward navigation would require a second rule, in which the *ss-* and *nw-*patterns of the current rule are reversed.

[15] Also called eternal sentences (Quine 1960).

4. Concept Types and Concept Tokens

Having outlined the external interfaces, the data structure, and the algorithm of a talking robot, we turn now to a rather sensitive topic: *meaning*. We approach this notion on the basis of a straightforward task, namely the artificial agent's ability to recognize new objects of a known type, like a brand new pair of shoes. We would like the system to be forgiving in marginal cases, like clogs, but give a clear "no" when it comes to wheelchairs or shovels. This kind of classification requires the ability to distinguish between necessary and accidental properties.

Our solution consists in applying the type–token distinction[1] to concepts: Concepts are defined as feature structures such that concept types represent accidental properties by means of variables, while concept tokens instantiate them by means of constants (cf. FoCL'99, Sect. 3.3). This way of utilizing the distinction between constants and variables for characterizing the type–token relation in concepts is not only intuitively adequate, but provides also for a straightforward computational implementation.

Concepts are integrated into the framework of Database Semantics as the core values of certain proplets, whereby some proplets take concepts types and others concept tokens. A computationally realized type–token correspondence in concepts has important uses. It is employed here in the following locations (cf. 2.4.1): (i) The "middle part" of reference, i.e., the internal matching between the language and the context level, (ii) the "lower interface," i.e., contextual recognition and action, and (iii) the "upper interface," i.e., language interpretation and production.

4.1 Kinds of Proplets

A proplet is composed of attributes and their values. Jointly they are the basis for two kinds of relations to other proplets: The "horizontal" relations concern the semantic relations of functor–argument structure, coordination, and coreference, intra- and extrapropositionally; the "vertical" ones concern the reference relation between language proplets and context proplets, in the speaker and the hearer mode (cf. 3.2.4).

In Database Semantics, these relations are coded by means of only three basic kinds of proplets for representing propositions. They reflect the ontological distinction between (i) object, (ii) relation, and (iii) property.[2] The corresponding distinction in lan-

---

[1] The notions of type and token were introduced by Peirce (CP, Vol.4, p. 537).

[2] See FoCL'99, Sect. 3.4, for a more detailed discussion of propositions.

guage is between the traditional parts of speech, (i) noun, (ii) verb, and (iii) adjective. The corresponding logical notions are (i) argument, (ii) functor, and (iii) modifier.

The distinction between the three basic kinds of proplets is formally expressed in terms of the core attributes (i) noun, (ii) verb, and (iii) adj – at the language and the context level. Apart from their core attributes, proplets employ partially the same and partially different attributes, as illustrated by the following examples:

4.1.1 EXAMPLES OF THE THREE MAIN KINDS OF PROPLETS

noun proplet   *verb proplet*   *adj proplet*

$$
\begin{bmatrix}
\text{sur:} \\
\text{noun: book} \\
\text{cat: sn} \\
\text{sem: def sg} \\
\text{mdr: blue} \\
\text{fnc: buy} \\
\text{idy: 3} \\
\text{nc:} \\
\text{pc:} \\
\text{prn: 11}
\end{bmatrix}
\quad
\begin{bmatrix}
\text{sur:} \\
\text{verb: read} \\
\text{cat: decl} \\
\text{sem: pres} \\
\text{mdr:} \\
\text{arg: John book} \\
\text{pc: 15 sit} \\
\text{nc: 17 sleep} \\
\text{prn: 16}
\end{bmatrix}
\quad
\begin{bmatrix}
\text{sur:} \\
\text{adj: blue} \\
\text{cat: adn} \\
\text{sem:} \\
\text{mdr: B} \\
\text{mdd: book 3} \\
\text{idy: B} \\
\text{nc:} \\
\text{pc:} \\
\text{prn: 20}
\end{bmatrix}
$$

The attributes of a proplet may be classified as follows:

4.1.2 PROPLET ATTRIBUTES AND THEIR VALUES

1. Surface attribute: sur
   All proplets have a surface attribute. If it has the value NIL, the proplet is a context proplet. In language proplets, it gets its non-NIL value from the lexicon.

2. Core attributes: noun, verb, adj
   The core attribute of a proplet gets its unique value from the lexicon. From a sign-theoretic point of view,[3] the core values may be a *concept*, a *pointer*, or a *marker*, which correspond to the sign kinds of *symbol, indexical* and *name*.

3. Grammatical attributes: cat, sem
   The grammatical attributes cat (category) and sem (semantics) get their initial values from the lexicon; they may be modified during the derivation.

4. Intrapropositional continuation attributes: fnc, arg, mdd, mdr
   The intrapropositional continuation attributes get their value(s) by copying during the time-linear composition of proplets (cf. 3.4.2). The values consist of characters (char), which represent the names of other proplets. In complete propositions, the values of fnc (functor), arg (argument), and mdd (modified) must be non-NIL (obligatory continuation attributes), while that of mdr (modifier) may be NIL (optional continuation attribute).

---

[3] See Sect. 2.6 above, and FoCL'99, Chapt. 6.

5. Extrapropositional continuation attributes: nc, pc, idy
   The extrapropositional continuation attributes nc (next conjunct), pc (previous conjunct), and idy (identity) are used extra- and intrapropositionally. Their extrapropositional use is obligatory (in a text, at least one of these attributes must have a non-NIL value), while their intrapropositional use is optional. Like intrapropositional continuation attributes, they get their values by copying.[4]

6. Bookkeeping attribute: prn
   The bookkeeping attribute prn (proposition number) gets its value from the control structure of the parser and consists of a number (integer). Additional bookkeeping attributes are wrn (word number), and trc (transition counter), which serve in the implementation.

For reasons of simplicity, attributes which are not relevant for the discussion at hand will usually be omitted.

To generalize over attributes and values in certain rules or for purposes of designing the lexicon, Database Semantics uses the replacement variables RA.n for attributes and RV.n for values. In contrast to a "binding variable" (for example, α in 3.6.8), a replacement variable is not bound to a value, but replaced by it. A lexical proplet which has a replacement variable RV.n as its core value is called a proplet *shell*:

4.1.3 SUBSTITUTING A REPLACEMENT VARIABLE WITH A CORE VALUE

semantic core	proplet shell	lexical proplet
apple	$\begin{bmatrix} \text{noun: RV.1} \\ \text{fnc:} \\ \text{mdr:} \\ \text{prn:} \end{bmatrix}$	$\begin{bmatrix} \text{noun: apple} \\ \text{fnc:} \\ \text{mdr:} \\ \text{prn:} \end{bmatrix}$

The lexical proplet results from substituting the replacement variable RV.1 of the core attribute noun in the proplet shell with the concept *apple*.

If the replacement variable of a proplet shell is replaced by a binding variable, the result is a rule pattern suitable to match a lexical proplet:

4.1.4 RELATING PROPLET SHELLS, LEXICAL ITEMS, AND RULE PATTERNS

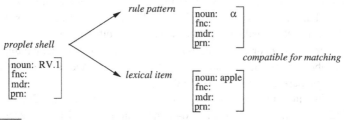

---

[4] nc and pc were used in 3.1.1 ff. and will be formally introduced in 11.2.5. idy is discussed in Chapt. 10 and Appendix A.

The proplet shell, the rule pattern, and the lexical item differ only in their core values. The core value of the proplet shell is the replacement variable RV.1. The core value of the lexical item is the concept *apple*. The core value of the rule pattern is the binding variable α, which can be vertically bound to any core value during a rule application (cf. 3.4.3).

While the *content* of a proplet is represented by the value of its core attribute, its *combinatorics* is represented by (i) the obligatory continuation attribute(s), e.g., fnc, (ii) the optional continuation attribute(s), e.g., mdr, and (iii) the bookkeeping attribute(s), e.g., prn. This way of separating the content and the combinatorial aspect of a proplet allows to treat the combinatorics relatively independently of the content and vice versa.

For handling the combinatorial aspect of proplets, the core values may be represented by placeholders, i.e., names which have no explicitly defined referents (e.g., concepts). A working model of communication (talking robot), however, requires core values which have declarative specifications with adequate procedural counterparts.

For example, if we present different geometric objects to a talking robot and tell it to pick up a square, it must be able to (i) interpret the word square at the language level, (ii) distinguish the shape in question at the context level, and (iii) relate the language meaning to the corresponding contextual referent. As a sign, the word square is of the kind *symbol*, and thus takes a concept as the value of its core attribute.

Correspondingly, if a feature like [noun: *apple*] appears as the core value of a proplet, then the value *apple* should not be merely a placeholder, but represent a concept suitable for recognizing appropriate referents. For this, the concept must have been implemented as an effective recognition procedure of the cognitive agent (robot).

4.2 Type–Token Relation for Establishing Reference

In order for a language and a context proplet to match, the value condition 3.2.3 (2) requires that the values of corresponding attributes must be compatible. To get an upper bound on the cost of fulfilling this condition let us see which kind of features would be the most challenging for a computational implementation of matching.

Of the six kinds described in 4.1.2, neither the sur attribute nor the bookkeeping attributes are relevant for matching between the language and the context level. The continuation attributes are relevant, but the compatibility of their values is not difficult to implement because these values are merely names for other proplets (whereby the names must agree in order for matching to be successful). The only demanding cases are the core attributes with their values of concepts, pointers, and markers. Of these, the concepts are perhaps the most demanding.

The considerable literature on concepts presents the schema (Piaget 1926; Stein and Trabasso 1982), the template (Neisser 1964), the feature (Hubel and Wiesel 1962; Gibson 1969), the prototype (Bransford and Franks 1971; Rosch 1975), and the geon

(Biederman 1987) approach. For simplicity, let us join the debate at a slightly higher level of abstraction by beginning with a distinction which should be common to all of these approaches, namely the distinction between concept *types* and concept *tokens*.

For present purposes, we define concepts as feature structures, i.e., as sets of features, each defined as an attribute-value pair – like proplets. The necessary properties of a type are represented by the attributes and certain constant values. These are shared with the tokens. The accidental properties are represented in the type by certain variable values, which are instantiated in different tokens as different constants. Thus, to a given type there corresponds an infinite number of tokens which differ from their type in that the type's variables have been replaced by specific values.

To simplify the explanation of the most basic notions, we use here a preliminary holistic representation, which will have to be replaced by the declarative specification of incremental, time-linear procedures for recognizing concepts based on geons, and geons based on features (cf. L&I'05).[5] Consider the following example using the preliminary holistic representation:

4.2.1 TYPE AND TOKEN OF THE CONCEPT *square*

type	*token*
$\begin{bmatrix} \text{edge 1: } \alpha \\ \text{angle 1/2: } 90° \\ \text{edge 2: } \alpha \\ \text{angle 2/3: } 90° \\ \text{edge 3: } \alpha \\ \text{angle 3/4: } 90° \\ \text{edge 4: } \alpha \\ \text{angle 4/1: } 90° \end{bmatrix}$	$\begin{bmatrix} \text{edge 1: 2 cm} \\ \text{angle 1/2: } 90° \\ \text{edge 2: 2 cm} \\ \text{angle 2/3: } 90° \\ \text{edge 3: 2 cm} \\ \text{angle 3/4: } 90° \\ \text{edge 4: 2 cm} \\ \text{angle 4/1: } 90° \end{bmatrix}$

The necessary properties, shared by the type and its token, are represented by four attributes for edges and four attributes for angles. Furthermore, all angle attributes have the same value, namely the constant "90 degrees" in the type and the token. The edge attributes also have the same value, though it is different for the type and the token.

The accidental property of a square is the edge *length*, represented by the variable α in the type. In the token, all occurrences of this variable have been instantiated

---

by a constant, here 2 cm. Because of its variable, the type of the concept square is compatible with infinitely many corresponding tokens, each with another edge length.

We have chosen this simple example to illustrate (i) how concepts are embedded into proplets as core values and (ii) how they play a central role in the internal matching between the language and the context level, based on the type–token relation:

4.2.2 CONCEPTS AS VALUES OF THE CORE ATTRIBUTES

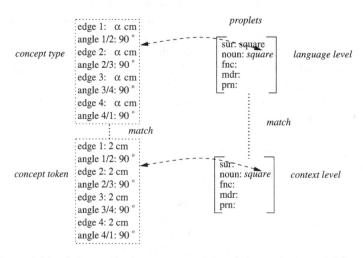

The matching between the language proplet and the context proplet is successful because (i) the language proplet and the context proplet have the same attributes and (ii) the values of their respective core attributes noun are compatible – due to the fact that they happen to be the type and a token of the same concept (other values have been omitted for simplicity).

The great utility of the type–token relation in the matching between language and context proplets wich contain concepts as values may be summarized as follows:

4.2.3 WHY THE TYPE–TOKEN RELATION IS IMPORTANT

Type–token relations based on feature structures with variables and constants are easily computed. Procedures matching the concept type of a language proplet with the concept token of a context proplet enable the language proplet to refer in different utterance situations to different context proplets, including reference to items never encountered before.

Let us assume, for example, that the robot is shown new geometrical objects which differ from previous ones in terms of their size. If we say: Pick the square!, then at least the middle part of the robot's reference mechanism, i.e., the matching between the language and the context level, will be able to do it (as shown by 4.2.2). The associated upper and lower interfaces, consisting of recognition and action at the language and context levels, are the topics of the following sections 4.3 and 4.4.

4.3 Context Recognition

The type–token relation of concepts is central also to the external interfaces at the context level. In contextual recognition, concept type and concept token function together as follows:

4.3.1 CONCEPT TYPE AND CONCEPT TOKEN IN CONTEXTUAL RECOGNITION

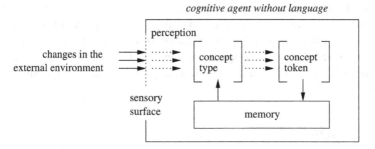

The sensory surface produces incoming parameter values, for example, in the form of a bitmap, which are matched by a concept type provided by the database. Thereby, the variables of the type are instantiated by constants. The resulting concept token may be stored in memory.

The matching process shown in 4.3.1 is illustrated below in more detail with the recognition of a square:

4.3.2 CONCEPT TYPE AND CONCEPT TOKEN IN RECOGNIZING A SQUARE

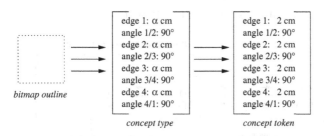

The type can be matched with the outline of all kinds of different squares, whereby its variables are instantiated accordingly.

Our preliminary holistic method of representing the concept **square** may be applied to other polygons, using the same recognition procedure based on matching concept types with bitmap outlines. The approach may also be extended to other kind of data, such as the recognition of colors, defining concept types as certain intervals in the electromagnetic spectrum and the tokens as particular constant values in such an interval (cf. CoL'89, pp. 296 ff.). The method is even suitable to implement the recognition of relations like "A is contained in B."

Today, there already exist pattern recognition programs which are quite good at recognizing geometric objects. They differ from our approach in that they are based almost completely on statistics. However, even if the terms of type and token may not be found in their theoretical descriptions, the type–token distinction is nevertheless implicit in any pattern recognition process. Furthermore, the rule-based, incremental procedures of pattern recognition presented in L&I'05 are well-suited to be combined with statistical methods.

As shown by the work of Steels (1999), suitable algorithms can evolve new types automatically from similar data by abstracting from what they take to be accidental. For Database Semantics, the automatic evolution of types has to result in concepts which correspond to those of a language community. This may be achieved by presenting the artificial agent with properly selected data in combination with human guidance.

4.4 Context Action

Having examined incoming data in terms of perception and recognition, let us turn to the outgoing data, which are analyzed in terms of intention and action. Intention is the process of developing an action cognitively, while action is the mechanism of realizing an intention by changing the environment.

Like recognition, action is based on concept types and concept tokens, but in the inverse order: While recognition is based on the sequence *periphery–type–token*, action is based on the sequence *token–type–periphery*, as shown in the following schema:

4.4.1 CONCEPT TYPES AND CONCEPT TOKENS IN ACTION

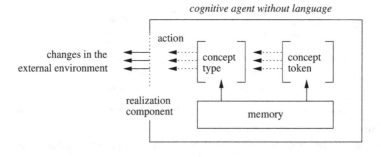

The input to an action is an intention. Intentions (in the sense of wanting to act in a certain way) must be specific with respect to time and space as well as to the properties of the objects involved. Therefore, intentions are defined as concept tokens.

Actions, as the corresponding concept types, are defined as general realization procedures, for example, drinking from a cup. They are provided by the database for a given intention. The action procedure (type) is matched with the intention (token), whereby the variables of the action type are instantiated by the constants of the intention (specialization). The specialized action is realized by peripheral cognition as changes in the environment. Tasks for which no standard action is available, like the creative opening of a difficult lock in an unfamiliar door, are realized by trying different combinations of smaller standard actions.

4.5 Sign Recognition and Production

From the recognition and action procedures at the context level let us turn next to the corresponding procedures at the language level. There, recognition is called *interpretation* and action is called *production*.

Taking the view point of evolution, we regard sign interpretation and production at the language level as a secondary use of recognition and action at the context level. Just as the recognition of the *object* of a square at the context level is based on parameter values in a certain modality (here vision) which are matched by a concept type and instantiated as a concept token, the recognition of the *surface* of the word square is based on parameter values in a certain modality (e.g., hearing) which are matched by a surface type and instantiated as a surface token, and similarly for surface synthesis in language production. In short, the surface types and tokens used at the language level are a special kind of the concept types and tokens used at the context level.

As physical objects, e.g., as sound waves or dots on paper produced by the speaker and perceived by the hearer, the surfaces carry neither a syntactic category nor a semantic representation nor any other grammatical property. Within cognition, however, the surfaces serve as *keys*: For the hearer, each recognized external surface provides access to a lexical entry stored in memory, which contains a corresponding surface:

4.5.1 LEXICAL LOOKUP OF GERMAN Apfel IN THE HEARER MODE

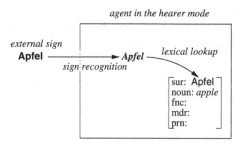

Within the lexical entry, the surface is firmly attached to a battery of properties, such as a specific part of speech (here noun), morpho-syntactic properties (omitted), and a literal meaning (here *apple*). In Database Semantics, these properties are represented in the form of an isolated proplet. The connection between the surface of a lexical entry and the associated set of grammatical properties is established by conventions,[6] which each member of the language community has to learn.

The processing of surfaces in the speaker and the hearer mode constitutes the third application based on the type–token relation between concepts (besides recognition and action at the context level, and the vertical matching between the language and the context level). The threefold function of the type–token relation in the cycle of natural language communication may be summarized as follows:

4.5.2 THREE TYPE–TOKEN RELATIONS IN THE CYCLE OF COMMUNICATION

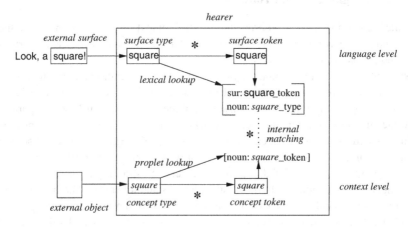

The three instances of a type–token relation are indicated by *. As shown in FoCL'99, Sect. 23.5, there are altogether 10 different variants of 4.5.2, depending on different combinations of recognition and action at the language and the context level. In 4.5.2, the hearer mode is shown in a constellation of immediate reference (SLIM 8, cf. FoCL'99, 23.5.8).

At the language level, recognition of the external surface square is based on matching it with a surface type and instantiating it as a token. The type triggers the lexical lookup of an appropriate proplet. The surface token replaces[7] the original type value of the sur attribute (indicated as [sur: square_token]). The lexical value of the core attribute noun is the concept type *square* (indicated as [noun: *square*_type]).

---

[6] The convention-based connection between surface and meaning was described in 1913 by de Saussure in his first principle as *l'arbitraire du signe*. For further discussion see FoCL'99, Sect. 6.2

[7] This is because the hearer remembers the pronunciation of a word. Also, we would like to maintain symmetry with the context level. The current JSLIM implementation simplifies the issue by turning language proplets into context proplets right after lexical lookup by deleting the surface values.

At the context level, recognition of the external object is based on a concept type, which is instantiated as a concept token. The type triggers lookup of a corresponding context proplet. The token replaces the original type value[8] of the core attribute of the context proplet (indicated as [noun: *square*_token]). As a result, the feature [noun: *square*_type] at the language level can be matched with the feature [noun: *square*_token] at the context level.

Apart from the vertical internal matching of types with tokens, there is also the possibility of matching types with types. This case arises in the interpretation of absolute, rather than episodic, propositions (cf. Sect. 5.2). For example, in the proposition *A square has four corners*, the context proplet *square* would contain the concept type rather than a token as its core value. This is no problem for matching with a corresponding language proplet, however, because matching a type with a type is structurally straightforward.

4.6 Universal versus Language-Dependent Properties

Given that the function of natural language is communication and that form (including the form of language) follows function, Database Semantics, as an abstract declarative specification, is common to all natural languages – simply for reasons of how natural language communication works. Consequently, all the differences between the various natural languages like English, Chinese, Tagalog, or Quechua have no effect on the basic framework of Database Semantics. This raises the following questions:

- What are the differences between natural languages?
- How should these differences be integrated into Database Semantics?

The most obvious difference between natural languages are in their surfaces. This difference is handled in the lexical proplets by having different values of the sur attribute (cf. 3.2.1). If two languages are sufficiently close to have similar concepts in content words, this is expressed by using the same core value (cf. 3.2.2).

For two languages or groups of languages to be unrelated, the traditional criterion is their having different *roots*, for example, the Indo-European languages versus the Finno-Ugric languages. If these roots represent well-defined, simple concepts like father, mother, or water, they can be represented by the same core values. Otherwise, new concepts have to be defined and the relation between incommensurable roots must be specified.

Finally, there are the language-dependent differences as to which grammatical relations and distinctions are coded *analytically* by means of function words (e.g., determiners, conjunctions, prepositions) or *synthetically* in terms of morphology (e.g.,

---

[8] In the current implementation, concepts are represented by placeholders. This is because without contextual interfaces (as in 2.5.1), concepts defined as effective procedures are not yet available. In placeholders, the distinction between concept types and concept tokens is in name only.

inflection, agglutination, derivation, composition). In Database Semantics, these aspects are treated by language-dependent LA-grammars with a suitable lexicon and associated systems of automatic word form recognition and production, restrictions on variables (e.g., 13.2.2) for handling agreement (e.g., 13.2.3), and a rule system for handling word order (e.g., 13.2.4).

From a functional point of view, Database Semantics treats the differences between natural languages as relatively minor variations at certain low-level locations, such as the values of certain attributes. From a linguistic point of view, however, the handling of the universal versus language-dependent aspects of natural language in Database Semantics may be characterized in terms of the following hierarchy:

4.6.1 HIERARCHY OF NOTIONS AND DISTINCTIONS IN DATABASE SEMANTICS

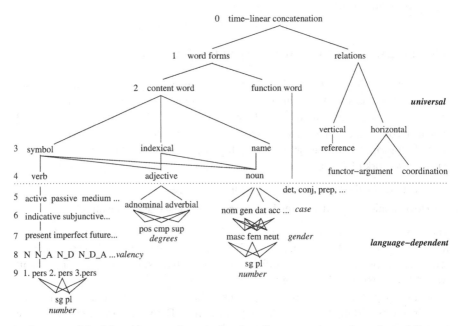

At the root of the hierarchy tree there is the time-linear concatenation of word forms (level 0). This most basic structural property of natural language is illustrated by the DBS-letter system defined in Sect. 3.6.

Level 1 is divided into (i) word forms and (ii) relations. The word forms are divided into content words and function words (level 2), while the relations are divided into vertical and horizontal relations.

The content words are divided into the three basic kinds of signs, namely symbol, indexical, and name (level 3). In the branch of relations, the kinds of signs serve the vertical relation of reference (level 3), implemented as a matching between the levels of language and context (cf. 3.2.4).

The kinds of signs (level 3) are correlated with the parts of speech (level 4). Symbols can be verbs, adjectives, or nouns; indexicals can be adjectives or nouns; and names can be nouns only. This is shown graphically by the lines relating the kinds of signs and the parts of speech. In the branch of relations, the parts of speech serve the horizontal relations (cf. 3.2.4) of functor–argument structure and coordination.

The structures shown above the dotted line separating levels 4 and 5 are universal: All natural languages are based on a time-linear concatenation of word forms, the distinction between content and function words, the three kinds of signs, the three parts of speech,[9] the vertical relation of reference, and the horizontal relations of functor–argument structure and coordination.

The structures shown below the dotted line are language-dependent. For the verbs of the Indo-European languages, for example, this holds for the genus, modus, and tempus verbi (levels 5, 6, and 7), the valency structure (level 8), as well as the person and number distinction (level 9). For the adjectives, it holds for the distinction between adnominal and adverbial use, and for the synthetic handling of the degrees (positive, comparative, superlative). For the nouns, it holds for the different case systems, and the number and gender distinctions (which are absent,[10] for example, in Korean).

---

[9] Typologically speaking, this applies to the "functional" level, i.e., the level of the semantic representations, rather than the "formal" level, i.e., the level of structural surface properties (cf. Stassen 1985, pp. 14–15; Croft 1995, pp. 88–89).

[10] In the sense that they are not inherent in the nouns and do not impose any combinatorial restrictions such as agreement. Cf. Choe et al. (2006).

5. Forms of Thinking

Section 5.1 shows that the DBS data structure is well-suited for question answering. Furthermore, the data structure is easily extended[1] to the distinction between episodic and absolute propositions (Sect. 5.2), which in turn is the basis for implementing inferences, here *modus ponens* (Sect. 5.3). This inference is employed for implementing an indirect use of language (Sect. 5.4). Finally, it is shown how the intuitive meaning of a word is composed of several ingredients, some of which are derived from the agent's personal experiences and socio-cultural background (Sects. 5.5 and 5.6).

5.1 Retrieving Answers to Questions

So far, the data structure of a Word Bank, consisting of ordered token lines listing connected proplets with the same core value (cf. 3.3.1, 3.6.6), has been used (i) for the storage in the hearer mode and (ii) for the retrieval of successor proplets in the most basic kind of the think mode, namely free association based on fixed patterns, serving as an example of the speaker's conceptualization. We turn now to another kind of thinking supported by this data structure, namely (iii) moving along a token line.

Consider an agent thinking about girls. This means activating the corresponding token line, such as the following example:

5.1.1 EXAMPLE OF A TOKEN LINE

owner record   *member records*

$$\begin{bmatrix} \text{noun: } girl \end{bmatrix} \quad \begin{bmatrix} \text{noun: girl} \\ \text{fnc: walk} \\ \text{mdr: young} \\ \text{prn: 10} \end{bmatrix} \begin{bmatrix} \text{noun: girl} \\ \text{fnc: sleep} \\ \text{mdr: blond} \\ \text{prn: 12} \end{bmatrix} \begin{bmatrix} \text{noun: girl} \\ \text{fnc: eat} \\ \text{mdr: small} \\ \text{prn: 15} \end{bmatrix} \begin{bmatrix} \text{noun: girl} \\ \text{fnc: read} \\ \text{mdr: smart} \\ \text{prn: 19} \end{bmatrix}$$

As indicated by the fnc and mdr values of the connected proplets (member records), the agent happened to observe or hear about a young girl walking, a blonde girl sleeping, a small girl eating, and a smart girl reading.

Traversing the token line of any given concept is powered by the following LA-think grammar, called LA-think.LINE:

---

[1] That a framework developed for certain purposes turns out to be suitable for other purposes as well is a kind of convergence. Convergence is one of most significant indicators in science for being on the right track (cf. FoCL'99, Sect. 9.5).

5.1.2 DEFINITION OF **LA-think.LINE**

ST_S: $\{([RA.1:\alpha]\{1\ r_{forwd}\ 2\ r_{bckwd}\})\}$

r_{forwd} $\begin{bmatrix} RA.1:\alpha \\ prn:\ n \end{bmatrix}$ $\begin{bmatrix} RA.1:\alpha \\ prn:\ n+1 \end{bmatrix}$ output position nw $\{r_{forwd}\}$

r_{bckwd} $\begin{bmatrix} RA.1:\alpha \\ prn:\ n \end{bmatrix}$ $\begin{bmatrix} RA.1:\alpha \\ prn:\ n-1 \end{bmatrix}$ output position nw $\{r_{bckwd}\}$

ST_F: $\{([RA.1:\alpha]\ rp_{forwd}),\ ([RA.1:\alpha]\ rp_{bckwd})\}$

The core attribute is represented by the replacement variable RA.1 (cf. 4.1.3, C.3.2), which is restricted to the attributes noun, verb, or adj. The prn values n, $n+1$ and $n-1$ follow the convention that $n+1$ stands for the proplet immediately following the current proplet n in the token line, and $n-1$ for the proplet immediately preceding. The rule r_{forwd} traverses a token line from left to right (forward), following the temporal order, while the rule r_{bckwd} moves right to left in the antitemporal order (backward).

Consider the application of r_{forwd} to the proplet with the prn value 12 in 5.1.1:

5.1.3 EXAMPLE OF AN **LA-think.LINE** RULE APPLICATION

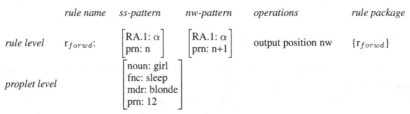

	rule name	ss-pattern	nw-pattern	operations	rule package
rule level	r_{forwd}:	$\begin{bmatrix} RA.1:\alpha \\ prn:\ n \end{bmatrix}$	$\begin{bmatrix} RA.1:\alpha \\ prn:\ n+1 \end{bmatrix}$	output position nw	$\{r_{forwd}\}$
proplet level		$\begin{bmatrix} noun:\ girl \\ fnc:\ sleep \\ mdr:\ blonde \\ prn:\ 12 \end{bmatrix}$			

During matching, the replacement variable RA.n is substituted by the attribute noun, and the binding variables α and n are bound to the values girl and 12, respectively. The application of this rule to the token line example 5.1.1 has the following result:

5.1.4 RESULT OF THE **LA-think.LINE** RULE APPLICATION

$\begin{bmatrix} noun:\ girl \\ fnc:\ sleep \\ mdr:\ blonde \\ prn:\ 12 \end{bmatrix}$ $\begin{bmatrix} noun:\ girl \\ fnc:\ eat \\ mdr:\ small \\ prn:\ 15 \end{bmatrix}$

Such moving along the token line of an activated concept is naturally extendable to answering questions. There are two kinds of basic query, called (i) *wh questions* and (ii) *yes/no questions*,[2] illustrated below with examples relating to the token line example 5.1.1.

5.1.5 BASIC KINDS OF QUERY IN NATURAL LANGUAGE

wh question	*yes/no question*
Which girl walked?	Did the young girl walk?

---

[2] The expressions used in these questions are of the sentence mood *interrogative*. Explicit syntactic–semantic derivations of interrogatives, including long distance dependency, are shown in Sect. 9.5.

In Database Semantics, these questions translate into the following proplet patterns:

5.1.6 SEARCH PROPLETS ILLUSTRATING THE TWO BASIC TYPES OF QUESTIONS

In the search proplet of the wh question, the mdr attribute has the variable σ and the prn attribute the variable n as value; in the search proplet of the yes/no question, only the prn attribute has a variable as value. Technically, the answer to a question consists in binding the variables of the search proplet to suitable values. Consider the application of the wh question search pattern in 5.1.6 to the token line 5.1.1:

5.1.7 WH SEARCH PATTERN CHECKING A TOKEN LINE

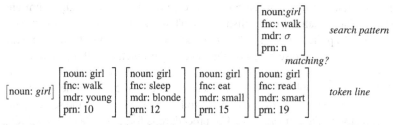

The indicated attempt at matching fails because the fnc values of the proplet pattern (i.e., walk) and of the proplet token (i.e., read) are incompatible. The same holds after moving the pattern one proplet to the left. Only after reaching the leftmost proplet is the matching successful. Now the variable σ is bound to young and the variable n to 10. Accordingly, the answer provided to the question Which girl walked? is The young girl (walked). This procedure is formalized by the following LA-think grammar:

5.1.8 DEFINITION OF **LA-think.Q1** (*wh question*)

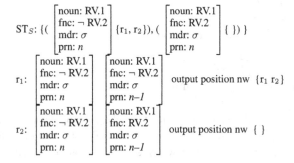

$$ST_F: \{(\begin{bmatrix} \text{noun: RV.1} \\ \text{fnc: } \neg \text{ RV.2} \\ \text{mdr: } \sigma \\ \text{prn: } n{-}1 \end{bmatrix} \text{rp}_1), (\begin{bmatrix} \text{noun: RV.1} \\ \text{fnc: RV.2} \\ \text{mdr: } \sigma \\ \text{prn: } n{-}1 \end{bmatrix} \text{rp}_2) \}$$

The proplets in the start states, the rules, and the final states represent search patterns, whereby RV.1 and RV.2 are replacement variables for a core and a continuation value, respectively, while σ, n, and $n{-}1$ are binding variables. For example, applied to the wh search pattern of 5.1.6, RV.1 is replaced with girl and RV.2 with walk.

For the feature [fnc: $\neg$ RV.2] to match it must *not* be compatible with the input. In the definition of LA-think.Q1 in 5.1.8, this is specified for the first start state, the sentence start and the next word of r_1, the sentence start of r_2, and the first final state. In contrast, the corresponding feature [fnc: RV.2] in the second sentence start, the next word of r_2, and second final state, does have to be compatible to match the input.

If the last proplet of a token line does not match the search pattern, the rules r_1 and r_2 are both activated (cf. rule package of the first start state). If the next to last proplet does not match either, r_1 is successful; otherwise r_2 is successful. As long as there are proplets in the token line for r_1 to apply successfully (i.e., matching fails), the derivation continues; when no token remains, the grammar algorithm enters the first final state, realized in English as I don't know. If the derivation completes with a successful application of r_2, the grammar enters the second final state, realized in English as a noun phrase based on the matching proplet, here the young girl.

A yes/no question is handled in a similar manner. For example, Did the young girl walk?, based on applying the yes/no search pattern of 5.1.6 to the token line 5.1.1, results in the answer yes, due to a successful matching between the search pattern and the proplet with the prn value 10. The procedure is formalized as LA-think.Q2:

5.1.9 DEFINITION OF **LA-think.Q2** (*yes/no question*)

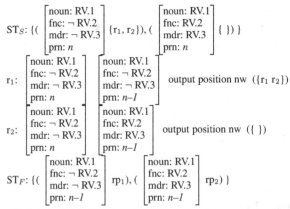

In LA-think.Q2, RV.1, RV.2, and RV.3 are replacement variables, while n and $n{-}1$ are binding variables. The answers are based on the final states ST_F, the first of which represents the answer no and the second the answer yes. For example, in the attempt to answer the question Did the blonde girl walk? relative to the token line 5.1.1, the search will be in vain; having applied r_1 to all proplets in the token line, LA-think.Q2 terminates in the first final state, which is realized in English as the answer no. The question Did the young girl walk?, in contrast, results in the second final state, which is realized in English as the answer yes. For further discussion see Sect. 9.5.

5.2 Episodic versus Absolute Propositions

Another kind of thinking, besides (i) navigating along interproplet relations (cf. 3.5.1) and (ii) moving along token lines (cf. 5.1.3), are (iii) inferences. In Database Semantics, inferences are based on *absolute* propositions, as opposed to *episodic* propositions (cf. FoCL'99, Sect. 22.4; AIJ'01).

Absolute propositions represent content which holds independently of any STAR (cf. 2.6.2), such as scientific or mathematical content, but also personal beliefs like Mary takes a nap after lunch. Episodic propositions, in contrast, require specification of the STAR in order for the content to be coded correctly.[3]

In DBS, episodic and absolute propositions are distinguished by the value of their prn attribute, as illustrated by the following example showing the proplets of the propositions A dog is an animal (absolute) and the dog is tired (episodic):

5.2.1 ABSOLUTE AND EPISODIC PROPLETS IN A WORD BANK (context level)

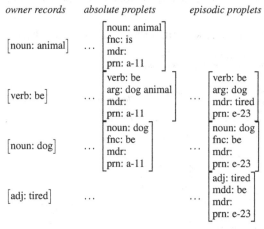

In addition to the different prn values, here a-11 versus e-23, absolute and episodic proplets differ in that the core value of absolute proplets is a concept type, while the core value of episodic proplets is a concept token:

---

[3] Absolute propositions of the context level are coded in language as *generic* sentences which express their atemporal character by using present tense. Episodic propositions of the context level are coded in language as sentences which usually contain temporal and local adjectives, and a verb which is not in present tense.

5.2.2 CORE VALUES AS CONCEPT TYPES AND CONCEPT TOKENS

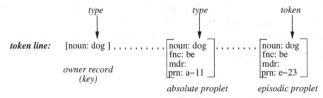

Thus, at the context level the core values of episodic proplets are typed indirectly by the associated owner record.

The distinction between absolute and episodic proplets leads to an additional division of fields in a Word Bank, both in the area of context and of language proplets:

5.2.3 AREAS OF EPISODIC VS. ABSOLUTE PROPLETS IN A WORD BANK

context owner records	absolute context proplets	episodic context proplets	episodic language proplets	absolute language proplets	language owner records
1	2	3	4	5	6

To obtain matching frontiers (cf. 3.3.1) between the areas of context and language for the absolute as well as the episodic propositions, absolute and episodic proplets are stored conceptually in two levels, as indicated by the following representation:

5.2.4 MATCHING FRONTIERS IN A THREE-DIMENSIONAL REPRESENTATION

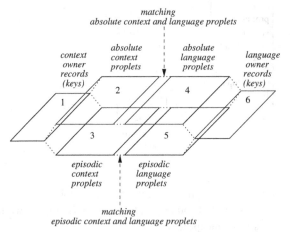

Presenting the absolute proplets above the episodic ones is motivated by the transition of frequent episodic propositions of the same content into an absolute proposition, as illustrated below:

5.2.5 FROM EPISODIC PROPOSITIONS TO AN ABSOLUTE PROPOSITION

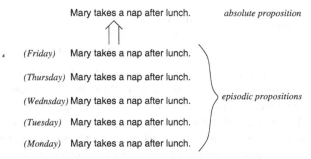

Episodic propositions represent isolated events, bound to a particular STAR. If their STAR grounding turns out to be redundant (because it does not seem to matter), they may be summarized as an absolute proposition, in which the STAR is omitted.

From a technical point of view, it must be emphasized that the structuring of a Word Bank indicated in 5.2.4 is purely conceptual and does not restrict the storage locations in the actual implementation of the database. This is because relations between proplets are coded solely in terms of attributes and their values.

5.3 Inference: Reconstructing *Modus Ponens*

Before we turn to the handling of inferences in Database Semantics, let us consider the classical inferences of Propositional Calculus. In the following summary, A and B are true propositions, $\neg$ is sentential negation, & is logical and, $\vee$ is logical or, $\rightarrow$ is logical implication, the expressions above the horizontal line are the premise or premises, and the expression below is the conclusion, indicated by $\vdash$:

5.3.1 INFERENCE SCHEMATA OF PROPOSITIONAL CALCULUS

$$1.\ \frac{A, B}{\vdash A\&B} \qquad 2.\ \frac{A \vee B, \neg A}{\vdash B} \qquad 3.\ \frac{A \rightarrow B, A}{\vdash B} \qquad 4.\ \frac{A \rightarrow B, \neg B}{\vdash \neg A}$$

$$5.\ \frac{A\&B}{\vdash A} \qquad 6.\ \frac{A}{\vdash A \vee B} \qquad 7.\ \frac{\neg A}{\vdash A \rightarrow B} \qquad 8.\ \frac{\neg\neg A}{\vdash A}$$

In the inference schema 1, called *conjunction*, the truth of two arbitrary propositions A and B implies the truth of the complex proposition $A\&B$. If the inference of *conjunction* were reconstructed in Database Semantics, it would amount to an operation which establishes new extrapropositional relations between arbitrary propositions, based on the conjunction and. This operation may be characterized as the following LA-grammar rule.

5.3.2 LA-RULE FOR THE INFERENCE OF *conjunction* (HYPOTHETICAL)

$$\text{inf}_1: \begin{bmatrix} \text{verb: } \alpha \\ \text{prn: } m \end{bmatrix} \begin{bmatrix} \text{verb: } \beta \\ \text{prn: } n \end{bmatrix} \implies \begin{bmatrix} \text{verb: } \alpha \\ \text{prn: } m \\ \text{cnj: } m \text{ and } n \end{bmatrix} \begin{bmatrix} \text{verb: } \beta \\ \text{prn: } n \\ \text{cnj: } m \text{ and } n \end{bmatrix}$$

The patterns to the left of the arrow each match the verb proplet of some arbitrary proposition, thereby binding the variables α, β, m, and n. To the right of the arrow the same patterns are shown with the additional feature [cnj: m and n]. Thus, inf1 produces the extrapropositional relation of coordination between two arbitrary propositions m and n by adding cnj attributes with values to their proplets in the word bank. These new connections enable new navigations, from any proposition to any other proposition asserted in the Word Bank.

In its Truth-Conditional Semantics interpretation, the inference in question expresses a conjunction of truth and is, as such, intuitively obvious. From this point of view, it is not relevant which propositions are conjoined. The only condition for the inference to be valid is that the two propositions in the premise happen to be true.

From the view point of Database Semantics, in contrast, there arises the question of *why* two – previously unconnected – propositions should be concatenated with and. For example, even though conjoining Lady Marion smiled at Robin Hood and The glove compartment was open might not result in asserting a falsehood, it would make little sense. Because an uncontrolled application of inf$_1$ would create new, unmotivated connections between hitherto unconnected propositions, the coherence of content in a word bank would be destroyed by it.

The example of *conjunction* has shown how a classical inference can be reconstructed in Database Semantics. We have also seen that the classical inference schemata may change their character substantially when transferred to Database Semantics. Therefore they should not be transferred blindly.

Let us turn now to *modus ponens*. Its inference schema (cf. 3 in 5.3.1) may be illustrated in Propositional Calculus as follows:

5.3.3 *modus ponens* IN PROPOSITIONAL CALCULUS

Premise 1:	If the sun is shining, Mary takes a walk.	$A \rightarrow B$
Premise 2:	The sun is shining.	A
Conclusion:	Mary takes a walk.	$\vdash B$

Because Propositional Calculus treats propositions as unanalyzed constants. e.g., A and B, this form of *modus ponens* is suitable to assert the inference relation between sentences, but not between individuals. Let us therefore consider *modus ponens* in Predicate Calculus (cf. Bochenski 1961, 16.07 ff., 43.16 ff.), which analyzes the internal structure of propositions using the connectives $\neg$, &, $\vee$, and $\rightarrow$ of Propositional Calculus plus one- and two-place functor constants like f, g, and h, and the quantifiers $\exists$ and $\forall$ horizontally binding the variables x, y, z:

5.3.4 *modus ponens* IN PREDICATE CALCULUS

$$\frac{\forall x[f(x) \rightarrow g(x)],\ \exists x[f(x)\ \&\ h(x)]}{\vdash\ \exists x[g(x)\ \&\ h(x)]}$$

Thus, if f is realized as dog, g as animal, and h as tired, the inference would read:

Premise 1:   For all x, if x is a dog, then x is an animal. $\forall x[dog(x) \rightarrow animal(x)]$
Premise 2:   There exists an x, x is a dog and x is tired. $\exists x[dog(x)\ \&\ tired(x)]$
Conclusion: There exists an x, x is an animal and x is tired. $\vdash\ \exists x[animal(x)\&tired(x)]$

Because the binding of variables in Prepositional Calculus is horizontal (e.g., $\exists x\ [... x]$), but vertical in Database Semantics, and because the parts of a logical formula are ordered, while proplets are unordered, this inference cannot be transferred to Database Semantics directly. Instead, *modus ponens* may be reconstructed by representing (i) the premise with the universal quantifier as an absolute proposition, e.g., A dog is an animal, (ii) the premise with the existential quantifier as an episodic proposition, e.g., The dog was tired, and (iii) the conclusion as the following rule:

5.3.5 INFERENCE RULE INF$_2$ FOR RECONSTRUCTING *modus ponens*

$$
\text{inf}_2:
\begin{bmatrix} \text{verb: be} \\ \text{arg: } \alpha \\ \text{mdr: } \beta \\ \text{prn: } e\text{-}n \end{bmatrix}
\begin{bmatrix} \text{noun: } \alpha \\ \text{fnc: be} \\ \text{prn: } e\text{-}n \end{bmatrix}
\begin{bmatrix} \text{adj: } \beta \\ \text{mdd: be} \\ \text{mdr:} \\ \text{prn: } e\text{-}n \end{bmatrix}
\begin{bmatrix} \text{verb: is-a} \\ \text{arg: } \delta\ \gamma \\ \text{prn: } a\text{-}m \end{bmatrix}
\begin{matrix} \text{if } \alpha \text{ instantiates } \delta, \\ \text{replace } \alpha \text{ with } \gamma \\ \text{and replace } e\text{-}n \text{ with } e\text{-}n' \end{matrix}
\quad \{\,...\,\}
$$

The proplets with the prn value *e-n* represent the episodic premise, the one with the prn value *a-m* the absolute premise, and the operation realizes the conclusion.

This inference rule may be restated informally as the following abstract paraphrase:

5.3.6 ABSTRACT PARAPHRASE

1. Absolute premise: noun type δ is-a noun type γ.
2. Episodic premise: noun token α happens to be adjective β.
3. Episodic conclusion: If noun token α instantiates noun type δ, then noun token γ happens to be adjective β.

This reconstruction is based semantically on equating the grammatical terms *noun, verb,* and *adjective* with the logical terms *argument, functor,* and *modifier,* and the ontological terms *object/individual, relation,* and *property,* respectively (cf. FoCL'99, Sect. 3.4). Furthermore, while the two premises of *modus ponens* in Predicate Calculus are connected – roughly speaking – by a quantifier-kind of Substitutivity of Identicals (cf. FoCL'99, Sect. 20.1), in Database Semantics the connection is based on the type–token relation "*instantiates.*" This is shown by the following example, which realizes the variables of the abstract paraphrases as concrete terms:

5.3.7 CONCRETE EXAMPLE BASED ON THE ABSTRACT PARAPHRASE

1. Absolute premise: *dog* type is-a(n) *animal* type.
2. Episodic premise: *dog* token happens to be *tired*.
3. Episodic conclusion: If *dog* token instantiates *dog* type, then *animal* token happens to be *tired*.

In the formal definition of the rule inf_2, the distinction between concept tokens and concept types is left implicit for simplicity.[4]

Consider the application of the rule inf_2 to proplets in the Word Bank 5.2.1:

5.3.8 APPLYING INF$_2$ TO THE WORD BANK 5.2.1

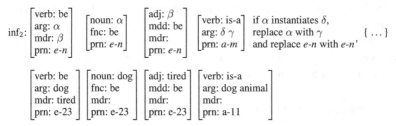

In this example, the first three patterns of the rule are matched with the episodic proplets *be, dog,* and *tired*, thereby vertically binding the variable α to the value dog and the variable β to the value tired. The fourth pattern is matched with an absolute proplet. The variables δ and γ are vertically bound to the values dog and animal, respectively. Because the token bound to the variable α instantiates the type bound to variable δ, the operation of the rule replaces α with γ, resulting in the following new proposition, which represents the conclusion of the inference:

5.3.9 RESULT OF APPLYING INF$_2$ TO THE WORD BANK 5.2.1

$$
\begin{bmatrix} \text{verb: be} \\ \text{arg: animal} \\ \text{mdr: tired} \\ \text{prn: e-23'} \end{bmatrix}
\begin{bmatrix} \text{noun: animal} \\ \text{fnc: be} \\ \text{mdr:} \\ \text{prn: e-23'} \end{bmatrix}
\begin{bmatrix} \text{adj: tired} \\ \text{mdd: be} \\ \text{mdr:} \\ \text{prn: e-23'} \end{bmatrix}
$$

In this way, the original episodic proposition the dog is tired with the prn value e-23 is complemented by the variant the animal is tired with the prn value e-23'.

Therefore, prior to this application of *modus ponens*, querying the Word Bank 5.2.1 with the question Was the animal tired? would result in the answer no. Once the inference is applied, however, the answer is yes – which is in concord with intuition. Technically, the application of inf_2 is an instance of nonmonotonic reasoning.

The method of inferring illustrated with inf_2 may be extended to episodic propositions of other structures, e.g., one-place main verbs, two-place main verbs, etc., and applied to proplets of all absolute propositions with the verb is-a, i.e., to all the elements of the *is-a* hierarchy. Similar rules may be defined for the other hierarchies.

5.4 Indirect Uses of Language

The strict correspondence between language and context proplets illustrated in 3.2.4 raises the question of how to extend internal matching to nonliteral uses. As an example (borrowed from FoCL'99, p. 92), consider a hearer who has just entered a room containing only an orange crate. If the speaker commands Put the coffee on the table!, the hearer will infer that table refers to the orange crate. Given the small number of referential candidates in this limited context of use, the minimal meaning$_1$ of the word table best fits the structure of the orange crate (*best match*).

5.4.1 NONLITERAL USE OF THE WORD table

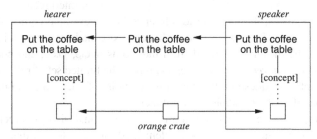

However, if a prototypical table were placed next to the orange crate, the hearer would interpret the sentence differently, putting the coffee not on the orange crate, but on the table. This is not caused by a change in the meaning$_1$ of table, but by the fact that the context of use has changed, providing an additional candidate for best match.[5]

The importance of metaphor as a basic principle of natural language communication has been emphasized by Lakoff and Johnson (1980) and subsequent work. However, their approach is quite different from ours because it is based on the following meaning definition by Grice:

5.4.2 GRICE'S DEFINITION OF MEANING

Definiendum: U meant something by uttering x.
Definiens: For some audience A, U intends his utterance of x to produce in A some effect (response) E, by means of A's recognition of the intention.[6]

One problem with this definition is that it is not suitable for a computational model.[7]

---

[4] Whether a concept happens to be a type or a token may be inferred from the distinction between absolute and episodic propositions, formally marked by the prn values.

[5] The principle of best match can only function properly if the choice of possible candidates is restricted. Therefore the selection and delimitation of the context of use based on the sign's STAR is crucial for the successful interpretation of natural language. Cf. 2.6.2 above. For a more detailed discussion see FoCL'99, pp. 93 ff., Sect. 5.3.

[6] Cf. Grice (1957) and (1965).

[7] For a more detailed discussion see FoCL'99, pp. 84–86.

Regarding metaphor, the difference between the two approaches may be demonstrated with the following example from Lakoff and Johnson (1980, p. 12). They present the utterance Please sit in the apple juice seat as referring to the seat with the apple juice setting, and continue: "In isolation this sentence has no meaning at all, since the expression 'apple juice seat' is not a conventional way of referring to any kind of object." For the SLIM theory of language, the question is whether Lakoff and Johnson use the term "meaning" as the $meaning_1$ of the sign, or the $meaning_2$ of the utterance (cf. 2.6.1). If "meaning" is to be interpreted as the literal $meaning_1$ of the sign apple juice seat, then the sentence clearly does have such a meaning, compositionally derived from the $meaning_1$ of its words. If "meaning" is to be interpreted as $meaning_2$, however, then it holds by definition that no sentence has a $meaning_2$ *in isolation*, i.e., as a sign type and without an associated context of interpretation.

According to our analysis, the metaphoric reference in this example comes about by matching the $meaning_1$ of the expression with a context containing a seat with an apple juice setting. The $meaning_1$ derived from the words apple, juice, and seat is minimal in the sense of *seat related to apple juice*. Given the limited set of referential candidates in the context in question, this literal meaning is sufficient to pick out the intended referent based on the principle of best match.

For Database Semantics, the crucial question raised by this analysis of indirect use is how the principle of best match should be implemented formally. Rather than loosening the matching conditions defined in 3.2.3 (as would be suggested by the intuitive approach illustrated in 5.4.1), Database Semantics handles nonliteral (indirect) language uses on the basis of inferencing.

Direct and indirect uses differ as follows: In direct use, the language and the context proplets match in accordance with the matching condition 3.2.3, as illustrated in 3.2.4, whereas in indirect use, inferences first map some of the context proplets into a *secondary coding* that is then matched by corresponding language proplets directly, again in accordance with the matching condition 3.2.3.[8] For example, if the contextual content *the dog is tired* is to be coded into language as the animal is tired, then is tired is a direct use while the animal is an indirect use based on the absolute proposition *a dog is an animal* (see 5.3.5–5.3.9):

5.4.3 CONTEXTUAL INFERENCE UNDERLYING A NONLITERAL USE

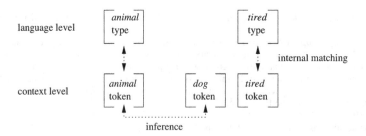

In the speaker mode, the proposition *dog tired* is extended at the context level into the secondary coding *animal tired*. This secondary coding is matched directly with language proplets. In the hearer mode, the language proplets *animal tired* are matched directly with corresponding context proplets. By looking for an appropriate instantiation of *animal* at the context level, the hearer reconstructs the primary coding from the secondary coding via an inference.

With this approach, direct and indirect uses of language differ solely in whether or not the proplet representing the referent is the referent itself (primary coding) or instead some other proplet related to the referent via an inference (secondary coding). This way of handling inferences, secondary codings, and indirect language uses has the following advantages:

5.4.4 ADVANTAGES OF HANDLING INDIRECT USES VIA INFERENCES

1. Direct and indirect uses of language are based on the same method of strict internal matching (cf. 3.2.3), which greatly facilitates computational realization.
2. The inferencing underlying indirect uses is restricted to the level of context. Therefore, agents with and without language can use the same cognitive system.
3. Inferencing at the level of context is much more powerful and flexible than the traditional inferencing based on isolated signs of language.
4. Assuming that natural language directly reflects the contextual coding, the contextual inferences can be studied by analyzing their language reflections.

Let us consider the inference, the secondary coding, and the indirect use of language in a few more examples. Another kind of indirect use, called *pars pro toto*, is based on the inference of choosing a prominent property of the referent, as when observing *girl with pink dress wants to sing* (context level) and expressing it with the sentence The pink dress wants to sing (language level).

Other inferences underlying a secondary coding select a characteristic behavior to refer to an individual, as in The man eater went back into the jungle, where the subject refers to a tiger preying on humans. Indirect uses arise also with absolute propositions. For example, The master of the animal kingdom lives in Africa (language level) may be used to express *The lion lives in Africa* (context level).

Indirect uses and the inferences on which they are based apply to all three parts of speech. An indirect use of a verb is illustrated by Julia did the dishes. Here an inference selects the verb from a higher place in the semantic hierarchy associated with *wash*, just as in our initial nominal example of referring to a dog with the word animal. The indirect use of an adjective, finally, is illustrated by easy money, where *easy* is a secondary coding expressing the manner in which the money is obtained.

---

[8] For example, the inference underlying 5.4.1 is based on the absolute propositions A table has a flat surface and An orange crate has a flat surface. Rather than formally reconstructing this inference, we use the inference defined in the previous section for the following Example 5.4.3.

Indirect uses arise not only with the sign kind of symbols, as when referring to the context proplet *dog* using the symbolic language proplet animal, but also with indexicals and names. For example, there are indirect uses of referring with a concept to a referent represented by a name proplet, as in calling *Richthofen* the red baron, referring with an indexical to a name proplet, as in calling *Julia* she, referring with an indexical to a referent represented by a concept proplet, as in calling the book in front of me it, etc. All these forms of reference are based on a secondary coding with associated inferencing at the level of context.

5.5 Secondary Coding as Perspective Taking

The derivation of secondary codings, defined solely at the level of context, is independent of whether or not the agent has the language faculty. Accordingly, even a dog, for example, could view an entity from a certain subjective perspective, such as viewing the mail man as an enemy. The role of secondary codings in agents with and without language may be shown schematically as follows:

5.5.1 CODING LEVELS IN AGENTS WITH AND WITHOUT LANGUAGE

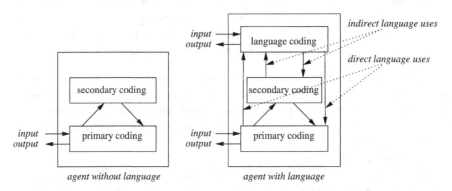

agent without language   *agent with language*

In terms of evolution, the levels of primary and secondary coding in agents without language are being reused essentially unchanged in agents with language. The whole machinery of inferencing and secondary coding is already present when language is added. The adding of language is based on matching the primary and the secondary codings directly (vertical arrows).

The functions of the three kinds of coding may be summarized as follows:

5.5.2 FUNCTIONS OF CODING LEVELS IN DATABASE SEMANTICS

1. *Primary coding* at the context level:
   Represents contextual recognition and action at a low level of abstraction in a simple standardized format in order to ensure veracity.

2. *Secondary coding* at the context level:
Consists of inferencing over the primary coding in order to obtain sufficient expressive power at varying levels of abstraction.

3. *Language coding*:
Represents primary and secondary context coding in a natural language.

Primary and secondary codings are related to each other by inferences. They are related to the language coding by a strict method of internal matching.

The combination of primary and secondary coding allows content to be represented from different points of view at different levels of abstraction. Thereby the primary contextual coding can be left intact, at least in short-term memory. Long-term storage, however, may involve a fusion of primary and secondary coding into a condensed form – depending on the amount of content and the limits of storage.

While the primary coding of a given content is basically the same in different agents, their secondary codings may vary widely, depending on their knowledge and purposes. For example, an experienced scout and a greenhorn may see the same broken twig in primary coding. In secondary coding, however, the scout may spontaneously see the twig as a trace of whatever they pursue, while the greenhorn does not. Using language, however, the scout may adjust the greenhorn's secondary coding to his own.

5.6 Shades of Meaning

It seems to be taken for granted that a native speaker's intuitions about the meaning of a word could never be modeled in an artificial agent. This, however, is an unjustified assumption. In fact, the meaning of a word consists of several well-defined ingredients. That some of them consist of (i) personal experiences and (ii) implicit assumptions of the surrounding culture does not mean that they cannot be modeled.

The ingredients of a word meaning are based on the distinctions (i) between concept types and concept tokens, (ii) between episodic and absolute propositions, and (iii) between primary and secondary codings. Consider the word dog, for example.

First, there is the result of lexical lookup:

5.6.1 LEXICAL LOOKUP OF THE WORD dog

$$
\begin{bmatrix}
\text{sur: dog} \\
\text{noun: } dog \\
\text{fnc:} \\
\text{mdr:} \\
\text{prn:}
\end{bmatrix}
$$

Lexical lookup provides the semantic core, here *dog*, defined as a concept type and serving as the meaning$_1$.

Then there are all the absolute proplets containing the concept type *dog* listed in the absolute part of the token line of this concept (cf. 5.2.3 and 5.2.4, field 2):

5.6.2 ABSOLUTE PART OF THE TOKEN LINE OF *dog*

$$
\begin{bmatrix} \text{noun: } dog \end{bmatrix}
\quad
\begin{bmatrix} \text{noun: dog} \\ \text{fnc: be} \\ \text{mdr:} \\ \text{prn: a-1} \end{bmatrix}
\begin{bmatrix} \text{noun: dog} \\ \text{fnc: have} \\ \text{mdr:} \\ \text{prn: a-2} \end{bmatrix}
\quad \ldots
$$

These absolute proplets are connected: Based on their continuation values, all the absolute propositions about dogs may be activated, lighting up a subnetwork in the Word Bank. In this way, the semantic core of the lexical proplet (meaning$_1$) is complemented compositionally with the agent's general knowledge about dogs. This aspect of meaning is represented in the following schema as the second circle, called *absolute connections*:

5.6.3 COMPLEMENTATION OF A LITERAL MEANING$_1$ (CONCEPT TYPE)

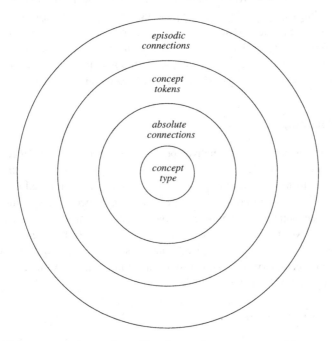

In addition to complementing a literal meaning$_1$, represented by a concept type, with all the absolute connections related to it there are the episodic proplets in the token line of the concept (cf. 5.2.3 and 5.2.4, field 3). If the concept is *dog*, for example, then the episodic proplets in its token line complement the core value type of the lexical item, e.g., 5.6.1, with all the core value tokens of dogs the agent has encountered and stored so far. These core value tokens may have any degree of detail, such as the kind of dog, the color of fur, the sound of barking, etc., depending on the memory available to the agent as well as the individual importance of each token. Given that these tokens arise at the level of context, they constitute an aspect of meaning which is generalized in the sense that it is independent of a particular utterance (cf. *concept tokens* in 5.6.3).

Finally, the episodic proplets in the token line of *dog* are the starting points of all the episodic propositions involving dogs, including secondary codings based on inferences. Using the retrieval mechanism of the Word Bank, the proplets of these propositions may be activated. In this way, the generalized aspect of meaning represented by the set of dog tokens is complemented compositionally with the agent's individual dog experiences (cf. *episodic connections* in 5.6.3).

Thus, the build-up of structure, from concepts types to absolute connections to concept tokens to episodic connections can well explain why a concept type, as the minimal literal meaning$_1$ used for matching between the language and the context level (cf. 4.2.2), is intuitively shrouded behind a cloud of individual differentiations. These consist of the agent's various tokens of the concept instantiating the type (content aspect of the word) and the various absolute and episodic connections (combinatorial aspects of the word). Due to the data structure of a Word Bank, they can all be activated with great ease, and jointly represent the associations an agent may have with a word's concept.[9]

---

[9] In some natural languages, e.g., German, the meaning of a sentence or phrase may be shaded by using a fairly large number of "particles." Examples in German (cf. Weydt (1969), Engel (1991), Ickler (1994)) are aber (but), auch (also), bloss (merely), as in Das ist aber schön! (That is but beautiful!), Sind Sie auch zufrieden? (Are you also content?), Was hat sie sich bloss gedacht?! (What has she herself merely thought?!), etc. Their main contribution to the overall interpretation is the triggering of certain inferences about the speaker's perspective.

Remark Concluding Part I

This part has presented a high-level description of Database Semantics (DBS). As an abstract model of natural language communication between humans, it provides the theoretical foundation for building artificial cognitive agents which human users can communicate with freely in their accustomed language.

The more this goal is being reached, the more the use of programming languages may be relegated to the maintenance routines of specialized "robot doctors." Accordingly, the keyboard and the screen of today's computers may be reduced to the artificial agent's service channel, while the communication with the user is entrusted to the newly developed auto-channel (cf. 1.4.3) using natural language.

In the following Part II, the focus changes from the interfaces and components of a cognitive agent to a systematic analysis of the major constructions of language, using English as our example. The purpose of these analyses is to show (i) how the compositional aspect of natural language meaning is coded in the semantic representations of DBS, (ii) how this coding is derived from the natural surface in the hearer mode, and (iii) how the correct natural surface is derived from the semantic representation in the speaker mode.

Part II

The Major Constructions of Natural Language

6. Intrapropositional Functor–Argument Structure

The major constructions of natural language consist of the primary relations of (i) functor–argument structure and (ii) coordination, and the secondary relation of (iii) coreference, occurring (a) intra- as well as (b) extrapropositionally. Analyzing these six basic constellations requires the use of examples. Moreover, in order to be concrete, these examples must be from at least one real natural language. Thus, the task at hand has a strongly sign-oriented aspect.

Nevertheless, our approach is also agent-oriented insofar as the examples are analyzed in the speaker mode and the hearer mode. In the hearer mode, an LA-hear grammar maps the language-dependent surface into a set of proplets suitable to be stored in a Word Bank. In the speaker mode, an LA-think grammar navigates along the grammatical relations established between the language-independent proplets in the Word Bank while an LA-speak grammar realizes the traversed proplets in a natural language of choice, here English.

In this chapter, we begin the systematic investigation of the major constructions with the analysis of intrapropositional functor–argument structure. The grammatical analyses are presented at an intermediate level of abstraction, using the formats illustrated in 3.4.2 and 3.5.3 for the hearer mode and the speaker mode, respectively.

6.1 Overview

In Database Semantics, the analysis of a grammatical construction comprises three basic tasks: (i) Designing the semantic representation of the relevant natural language example as a set of proplets, (ii) automatically deriving the semantic representation from the example surface (hearer mode) and (iii) automatically deriving the surface from the semantic representation (speaker mode).

The semantic representation of an intrapropositional functor–argument structure is the set of proplets of an elementary proposition (cf. FoCL'99, p. 62). It consists of one verb (relation, functor) with one, two, or three nouns (objects, arguments), the number of which is determined by the verb. There may be adjectives (properties, modifiers) modifying either the verb (adverbial use) or a noun (adnominal use).

To emphasize that the set of proplets serving as a semantic representation is unordered, the following examples present the proplets in the alphabetical order of their core values (rather than the order suggested by the natural surface).

6.1.1 Examples of Intrapropositional Functor–Argument Structure

1. Representing *The man gave the child an apple* (three-place verb)

$$
\begin{bmatrix} \text{noun: apple} \\ \text{fnc: give} \\ \text{mdr:} \\ \text{prn: 1} \end{bmatrix}
\begin{bmatrix} \text{noun: child} \\ \text{fnc: give} \\ \text{mdr:} \\ \text{prn: 1} \end{bmatrix}
\begin{bmatrix} \text{verb: give} \\ \text{arg: man child apple} \\ \text{mdr:} \\ \text{prn: 1} \end{bmatrix}
\begin{bmatrix} \text{noun: man} \\ \text{fnc: give} \\ \text{mdr:} \\ \text{prn: 1} \end{bmatrix}
$$

2. Representing *The little black dog barked* (adnominal adjectives)

$$
\begin{bmatrix} \text{verb: bark} \\ \text{arg: dog} \\ \text{mdr:} \\ \text{prn: 2} \end{bmatrix}
\begin{bmatrix} \text{adj: black} \\ \text{mdd: dog} \\ \text{mdr:} \\ \text{prn: 2} \end{bmatrix}
\begin{bmatrix} \text{adj: little} \\ \text{mdd: dog} \\ \text{mdr:} \\ \text{prn: 2} \end{bmatrix}
\begin{bmatrix} \text{noun: dog} \\ \text{fnc: bark} \\ \text{mdr: little black} \\ \text{prn: 2} \end{bmatrix}
$$

3. Representing *Julia has been sleeping deeply* (adverbial adjective)

$$
\begin{bmatrix} \text{adj: deep} \\ \text{mdd: sleep} \\ \text{mdr:} \\ \text{prn: 3} \end{bmatrix}
\begin{bmatrix} \text{noun: Julia} \\ \text{fnc: sleep} \\ \text{mdr:} \\ \text{prn: 3} \end{bmatrix}
\begin{bmatrix} \text{verb: sleep} \\ \text{arg: Julia} \\ \text{mdr: deep} \\ \text{prn: 3} \end{bmatrix}
$$

These semantic representations show the coding of grammatical relations. The function words have been absorbed by fusing them with the associated content words. The contributions of the function words as well as other morpho-syntactic details are specified in the attributes cat (for category) and sem (for semantics), which are omitted here for simplicity.[1] For complete semantic representations see Part III.

In Example 1, the verb *give* takes the noun arguments *man*, *child*, and *apple*. These grammatical relations are coded by the value give in the fnc slot of the noun proplets *man*, *child*, and *apple*, and by the values man, child, and apple in the arg slot of the verb proplet *give*. The different case roles of the arguments are specified in terms of their order in the arg slot of the verb proplet. The lexical proplets of the determiners have been fused with their noun proplets, whereby their contributions are represented as values of the cat and sem attributes (not shown, cf. Sect. 13.4).

In Example 2, the noun *dog* is modified by the adnominal adjectives *little* and *black*. These grammatical relations are coded by the value dog in the mdd slot of the adjective proplets *little* and *black*, and by the values little and black in the mdr slot of the noun proplet *dog*. The adnominal use of the adjectives is specified as the value adn of the cat attribute (not shown, cf. Sect. 13.3) of the adjective proplets.

In Example 3, the verb *sleep* is modified by the adverbial adjective *deep*. This relation is coded by the value sleep in the mdd slot of the proplet *deep*, and by the value deep in the mdr slot of the verb proplet *sleep*. The adverbial use of the adjective is specified as the value adv of the cat attribute (not shown) of the adjective proplet.

---

[1] For example, in the derivation of Example 3 from the surface Julia has been sleeping deeply, the contributions of the auxiliaries has been and the progressive form are specified in the verb proplet by the feature [sem: hv_pres perf prog] to indicate the tense of the input sentence (cf. 13.4.7).

6.2 Determiners

We turn now to deriving the semantic representation 6.1.1 (1) from a suitable English surface (hearer mode). The result is an intrapropositional functor–argument structure consisting of a three-place verb and its arguments. The derivation illustrates how determiners and their nouns are fused by absorbing the noun into the determiner.

6.2.1 THREE-PLACE PROPOSITION: The man gave the child an apple

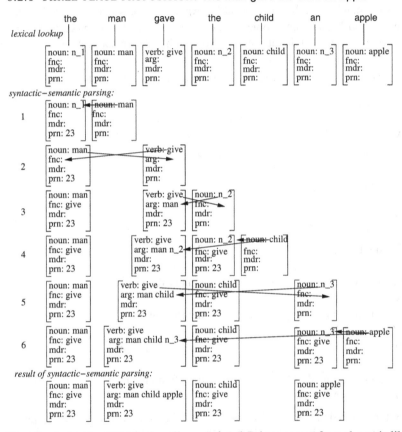

That the derivation 6.2.1 is time-linear (cf. 1.6.5) is apparent from the stair-like structure resulting from adding exactly one new "next word" in each new proplet line. The derivation is also surface compositional (cf. 1.6.1) because each word form in the surface has a lexical analysis and there are no "zero elements" postulated in the input.

In line 1, the substitution value n_1 of the determiner proplet is replaced by the value man of the noun proplet, which is then discarded (function word absorption). The result is shown in the first proplet of line 2. In the combination of the proplets *man* and *give*, the core value of *man* is copied into the arg slot of the verb and the core value of *give* into to fnc slot of the noun. In line 3, the value give is copied into the fnc attribute of the next word proplet *the*, and the substitution value n_2 of *the* is copied into the arg slot of the verb.[2] In line 4, both instances of the substitution value n_2 are replaced by the value child of the next word. Integration of the noun proplet *apple* in lines 5 and 6 is analogous to that of *child* in lines 3 and 4. The result of the derivation is shown in the bottom line, using the natural surface order.

Once these proplets have been stored in the Word Bank, they support various LA-think traversals which use the relations between proplets for retrieval. One of these traversals is the standard VNNN navigation (cf. Appendix A), where the first N is the subject, the second N the indirect object, and the third N the direct object. Consider the production of the English input sentence from such a VNNN navigation:

6.2.2 SCHEMATIC PRODUCTION FROM A THREE-PLACE PROPOSITION

	activated sequence	*realization*
i		
	... V	
i.1	d	d
	V N	
i.2	d nn	d nn
	V N	
i.3	fv d nn	d nn fv
	V N	
i.4	fv d nn d	d nn fv d
	V N N	
i.5	fv d nn d nn	d nn fv d nn
	V N N	
i.6	v d nn d nn d	d nn v d nn d
	V N N N	
i.7	fv d nn d nn d nn	d nn fv d nn d nn
	V N N N	
i.8	fv p d nn d nn d nn	d nn fv d nn d nn p
	V N N N	

Like 3.5.3, this derivation shows the handling of word order, function word precipitation, and the switching between LA-think and LA-speak. The abstract surfaces d, nn, fv, and p stand for determiner, noun, finite verb, and punctuation, respectively.

In Database Semantics, the meaning of the determiners (here the) is handled in terms of the atomic values exh, sel, sg, pl, def, and indef (cf. 6.2.9) in the sem attribute (cf. 6.2.7) of the noun proplets. This is different from the treatment of determiners as quantifiers in Predicate Calculus, beginning with Russell's (1905) celebrated analysis

---

[2] To distinguish different determiners, the substitution values n_1, n_2, n_3, etc., are automatically incremented during lexical lookup (cf. 13.3.5, 13.5.4, and 13.5.6).

of "definite descriptions" and still being expanded within the framework associated with Montague (1974), e.g., Barwise and Perry (1983); Kamp and Reyle (1993); and others. Consider the following example:

6.2.3 PREDICATE CALCULUS ANALYSIS OF All girls sleep

$$\forall x \, [girl(x) \rightarrow sleep(x)]$$

The interpretation of such a formula is defined with respect to a model and a variable assignment. Following Montague (1974), the model @ is defined as a tuple (A,F), where A is a set of individuals, e.g., $\{a_0, a_1, a_2, a_3\}$, and F is an assignment function which assigns to every one-place predicate in the formal language an element of 2^A (i.e., the power set of A) as an interpretation (and accordingly for two-place predicates, etc.). For example, F(girl) might be defined in @ as $\{a_1, a_2\}$ and F(sleep) as $\{a_0, a_2\}$. This means that a_1 and a_2 in the model are girls, while a_0 and a_2 are sleeping.

The dependence of the truth-value of a formula on the actual definition of the model and a variable assignment is represented by Montague by adding @ and g as superscripts to the end of the formula:

6.2.4 INTERPRETATION RELATIVE TO A MODEL

$$\forall x \, [girl(x) \rightarrow sleep(x)]^{@,g}$$

The interpretation of the quantifier $\forall$ is based on the variable assignment g as follows: The whole formula is true relative to the model @ if it holds for *all* possible variable assignments g' that the formula without the outermost quantifier is true:

6.2.5 ELIMINATION OF THE OUTERMOST QUANTIFIER

$$[girl(x) \rightarrow sleep(x)]^{@,g'}$$

The purpose of eliminating the quantifier is to reduce the Predicate Calculus formula to Propositional Calculus and its truth tables (cf. Bochenski 1961). This is achieved by systematically assigning all possible values in the set of individuals A $=_{def}$ $\{a_0, a_1, a_2, a_3\}$ to the variable x and determining the truth-value of the subformulas girl(x) and sleep(x) for each assignment. Thus, g' first assigns to the variable x the value a_0, then the value a_1, etc. Given the definition of the model @ $=_{def}$ (A,F), we can now check for each such assigment whether or not it makes the formula 6.2.5 true.

For example, the first assignment $g'(x) = a_0$ makes the formula true: a_0 is not in the set denoted by F(girl) in @; therefore, based on the truth table of p $\rightarrow$ q in Propositional Calculus, the formula in 6.2.5 is true for this assignment. The second assignment $g'(x) = a_1$, in contrast, makes the formula in 6.2.5 false: a_1 is in the set denoted by F(girl), but not in the set denoted by F(sleep) in @. Having shown that *not all* variable assignments g' make the formula in 6.2.5 true, the interpretation of the formula in 6.2.3 is determined to be false relative to @. Given how the model @ $=_{def}$ (A,F) was defined, this is in accordance with intuition.

This method of treating determiners at the highest level of the logical syntax leads to ambiguities because the quantifiers may have different orders.[3] For example, the Predicate Calculus analysis of Every man loves a woman has the following readings:

6.2.6 ANALYZING Every man loves a woman IN PREDICATE CALCULUS

Reading 1: $\forall x$ [man(x) $\rightarrow$ $\exists y$ [woman(y) & love(x,y)]]

Reading 2: $\exists y$ [woman(y) & $\forall x$ [man(x) $\rightarrow$ love(x,y)]]

On reading 1, it holds for every man that there is some woman whom he loves. On reading 2, there is a certain woman, e.g., Marilyn Monroe, who is loved by every man.

The two formulas of Predicate Calculus are based on the notions of functor–argument structure, coordination, and coreference, though in a manner different from their use in Database Semantics. Functor–argument structure is used in man(x), woman(y), and love(x,y); coordination is used in [man(x) $\rightarrow$ P] and [woman(y) & Q]; and coreference is expressed by the quantifiers and the horizontally bound variables in $\forall x$ [man(x) ... love(x,y)] and $\exists y$ [woman(y)... love(x,y)].

In Database Semantics, in contrast, the meanings of the determiners every and a are expressed by atomic values pl exh of the sem attribute of the noun proplets:

6.2.7 RESULT OF PARSING Every man loves a woman IN DBS

$$
\begin{bmatrix}
\text{sur:} \\
\text{noun: } man \\
\text{cat: snp} \\
\text{sem: pl exh} \\
\text{mdr:} \\
\text{fnc: love} \\
\text{idy: 1} \\
\text{prn: 1}
\end{bmatrix}
\begin{bmatrix}
\text{sur:} \\
\text{verb: } love \\
\text{cat: v} \\
\text{sem: pres} \\
\text{mdr:} \\
\text{arg: man woman} \\
\text{prn: 1}
\end{bmatrix}
\begin{bmatrix}
\text{sur:} \\
\text{noun: } woman \\
\text{cat: snp} \\
\text{sem: indef sg} \\
\text{mdr:} \\
\text{fnc: love} \\
\text{idy: 2} \\
\text{prn: 1}
\end{bmatrix}
$$

In this analysis, the sentence is not ambiguous: It has only reading 1 of 6.2.6 – which is entailed by reading 2 (i.e., reading 1 is true whenever reading 2 is true, but not vice versa). In other words, whether or not some (or even all) of the men happen to love the same woman is treated as a private matter in Database Semantics.

Furthermore, the Database Semantics analysis uses only intrapropositional functor–argument structure: As in the natural surface, there is neither coordination nor coreference. Treated as determiners, the "quantifiers" every and a are each fused with their noun into a single proplet (similar to 6.2.1, 6.3.1, 6.5.1, 6.6.2, 8.2.1, and 8.3.2).

The atomic values exh (exhaustive), sel (selective), sg (singular), pl (plural), def (definite), and indef (indefinite) are used in different combinations to characterize the following kinds of noun phrases in English:

---

[3] Cf. Kempson and Cormack (1981). In recent years, Minimal Recursion Semantics (MRS, Copestake, Flickinger et al. 2006) has devoted much work to avoid the unnatural proliferation of readings caused by different quantifier scopes, using "semantic under-specification." In MRS, under-specification is limited to quantifier scope (see also Steedman 2005). In Database Semantics, which has neither quantifiers nor quantifier scope, semantic under-specification applies to *all* content coded at the language level and is being used for the matching with a delimited context of use (cf. FoCL'99, Sect. 5.2).

6.2.8 THE sem VALUES OF DIFFERENT DETERMINER–NOUN COMBINATIONS

a girl	[sem: indef sg]
some girls	[sem: indef pl sel]
all girls	[sem: exh pl]
the girl	[sem: def sg]
the girls	[sem: def pl]

The atomic values have the following set-theoretic interpretations:

6.2.9 SET-THEORETIC INTERPRETATION OF exh, sel, sg, pl, def, indef

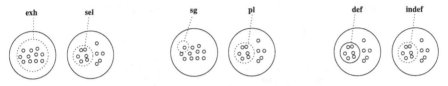

The value exh refers to all members of a set, called the domain, while sel refers only to some. The value sg refers to a single member of the domain, while pl refers to more than one. The value def refers to a prespecified subset of the domain, while no such subset is presumed by indef.

Each value can only be combined with a value from the other pairs. Thus exh cannot combine with sel, sg cannot combine with pl, and def cannot combine with indef. However, the combinations exh pl, sel sg, sel pl, def sg, def pl, indef sg, indef pl, etc., are legitimate and have different meanings. The combination exh sg is theoretically possible, but makes little sense (pace Russell 1905) because the domain would have to be a unit set.

Regarding the interpretation of determiners in Database Semantics during communication, consider a robot in the speaker mode. If it perceives the set-theoretic situation corresponding to exh and pl as shown in 6.2.9, it will use the determiner all, and similarly with the other values. Correspondingly, if a robot in the hearer mode hears the noun phrase all girls, for example, it will be able to draw the corresponding set-theoretic situation or to choose the right schema from several alternatives.

The Database Semantics approach differs from Predicate Calculus in that Predicate Calculus uses the words *some* and *all* in the metalanguage to define the words some and all in the object-language (as shown by the use of the variable assignment function g' described above), while Database Semantics is based on a procedural interpretation. This difference is based on profoundly different ontological assumptions of the two approaches, illustrated in 2.3.1 with the most simple sentence Julia sleeps.

A related difference is that the semantics of Predicate Calculus is based on truth-conditions, while that of Database Semantics is not. Instead, Database Semantics handles truth as procedural assertions. For example, if a robot observes correctly that every girl is sleeping and communicates this fact by saying every girl is sleeping, it is speaking truly. Semantically, every girl is sleeping asserts that there is a set of more than one girl and all elements of the set participate in whatever is asserted by the verb.

6.3 Adjectives

A form of noun phrase more complex than the determiner–noun combination shown above includes one or more adnominal adjectives, as illustrated by the following example of a (short) modifier recursion:

6.3.1 PARSING The little black dog barked IN THE HEARER MODE

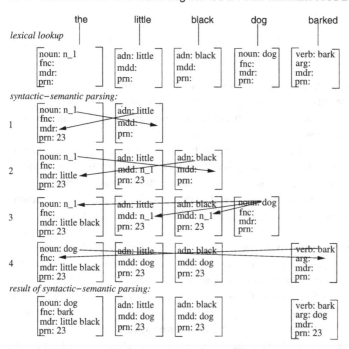

In line 1, the core value of the adnominal adjective *little* is copied into the mdr slot of the determiner, and the substitution value n_1 is copied into the mdd slot of the proplet *little*. In line 2, the core value of the adnominal adjective *black* is copied and added to the mdr slot of the determiner, and the substitution value n_1 is copied into the mdd slot of the proplet *black*. In line 3, all three instances of the substitution value n_1 are simultaneously replaced by the core value of the lexical proplet *dog*, which is then discarded. In line 4, the core value of the former determiner proplet is copied into the arg slot of the verb proplet *bark*, and the core value of the verb is copied into the fnc slot of the former determiner proplet. As a result any adnominal, e.g., *black*, allows the retrieval of the associated noun, here *dog*, and any noun allows the retrieval of the associated adnominal(s), here *little* and *black*.

The (re)production of the input sentence from a standard VNAA navigation in the speaker mode is characterized below.

6.3.2 SCHEMATIC PRODUCTION OF THE The little black dog barked

activated sequence				*realization*
i				
	V			
i.1	d			d
	V	N		
i.2	d	an		d an
	V	N	A	
i.3	d	an an		d an an
	V	N	A A	
i.4	d nn	an an		d an an nn
	V	N	A A	
i.5	fv d nn	an an		d an an nn fv
	V	N	A A	
i.6	fv p d nn	an an		d an an nn fv p
	V	N	A A	

The abstract surfaces d, an, nn, fv, and p stand for determiner, adnominal, noun, finite verb, and punctuation, respectively.

Next consider the time-linear derivation of a sentence with an adverbial adjective:

6.3.3 PARSING Fido barked loudly IN THE HEARER MODE

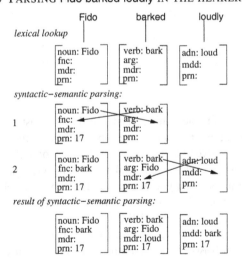

In adverbial use, the adjective proplet contains a copy of the core value of the modified *verb* in its mdd slot – in contrast to adnominal use, in which the adjective proplet contains a copy of the core value of the modified *noun*. Furthermore, in adverbial use it is the verb which contains a copy of the adjective's core value in its mdr slot, while in adnominal use it is the noun.

The (re)production of the input sentence from a standard VNA navigation in the speaker mode is characterized below:

6.3.4 SCHEMATIC PRODUCTION OF THE Fido barked loudly

	activated sequence			*realization*
i				
	V			
i.1		n		n
	V	N		
i.2	fv	n		n fv
	V	N		
i.3	fv	n	av	n fv av
	V	N	A	
i.4	fv p	n	av	n fv av p
	V	N	A	

The abstract surfaces n and av stand for name and adverbial, respectively.

In Database Semantics, adnominal and adverbial modifiers are treated as variants of the same part of speech: adjective. The Latin root of this term means "what is thrown in," which aptly characterizes the optional quality of modifiers in general.

6.3.5 RELATION OF THE TERMS Adjective, Adnominal, and Adverbial IN DBS

The morphological motivation for treating adnominals and adverbials as instances of the same part of speech is their similarity. Consider, for example, the adnominal adjective beautiful and the adverbial adjective beautifully in English, or schöne, schöner, schönes, etc., (adnominal adjectives) and schön (adverbial adjective) in German. The two uses resemble each other also in their analytic degrees, as in more beautiful (adnominal) and more beautifully (adverbial). In synthetic degrees, as in faster, the adnominal and the adverbial form are not even distinguished in English.

Modifier proplets have the core attribute adj, which represents the part of speech. If there is no morphological distinction between the adnominal and adverbial use of a modifier and its grammatical role is still undefined, it is called an adjective. Modifiers which are restricted morphologically or by their syntactic environment to adnominal use are called adnominals, and accordingly for adverbials. Just as there are elementary nouns like Fido and complex nouns like the little black dog, there are elementary adjectives like fast and complex adjectives like in ten seconds.

6.4 Auxiliaries

Another kind of function word besides determiners are auxiliaries. They combine with nonfinite forms of the main verb to form complex constructions:

6.4.1 COMPLEX VERB PHRASE: Fido has been barking

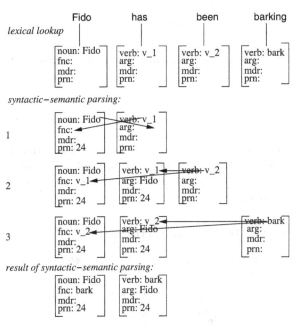

Just as the determiners have the substitution values n_1, n_2, etc., (cf. 6.2.1), the auxiliaries have the substitution values v_1, v_2, etc.,, as their core values.

In line 1, the value v_1 is copied into the fnc slot of *Fido*, and the core value of *Fido* is copied into the arg slot of the first auxiliary. In line 2, the two instances of v_1 are replaced by the value v_2 serving as the core value of the second auxiliary. In line 3, the two instances of v_2 are replaced by the core value of the proplet *bark*, which is then discarded (function word absorption). The contribution of the two auxiliaries and the progressive form of the nonfinite main verb is represented by the values of the cat and sem attributes (not shown, cf. Sect. 13.4) of the resulting verb proplet.

The production of auxiliaries (function word precipitation) is derived as follows:

6.4.2 SCHEMATIC PRODUCTION OF Fido has been barking

	activated sequence		*realization*
i.			
	V		
i.1		n	n
	V	N	
i.2	ax	n	n ax
	V	N	
i.3	ax ax	n	n ax ax
	V	N	
i.4	ax ax nv	n	n ax ax nv
	V	N	
i.6	ax ax nv p	n	n ax ax nv p
	V	N	

Here, the abstract surfaces n, ax, nv, and p stand for name, auxiliary, nonfinite verb, and punctuation, respectively.

6.5 Passive

Another kind of complex verb construction is passive. In grammar, active and passive are called the *genus verbi* or *voice of the verb*. In Database Semantics, passive is viewed as a certain perspective (cf. Sect. 5.5) on a propositional content, resulting from backward navigation (see also Sect. 9.6).

6.5.1 INTERPRETATION OF PASSIVE: The book was read by John

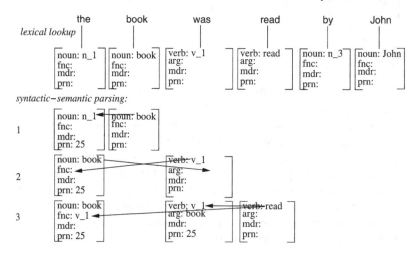

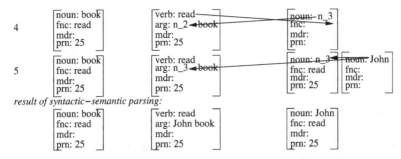

result of syntactic−semantic parsing:

$$\begin{bmatrix} \text{noun: book} \\ \text{fnc: read} \\ \text{mdr:} \\ \text{prn: 25} \end{bmatrix} \quad \begin{bmatrix} \text{verb: read} \\ \text{arg: John book} \\ \text{mdr:} \\ \text{prn: 25} \end{bmatrix} \quad \begin{bmatrix} \text{noun: John} \\ \text{fnc: read} \\ \text{mdr:} \\ \text{prn: 25} \end{bmatrix}$$

Up to line 2, the voice of the verb is undecided: The sentence start the book was could be continued as an active, as in the book was lying on the table, or as the passive in question. However, as soon as the past participle of *read* is added in line 3, the order of the values in the arg attribute of the verb proplet is adjusted by inserting the nominal substitution value n_2, fixing the switch to passive. The result is shown by the verbal proplet in line 4.

At this point, the sentence could be completed as The book was read. Such a suppression of the agent is an option typical of passive. In our derivation, it is expressed by the feature [arg: n_2 book] of the verb proplet. It would be up to inferencing to determine the agent by finding a suitable value for n_2. However, as the sentence continues with the *by*-phrase, the value n_2 is replaced by the value n_3. The nominal proplet John is added and absorbed into the *by*-proplet, replacing all occurrences of n_3 with the value John. The result is the same set of proplets as would be derived from the corresponding active.

Once the proplets have been stored in the Word Bank, they can be traversed forward or backward. A simple way to characterize a standard forward navigation is by showing the steps as V . VN . VNN, while the alternative backward navigation through the same set of proplets is shown as the steps V . V_N . VNN. This method presupposes that the role of the verbal arguments is expressed by their order: The first N is the agent or (deep) subject and the second N the patient or object; if there is a third N, the second N is the indirect object and the third N is the direct object. In other words, the same order is used in the arg attribute of verbal proplets, regardless of verbal voice.[4]

Based on a V . V_N . VNN navigation, the input sentence is (re)produced as follows:

6.5.2 SCHEMATIC PRODUCTION OF The book was read by John

activated sequence   *realization*

i

V

i.1   d   d

V   N

---

[4] Expressing the grammatical role in terms of order is a terminological choice. The same content could be expressed by introducing additional attributes like agent. We do not take this option in order to

i.2			d nn		d nn
	V		N		
i.3	ax		d nn		d nn ax
	V		N		
i.4	ax nv		d nn		d nn ax nv
	V		N		
i.5	ax nv	by	d nn		d nn ax nv by
	V	N	N		
i.6	ax nv	by n	d nn		d nn ax nv by n
	V	N	N		
i.7	ax nv p	by n	d nn		d nn ax nv by n p
	V	N	N		

The corresponding active is produced from the same set of proplets, but is activated in the standard V . VN . VNN navigation order. A production of passive in the interrogative mood is shown in A.5.2. For a more detailed analysis of passive in Database Semantics, see Twiggs (2005).

6.6 Prepositions

We conclude our survey of intrapropositional functor–argument structures with prepositional phrases in adnominal and adverbial use ("PP attachment"). In certain positions, both interpretations are possible. For example, in Julia ate the apple on the table, the prepositional phrase on the table can modify *eat* (in the sense of Julia sitting on the table while eating) or *apple* (in the sense of eating the apple which was on the table). In DBS, this ambiguity is handled in terms of semantic doubling:[5]

6.6.1 SEMANTIC DOUBLING OF A PREPOSITIONAL PHRASE

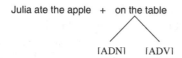

According to this analysis, the example, is unambiguous syntactically because only one representation is derived. It is ambiguous semantically, however, in that the prepositional phrase has an ADN (adnominal) and an ADV (adverbial) meaning attached to it. It is assumed that the alternative ADN and ADV meanings are positioned relative to the context of use, whereby the choice between the alternatives is based on the principle of best match.

The formal realization of semantic doubling is shown by the following derivation:

_____

maintain the flat (nonrecursive) feature structure of proplets.
[5] The method of semantic doubling was first proposed in CoL'89, pp. 219–232 and pp. 239–247. See also FoCL'99, pp. 234 ff.

6.6.2 ADJECTIVAL PHRASE: Julia ate the apple on the table

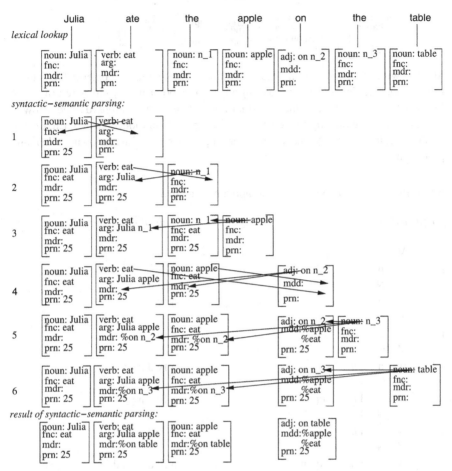

In line 4, the adj value of the preposition is copied into the mdr slot of both the verb proplet *eat* and the noun proplet *apple*. Furthermore, the core values of the verb and the noun are both copied into the mdd slot of the preposition *on*. To indicate that the copied values are only one of several possible interpretations (here two), they are preceded by % (cf. line 5). The fusion of the proplets *on*, *the*, and *table* into one is another instance of function word absorption.

When the resulting proplets are stored, the ambiguity may be resolved by an inference which removes a pair of %-values, for example, %on table in the mdr-slot of the *eat* proplet and %eat in the mdd-slot of the *on table* proplet. However, the proplets may also remain as they are, leaving the ambiguity in place.

Turning to the (re)production of the input sentence in its two interpretations, consider the retrieval connections of the output of 6.6.2:

6.6.3 RETRIEVAL DURING NAVIGATION

$$
\begin{array}{llll}
\begin{bmatrix} \text{noun: Julia} \\ \text{fnc: eat} \\ \text{mdr:} \\ \text{prn: 25} \end{bmatrix} &
\begin{bmatrix} \text{verb: eat} \\ \text{arg: Julia apple} \\ \text{mdr:\%on table} \\ \text{prn: 25} \end{bmatrix} &
\begin{bmatrix} \text{noun: apple} \\ \text{fnc: eat} \\ \text{mdr:\%on table} \\ \text{prn: 25} \end{bmatrix} &
\begin{bmatrix} \text{adj: on table} \\ \text{mdd:\%apple} \\ \qquad \text{\%eat} \\ \text{prn: 25} \end{bmatrix}
\end{array}
$$

Starting with the V proplet *eat*, the navigation retrieves the N proplet *Julia*, returns to the V, and retrieves the N proplet *apple*. At this point it may either return to the V to continue from there to the adverbial interpretation of *on table* (dashed arrows), or it may continue directly to the adnominal interpretation (dotted arrow). Either case produces a standard VNNA navigation, serving as the basis of the following schematic production:

6.6.4 PRODUCTION OF Julia ate the apple on the table

	activated sequence				*realization*
i					
	V				
i.1		n			n
	V	N			
i.2	fv	n			n fv
	V	N			
i.3	fv	n	d		n fv d
	V	N	N		
i.4	fv	n	d n		n fv d n
	V	N	N		
i.5	fv	n	d n	pp	n fv d n pp
	V	N	N	A	
i.6	fv	n	d n	pp d	n fv d n pp d
	V	N	N	A	
i.7	fv	n	d n	pp d nn	n fv d n pp d nn
	V	N	N	A	
i.8	fv p	n	d n	pp d nn	n fv d n pp d nn p
	V	N	N	A	

The abstract surface pp stands for a preposition.

Treating "PP-attachment" by means of semantic doubling is especially beneficial in more complex examples containing potentially unlimited sequences of prepositional phrases, as in *Julia ate the apple on the table in the garden behind the tree* .... There, semantic doubling reduces the mathematical complexity from the exponential complexity of the Nativist approach to linear complexity.[6] For a detailed analysis of "prepositional phrase attachment" in the hearer mode see Chapt. 15.

---

[6] Cf. FoCL'99, Sect. 12.5.

7. Extrapropositional Functor–Argument Structure

In natural language, extrapropositional relations can be intrasentential or extrasentential. This distinction is best explained with extrapropositional coordination. For example, Julia sleeps and Susanne sings. is *intrasentential* extrapropositional, while Julia sings. Susanne sleeps. is *extrasentential* extrapropositional.

Extrapropositional functor–argument structure is always intrasentential. In the simplest case, there are two propositions, one representing the higher and the other the lower clause. The lower clause serves in the higher clause as (i) a sentential argument or (ii) a sentential modifier.

In sentential arguments, the subordinate proposition functions like a noun, serving as the *subject* or as an *object*. In sentential modifiers, the subordinate proposition functions like an adjective, serving as an *adnominal* or as an *adverbial*. Adnominal sentential modifiers are also known as relative clauses.

7.1 Overview

The two propositions of a simple extrapropositional functor–argument structure are each represented by a set of proplets. The proplets of the first proposition are held together by being *co-indexed*, in the sense of having the same prn value. The proplets of the other proposition are co-indexed as well, and distinguished from the first by having a different prn value.

In sentential argument and adverbial modifier constructions, the connection between the higher and the lower proposition is established by the *verb* proplet of the higher proposition taking the prn and the core value of the verb proplet of the lower proposition as one of its arg or mdr values, for example, [arg: 27 bark   Mary] (subject sentence), [arg: John   31 bark] (object sentence), or [mdr: 36 bark] (adverbial sentence). In adnominal modifier constructions (relative clauses), the connection in question is established by a *noun* proplet in the higher proposition taking the prn and the core value of the lower verb as the values of its mdr attribute.

The inverse connection between the lower and the higher proposition is based on two new kinds of proplets with the core attributes n/v and a/v. The attribute n/v indicates that the verb proplet of a sentential argument proposition functions (i) as a nominal argument in the higher and (ii) as the verb of the lower proposition. Similarly, the attribute a/v indicates that the verb of a sentential modifier proposition functions (i) as an adjective in the higher and (ii) as the verb of the lower proposition.

The essential attributes and values of n/v and a/v proplets in sentential arguments, adverbials, and adnominals may be shown schematically as follows:

7.1.1 VERB PROPLETS OF SUBORDINATE CLAUSES

subject or object sentence

```
⎡ n/v: verb of the subclause    ⎤
⎢ arg: noun(s) of the subclause ⎥
⎢ fnc: verb of the higher clause ⎥
⎣ prn: number of the subclause  ⎦
```

adverbial sentence

```
⎡ a/v: verb of the subclause    ⎤
⎢ arg: noun(s) of the subclause ⎥
⎢ mdd: verb of the higher clause ⎥
⎣ prn: number of the subclause  ⎦
```

adnominal sentence

```
⎡ a/v: verb of the subclause    ⎤
⎢ arg: noun(s) of the subclause ⎥
⎢ mdd: noun of the higher clause ⎥
⎣ prn: number of the subclause  ⎦
```

To serve as a noun of the higher clause, an n/v proplet must have a fnc attribute. To serve as an adjective in the higher clause, an a/v proplet must have an mdd attribute.

As in the preceding chapter, we begin with the semantic representations of the different constructions by analyzing them as sets of proplets, concentrating on the grammatical relations. To facilitate understanding, the proplets are shown in the order which would result from the time-linear analysis of the surfaces specified in English (rather than in the alphabetical order of their core values, as in 6.1.1).

7.1.2 EXAMPLES OF EXTRAPROPOSITIONAL FUNCTOR–ARG. STRUCTURE

1. Representing That Fido barked amused Mary (subject sentence)

```
⎡ n/v: that bark ⎤ ⎡ noun: Fido ⎤ ⎡ verb: amuse          ⎤ ⎡ noun: Mary ⎤
⎢ arg: Fido      ⎥ ⎢ fnc: bark  ⎥ ⎢ arg: 27 bark   Mary  ⎥ ⎢ fnc: amuse ⎥
⎢ fnc: 28 amuse  ⎥ ⎢ mdr:       ⎥ ⎢ mdr:                 ⎥ ⎢ mdr:       ⎥
⎣ prn: 27        ⎦ ⎣ prn: 27    ⎦ ⎣ prn: 28              ⎦ ⎣ prn: 28    ⎦
```

2. Representing John heard that Fido barked (object sentence)

```
⎡ noun: John ⎤ ⎡ verb: hear           ⎤ ⎡ n/v: that bark ⎤ ⎡ noun: Fido ⎤
⎢ fnc: hear  ⎥ ⎢ arg: John   31 bark  ⎥ ⎢ arg: Fido      ⎥ ⎢ fnc: bark  ⎥
⎢ mdr:       ⎥ ⎢ mdr:                 ⎥ ⎢ fnc: 30 hear   ⎥ ⎢ mdr:       ⎥
⎣ prn: 30    ⎦ ⎣ prn: 30              ⎦ ⎣ prn: 31        ⎦ ⎣ prn: 31    ⎦
```

3. Representing The dog which saw Mary barked (adnominal sent., subject gap)

```
⎡ noun: dog   ⎤ ⎡ a/v: see    ⎤ ⎡ noun: Mary ⎤ ⎡ verb: bark ⎤
⎢ fnc: bark   ⎥ ⎢ arg: # Mary ⎥ ⎢ fnc: see   ⎥ ⎢ arg: dog   ⎥
⎢ mdr: 33 see ⎥ ⎢ mdd:32 dog  ⎥ ⎢ mdr:       ⎥ ⎢ mdr:       ⎥
⎣ prn: 32     ⎦ ⎣ prn: 33     ⎦ ⎣ prn: 33    ⎦ ⎣ prn: 32    ⎦
```

4. Representing The dog which Mary saw barked (adnominal sent., object gap)

```
⎡ noun: dog   ⎤ ⎡ a/v: see    ⎤ ⎡ noun: Mary ⎤ ⎡ verb: bark ⎤
⎢ fnc: bark   ⎥ ⎢ arg: Mary # ⎥ ⎢ fnc: see   ⎥ ⎢ arg: dog   ⎥
⎢ mdr: 35 see ⎥ ⎢ mdd:34 dog  ⎥ ⎢ mdr:       ⎥ ⎢ mdr:       ⎥
⎣ prn: 34     ⎦ ⎣ prn: 35     ⎦ ⎣ prn: 35    ⎦ ⎣ prn: 34    ⎦
```

5. Representing When Fido barked Mary smiled (adverbial sentence)

```
⎡ a/v: when bark ⎤ ⎡ noun: Fido ⎤ ⎡ noun: Mary ⎤ ⎡ verb: smile  ⎤
⎢ arg: Fido      ⎥ ⎢ fnc: bark  ⎥ ⎢ fnc: smile ⎥ ⎢ arg: Mary    ⎥
⎢ mdd:37 smile   ⎥ ⎢ mdr:       ⎥ ⎢ mdr:       ⎥ ⎢ mdr: 36 bark ⎥
⎣ prn: 36        ⎦ ⎣ prn: 36    ⎦ ⎣ prn: 37    ⎦ ⎣ prn: 37      ⎦
```

Extrapropositional values are preceded by a prn number, e.g., [fnc: 28 amuse].

In sentential argument constructions, there is a gap in the higher clause. Located in the arg slot of the higher verb proplet, it is filled by a pointer to the lower clause, e.g., [arg: 27 bark Mary] (with 27 bark serving as a subject sentence, cf. 7.1.2, 1) and [arg: John 31 bark] (with 31 bark serving as an object sentence, cf. 7.1.2, 2).

In adnominal modifiers, there is a gap in the lower clause. Because a relative clause modifies a noun in the higher clause, the pointer to it must be located in the mdd slot of the a/v proplet, e.g., [mdd: 32 dog]. As a consequence, the gap in the arg slot of the lower a/v proplet remains unfilled and is represented by #, e.g., [arg: # Mary] (subject gap, cf. 7.1.2, 3) and [arg: Mary #] (object gap, cf. 7.1.2, 4).

The distribution and grammatical function of gaps in extrapropositional functor–argument structures is indicated schematically below (in corelation with 7.1.2):

7.1.3 EXTRAPROPOSITIONAL FUNCTOR–ARGUMENT STRUCTURES

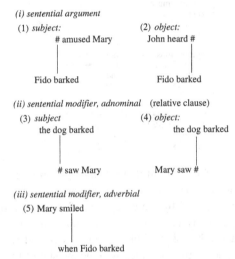

(i) sentential argument

(1) *subject:*
    # amused Mary

Fido barked

(2) *object:*
    John heard #

Fido barked

(ii) sentential modifier, adnominal (relative clause)

(3) *subject*
    the dog barked

saw Mary

(4) *object:*
    the dog barked

Mary saw #

(iii) sentential modifier, adverbial

(5) Mary smiled

when Fido barked

In the adverbial modifier construction *(iii)* there is no gap. Instead, the grammatical relation between the higher and the lower proposition is established by the mdr attribute of the higher verb, e.g., [mdr: 36 bark], and the mdd attribute of the lower verb, e.g., [mdd: 37 smile] (cf. 7.1.2, 5).

7.2 Sentential Argument as Subject

In the time-linear derivation of the subject sentence construction That Fido barked amused Mary, the lexical analysis of the function word that (subordinating conjunction) provides the attributes n/v and fnc. Because the verb is absorbed into the conjunction, the standard lexical analysis of the verb (as in 6.3.1, 6.4.1) is sufficient:

7.2.1 INTERPRETATION OF That Fido barked amused Mary

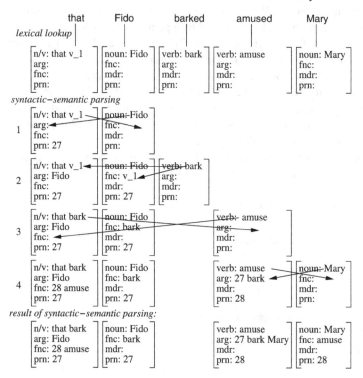

In line 1, the substitution value v_1 of the n/v attribute of *that* is copied into the fnc slot of *Fido*, and the core value of *Fido* is copied into the arg slot of *that*. In line 2, the two instances of v_1 are replaced by the core value of the *bark* proplet, which is then discarded. As in 6.4.1, this is an instance of function word absorption involving a verb. In line 3, the bark value of the initial proplet is copied into the arg slot of the verb proplet *amuse*, and amuse is copied into the fnc slot of the *bark* proplet, establishing the desired connection between the subordinate subject sentence and the higher clause. For unique identification, the copied (clause-external) values are preceded by the proposition number of their proplets, as shown in line 4.

The (re)production of the input sentence is based on a VNVN navigation:

7.2.2 PRODUCTION OF That Fido barked amused Mary

1.2	sc	n			sc	n				
	V	N								
1.3	sc fv	n			sc	n	fv			
	V	N								
2.1	sc fv	n	fv		sc	n	fv	fv		
	V	N	V							
2.2	sc fv	n	fv n		sc	n	fv	fv	n	
	V	N	V N							
2.3	sc fv	n	fv p n		sc	n	fv	fv	n	p
	V	N	V N							

The abstract surface **sc** stands for *subordinating conjunction*. It is produced from the verb proplet of the lower clause.

7.3 Sentential Argument as Object

Next consider the interpretation of an object sentence. In this example, the verb proplet *bark* represents the subclause, serving as the object of the higher clause:

7.3.1 INTERPRETATION OF John heard that Fido barked

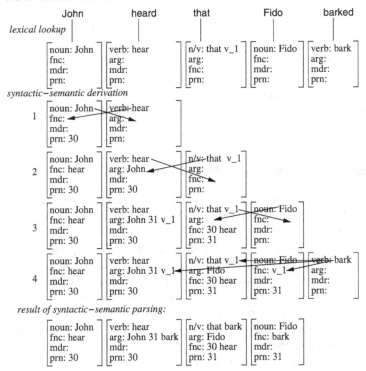

In line 2, the core value of the proplet *that*, i.e., the substitution value v_1, is copied into the arg slot of the proplet *hear*, taking second (i.e., object) position. Also, the core value of the proplet *hear* is copied into the fnc slot of the proplet *that*. In line 3, v_1 is copied into the fnc slot of the *Fido* proplet, and the core value Fido is copied into the arg slot of the *that* proplet. In line 4, the three instances of v_1 are simultaneously replaced by the core value of the proplet *bark*, which is then discarded.

The (re)production of this input sentence is based on a VNVN navigation:

7.3.2 SCHEMATIC PRODUCTION OF John heard that Fido barked

activated sequence					realization					
1										
	V									
1.1		n				n				
	V	N								
1.2	fv	n				n	fv			
	V	N								
2.1	fv	n	sc			n	fv	sc		
	V	N	V							
2.2	fv	n	sc	n		n	fv	sc	n	
	V	N	V	N						
2.3	fv	n	sc fv	n		n	fv	sc	n	fv
	V	N	V	N						
2.4	fv p	n	sc fv	n		n	fv	sc	n	fv	p
	V	N	V	N						

The abstract surface p (punctuation) is generated from the V proplet of the higher clause, while sc (subordinating conjunction) is generated from the V proplet of the lower clause – as in 7.2.2.

7.4 Adnominal Sentential Modifier with Subject Gap

Turning from sentential arguments to sentential modifiers, we start with the adnominals. Adnominal adjectives occur as elementary words, e.g., little (cf. 6.3.1), as prepositional phrases, e.g., on the table (cf. 6.6.2), and as adnominal sentences, such as which Mary saw (cf.7.1.2, 3, subject gap) and which saw Mary (cf.7.1.2, 4, object gap). In English, adnominal propositions are called relative clauses, and are connected to the higher clause by the function words who, whom, or which, which lexically introduce the core attribute a/v (with the core value v_1) and an mdd attribute.

Adnominal propositions differ from adverbial ones insofar as the core value of the lower verb proplet is copied into the mdr slot of a noun of the higher proposition (and not of the verb). Furthermore, the mdd attribute of the adnominal a/v proplet takes the core value of the higher noun proplet as its value (and not of the verb).

In the following example, a relative clause attaches to the higher noun with a subject gap. In order to show the compatibility between an extrapropositional adnominal modifier and an intrapropositional adverbial modifier, the example includes the adverb quickly. Due to its position, it is ambiguous between a reading modifying saw (7.4.1) and one modifying bark (7.4.2).

7.4.1 INTERPRETATION OF The dog which saw Mary quickly barked

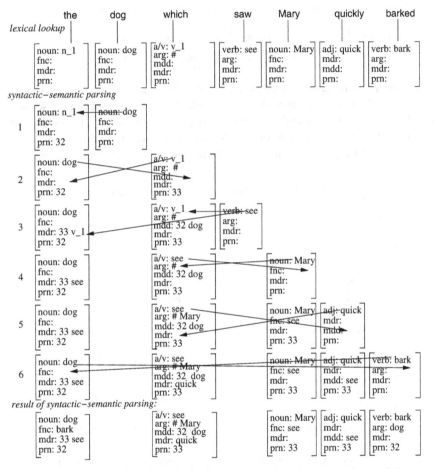

The a/v proplet *which* has the substitution value v_1 as its core value and the gap # in its arg slot. It also provides an mdd slot to take the head noun as value and an mdr attribute to accommodate the modifier quickly.

In line 2, the core value of *dog* is copied into the mdd of the a/v proplet, and the v_1 value of the a/v proplet is copied into the mdr slot of the *dog* proplet. In line 3, both occurrences of v_1 are replaced by the core value of the proplet *see*, which is then discarded. In line 4, the object of the relative clause is added by copying Mary as the second value into the arg slot of the a/v proplet, and the core value see of the a/v proplet into the fnc slot of the proplet *Mary*. In line 5, the adverb *quick* is added to the relative clause by copying see into the mdd slot of *quick*, and quick into the mdr slot of *see*. In line 6, the verb of the main clause is added by copying bark into the fnc slot of *dog* and dog into the arg slot of *bark*.

Next consider the other reading of this sentence:

7.4.2 SECOND READING OF 7.4.1 WITH quickly MODIFYING bark

$$
\begin{bmatrix} \text{noun: dog} \\ \text{fnc: bark} \\ \text{mdr: 33 see} \\ \text{prn: 32} \end{bmatrix}
\begin{bmatrix} \text{a/v: see} \\ \text{arg: \# Mary} \\ \text{mdd: 32 dog} \\ \text{mdr:} \\ \text{prn: 33} \end{bmatrix}
\begin{bmatrix} \text{noun: Mary} \\ \text{fnc: see} \\ \text{mdr:} \\ \text{prn: 33} \end{bmatrix}
\begin{bmatrix} \text{adj: quick} \\ \text{mdd: bark} \\ \text{mdr:} \\ \text{prn: 32} \end{bmatrix}
\begin{bmatrix} \text{verb: bark} \\ \text{arg: dog} \\ \text{mdr: quick} \\ \text{prn: 32} \end{bmatrix}
$$

The two readings are distinguished only in terms of different attribute values. On the first reading, the mdd attribute of the *quick* proplet has the value see, on the second, the value bark. Correspondingly, on the first reading, quick is the value of the mdr attribute of the proplet *see*, but of the proplet *bark* on the second reading.

The following (re)production of the first reading is based on a VNVNA navigation.

7.4.3 PRODUCTION OF The dog which saw Mary quickly barked

activated sequence						*realization*						
1												
	V											
1.1		d				d						
	V	N										
1.2		d nn				d nn						
	V	N	V									
2.1		d nn	wh			d	nn	wh				
	V	N	V									
2.2		d nn	wh fv			d	nn	wh	fv			
	V	N	V									
2.3		d nn	wh fv	n		d	nn	wh	fv	n		
	V	N	V	N								
1.3		d nn	wh fv	n	av	d	nn	wh	fv	n	av	
	V	N	V	N	A							
1.4	fv	d nn	wh fv	n	av	d	nn	wh	fv	n	av	fv
	V	N	V	N	A							
1.5	fv p	d nn	wh fv	n	av	d	nn	wh	fv	n	av	fv p
	V	N	V	N	A							

The abstract surface av represents the adverbial adjective quickly. The abstract surface wh stands for the relative pronoun, here which. Relative clauses resemble wh interrogatives (cf. Sections 5.1 and 9.5) in that both have a gap. This may be the reason why both kinds of sentences use wh words in English.

7.5 Adnominal Sentential Modifier with Object Gap

Next consider the derivation of a relative clause with an object gap. In the following example, the higher noun dog is modified (i) by the elementary adnominal little and (ii) the sentential adnominal (relative clause) which Mary saw, illustrating the compatibility of these two kinds of adnominal adjectives when modifying the same noun.

7.5.1 INTERPRETATION OF The little dog which Mary saw barked

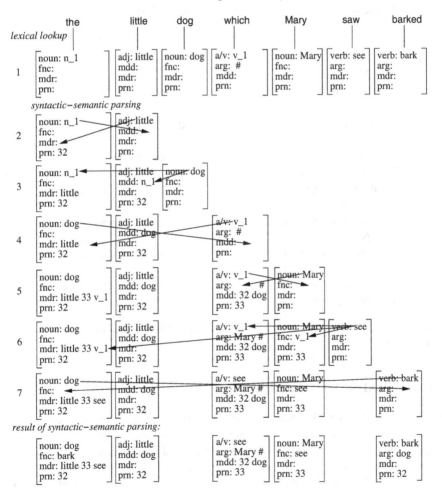

Up to line 4, this derivation is the same as in 7.4.1, apart from the elementary adnominal modifier little in 7.5.1. The derivations diverge in line 5: In 7.5.1, the core value of the proplet *Mary* is copied into the first position of the arg slot of the a/v proplet, thus pushing the gap indicator # into second (object) position. The remainders of the two derivations are again analogous, apart from the elementary adverbial modifier quickly in 7.4.1. For the semantic representation of 7.4.1 and 7.5.1 without elementary adjectives, see 7.1.2, 3 and 4, respectively.

The following (re)production of the input sentence is based on a VNAVN navigation.

7.5.2 PRODUCTION OF The little dog which Mary saw barked

activated sequence						realization							
1													
	V												
1.1		d				d							
	V	N											
1.2		d	an			d	an						
	V	N	A										
1.3		d nn	an			d	an	nn					
	V	N	A										
2.1		d nn	an	wh		d	an	nn	wh				
	V	N	A	V									
2.2		d nn	an	wh	n	d	an	nn	wh	n			
	V	N	A	V	N								
2.3		d nn	an	wh fv	n	d	an	nn	wh	n	fv		
	V	N	A	V	N								
1.4	fv	d nn	an	wh fv	n	d	an	nn	wh	n	fv	fv	
	V	N	A	V	N								
1.5	fv p	d nn	an	wh fv	n	d	an	nn	wh	n	fv	fv	p
	V	N	A	V	N								

In line 1.4, the second fv is realized from the initial V proplet, just as the punctuation p in line 1.5.

7.6 Adverbial Sentential Modifier

Finally, let us consider adverbial modifiers. Adverbial adjectives are like adnominal adjectives in that they occur as elementary word forms, e.g., loudly (cf. 6.3.4), as prepositional phrases, e.g., on the table (cf. 6.6.2), and as adverbial sentences, as in when Fido barked (cf 7.1.2, 5). The latter construction resembles the examples sentential subject 7.2.1 and sentential object 7.3.1 as well as adnominal adjective with subject gap 7.4.1 and object gap 7.5.1 insofar as the verb of the lower proposition is fused with a clause-initial function word, here *when*.

Like adnominal *which* (cf. 7.4.1 and 7.5.1), the lexical proplet of adverbial *when* introduces an a/v and a mdd attribute – in contradistinction to *that* (cf. 7.2.1 and 7.3.1), which introduces an n/v and a fnc attribute (see also 7.1.1):

7.6.1 INTERPRETATION OF When Fido barked Mary smiled

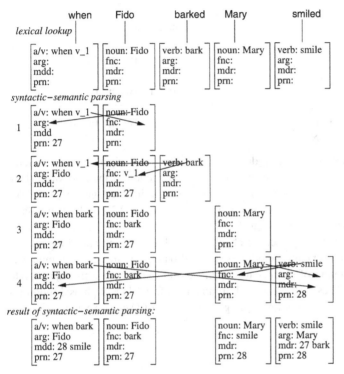

After completing the adverbial subclause in line 2, the subject Mary of the main clause is added to the set of proplets, but cannot be related grammatically to any previous proplet. Instead, it is *suspended* until the verb of the main clause is available for attachment (line 4).[1]

The production of the input sentence 7.6.1 is based on a VNVN navigation:

---

[1] Suspension is quite common in SOV languages like Korean. For example, in man$_{nom}$ her$_{dat}$ apple$_{acc}$ gave, all three arguments are suspended until the verb finally arrives (Lee 2002, 2004). Even though the same verb-final word order occurs in German subordinate clauses, there is no suspension due to the presence of a clause-initial function word, i.e., the subordinating conjunction, in which the arguments can be collected until the verb is absorbed into it.

7.6.2 PRODUCTION OF When Fido barked Mary smiled

	activated sequence						*realization*					
1												
	V											
1.1	sc						sc					
	V	N										
1.2	sc	n					sc	n				
	V	N										
1.3	sc fv	n					sc	n	fv			
	V	N										
2.1	sc fv	n		n			sc	n	fv	n		
	V	N	V	N								
2.2	sc fv̂	n	fv	n			sc	n	fv	n	fv	
	V	N	V	N								
2.3	sc fv	n	fv p	n			sc	n	fv	n	fv	p
	V	N	V	N								

Suspension also shows up in the production: In line 2.1, the navigation has to traverse the verb and the noun of the higher clause before production of the next word (here *Mary*) can take place. Other instances of suspension occur in object-gapping (cf. 8.6.1 and 8.6.4), extrapropositional coordination (cf. 9.2.1 and 9.2.2), and adverbials in prenominative position (cf. 15.3.7 and 15.3.10).

In summary, this and the preceding chapter have shown that the handling of sentential arguments and sentential modifiers is based on exactly the same grammatical relations as the handling of elementary arguments (cf. 3.4.2) and elementary modifiers (cf. 6.3.1, 6.3.3) as well as phrasal arguments (cf. 6.3.1) and phrasal modifiers (cf. 6.6.2). This is a substantial linguistic generalization of Database Semantics.

8. Intrapropositional Coordination

The other primary grammatical relation besides functor–argument structure (hypotaxis) is coordination (parataxis). While functor–argument structure typically combines different parts of speech, i.e., verbs with nouns, adjectives with nouns, and adjectives with verbs, coordination combines expressions of the same kind, i.e., nouns with nouns, verbs with verbs, and adjectives with adjectives.

The expressions being combined in a coordination are called *conjuncts*. The relations between conjuncts may be conjunctive, disjunctive, or adversative, as specified by the function words and, or, and but, respectively. These are called *coordinating conjunctions* (cc), in contradistinction to the subordinating conjunctions (sc), such as that (sentential argument, cf. Sects. 7.2 and 7.3) and when (adverbial modifier, cf. Sect. 7.6). In intrapropositional coordination, the conjuncts may be elementary or phrasal, and a conjunction is required. In extrapropositional coordination (cf. Chap. 9), the conjuncts are sentential and the conjunction is optional.

8.1 Overview

The semantic interpretation of coordination raises two fundamental questions. The first is how to build the relations between the conjuncts in a sequence, and applies to intra- and extrapropositional coordination alike. The second question is how to integrate a coordination into the functor–argument structure of a proposition, and is naturally restricted to intrapropositional coordination.

In Database Semantics, the conjuncts are connected by the values of their nc (next conjunct) and pc (previous conjunct) attributes. This is illustrated by the following example showing the proplet structure of an intrapropositional noun coordination:

8.1.1 GRAMMATICAL RELATIONS OF the man, the woman, and the child

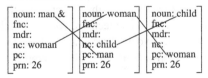

The nc attribute of the *man* proplet specifies woman as the next conjunct; the pc and nc attributes of the *woman* proplet specify man as the previous and child as the next conjunct, respectively; and the pc attribute of the *child* proplet specifies woman as the previous conjunct. The coordinating conjunction is indicated after the core value of the first conjunct (here [noun: man &]). The elements of the coordination are held together by a common proposition number (here [prn: 26]).[1]

The integration of such a coordination into the proposition's functor–argument structure is based on using only the initial conjunct for establishing the grammatical relation in question. This is shown by the following example in which the coordination the man, the woman, and the child (cf. 8.1.1) is combined with the verb sleep:

8.1.2 GRAMMATICAL RELATIONS OF The man, the woman, and the child slept

noun: man-&-	noun: woman	noun: child	verb:-sleep
fnc: sleep	fnc:	fnc:	arg:-man &
mdr:	mdr:	mdr:	mdr:
nc: woman	nc: child	nc:	nc:
pc:	pc: man	pc: woman	pc:
prn: 26	prn: 26	prn: 26	prn: 26

The arg slot of the verb proplet *sleep* has the value man &; thus, only the initial conjunct is specified as the verb's argument. Correspondingly, only the initial conjunct *man* has a core value marked with & and the fnc value sleep, while the noninitial conjuncts *woman* and *child* are unmarked and their fnc slots are empty. They are, however, connected to the initial conjunct via their nc and pc features (cf. 8.1.1).

Using only the initial conjunct for establishing the functor–argument structure provides a coding of grammatical relations in the semantic representation which is as complete as necessary and as parsimonious as possible – not only for modeling the time-linear interpretation and production of the surface, but also for supporting the required retrieval. For example, even though the *sleep* proplet in 8.1.2 does not explicitly specify child as its arg value, and the *child* proplet does not explicitly specify sleep as its fnc value, the correct answer to the question *Did a child sleep?* relative to a Word Bank containing 8.1.2 should be yes.

One method to answer the question is to look through all *sleep* proplets (cf. Sect. 5.1) and find the ones with the arg value child. Yet if child happens to be a noninitial conjunct, it will not be specified directly in the *sleep* proplet. However, if the arg slot of the verb proplet contains the conjunction marker & it will trigger a subnavigation through all the conjuncts of the associated coordination, ensuring that the *child* conjunct in 8.1.2 will not be overlooked. And correspondingly for the other method, which is to check all *child* proplets to find the ones with the fnc value sleep.

Different kinds of coordination may be distinguished with respect to (i) the parts of speech serving as conjuncts, i.e., nouns, verbs, or adjectives, (ii) the number of coordinated arguments in a proposition, i.e., one, two, or three, and (iii) the alternative between simple and complex coordinations. Consider the following examples:

---

[1] Our treatment of coordination as a grammatical relation like functor–argument structure, handled in terms of the attributes and values of proplets, differs from the approach of Lobin (1993a): "The best way of dealing with coordination is not to deal with it at all, but 'process it away immediately'."

8.1.3 DIFFERENT KINDS OF COORDINATIONS

1. *One simple noun coordination* (subject, cf. 8.2.1, 8.2.2)
   The man, the woman, and the child slept.

2. *One simple noun coordination* (object, 8.2.4, 8.2.5)
   John bought an apple, a pear, and a peach.

3. *Two simple noun coordinations* (subject object, cf. 8.2.3)
   The man, the woman, and the child bought an apple, a pear, and a peach.

4. *One simple verb coordination* (cf. 8.3.1, 8.3.2, 8.3.3)
   John bought, cooked, and ate the pizza.

5. *Three simple coordinations of noun, verb, and noun* (subject verb object)
   The man, the woman, and the child bought, cooked, and ate the steak, the pota-
   toes, and the broccoli.

6. *One simple adjective coordination* (adnominal, cf. 8.3.4)
   John loves a smart, pretty, and rich girl.

7. *One simple adjective coordination* (adverbial, cf. 8.3.5)
   John talked gently, slowly, and seriously.

8. *One simple noun coordination in a prepositional phrase*
   The company has offices in London, Paris, and New York.

9. *One simple noun coordination in a genitive construction*
   John visited the house of Julia, Susanne, and Mary.

10. *One complex verb–object coordination* (subject gapping, cf. 8.4.1, 8.4.5)
    Bob ate an apple, # walked his dog, and # read a paper.

11. *One complex subject–object coordination* (verb gapping, cf. 8.5.1, 8.5.4)
    Bob ate an apple, Jim # a pear, and Bill # a peach.

12. *One complex subject–verb coordination* (object gapping,[2] cf. 8.6.1, 8.6.4)
    Bob bought #, Jim peeled #, and Bill ate the peach.

The above examples have been limited to intrapropositional constructions excluding modifier recursion. This resulted in a short but essentially complete list of the most basic possibilities regarding the correlation of intrapropositional functor–argument structure and coordination. Once extrapropositional functor–argument structure (i.e., subordination, cf. Chap. 7) is included, however, the number of coordinations in a sentence (though not a proposition) is unlimited – at least in theory. Consider for example, The man, who bought an apple, a pear, and a peach, the woman, who read a paper, a novel, and a poem, etc.

In 8.1.3, the coordinations' part of speech is indicated in the subheadings. Examples 1, 2, 4, 6, 7, 8, and 9 contain one simple coordination each, 10, 11, and 12 contain

---

[2] This construction is also known as "right-node-raising." Cf. Jackendoff (1972); Hudson (1976); and Sag, Gazdar, Wasow, and Weisler (1985).

one complex coordination each, 3 contains two simple coordinations, and 5 contains three. The distinction between simple and complex coordination[3] concerns the relation between the conjuncts, as illustrated below:

8.1.4 COMPARING SIMPLE AND COMPLEX COORDINATION

(i) *two simple coordinations*
Bob, Jim, and Bill bought, peeled, and ate the peach.

(ii) *one complex coordination*
Bob bought #, Jim peeled #, and Bill ate the peach.

The two examples consist of exactly the same word forms, though in different order. Example (i) consists of two simple coordinations, one conjoining nouns, the other verbs. Example (ii) consists of one complex coordination, the conjuncts of which consist of noun-verb pairs. While (i) merely asserts that three subjects performed three actions as a group, (ii) associates each subject with only one of the three actions.

Regarding frequency, März (2005) determined the following results for German, using the LIMAS corpus.[4] It has a total of 77 500 sentences, of which 27 500 contain the coordinating conjunctions und (and), oder (or), or aber (but). The conjunction und was by far the most frequent, used in 21 420 sentences.

Of all the coordinations, 57% consist of nouns and 24.3% of verbs. Of the noun coordinations, 25% function in prepositional phrases (cf. 8.1.3, 8), 13% as subjects (cf. 8.1.3, 1), 7% as objects (cf. 8.1.3, 2), and 6.5% in genitives (cf. 8.1.3, 9). Gapping occurs in only 0.1% of the coordinations, with no example of object gapping (cf. 8.1.3, 12). Given that all of these constructions provide equally clear grammaticality intuitions, and may be found in a wide range of languages (such as Chinese, Tagalog, Russian, Georgian, Czech, and Korean),[5] the least frequent constructions are just as interesting for a systematic grammatical analysis as the most frequent ones.

8.2 Simple Coordination of Nouns in Subject and Object Position

Having characterized the grammatical relations of a functor–argument structure containing a coordination as a set of proplets (cf. 8.1.1 and 8.1.2), we turn next to the tasks of (i) deriving the semantic representation from the corresponding surface of English (hearer mode, interpretation) and (ii) deriving the surface of English from the semantic representation (speaker mode, production).

---

[3] The terminological distinction between simple and complex coordination follows Greenbaum and Quirk (1990, pp. 271ff). Within Nativism, simple coordination is called "constituent coordination," and complex coordination is called "nonconstituent coordination." Different kinds of complex coordination are distinguished here in terms of subject gapping, verb gapping, and object gapping.

[4] The LIMAS corpus (Heß, Lenders, et al. 1983) was designed as a balanced and representative corpus of German, built in analogy to the Brown corpus (Kučera and Francis 1967).

[5] I would like to thank Hsiao-Yun Huang (China), Guerly Soellch (The Philippines), Katja Kalender (Russia), Sofia Tkemaladze (Georgia), Marie Hučinova (Czech Republic), and Soora Kim (South Korea) for their native speaker grammaticality judgments during a seminar at CLUE.

8.2.1 NOUN COORDINAT. (SUBJECT): The man, the woman, and the child slept

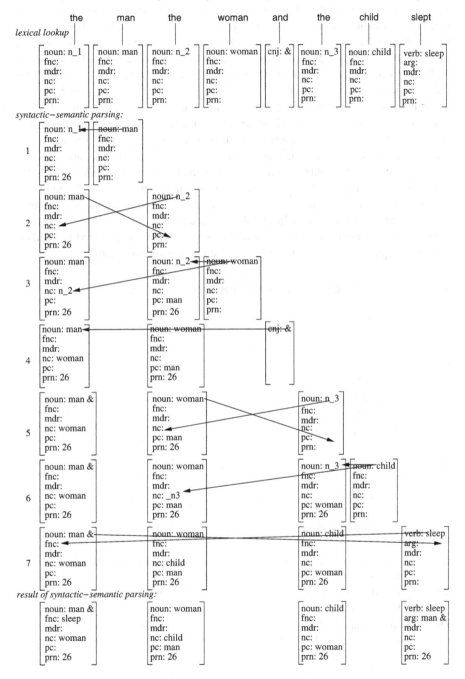

In line 1, the lexical proplets *the* and *man* are fused (function word absorption). In line 2, the core value n_2 of the second *the* is copied into the nc slot of *man*, and the core value of *man* is copied into the pc slot of *the*. In line 3, the two occurrences of the substitution value n_2 are replaced by the core value of the lexical proplet *woman*. In line 4, the core value of the conjunction is added to the core value of *man*. In line 5, the core value n_3 of the third *the* is copied into the nc slot of *woman*, and the core value of *woman* is copied into the pc slot of *the*. In line 6, the two occurrences of the substitution value n_3 are replaced by the core value of the lexical proplet *child*. In line 7, the core value of the initial conjunct, i.e., man &, is copied into the arg slot of *sleep*, and the core value of *sleep* is copied into the fnc slot of the initial conjunct.[6]

In the result, the initial conjunct *man* contains & in its core attribute, and specifies the verb *see* as its fnc value. The noninitial conjuncts *woman* and *child* have no fnc value. It may be obtained from the initial conjunct, however, to which the noninitial conjuncts are connected via their nc and pc features. The verb proplet *see* specifies only the initial conjunct man in its arg slot, marked by &.

The (re)production of this sentence from the set of proplets just derived is based on a VNNN sequence, whereby the three Ns constitute a noun coordination.

8.2.2 PRODUCTION OF The man the woman and the child slept

activated sequence				*realization*
i.				
V				
i.1	d			d
V	N			
i.2	d nn			d nn
V	N			
i.3	d nn	d		d nn d
V	N	N		
i.4	d nn	d nn		d nn d nn
V	N	N		
i.5	d nn cc	d nn		d nn d nn cc
V	N	N		
i.6	d nn cc	d nn	d	d nn d nn cc d
V	N	N	N	
i.7	d nn cc	d nn	d nn	d nn d nn cc d nn
V	N	N	N	
i.8	fv	d nn cc	d nn	d nn	d nn d nn cc d nn fv
V	N	N	N	
i.9	fv p	d nn cc	d nn	d nn	d nn d nn cc d nn fv p
V	N	N	N	

The coordinating conjunction cc is lexicalized from the first conjunct in line i.5. Due to this late realization, it appears between the penultimate and the ultimate conjunct.

While a coordination in subject position is built first and then combined with the verb, a coordination in object position is attached to the verb incrementally. This is indicated by the schematic characterization of the grammatical relations in the man, the woman, and the child bought an apple, a pear, and a peach:

8.2.3 SIMPLE COORDINATIONS OF SUBJECT AND OBJECT NOUNS

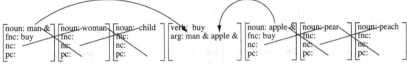

When the subject coordination is combined with the verb, the conjunction has been parsed, marking the initial conjunct, here [noun: man &]. Thus it is clear which proplet of the coordination must serve as the arg value of the verb. When the object noun is started, it is open whether or not it will turn out to be a coordination. In any case, the first object noun encountered will be the proper value for the arg slot of the verb.

The following example shows the incremental build-up of a noun coordination serving as the object, using a proper name as subject:

8.2.4 NOUN COORDIN. (OBJECT): John bought an apple, a pear, and a peach

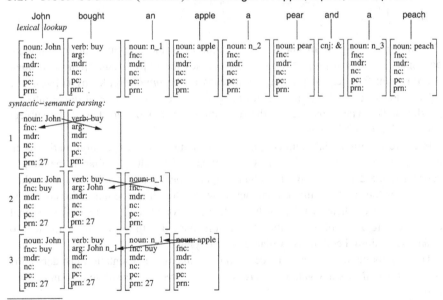

---

[6] Given the disambiguating function of the commas in the surface, they should eventually be represented as lexical proplets and added by suitable rules. For a syncategorematic treatment of commas see NEWCAT'86.

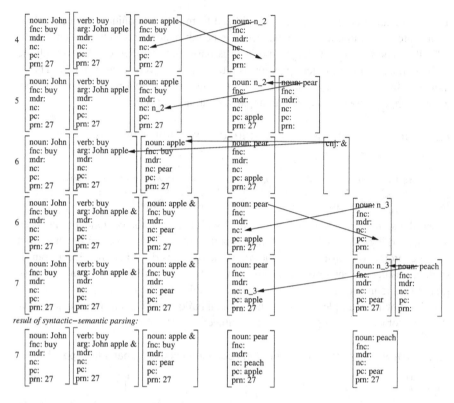

result of syntactic–semantic parsing:

The first three proplets in line 4 are the same as in the derivation of John bought an apple. The fourth proplet, however, continues the object noun *apple* as a noun coordination: The lexical proplet *the* attaches to the *apple* proplet by copying the substitution value n_2 into the nc slot of *apple* and the core value of *apple* into the pc slot of *the*. The remainder of the derivation is analogous to that of the subject coordination in 8.2.1, lines 1–6.

In the result, the initial noun conjunct *apple* contains the conjunction marker & in its core attribute, and specifies the verb buy as its fnc value (similar to the subject coordination 8.2.1). The noninitial noun conjuncts *pear* and *peach* have no fnc value. It is obtainable from the initial conjunct, however, to which the noninitial conjuncts are connected via their nc and pc values. The verb proplet contains the initial nominal conjunct, here as the object, in its arg slot. It is marked with &, which is sufficient to make the noninitial conjuncts available for querying as well.

The (re)production of this sentence from the semantic representation just derived is based on a VNNNN navigation, whereby the last three Ns constitute a noun coordination.

8.2.5 PRODUCTION OF John bought an apple, a pear, and a peach

activated sequence   *realization*

i.
```
        V
i.1     n                                                     n
        V   N
i.2     fv  n                                                 n fv
        V   N
i.3     fv  n      d                                          n fv d
        V   N      N
i.4     fv  n      d nn                                       n fv d nn
        V   N      N
i.5     fv  n      d nn     d                                 n fv d nn d
        V   N      N
i.6     fv  n      d nn     d nn                              n fv d nn d nn
        V   N      N        N
i.7     fv  n      d nn cc  d nn                              n fv d nn d nn cc
        V   N      N        N
i.8     fv  n      d nn cc  d nn    d                         n fv d nn d nn cc d
        V   N      N        N       N
i.9     fv  n      d nn cc  d nn  d nn                        n fv d nn d nn cc d nn
        V   N      N        N     N
i.10    fv p n     d nn cc  d nn  d nn                        n fv d nn d nn cc d nn p
        V    N     N        N     N
```

As in 8.2.2, the coordinating conjunction cc is lexicalized from the first conjunct, here in line i.7.

8.3 Simple Coordination of Verbs and of Adjectives

While the initial conjunct of a noun coordination serves as a value in the arg slot of the verb (cf. 8.2.3), the initial conjunct of a verb coordination serves as the value of the fnc slot of the noun(s). This partial inversion of the grammatical relations in the coordination of verbs versus nouns is shown by the distribution of & markers in the following schematic characterization of a coordination of two-place verbs:

8.3.1 COORDINATION OF TWO-PLACE VERBS

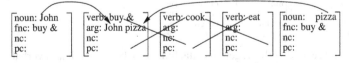

This example has the following time-linear derivation:

8.3.2 VERB COORDINATION: John bought, cooked, and ate the pizza

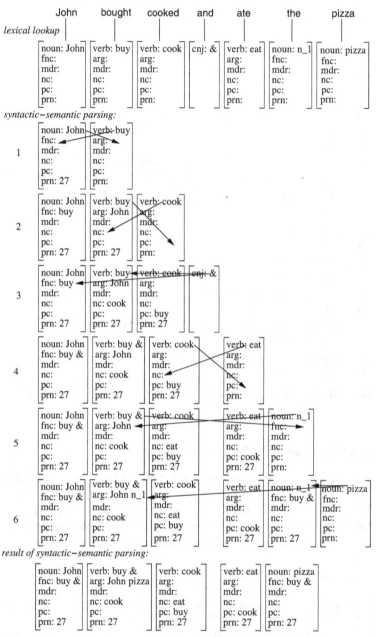

In line 2, the arrival of a second verb triggers its attachment to the first verb as a verbal conjunct, coded by copying the core value of *buy* into the pc slot of *cook* and the core value of *cook* into the nc slot of *buy*.[7] In line 3, the conjunction marker & is added to the core value of the initial verb conjunct *buy* and to the fnc value of the subject *John*. In line 4, the third verb conjunct *eat* is added. In line 5, the core value buy & of the initial verb conjunct is copied into the fnc slot of the beginning of the object, i.e., the determiner *the*. In line 6, the two occurrences of n_1 are replaced by the core value of the lexical proplet *pizza*, which is then discarded.

In the result, the initial verb conjunct *buy* contains & in its core attribute, and specifies the noun fillers John and pizza as its arg values. The noninitial verb conjuncts *cook* and *eat* have no arg values. They are obtainable from the initial conjunct, however, to which the noninitial conjuncts are connected via their nc and pc values. The noun proplets *John* and *pizza* specify only the initial verb conjunct, marked with &. This is sufficient to make the noninitial verb conjuncts available for querying.

The (re)production of this sentence from the proplets just derived is based on a VNVVN navigation, whereby the three Vs constitute a verb coordination.

8.3.3 PRODUCTION OF John bought, cooked, and ate the pizza

	activated sequence					realization
i	V					
i.1		n				n
	V	N				
i.2	fv	n				n fv
	V	N				
i.3	fv	n	fv			n fv fv
	V	N	V			
i.4	fv cc	n	fv			n fv fv cc
	V	N	V			
i.5	fv cc	n	fv	fv		n fv fv cc fv
	V	N	V	V		
i.6	fv cc	n	fv	fv	d	n fv fv cc fv d
	V	N	V	V	N	
i.7	fv cc	n	fv	fv	d nn	n fv fv cc fv d nn
	V	N	V	V	N	
i.8	fv cc p	n	fv	fv	d nn	n fv fv cc fv d nn p
	V	N	V	V	N	

Up to line i.2, the derivation resembles a sentence start without a verb coordination, e.g., John bought. When the navigation returns from *John* to *buy*, however, the conjunction marker (cf. result in 8.3.2) triggers the production of the verb coordination. Its end is indicated by the empty nc-attribute of *eat*, telling **LA-speak** to lexicalize the conjunction, using the & in the core attribute of the first conjunct *buy*.

---

[7] As mentioned before, a compositional treatment of commas is omitted here for simplicity.

We conclude the discussion of simple coordination with a look at the third basic part of speech, namely adjectives (modifiers[8]). For brevity, the time-linear interpretation and production of the surfaces is omitted, limiting the analysis to semantic representations which characterize the grammatical relations as sets of proplets.

Consider the semantic representation of coordinated adjectives in adnominal use:

8.3.4 ADNOMINAL COORDINATION: John loves a smart, pretty, and rich girl

$$
\begin{bmatrix} \text{noun: John} \\ \text{fnc: love} \\ \text{mdr:} \\ \text{nc:} \\ \text{pc:} \\ \text{prn: 21} \end{bmatrix}
\begin{bmatrix} \text{verb: love} \\ \text{arg: John girl} \\ \text{mdr::} \\ \text{nc:} \\ \text{pc:} \\ \text{prn: 21} \end{bmatrix}
\begin{bmatrix} \text{noun: girl} \\ \text{fnc: love} \\ \text{mdr: smart \&} \\ \text{nc:} \\ \text{pc:} \\ \text{prn: 21} \end{bmatrix}
\begin{bmatrix} \text{adj: smart \&} \\ \text{mdr: B} \\ \text{mdd: girl} \\ \text{nc: pretty} \\ \text{pc:} \\ \text{prn: 21} \end{bmatrix}
\begin{bmatrix} \text{adj: pretty} \\ \text{mdr: B} \\ \text{mdd:} \\ \text{nc: rich} \\ \text{pc: smart} \\ \text{prn: 21} \end{bmatrix}
\begin{bmatrix} \text{adj: rich} \\ \text{mdr: B} \\ \text{mdd:} \\ \text{nc:} \\ \text{pc: pretty} \\ \text{prn: 21} \end{bmatrix}
$$

The first adjective conjunct *smart* contains the conjunction marker & in its core attribute, and specifies the modified (here the noun *girl*) as its mdd value. The noninitial adjectival conjuncts *pretty* and *rich* have no mdd value. It is obtainable from the initial conjunct, to which the noninitial conjuncts are connected via their nc and pc values. The modified proplet *girl* contains & in its mdr slot, which specifies only the initial adjectival conjunct. Because elementary adnominals are intraphrasal in English, speaker–hearers seem to prefer modifier recursion (cf. 6.3.1) over coordination.

Next, consider the coordination of adjectives in adverbial use:

8.3.5 ADVERBIAL COORDINATION: John talked slowly, gently, and seriously

$$
\begin{bmatrix} \text{noun: John} \\ \text{fnc: talk} \\ \text{mdr:} \\ \text{nc:} \\ \text{pc:} \\ \text{prn: 29} \end{bmatrix}
\begin{bmatrix} \text{verb: talk} \\ \text{arg: John} \\ \text{mdr: slow \&} \\ \text{nc:} \\ \text{pc:} \\ \text{prn: 29} \end{bmatrix}
\begin{bmatrix} \text{adj: slow \&} \\ \text{mdr: B} \\ \text{mdd: talk} \\ \text{nc: gentle} \\ \text{pc:} \\ \text{prn: 29} \end{bmatrix}
\begin{bmatrix} \text{adj: gentle} \\ \text{mdr: B} \\ \text{mdd:} \\ \text{nc: serious} \\ \text{pc: slow} \\ \text{prn: 29} \end{bmatrix}
\begin{bmatrix} \text{adj: serious} \\ \text{mdr: B} \\ \text{mdd:} \\ \text{nc:} \\ \text{pc: gentle} \\ \text{prn: 29} \end{bmatrix}
$$

The first adjective conjunct *slow* contains the conjunction & in its core attribute, and specifies the modified (here the verb *talk*) as its mdd value. The noninitial adjective conjuncts have no mdd value. It is obtainable from the initial conjunct, to which they are connected via their nc and pc values. The modified proplet *talk* specifies only the initial adjectival conjunct, marked with &, in its mdr slot.

8.4 Complex Coordination of Verbs and Objects: Subject Gapping

We turn now to propositions with a complex coordination (gapping constructions), beginning with an example of subject gapping: Bob ate an apple, walked his dog, and read the paper. The parallel construction with two simple coordinations (cf. 8.1.4) would be *Bob ate, walked, and read an apple, his dog, and the paper, clearly indicating the need for different analyses of simple and complex coordinations:

---

[8] Modifier coordination is in competition with modifier recursion (cf. Sect. 6.3), the latter belonging to functor–argument structure.

8.4.1 Bob ate an apple, # walked his dog, and # read a paper

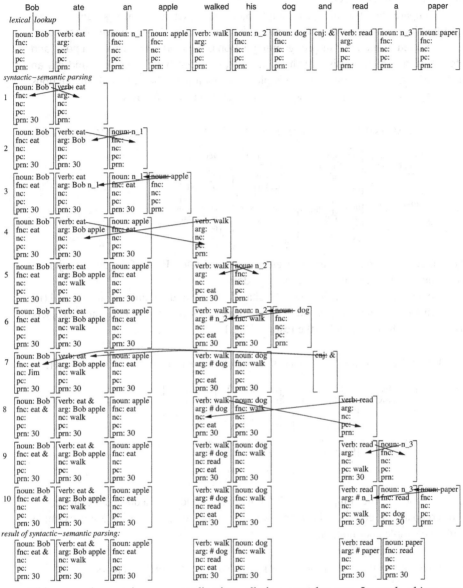

This example contains one coordination, albeit a complex one. Its *verb–object* conjuncts are *eat-apple*, *walk-dog*, and *read-paper*. The two proplets of a conjunct are connected by copying the core value of the verb, e.g., *walk*, into the fnc slot of the object, and the core value of the object, e.g., *dog*, into the second position of the arg slot of the verb; the first arg position of, e.g.,, *walk* is filled by #, thus characterizing the value dog as an object.

To compare the structure of Example 8.4.1 with that of a corresponding simple coordination, let us change the words without changing the grammatical structure. Our modified example of subject gapping is Bob bought an apple, peeled a pear, and ate a peach, which consists of the same words as Bob bought, peeled, and ate an apple, a pear, and a peach (two simple coordinations). The grammatical relations within the complex conjuncts may be shown graphically as follows:

8.4.2 Intraconjunct relations of complex verb–object coordinat.

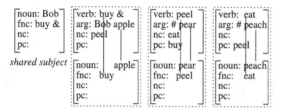

The intraconjunct relations are indicated by vertical lines. Each of the three conjuncts is surrounded by a rectangle consisting of dots.

The external relations (i) between the shared subject and the initial conjunct and (ii) between the conjuncts may be shown graphically as follows, using the same proplets as 8.4.2, which correspond to the result of 8.4.1:

8.4.3 Extraconjunct relations of complex verb–object coordinat.

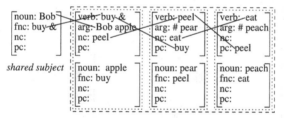

The conjuncts of the complex coordination are surrounded by a dashed rectangle.

In comparison, consider the grammatical relations of the corresponding example with two simple coordinations:

8.4.4 Corresponding simple verb and object coordinations

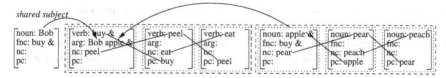

This representation of Bob bought, peeled, and ate an apple, a pear, and a peach shows two simple coordinations, each surrounded by a dashed rectangle, one serving as the verb, the other as the object. For the comparison with 8.4.2, the conjuncts are surrounded by dotted rectangles.

In contradistinction to the complex conjuncts in 8.4.2 and 8.4.3, the arg slots of the noninitial conjunct proplets *peel* and *eat* in 8.4.4 have no values, just as the fnc slots of the noninitial conjunct proplets *pear* and *peach*. These values may be obtained, however, by navigating to the initial conjuncts *buy* and *apple*, respectively. While in a complex verb–object coordination the number of verbs and objects must be equal, there is no such restriction in a simple coordination.

Based on the grammatical relations shown in 8.4.2 and 8.4.3, the surface of the complex coordination 8.4.1 is derived using a VNNVNVN navigation:

8.4.5 PRODUCTION OF Bob ate an apple, walked his dog, and read a paper

	activated sequence							*realization*
i	V							
i.1	n							n
	V	N						
i.2	fv	n						n fv
	V	N						
i.3	fv	n	d					n fv d
	V	N	N					
i.4	fv	n	d nn					n fv d nn
	V	N	N					
i.5	fv	n	d nn	fv				n fv d nn fv
	V	N	N	V				
i.6	fv	n	d nn	fv	d			n fv d nn fv d
	V	N	N	V	N			
i.7	fv	n	d nn	fv	d nn			n fv d nn fv d nn
	V	N	N	V	N			
i.8	fv cc	n	d nn	fv	d nn			n fv d nn fv d nn cc
	V	N	N	V	N			
i.9	fv cc	n	d nn	fv	d nn	fv		n fv d nn fv d nn cc fv
	V	N	N	V	N	V		
i.10	fv cc	n	d nn	fv	d nn	fv	d	n fv d nn fv d nn cc fv d
	V	N	N	V	N	V	N	
i.11	fv cc	n	d nn	fv	d nn	fv	d nn	n fv d nn fv d nn cc fv d nn
	V	N	N	V	N	V	N	
i.12	fv cc p	n	d nn	fv	d nn	fv	d nn	n fv d nn fv d nn cc fv d nn p
	V	N	N	V	N	V	N	

Up to line i.4, the derivation resembles that of Bob ate an apple without a coordination. When the navigation returns from *apple* to *eat*, however, the conjunction marker in the verb triggers the production of the complex verb–object coordination.

8.5 Complex Coordination of Subjects and Objects: Verb Gapping

The second kind of complex coordination is based on subject–object conjuncts sharing the verb (verb gapping). In contrast to 8.4.1, we illustrate the complex coordination with an example which is suitable to be reformulated as a simple coordination with a reasonable meaning. The complex coordination example is Bob ate an apple, Jim a pear, and Bill a peach, while the parallel example with two simple coordinations is Bob, Jim, and Bill ate an apple, a pear, and a peach.

8.5.1 VERB GAPPING: Bob ate an apple, Jim # a pear, and Bill # a peach

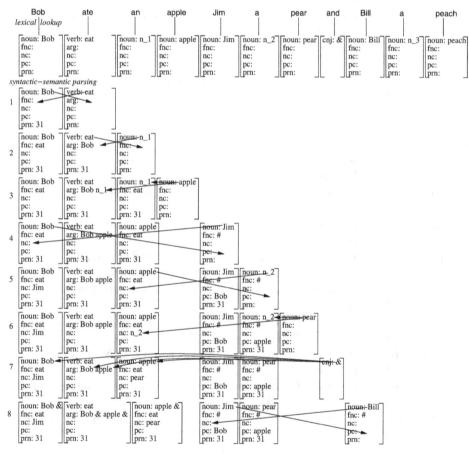

9
$$
\begin{bmatrix} \text{noun: Bob \&} \\ \text{fnc: eat} \\ \text{nc: Jim} \\ \text{pc:} \\ \text{prn: 31} \end{bmatrix}
\begin{bmatrix} \text{verb: eat} \\ \text{arg: Bob \& apple \&} \\ \text{nc:} \\ \text{pc:} \\ \text{prn: 31} \end{bmatrix}
\begin{bmatrix} \text{noun: apple \&} \\ \text{fnc: eat} \\ \text{nc: pear} \\ \text{pc:} \\ \text{prn: 31} \end{bmatrix}
\begin{bmatrix} \text{noun: Jim} \\ \text{fnc: \#} \\ \text{nc: Bill} \\ \text{pc: Bob} \\ \text{prn: 31} \end{bmatrix}
\begin{bmatrix} \text{noun: pear} \\ \text{fnc: \#} \\ \text{nc:} \\ \text{pc: apple} \\ \text{prn: 31} \end{bmatrix}
\begin{bmatrix} \text{noun: Bill} \\ \text{fnc: \#} \\ \text{nc:} \\ \text{pc: Jim} \\ \text{prn: 31} \end{bmatrix}
\begin{bmatrix} \text{noun: n\_3} \\ \text{fnc: \#} \\ \text{nc:} \\ \text{pc:} \\ \text{prn:} \end{bmatrix}
$$

10
$$
\begin{bmatrix} \text{noun: Bob \&} \\ \text{fnc: eat} \\ \text{nc: Jim} \\ \text{pc:} \\ \text{prn: 31} \end{bmatrix}
\begin{bmatrix} \text{verb: eat} \\ \text{arg: Bob \& apple \&} \\ \text{nc:} \\ \text{pc:} \\ \text{prn: 31} \end{bmatrix}
\begin{bmatrix} \text{noun: apple \&} \\ \text{fnc: eat} \\ \text{nc: pear} \\ \text{pc:} \\ \text{prn: 31} \end{bmatrix}
\begin{bmatrix} \text{noun: Jim} \\ \text{fnc: \#} \\ \text{nc: Bill} \\ \text{pc: Bob} \\ \text{prn: 31} \end{bmatrix}
\begin{bmatrix} \text{noun: pear} \\ \text{fnc: \#} \\ \text{nc: n\_1} \\ \text{pc: apple} \\ \text{prn: 31} \end{bmatrix}
\begin{bmatrix} \text{noun: Bill} \\ \text{fnc: \#} \\ \text{nc:} \\ \text{pc: Jim} \\ \text{prn: 31} \end{bmatrix}
\begin{bmatrix} \text{noun: n\_3} \\ \text{fnc: \#} \\ \text{nc:} \\ \text{pc: pear} \\ \text{prn: 31} \end{bmatrix}
\begin{bmatrix} \text{noun: peach} \\ \text{fnc:} \\ \text{nc:} \\ \text{pc:} \\ \text{prn:} \end{bmatrix}
$$

result of syntactic–semantic parsing:

$$
\begin{bmatrix} \text{noun: Bob \&} \\ \text{fnc: eat} \\ \text{nc: Jim} \\ \text{pc:} \\ \text{prn: 31} \end{bmatrix}
\begin{bmatrix} \text{verb: eat} \\ \text{arg: Bob \& apple \&} \\ \text{nc:} \\ \text{pc:} \\ \text{prn: 31} \end{bmatrix}
\begin{bmatrix} \text{noun: apple \&} \\ \text{fnc: eat} \\ \text{nc: pear} \\ \text{pc:} \\ \text{prn: 31} \end{bmatrix}
\begin{bmatrix} \text{noun: Jim} \\ \text{fnc: \#} \\ \text{nc: Bill} \\ \text{pc: Bob} \\ \text{prn: 31} \end{bmatrix}
\begin{bmatrix} \text{noun: pear} \\ \text{fnc: \#} \\ \text{nc: peach} \\ \text{pc: apple} \\ \text{prn: 31} \end{bmatrix}
\begin{bmatrix} \text{noun: Bill} \\ \text{fnc: \#} \\ \text{nc:} \\ \text{pc: Jim} \\ \text{prn: 31} \end{bmatrix}
\begin{bmatrix} \text{noun: peach} \\ \text{fnc: \#} \\ \text{nc:} \\ \text{pc: pear} \\ \text{prn: 31} \end{bmatrix}
$$

The one coordination of this example has three complex *subject–object* conjuncts, namely *Bob-apple*, *Jim-pear*, and *Bill-peach*. The grammatical relations within and between the complex conjuncts may be shown graphically as follows:

8.5.2 GRAMMATICAL RELATIONS IN COMPLEX SUBJECT–OBJECT COORDINAT.

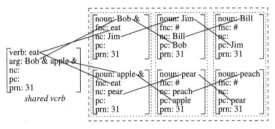

The three complex conjuncts are surrounded by dotted rectangles. They constitute one coordination surrounded by a dashed rectangle.

While the parts of a noninitial subject gapping conjunct, e.g., *read-paper* (cf. Sect. 8.4) can be naturally connected via the arg slot of the verb and the fnc slot of the noun, this is not possible for the two nouns constituting the parts of a noninitial verb gapping conjunct, e.g., *Bill-peach*. Instead, the connection between the two nouns must be established via the shared verb. The navigation traversing the shared verb is triggered by the # in the fnc slot of the noun proplets of the noninitial conjuncts. It represents the shared verb – just as # indicates the shared subject in 8.4.3.

Next consider the grammatical relations of the corresponding example Bob, Jim, and Bill ate an apple, a pear, and a peach. It contains the two simple coordinations *Bob, Jim, Bill* and *apple, pear, peach*.

8.5.3 GRAMMATICAL RELATIONS IN SIMPLE SUBJECT AND OBJECT COORDINAT.

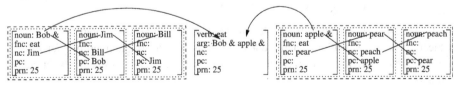

Leaving the spatial layout and the prn values aside, the only difference between the complex coordination 8.5.1/8.5.2 and the parallel simple coordinations 8.5.3 are the # markers in the fnc slots of the noninitial conjuncts in the complex coordination, which are missing in the simple coordinations.

Based on the grammatical relations shown in 8.5.2, the surface of the complex coordination 8.4.1 is derived using a VNNNNNN navigation, whereby the six N constitute three complex subject–object conjuncts:

8.5.4 PRODUCTION OF Bob ate an apple, Jim a pear, and Bill a peach

activated sequence							*realization*
i							
	V						
i.1		n					n
	V	N					
i.2	fv	n					n fv
	V	N					
i.3	fv	n	d				n fv d
	V	N	N				
i.4	fv	n	d nn				n fv d nn
	V	N	N				
i.5	fv	n	d nn	n			n fv d nn n
	V	N	N	N			
i.6	fv	n	d nn	n	d		n fv d nn n d
	V	N	N	N	N		
i.7	fv	n	d nn	n	d nn		n fv d nn n d nn
	V	N	N	N	N		
i.8	fv cc	n	d nn	n	d nn		n fv d nn n d nn cc
	V	N	N	N	N		
i.9	fv cc	n	d nn	n	d nn	n	n fv d nn fv d nn cc n
	V	N	N	N	N	N	
i.10	fv cc	n	d nn	n	d nn	n	d	n fv d nn n d nn cc n d
	V	N	N	N	N	N	N	
i.11	fv cc	n	d nn	n	d nn	n	d nn	n fv d nn n d nn cc n d nn
	V	N	N	N	N	N	N	
i.12	fv cc p	n	d nn	n	d nn	n	d nn	n fv d nn n d nn cc n d nn p
	V	N	N	N	N	N	N	

Up to line i.4, the derivation resembles that of Bob ate an apple without a complex subject–object coordination. Then the # value in the fnc slot of the noun proplet *Jim*, indicating the shared verb, triggers the production of the complex subject–object coordination.

8.6 Complex Coordination of Subjects and Verbs: Object Gapping

The third basic kind of complex coordination is based on subject–verb conjuncts sharing the object (object gapping).[9] Consider the following hearer mode derivation:

8.6.1 OBJECT GAPPING: Bob bought #, Jim peeled #, and Bill ate the peach

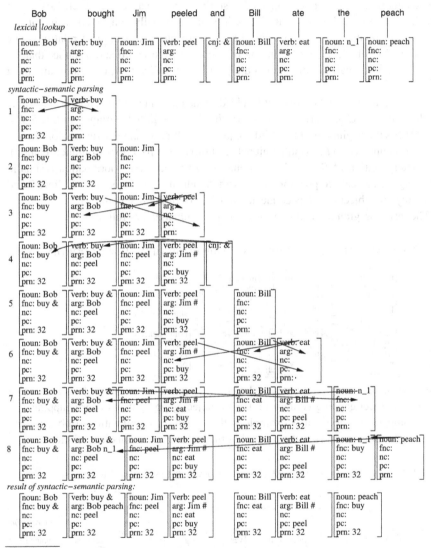

---

[9] This construction is also known as "right-node-raising," a technical term motivated by methods not used in Database Semantics. See Van Oirsouw (1987) for an overview of the Nativist literature on gapping.

The complex coordination consists of the three subject–object conjuncts *Bob-buy*, *Jim-peel*, and *Bill-eat*. The two proplets of a noninitial conjunct are connected by copying the core value of the verb, e.g., *eat*, into the fnc slot of the subject, and the core value of the subject, e.g., *Bill*, into the first position of the arg slot of the verb. The second arg position is filled by #, characterizing the other value as the subject.

Let us go through the derivation step by step. When the second subject *Jim* is attached in line 2, it cannot be connected, resulting in a suspension (cf. Sect. 7.6). When the second verb *peel* is added in line 3, it is bidirectionally connected with *Jim* (intraconjunct relation) as well as with the first verb *buy* (extraconjunct relation). The interpretation of *Jim* as the beginning of a subject–verb coordination rather than an object results in marking the second arg position of *peel* with #, indicating an object gap.

In line 4, the conjunction marker is added to the fnc value of *Bob* and the core value of the first verb, characterizing *buy* as (the head of) the initial conjunct. In line 5, *Bill* is added as the beginning of the third conjunct, resulting in another suspension. In line 6, *eat* is connected to *Bill* (intraconjunct relation) and to *peel* (extraconjunct relation). The interpretation of *Bill* as the beginning of a subject–verb coordination results in marking the second arg position of *eat* with #, indicating an object gap. In lines 7 and 8, finally, the object *peach* is connected to the verb of the first conjunct.

The resulting grammatical relations may be summarized as follows:

8.6.2 GRAMMATICAL RELATIONS IN COMPLEX SUBJECT–VERB COORDINATION

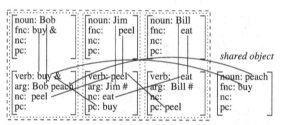

Because of the functor–argument relations between the two parts of each complex conjunct, object gapping is more similar to subject gapping than to verb gapping.

In comparison, the parallel example with two simple coordinations Bob, Jim, and Bill bought, peeled, and ate the peach has the following grammatical relations:

8.6.3 RELATIONS IN SIMPLE SUBJECT AND VERB COORDINATIONS

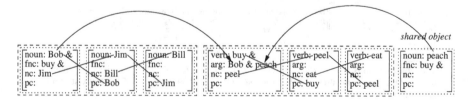

Based on the grammatical relations shown in 8.6.2, the surface of the complex co-ordination 8.6.1 is derived using a VNVNVNN navigation, whereby the VNVNVN sequence constitutes the three conjuncts of a complex subject–verb coordination:

8.6.4 PRODUCTION OF Bob bought, Jim peeled, and Bill ate the peach

	activated sequence							realization
i	V							
i.1		n						n
	V	N						
i.2	fv	n						n fv
	V	N						
i.3	fv	n		n				n fv n
	V	N	V	N				
i.4	fv	n	fv	n				n fv n fv
	V	N	V	N				
i.5	fv cc	n	fv	n				n fv n fv cc
	V	N	V	N				
i.6	fv cc	n	fv	n		n		n fv n fv cc n
	V	N	V	N	V	N		
i.7	fv cc	n	fv	n	fv	n		n fv n fv cc n fv
	V	N	V	N	V	N		
i.8	fv cc	n	fv	n	fv	n	d	n fv n fv cc n fv d
	V	N	V	N	V	N	N	
i.9	fv cc	n	fv	n	fv	n	d	n fv n fv cc n fv d nn
	V	N	V	N	V	N	N	
i.10	fv cc p	n	fv	n	fv	n	d nn	n fv n fv cc n fv d nn p
	V	N	V	N	V	N	N	

The two suspensions in the time-linear hearer mode derivation of this construction in 8.6.1 are clearly visible also in the time-linear speaker mode derivation (see lines i.3 and i.6).

Despite the fact that gapping constructions have a very low frequency in corpora, their grammaticality judgments are quite clear. For example, while Bob bought, Jim peeled, and Bill ate the peach (object gapping) is grammatical, *Bob bought the peach, Jim peeled, and Bill ate is not. Therefore, analyzing the time-linear build-up of gram-matical relations in the hearer mode (interpretation) and the production of surfaces from a time-linear navigation along these grammatical relations in the speaker mode (production) provides an insight into which kinds of content-coding are possible in human cognition and which are not.

For example, it is remarkable that complex subject–object coordination (verb gap-ping, cf. Sect. 8.5) correlates the noninitial conjuncts without any internal functor–

argument connection. Apparently, the nc and pc connections between the parts of the conjuncts, and the functor–argument relation within the initial conjunct are sufficient to establish the necessary grammatical relations in the noninitial conjuncts (cf. 8.5.2). Fortunately, the pattern-matching-based rules of LA-grammar are well-suited to handle these kinds of corelations without any increase in mathematical complexity.

It is also remarkable that the structure of intrasentential coordination, i.e., conjunct_1, conjunct_2, ..., conjunct_n-1, *conjunction* conjunct_n, turns out to be the same in many languages of the world[10] (disregarding interpunctuation). This must be seen in light of the fact that the coding of functor–argument structure – as it appears in the internal structure of complex noun phrases, complex verb phrases, word order, agreement, etc., – varies widely between different natural languages (cf. Nichols 1992).

---

[10] Apart from English, German, French, Italian, and Spanish, we know this of Czech, Russian, Georgian, Chinese, Korean, and Tagalog.

9. Extrapropositional Coordination

Extrapropositional coordination encodes the temporal sequence of incoming propositions (e.g., 3.1.1). At the language level, extrapropositional coordination may occur intrasententially, as in Julia sleeps and John sings. (complex sentence), and extrasententially, as in Julia sleeps. John sings. (sequence of sentences in a text or dialogue). Intrasentential extrapropositional coordination requires a conjunction word like and, placed between the last two conjuncts. In extrasentential coordination, the sequencing of sentences is sufficient; if there is a coordinating conjunction, it is placed at the beginning of a sentential conjunct.

9.1 Overview

In Database Semantics, the coordination of propositions is coded in their verb proplets' nc and pc attributes. Consider the following set of proplets representing Julia sang. Then Sue slept. John read.:

9.1.1 GRAMMATICAL RELATIONS BETWEEN CONCATENATED PROPOSITIONS

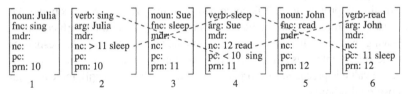

There are no proplets with values followed by a conjunction marker such as &. This is because without an integration of the coordination into a functor–argument structure there is no purpose to distinguish the initial conjunct from the noninitial ones (cf. 8.1.2). The extrapropositional nature of the coordination is indicated by the proposition numbers preceding the nc and pc values, e.g., [pc: 11 sleep] in proplet 6.

The optional conjunctions of extrapropositional coordination are specified in the nc and pc slots (in contradistinction to intrapropositional coordination, in which the conjunctions are obligatory and specified in the core attribute). For example, in 9.1.1 the coordinating conjunction then is added before the proposition number, e.g., [nc: > 11 sleep] in proplet 2 and [pc: < 10 sleep] in proplet 4, whereby then is represented as > or as <, depending on the direction of the connection.

Given that intrapropositional verb coordination (cf. 8.3.2) and extrapropositional coordination may be combined, they must be compatible. Intrapropositional conjunction assigns no value to either the first conjunct's pc attribute or the last conjunct's nc attribute. Therefore, these attributes are available for extrapropositional coordination.

As an example, consider Sue slept. John bought, cooked, and ate a pizza. Julia sang. This example consists of an extrasentential coordination of three propositions, whereby the middle one contains an intrapropositional verb coordination.

9.1.2 COMBINING INTRA- AND EXTRAPROPOSITIONAL COORDINATIONS

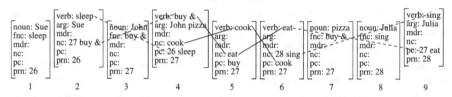

The relations of extrapropositional coordination are indicated by dashed lines, while those of the intrapropositional coordination are indicated by solid lines.

The first proposition 26 is connected extrapropositionally to the second proposition 27 by copying the core value sleep of proplet 2 into the pc slot of proplet 4, and the core value buy & of proplet 4 into the nc slot of proplet 2. As a consequence, the pc slot of proplet 4 (i.e., *buy* of the second proposition) is not empty any more. Nevertheless, proplet 4 is still characterized as the initial conjunct of an intrapropositional verb coordination because (i) its core value is followed by the conjunction marker ([verb: buy &]), and (ii) the value of its pc slot is preceded by a proposition number ([pc: 26 sleep]), indicating an extrapropositional relation.

Correspondingly, proposition 27 is conjoined with proposition 28 by copying the core value sing of proplet 9 into the nc slot of proplet 6, i.e., the final verb conjunct, and by copying the core value eat of proplet 6 into the pc slot of proplet 9. Despite its nonempty nc slot, proplet 6 is still characterized as a final intrapropositional conjunct because its nc value is preceded by a proposition number ([nc: 28 sing]), indicating an extrapropositional relation.

9.2 Interpretation and Production of Extrapropositional Coordination

The elements of an extrapropositional coordination may have any of the internal structures discussed in Chaps. 6–8, at any degree of complexity: Each one of them may be an intra- or an extrapropositional functor–argument structure with a one-, two-, or three-place verb, various adnominal and adverbial adjectives, and various simple or complex intrapropositional coordinations. While functor–argument structures of arbitrary complexity are always intrasentential at the level of language, their coordination may be either intra- or extrasentential.

In Database Semantics, the distinction between intra- and extrasentential coordination is a relatively minor surface phenomenon: If of two sentences in sequence the first one ends with a sentential punctuation mark such as ".", "?", or "!", the coordination is extrasentential; if the first sentence is continued with a coordinating conjunction such as and, or or but, in contrast, the coordination is intrasentential. In verb proplets representing extrapropositional conjuncts, punctuation marks are used not only to indicate the sentence mood, but are also treated as the default kind of an extrapropositional conjunction, which need not be explicitly listed in the nc and pc values.

The following time-linear derivations in the hearer mode (interpretation) and in the speaker mode (production) treat a simple extrasentential example:

9.2.1 DERIVATION OF Julia slept. John sang.

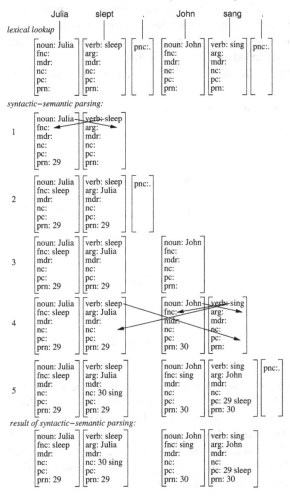

In line 2, the value "." of the pnc (punctuation) proplet is used to specify the sentence mood in the verb proplet as declarative (not shown here, but see 11.5.2); as the extrapropositional default, the core value of the punctuation/conjunction it is not added to the nc slot of *sleep*. In line 3, there is an instance of suspension (cf. 7.6.1 ff.): The subject of the second sentence is added to the set of proplets without being grammatically connected.

In line 4, there are two kinds of value copying. The first kind reconstructs the functor–argument structure of John sings, copying John into the arg slot of the proplet *sing*, and sing into the fnc slot of the proplet *John*. The second kind of value copying makes up for the suspension in line 3. It establishes the extrapropositional connections between the two verb proplets by copying sleep into the pc slot of the proplet *sing*, and sing into the nc slot of *sleep*.

Thus, even without an explicit conjunction, the two sentences are extrapropositionally conjoined: The nc slot of the first sentence specifies the proposition number and the core value of the verb proplet of the second sentence, while the pc slot of the second sentence specifies the corresponding values of the first.

The schematic production of this example from an VN VN navigation is as follows:

9.2.2 PRODUCTION OF Julia slept. John sang.

activated sequence					*realization*				
1									
	V								
1.1		n			n				
	V	N							
1.2	fv	n			n	fv			
	V	N							
1.3	fv p	n			n	fv p			
	V	N							
2.1	fv p	n		n	n	fv p	n		
	V	N	V	N					
2.2	fv p	n	fv	n	n	fv p	n	fv	
	V	N	V	N					
2.3	fv p	n	fv p	n	n	fv p	n	fv p	
	V	N	V	N					

After the initial LA-think navigation from V to N, LA-speak produces the abstract n fv p surface in lines 1.1–1.3. Thereby the sentence-final punctuation mark is lexicalized using the sentence mood specified in the verb proplet. Then LA-think traverses the second VN proplet sequence, from which LA-speak produces the second abstract n fv p surface in lines 2.1–2.3. The suspension shows up in line 2.1 in a way similar to example 7.6.2. See Chaps. 11 and 12 for the explicitly defined LA-hear, LA-think, and LA-speak grammars handling extrapropositional coordination.

9.3 Simple Coordinations as Sentential Arguments and Modifiers

The analysis of coordinations in Chap. 8 considered only intrapropositional functor–argument structures, for example, the man, the woman, and the child slept (simple coordination, cf. 8.2.1) and the man bought, the woman peeled, and the child ate the peach (complex coordination, object gapping, cf. 8.6.1). We turn now to the task of integrating coordinations into extrapropositional functor–argument structures.

In this section, we begin with simple coordination, going systematically through the constructions analyzed in Chap. 7, namely (i) sentential arguments serving as subject (subject sentences), (ii) sentential arguments serving as object (object sentences), (iii) sentential modifiers in adnominal use with a subject gap (relative clauses with the head serving as the subject), (iv) sentential modifiers in adnominal use with an object gap (relative clauses with the head serving as the/an object), and (v) sentential modifiers in adverbial use (adverbial sentences).

Given that the hearer and speaker mode derivations of extrapropositional functor–argument structure and intrapropositional coordination have already been presented in Chaps. 7 and 8, the following examples are analyzed as semantic representations only. As sets of proplets, they are by definition unordered. However, because their presentation requires the choice of some spatial lay-out, we choose to show them as sequences which are motivated in part by the surface order of the associated language example, and in part by the desire to bring out the relation between the coordination and the extrapropositional functor–argument structure as clearly as possible.

9.3.1 SIMPLE COORDINATIONS IN SENTENTIAL ARGUMENTS 1
(subject sentence, cf. 7.2, 8.2.1, 8.2.2)

1. Noun coordination as the subject of a subject sentence:
That the man, the woman, and the child slept surprised Mary.

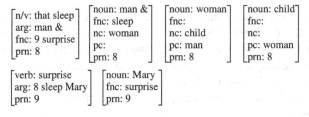

The grammatical relation between the subject sentence that the man ... slept and the main sentence # surprised Mary is established by the [fnc: 9 surprise] feature of the n/v proplet *sleep* and the [arg: 8 sleep Mary] feature of the verb proplet *surprise*. This example may be turned into the corresponding proposition without a coordination by deleting (i) the & markers, (ii) the noninitial conjunct proplets *woman* and *child*, and (iii) the value woman of the nc attribute in the initial conjunct proplet *man*.

2. Verb coordination in a subject sentence:

That the man bought, cooked, and ate the pizza surprised Mary.

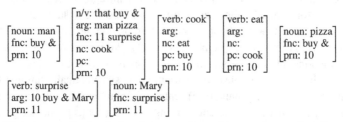

$$
\begin{bmatrix} \text{noun: man} \\ \text{fnc: buy \&} \\ \text{prn: 10} \end{bmatrix}
\begin{bmatrix} \text{n/v: that buy \&} \\ \text{arg: man pizza} \\ \text{fnc: 11 surprise} \\ \text{nc: cook} \\ \text{pc:} \\ \text{prn: 10} \end{bmatrix}
\begin{bmatrix} \text{verb: cook} \\ \text{arg:} \\ \text{nc: eat} \\ \text{pc: buy} \\ \text{prn: 10} \end{bmatrix}
\begin{bmatrix} \text{verb: eat} \\ \text{arg:} \\ \text{nc:} \\ \text{pc: cook} \\ \text{prn: 10} \end{bmatrix}
\begin{bmatrix} \text{noun: pizza} \\ \text{fnc: buy \&} \\ \text{prn: 10} \end{bmatrix}
$$

$$
\begin{bmatrix} \text{verb: surprise} \\ \text{arg: 10 buy \& Mary} \\ \text{prn: 11} \end{bmatrix}
\begin{bmatrix} \text{noun: Mary} \\ \text{fnc: surprise} \\ \text{prn: 11} \end{bmatrix}
$$

The grammatical relation between the subject sentence that the man bought ... the pizza and the main sentence # surprised Mary is established by the [fnc: 11 surprise] feature of the n/v proplet *buy* and the [arg: 10 buy & Mary] feature of the higher verb proplet *surprise*. The conjunction markers & ensure that the noninitial conjuncts of the verb coordination can be accessed from the subject and the object of the lower, and from the arg value of the higher proposition. The example may be turned into the corresponding construction without a coordination by deleting (i) the & markers, (ii) the noninitial conjunct proplets *cook* and *eat*, and (iii) the value cook of the nc attribute in the initial conjunct proplet *buy*.

3. Noun coordination as the object of a subject sentence:

That Bob ate an apple, a pear, and a peach, surprised Mary.

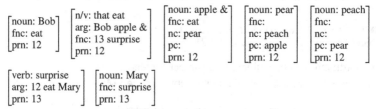

$$
\begin{bmatrix} \text{noun: Bob} \\ \text{fnc: eat} \\ \text{prn: 12} \end{bmatrix}
\begin{bmatrix} \text{n/v: that eat} \\ \text{arg: Bob apple \&} \\ \text{fnc: 13 surprise} \\ \text{prn: 12} \end{bmatrix}
\begin{bmatrix} \text{noun: apple \&} \\ \text{fnc: eat} \\ \text{nc: pear} \\ \text{pc:} \\ \text{prn: 12} \end{bmatrix}
\begin{bmatrix} \text{noun: pear} \\ \text{fnc:} \\ \text{nc: peach} \\ \text{pc: apple} \\ \text{prn: 12} \end{bmatrix}
\begin{bmatrix} \text{noun: peach} \\ \text{fnc:} \\ \text{nc:} \\ \text{pc: pear} \\ \text{prn: 12} \end{bmatrix}
$$

$$
\begin{bmatrix} \text{verb: surprise} \\ \text{arg: 12 eat Mary} \\ \text{prn: 13} \end{bmatrix}
\begin{bmatrix} \text{noun: Mary} \\ \text{fnc: surprise} \\ \text{prn: 13} \end{bmatrix}
$$

The grammatical relation between the subject sentence that Bob ate an apple... and the main sentence # surprised Mary is established by the [fnc: 13 surprise] feature of the n/v proplet *buy* and the [arg: 12 eat Mary] feature of the higher verb proplet *surprise*. This example may be turned into the corresponding proposition without a coordination by deleting (i) the & markers, (ii) the noninitial conjunct proplets *pear* and *peach*, and (iii) the value pear of the nc attribute in the initial conjunct proplet *apple*.

9.3.2 SIMPLE COORDINATIONS IN SENTENTIAL ARGUMENTS 2
(object sentence, cf. 7.3, 8.2.4, 8.2.5)

The crucial difference between the following three examples and those in 9.3.1 above is that the sentential and nonsentential arg values of the higher verb proplets (*surprise*, *see*) are in inverse order: In 9.3.1(1) they are [arg: 8 sleep Mary] (subject sentence), while in 9.3.2(1) they are [arg: Mary 15 sleep] (object sentence); in 9.3.1(2) they are [arg: 10 buy & Mary] (subject sentence), while in 9.3.2(2) they are [arg: Mary 17 buy &] (object sentence); and in 9.3.1(3) they are [arg: 12 buy Mary] (subject sentence), while in 9.3.2(3) they are [arg: Mary 19 buy] (object sentence).

1. Noun coordination as the subject of an object sentence:
   Mary saw that the man, the woman and the child slept.

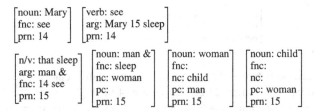

2. Verb coordination in an object sentence:
   Mary saw that the man bought, cooked, and ate the pizza.

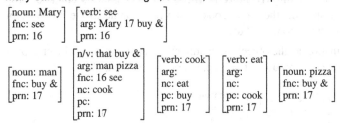

3. Noun coordination as the object of an object sentence::
   Mary saw that Bob bought an apple, a pear, and a peach.

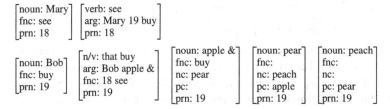

The reductions of the above examples to propositions without coordinations are analogous to those in 9.3.1.

9.3.3 SIMPLE COORDINATIONS IN SENTENTIAL MODIFIERS 1
(adnominal sentence/relative clause with a subject gap, cf. 7.4, 8.3.2, 8.3.3)

1. Noun coordination as the subject of an adnominal sentence with a subject gap:
   structurally excluded!

   A relative clause with a subject gap cannot have a subject coordination because the gap (represented in English by a relative pronoun) cannot be part of a noun coordination.

2. Verb coordination in an adnominal sentence with a subject gap:
   Mary saw the man who bought, cooked, and ate the pizza.

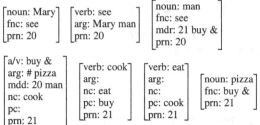

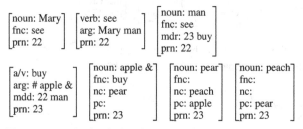

The grammatical relation between the noun man and the relative clause # buy ... pizza is established by (i) the [mdr: 21 buy &] feature of the higher noun proplet *man* and (ii) the [arg: # pizza] and the [mdd: 20 man] features of the a/v proplet *buy*. This example may be turned into the corresponding proposition without a coordination by deleting (i) the & markers, (ii) the noninitial conjunct proplets *cook* and *eat*, and (iii) the value cook of the nc attribute in the initial conjunct proplet *buy* with the core attribute a/v.

3. Noun coordination as the object of an adnominal clause with a subject gap:
   Mary saw the man who bought an apple, a pear, and a peach.

$$\begin{bmatrix} \text{noun: Mary} \\ \text{fnc: see} \\ \text{prn: 22} \end{bmatrix} \begin{bmatrix} \text{verb: see} \\ \text{arg: Mary man} \\ \text{prn: 22} \end{bmatrix} \begin{bmatrix} \text{noun: man} \\ \text{fnc: see} \\ \text{mdr: 23 buy} \\ \text{prn: 22} \end{bmatrix}$$

$$\begin{bmatrix} \text{a/v: buy} \\ \text{arg: # apple &} \\ \text{mdd: 22 man} \\ \text{prn: 23} \end{bmatrix} \begin{bmatrix} \text{noun: apple &} \\ \text{fnc: buy} \\ \text{nc: pear} \\ \text{pc:} \\ \text{prn: 23} \end{bmatrix} \begin{bmatrix} \text{noun: pear} \\ \text{fnc:} \\ \text{nc: peach} \\ \text{pc: apple} \\ \text{prn: 23} \end{bmatrix} \begin{bmatrix} \text{noun: peach} \\ \text{fnc:} \\ \text{nc:} \\ \text{pc: pear} \\ \text{prn: 23} \end{bmatrix}$$

The grammatical relation between the noun man and the relative clause # buy apple ... is established by (i) the [mdr: 23 buy] feature of the higher noun proplet *man* and (ii) the [arg: # apple &] and the [mdd: 22 man] features of the a/v proplet *buy*. This example may be turned into the corresponding proposition without a coordination by deleting (i) the & markers, (ii) the noninitial conjunct proplets *pear* and *peach*, and (iii) the value pear of the nc attribute in the initial conjunct proplet *apple*.

9.3.4 SIMPLE COORDINATIONS IN SENTENTIAL MODIFIERS 2
(adnominal sentence/relative clause with an object gap, cf. Sect. 7.5)

The crucial difference between the following three examples and those in 9.3.3 above is the position of the gap marker # in the arg values of the respective lower a/v proplets *buy* and *see*: in 9.3.3(2) the values are [arg: # pizza] (subject gap), while in 9.3.4(1) they are [arg: Bob & #] (object gap); and in 9.3.3(3) the values are [arg: # apple &] (subject gap), while in 9.3.4(2) they are [arg: man #] (object gap),

1. Noun coordination as the subject of an adnominal clause with an object gap:
   Mary saw the pizza which Bob, Jim, and Bill ate.

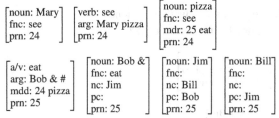

The grammatical relation between the noun *pizza* and the relative clause with object gap Bob ... eat # is established by (i) the [mdr: 25 eat] feature of the higher noun proplet *pizza* and (ii) the [arg: Bob & #] and the [mdd: 24 pizza] features of the a/v proplet *eat*. This example may be turned into the corresponding proposition without a coordination by deleting (i) the & markers, (ii) the noninitial conjunct proplets *Jim* and *Bill*, and (iii) the value Jim of the nc attribute in the initial conjunct proplet *Bob*.

2. Verb coordination in an adnominal clause with an object gap:
   Mary saw the pizza which the man bought, cooked, and ate.

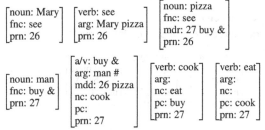

The grammatical relation between the noun *pizza* and the relative clause with object gap man buy ... # is established by (i) the [mdr: 27 buy &] feature of the higher noun proplet *pizza* and (ii) the [arg: man #] and the [mdd: 26 pizza] features of the a/v proplet *buy*. This example may be turned into the corresponding proposition without a coordination by deleting (i) the & markers, (ii) the noninitial conjunct proplets *cook* and *eat*, and (iii) the value cook of the nc attribute in the initial conjunct proplet *buy* with the core attribute a/v.

3. Noun coordination as the object of the adnominal clause with an object gap:
   structurally excluded!
   A relative clause with an object gap cannot have an object coordination because

the gap (represented in English by a relative pronoun) cannot participate in a coordination.

9.3.5 SIMPLE COORDINATIONS IN SENTENTIAL MODIFIERS 3
(adverbial sentence, cf. Sect. 7.6)

1. Noun coordination as the subject of an adverbial sentence:
Mary arrived after Bob, Jim, and Bill had eaten a pizza.

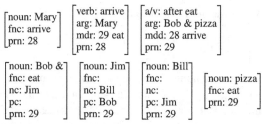

The grammatical relation between the main sentence Mary arrived and the adnominal sentence after Bob... had eaten a pizza is established by the [mdr: 29 eat] feature of the higher verb proplet *arrive* and the [mdd: 28 arrive] feature of the a/v proplet *eat*. This example may be turned into the corresponding proposition without a coordination by deleting (i) the & markers, (ii) the noninitial conjunct proplets *Jim* and *Bill*, and (iii) the value Jim of the nc attribute in the initial conjunct proplet *Bob*.

2. Verb coordination in an adverbial sentence:
After Bob had bought, cooked, and eaten the pizza, Mary arrived.

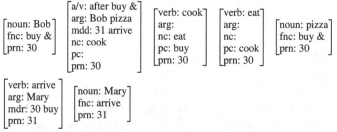

The grammatical relation between the main sentence Mary arrived and the adverbial sentence after Bob had bought ... the pizza is established by the [mdd: 31 arrive] feature of the a/v proplet *buy* and the [mdr: 30 buy] feature of the higher verb proplet *arrive*. This example may be turned into the corresponding proposition without a coordination by deleting (i) the & markers, (ii) the noninitial conjunct proplets *cook* and *eat*, and (iii) the value cook of the nc attribute in the initial conjunct proplet *buy* with an a/v core attribute.

3. Noun coordination as the object of an adverbial sentence:
   Mary arrived after Bob had eaten an apple, a pear, and a peach.

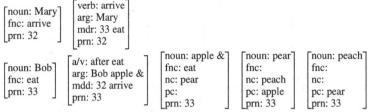

This example may be turned into the corresponding proposition without a coordination in the same way as 9.3.1 (3).

9.4 Complex Coordinations as Sentential Arguments and Modifiers

Corresponding to the grammatical analysis of simple subject, verb, and object coordinations in extrapropositional functor–argument structures, we turn now to complex verb–object, subject–object, and subject–verb coordinations (i.e., subject, verb, and object gapping, respectively). As before, their grammatical function is investigated in a (i) subject sentence, (ii) an object sentence, (iii) an adnominal sentence with subject gap, (iv) an adnominal sentence with object gap, and (v) an adverbial sentence.

9.4.1 COMPLEX COORDINATIONS IN SENTENTIAL ARGUMENTS 1
   (subject sentence, cf. Sect. 7.2)

1. Verb–object coordination (subject gapping, cf. 8.4) in a subject sentence:
   That Bob ate an apple, walked his dog, and read a paper, amused Mary.

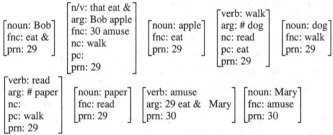

The grammatical relation between the main sentence # amused Mary and the subject sentence that Bob ate an apple ... is established by the [fnc: 30 amuse] feature of the n/v proplet *eat* and the [arg: 29 eat & Mary] feature of the higher verb proplet *amuse*. This example may be turned into the corresponding proposition without complex coordination by deleting (i) the & markers, (ii) the noninitial conjunct proplets *walk*, *dog*, *read*, and *paper*, and (iii) the value walk of the nc attribute in the initial conjunct proplet *eat* with the core attribute n/v.

2. Subject–object coordination (verb gapping, cf. 8.5) in a subject sentence:
That Bob ate an apple, Jim a pear, and Bill a peach, amused Mary.

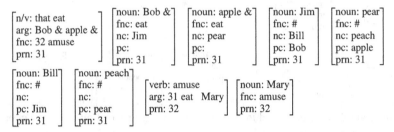

The grammatical relation between the main sentence # amused Mary and the subject sentence that Bob ate an apple ... is established by the [fnc: 32 amuse] feature of the n/v proplet *eat* and the [arg: 31 eat Mary] feature of the higher verb proplet *amuse*. This example may be turned into the corresponding proposition without a complex coordination by deleting (i) the & markers, (ii) the noninitial conjunct proplets *Jim, pear, Bill*, and *peach*, and (iii) the values Jim and pear of the nc attributes in the initial conjunct proplets *Bob* and *apple*, respectively.

3. Subject–verb coordination (object gapping, cf. 8.6) in a subject sentence:
That Bob bought, Jim peeled, and Bill ate the peach, amused Mary.

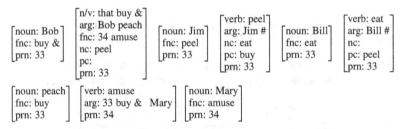

The grammatical relation between the main sentence # amused Mary and the subject sentence that Bob bought ... the peach is established by the [fnc: 34 amuse] feature of the n/v proplet *buy* and the [arg: 33 buy & Mary] feature of the verb proplet *amuse*. This example may be turned into the corresponding proposition without a complex coordination by deleting (i) the & markers, (ii) the noninitial conjunct proplets *Jim, peel, Bill*, and *eat*, and (iii) the value peel of the nc attribute in the initial conjunct proplet *buy* with the core attribute n/v.

9.4.2 COMPLEX COORDINATIONS IN SENTENTIAL ARGUMENTS 2
(object sentence, cf. Sect. 7.3)

The relation between subject and object sentences with complex coordinations is analogous to that between subject and object sentences with simple coordinations (cf. 9.3.1 and 9.3.2). The crucial difference between the following three examples and those in 9.4.1 above is that the sentential and nonsentential arg values of the higher verb proplets (*amuse*, *see*) are in inverse order: in 9.4.1(1) they are [arg: 29 eat & Mary] (subject sentence), while in 9.4.2(1) they are [arg: Mary 35 eat &] (object sentence); in 9.4.1(2) they are [arg: 31 eat Mary] (subject sentence), while in 9.4.2(2) they are [arg: Mary 37 eat] (object sentence); and in 9.4.1(3) they are [arg: 33 buy & Mary] (subject sentence), while in 9.4.2(3) they are [arg: Mary 39 buy &] (object sentence).

1. Verb–object coordination (subject gapping, cf. 8.4) in an object sentence:
   Mary saw that Bob ate an apple, walked his dog, and read a paper.

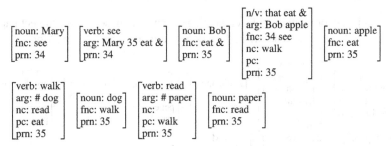

2. Subject–object coordination (verb gapping, cf. 8.5) in an object sentence:
   Mary saw that Bob ate an apple, Jim a pear, and Bill a peach.

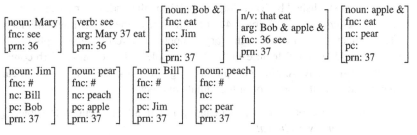

3. Subject–verb coordination (object gapping, cf. 8.6) in an object sentence:
   Mary saw that Bob bought, Jim peeled, and Bill ate the peach .

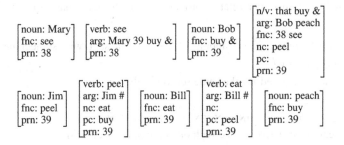

The reductions of the above examples to propositions without complex coordinations are analogous to those in 9.4.1.

9.4.3 COMPLEX COORDINATION IN SENTENTIAL MODIFIERS 1
  (adnominal sentence/relative clause with subject gap, cf. Sect. 7.4)

The following relative clause example(s) containing complex coordinations are analogous to those in 9.3.3, which contain simple coordinations. However, in relative clauses with complex coordinations two constructions are structurally excluded, in contrast to simple coordinations, which exclude only one.

1. Verb–object coordination (subject gapping) in an adnom. sent. with subject gap:
   The man who ate an apple, walked his dog, and read a paper loves Mary.

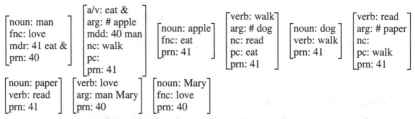

   The grammatical relation between the noun man and the relative clause # ate an apple ... is established by (i) the [arg: # apple] and the [mdd: 40 man] features of the a/v proplet *eat* and (ii) the [mdr: 41 eat &] feature of the higher noun proplet *man*. The subject gap indicated in the [arg: # apple] feature of *eat* is implicitly filled by the [mdd: 40 man] feature in the same proplet. The noninitial verb conjuncts *walk* and *read* have similar gaps in their arg attributes, the filler of which can be recovered from the mdd slot of the initial conjunct *eat*.

2. Subject–object coordination (verb gapping) in an adnom. sent. with subject gap:
   structurally excluded!

   A subject–object coordination as the subject of a relative clause with the head serving as the subject is excluded, because the subject position is taken by the gap (represented in English by a relative pronoun) – which cannot participate in a coordination.

3. Subject–verb coordination (object gapping) in a adnominal sent. with subject gap:
   structurally excluded!

   This construction is excluded for the same reason as the one above.

9.4.4 COMPLEX COORDINATION IN SENTENTIAL MODIFIERS 2
  (adnominal sentence/relative clause with object gap, cf. Sect. 7.5)

The following relative clause example(s) containing complex coordinations are analogous to those in 9.3.4, which contain simple coordinations. However, as in the subject–gap relative clauses 9.4.3 with complex coordinations, two constructions are excluded, in contrast to simple coordinations, which exclude only one.

1. Verb–object coordination (subject gapping) in a adnominal sent. with object gap:
   structurally excluded!

   A verb–object coordination as the object of a relative clause with the head serving as the object is excluded, because the object position is taken by the gap (represented in English by a relative pronoun) – which cannot participate in a coordination.

2. Subject–object coordination (verb gapping) in an adnominal sent. with object gap:
   structurally excluded!

   This construction is excluded for the same reason as the one above.

3. Subject–verb coordination (object gapping) in an adnominal sent. with object gap:

   Mary saw the peach which Bob bought, Jim peeled, and Bill ate.

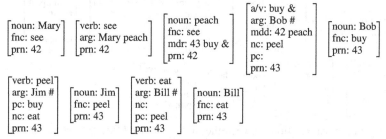

   The grammatical relation between the noun **peach** and the relative clause which Bob bought, ... is established by (i) the [arg: Bob #] and [mdd: 42 peach] features of the a/v proplet *buy* and (ii) the [mdr: 43 buy &] feature of the higher noun proplet *peach*. The object gap indicated in the [arg: Bob #] feature of *buy* is implicitly filled by the [mdd: 42 peach] feature in the same proplet. The noninitial verb proplets *peel* and *eat* have similar gaps in their arg attributes, the filler of which can be recovered from the mdd slot of the initial conjunct *buy*.

9.4.5 COMPLEX COORDINATIONS IN SENTENTIAL MODIFIERS 3
   (adverbial sentence, cf. Sect. 7.6)

1. Verb–object coordination (subject gapping, cf. 8.4) in an adverbial sentence:
   Mary arrived after Bob had eaten an apple, walked his dog, and read a paper.

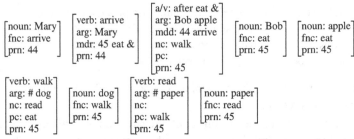

The grammatical relation between the main sentence Mary arrived and the adverbial sentence after Bob had eaten an apple... is established by the [mdr: 45 eat &] feature of the higher verb proplet *arrive* and the [mdd: 44 arrive] feature of the a/v proplet *eat*. This example may be turned into a corresponding proposition without a complex coordination by deleting (i) the & markers, (ii) the noninitial conjunct proplets *walk, dog, read,* and *paper,* and (iii) the nc value walk in the initial conjunct proplet *eat* with the core attribute a/v.

2. Subject–object coordination (verb gapping, cf. 8.5) in an adverbial sentence:
   After Bob had eaten an apple, Jim a pear, and Bill a peach, Mary arrived.

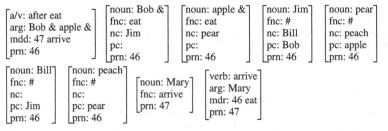

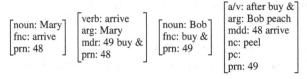

The grammatical relation between the main sentence Mary arrived and the adverbial sentence after Bob had eaten an apple... is established by the [mdr: 46 eat] feature of the higher verb proplet *arrive* and the [mdd: 47 arrive] feature of the a/v proplet *eat*. This example may be turned into a corresponding proposition without a complex coordination by deleting (i) the & markers, (ii) the noninitial conjunct proplets *Jim, pear, Bill,* and *peach,* and (iii) the nc values Jim and apple in the initial conjunct proplets *Bob* and *apple,* respectively.

3. Subject–verb coordination (object gapping, cf. 8.6) in an adverbial sentence:
   Mary arrived after Bob had bought, Jim had peeled, and Bill had eaten the peach.

$$\begin{bmatrix} \text{noun: Jim} \\ \text{fnc: peel} \\ \text{prn: 49} \end{bmatrix} \begin{bmatrix} \text{verb: peel} \\ \text{arg: Jim \#} \\ \text{nc: eat} \\ \text{pc: buy} \\ \text{prn: 49} \end{bmatrix} \begin{bmatrix} \text{noun: Bill} \\ \text{fnc: eat} \\ \text{prn: 49} \end{bmatrix} \begin{bmatrix} \text{verb: eat} \\ \text{arg: Bill \#} \\ \text{nc:} \\ \text{pc: peel} \\ \text{prn: 49} \end{bmatrix} \begin{bmatrix} \text{noun: peach} \\ \text{fnc: buy} \\ \text{prn: 49} \end{bmatrix}$$

The grammatical relation between the main sentence Mary arrived and the adverbial sentence after Bob had bought ... the peach is established by the [mdr: 49 buy &] feature of the higher verb proplet *arrive* and the [mdd: 48 arrive] feature of the a/v proplet *buy*. This example may be turned into a corresponding proposition without complex coordination by deleting (i) the & markers, (ii) the noninitial conjunct proplets *Jim, peel, Bill*, and *eat*, and (iii) the nc value peel of the initial conjunct proplet *buy* with the core attribute a/v.

9.5 Turn-Taking in Questions and Answers

Having analyzed extrapropositional coordination in a sequence of sentences, as in a text (Sect. 9.2), and the integration of intrapropositional coordination into extrapropositional functor–argument structures (Sects. 9.3 and 9.4), we turn now to extrapropositional coordination in a dialog (turn-taking, cf. 1.1.1). While in a text, the sequence of propositions is produced by the same agent, in a dialog the propositions, or even just parts of propositions, in the sequence are produced by different agents.

This difference is formally characterized by the STAR of the propositions (cf. 2.6.2). Consider the following examples, showing the STAR as superscripts:

9.5.1 COMPARING COORDINATION IN A TEXT AND A DIALOG

1. *Coordination of two propositions in a text*
   Julia ate an apple.^{STAR} Susanne ate a pear.$^{(\text{STAR})}$

2. *Coordination of two propositions in a dialog*
   Julia ate an apple.^{STAR} Susanne ate a pear.$^{\text{STA}'\text{R}'}$

3. *Coordination of a question and an answer in a dialog*
   Who is singing? ^{STAR} Julia.$^{\text{STA}'\text{R}'}$

Example 1 is a simple text consisting of two propositions, both of which were produced by the same author A and intended for the same recipient R (two identical STARs). Example 2 consists of the same propositions as Example 1, but was produced by two different authors, A and A$'$, for two different recipients R and R$'$, such that R=A$'$ and R$'$=A (STAR versus STA$'$R$'$). Example 3 resembles Example 2 except that parts of only one proposition are coordinated by the two authors.

For reasons explained in FoCL'99, Sects. 5.3–5.5, the STAR is essential for connecting an episodic proposition (i) to past, present, and future states of the world, and (ii) to content in the database. Formally, the STAR is coded as the value of an additional proplet attribute. We have omitted the STAR to this point for clarity of exposition.

In complete propositions of arbitrary complexity, the STAR is coded in the main verb proplet. In a continuous text, as in Example 1, it is usually sufficient to specify the STAR only once in a while. However, if the propositions are produced by different authors, as in example 2, the STAR must be specified after each turn-taking. In a question–answer sequence, as in Example 3, the two parts may be treated as belonging to the same proposition, sharing a common prn value, yet be properly separated by different STAR values.

These distinctions are illustrated below by simplified versions of the examples in 9.5.1, formalized as sets of proplets:

9.5.2 ILLUSTRATING KINDS OF COORDINATION AS SETS OF PROPLETS

1. Julia is singing.^{STAR} Susanne is dreaming.$^{(STAR)}$

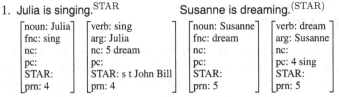

In this minimal text, the STAR of the second verb is redundant because its values are the same as those of the first verb's STAR attribute, namely S = s, T = t, A = John, and R = Bill. The two propositions are distinguished by prn values, here 4 and 5, and connected by the nc and pc values of their verb proplets.

2. Julia is singing.^{STAR} Susanne is dreaming.$^{STA'R'}$

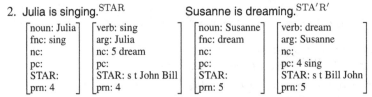

In this minimal dialog, the STAR attributes of the two verb proplets *sing* and *dream* have inverse values: the STAR attribute of *sing* specifies the values S = s, T = t, A = John, and R = Bill, while the STAR attribute of *dream* specifies the values S = s, T = t, A = Bill, and R = John. Otherwise the two propositions are distinguished and connected as in Example 1.

3. Who is singing? ^{STAR} Julia.$^{STA'R'}$

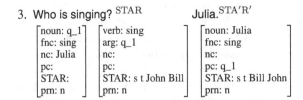

A common prn value, n, marks the elements of this question–answer pair as belonging to the same proposition. Unlike the two previous examples, the coordination is here between two nouns, as indicated by the nc value of *who* and the pc value of *Julia*. Thus, this kind of question–answer pair is analyzed as an intrapropositional noun coordination. While the *who* proplet inherits its STAR values implicitly from the verb *sing*, the answer proplet *Julia* must specify its own STAR values.

The interpretation and production of a question–answer pair may be experienced by an agent in the following constellations: (i) as the hearer of the question and the speaker of the answer, (ii) as the speaker of the question and the hearer of the answer, and (iii) as the hearer of the question and the answer (i.e., as an observer). These differences appear only in the STAR and the prn values, without affecting the grammatical analysis of the expressions used. Consider the following example:

9.5.3 DERIVATION OF A WH INTERROGATIVE IN THE HEARER MODE

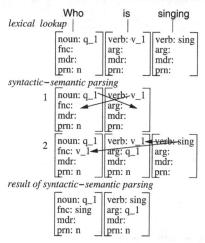

The hearer's pragmatic use of this expression for querying consists in applying the verb proplet to the token line of *sing* (cf. Sect. 5.1):

9.5.4 FINDING THE ANSWER

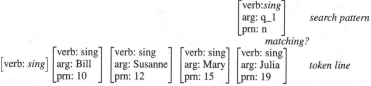

Given the present progressive tense of the question, the search pattern is matched with the last (and thus most recent) item in the token line of *sing*, thereby binding the variable q_1 to Julia and the variable n to 19. Thus the proplet underlying the answer to the question may be derived by navigating from *sing* to *Julia*, using the latter to produce the answer:

9.5.5 DERIVATION OF THE ANSWER

$$\begin{bmatrix} \text{verb: sing} \\ \text{arg: Julia} \\ \text{prn: 19} \end{bmatrix} \begin{bmatrix} \text{noun: Julia} \\ \text{fnc: sing} \\ \text{prn: 19} \end{bmatrix}$$

The interrogatives used in wh questions and yes/no questions (cf. Sect. 5.1) may be arbitrarily complex, based on sentential arguments and modifiers. "Long-distance dependencies" are particularly interesting constructions in English:

9.5.6 DERIVING Who did John say that Bill believes that Mary loves?

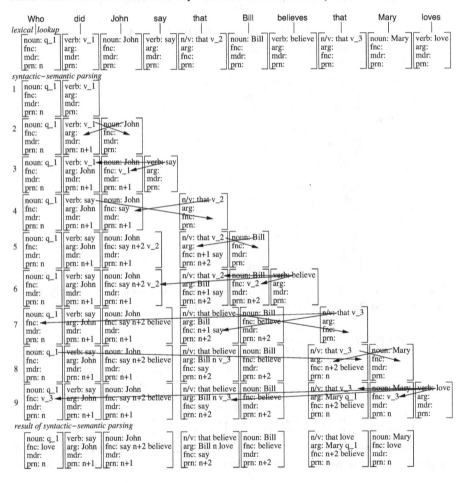

This construction is based on a recursion of two object sentences (cf. Sect. 7.3).

During the derivation, two local ambiguities occur. One arises when the first verb is added, resulting in:

Who did John say

This could be a complete interrogative, provided who was changed to what, or say to see. As soon, however, as the very next word, that, is added, this possibility is discarded. The same kind of local ambiguity arises when the verb believes is added – and just as soon discarded. For a discussion of ambiguity in LA-grammar see FoCL'99, Sect. 11.3. For automatically derived LA-grammar analyses of interrogatives, including several with long-distance dependencies, see NEWCAT'86, pp. 448–474.

9.6 Complex Propositions as Thought Structures

In Database Semantics, there is a fundamental distinction between the *representation* of content and its *activation* (cf. FoCL'99, Sect. 23.1). The representation of content is based on encoding all intra- and extrapropositional relations between proplets in a distributed, bidirectional manner by means of features. The activation of content is based on the principle of navigation: the intra- and extrapropositionally connected proplets provide a kind of railroad system for navigating through a proposition and from one proposition to the next.

This setup allows for the possibility that one and the same content may be traversed in alternative ways, depending on where the thought path is coming from and where it is going (cf. Appendix, Sect. A.1). Such alternative navigations explain certain alternative language surfaces. Consider the following example:

9.6.1 SIMPLE EXTRAPROPOSITIONAL COORDINAT. OF SIMPLE PROPOSITIONS

1. Extrapropositional forward navigation:

Peter left the house. Then Peter crossed the street.

⌈noun: Peter⌉	⌈verb: leave ⌉	⌈noun: house⌉	⌈noun: Peter⌉	⌈verb: cross ⌉	⌈noun: street⌉
fnc: leave	arg: Peter house	fnc: leave	fnc: cross	arg: Peter street	fnc: cross
nc:	nc: > 2 cross	nc:	nc:	nc:	nc:
pc:	pc:	pc:	pc:	pc: < 1 leave	pc:
⌊prn: 1 ⌋	⌊prn: 1 ⌋	⌊prn: 1 ⌋	⌊prn: 2 ⌋	⌊prn: 2 ⌋	⌊prn: 2 ⌋

2. Extrapropositional backward navigation:

Peter crossed the street. Before that Peter left the house.

⌈noun: Peter⌉	⌈verb: cross ⌉	⌈noun: street⌉	⌈noun: Peter⌉	⌈verb: leave ⌉	⌈noun: house⌉
fnc: cross	arg: Peter street	fnc: cross	fnc: leave	arg: Peter house	fnc: leave
nc:	nc: < 1 leave	nc:	nc:	nc: > 2 cross	nc:
pc:	pc:	pc:	pc:	pc:	pc:
⌊prn: 2 ⌋	⌊prn: 2 ⌋	⌊prn: 2 ⌋	⌊prn: 1 ⌋	⌊prn: 1 ⌋	⌊prn: 1 ⌋

The two sequences consist of exactly the same proplets. Thus, as representations of *content* in the Word Bank they are the identical. However, if we interpret the difference in order as alternative *activations*, the two sequences may be associated with the different language surfaces specified above the proplets.

The surfaces differ (i) in the order of the two sentences and (ii) in the realization of the coordinating conjunction, i.e., then (forward navigation) versus before that (backward navigation). The distinction between forward and backward navigation arises also intrapropositionally, as shown by the alternative between active and passive (cf. Sect. 6.5).

It would be nice if different surface realizations of the same (or closely related) content could all be based solely on alternative traversal orders of simple coordinations of simple propositions. However, our analyses of sentential arguments, sentential modifiers, and complex coordination have resulted in different representations even for similar contents. This is illustrated below with two complex propositions representing contents which are closely related to that of 9.6.1.

9.6.2 DIFFERENT EXTRAPROPOSITIONAL FUNCTOR–ARGUMENT STRUCTURES

1. Adnominal sentence with subject gap:
   Peter, who had left the house, crossed the street.

$$
\begin{bmatrix} \text{noun: Peter} \\ \text{fnc: cross} \\ \text{mdr: 2 leave} \\ \text{prn: 1} \end{bmatrix}
\begin{bmatrix} \text{a/v: leave} \\ \text{arg: \# house} \\ \text{mdd: 1 Peter} \\ \text{prn: 2} \end{bmatrix}
\begin{bmatrix} \text{noun: house} \\ \text{fnc: leave} \\ \text{prn: 2} \end{bmatrix}
\begin{bmatrix} \text{verb: cross} \\ \text{arg: Peter street} \\ \text{prn: 1} \end{bmatrix}
\begin{bmatrix} \text{noun: street} \\ \text{fnc: cross} \\ \text{prn: 1} \end{bmatrix}
$$

2. Adverbial sentence:
   After Peter had left the house, he crossed the street.

$$
\begin{bmatrix} \text{noun: Peter} \\ \text{fnc: leave} \\ \text{prn: 1} \end{bmatrix}
\begin{bmatrix} \text{a/v: leave} \\ \text{arg: Peter house} \\ \text{mdd: > 2 cross} \\ \text{prn: 1} \end{bmatrix}
\begin{bmatrix} \text{noun: house} \\ \text{fnc: leave} \\ \text{prn: 1} \end{bmatrix}
\begin{bmatrix} \text{noun: Peter} \\ \text{fnc: cross} \\ \text{prn: 2} \end{bmatrix}
\begin{bmatrix} \text{verb: cross} \\ \text{arg: Peter street} \\ \text{mdr: < 1 leave} \\ \text{prn: 2} \end{bmatrix}
\begin{bmatrix} \text{noun: street} \\ \text{fnc: cross} \\ \text{prn: 2} \end{bmatrix}
$$

These two representations are different from those in 9.6.1, and different from each other.

More specifically, as extrapropositional functor–argument structures, both examples in 9.6.2 background the content of proposition 2 (hypotaxis) – in contradistinction to the examples of extrapropositional coordination in 9.6.1 (parataxis). The two examples in 9.6.2 differ from each other, furthermore, in that they represent alternative perspectives on the content: The adnominal (or relative) clause attaches the background content to the noun *Peter* while the adverbial clause attaches it to the verb *cross*.

This raises the question of whether the special representations of complex propositions (i.e., sentential arguments, sentential modifiers, and complex conjunctions) should (i) be used at the language and the context level, or (ii) be limited to the language level by transforming the special representations into simple coordinations of simple propositions at the context level (hearer mode), and vice versa (speaker mode). Let us consider these two alternatives.

Alternative (ii) has the disadvantage that it requires a transformation of a complex proposition (language level) into a simple coordination of simple propositions (context level) during language interpretation, and a transformation of a simple coordination of simple propositions (context level) into a complex proposition (language level) during language production. Moreover, the contents represented by simple coordinations of simple propositions and by the related special representations as complex propositions are not really the same, making the required transformations awkward and unnatural. The apparent advantage of this costly procedure, however, would be that inferencing at the context level would not have to deal with complex propositions.

Alternative (i) has the advantage that the language and the context level use the same coding, thus making any transformations unnecessary. Furthermore, the inferencing in LA-grammar (cf. Sect. 5.3) is sufficiently powerful to derive all the required conclusions from the simple as well as from the special representations. For example, both special representations in 9.6.2 support inferring the answer yes to the question Did Peter leave the house – as do both simple representations in 9.6.1.

The remaining question is whether or not it is correct to assume that complex propositions, such as extrapropositional functor–argument structure, complex intrapropositional coordination, and their combination, should actually arise at the level of context – and thus represent thought structures which might potentially be present even in agents without language. To answer this question let us consider a related issue, namely the representation of temporal information.

At the levels of context and language, the order of proplets in the token lines reflects the order in which the information is coming in (like sediment), and is going out. At the level of language this principle applies to the moment of production in the speaker mode and the moment of interpretation in the hearer mode. It does not apply, however, to the temporal information coded within the language expressions.

Assume, for example, that agent A observes on Monday that *Mary arrives* and tells this on Tuesday to agent B by saying Mary arrived yesterday. This communication event is stored by agent B at the Tuesday STAR. Agent B's interpretation of the sign, however, raises the question of whether B should store its content (i) as *Mary arrived yesterday* at the Tuesday STAR or (ii) as *Mary arrives* at the Monday STAR. Alternative (ii) requires not only a transformation of the content, but also finding the correct new storage position, while alternative (i) requires neither. Moreover, alternative (i) allows one to infer the correct temporal location whenever needed, whereby the incoming information may continue to accumulate in agent B's database undisturbed.

Alternative (i) receives additional support from a slight change of the example. Let us assume that agent A observes on Monday that *Mary arrives* and tells this on Friday to agent B by saying Mary arrived a few days ago. Now it is impossible for agent B to do find the correct new storage location, as required by alternative (ii). This is because the vague temporal information in the language sign does not permit agent B to determine a sufficiently precise STAR for the proposition *Mary arrives*.

Our choice of alternative (i) implies that the perspectives represented by extrapropositional functor–argument structure (cf. Chap. 7), complex intrapropositional coordination (cf. Sects. 8.4–8.6) and their combination (cf. Sect. 9.4) are essentially thought structures. They are perspectives which arise already at the level of context and are merely reflected in language – just as the secondary coding underlying indirect (e.g., metaphoric) uses of language described in Sects. 5.4 and 5.5.[1]

---

[1] Another related issue is pattern completion (cf. L&I'05), which raises the question of whether an unknown object of a known kind, e.g., a car, should be stored in memory including a hypothetical reconstruction of the unseen side(s), or solely from the perspective actually seen so that the unseen side is reconstructed hypothetically only when needed. For an explanation of the reconstruction on the basis of *frames*, see Barsalou (1999).

10. Intrapropositional and Extrapropositional Coreference

In this chapter we turn to the secondary grammatical relation of coreference. The distinction between primary and secondary relations is defined as follows: Primary relations are built directly during a time-linear derivation (hearer mode). This applies to functor–argument structure and to coordination. Secondary relations, in contrast, (i) presuppose the primary relations and (ii) modify or complement some of the values assigned by the primary relations. In Database Semantics, secondary relations are implemented as inferences (cf. Sect. 5.3).

An important kind of secondary relation is identity. During a time-linear derivation in the hearer mode, noncoreference between different noun proplets is assumed as the default: The value of the idy (identity) attribute of each new noun proplet is automatically incremented, regardless of whether the noun is a symbol (cf. 2.6.4), an indexical (cf. 2.6.5), or a name (cf. 2.6.7). Under certain conditions, the default values are modified by inferences which establish coreference between certain nonindexical and indexical nouns (pronouns) by setting their identity values to be equal.

10.1 Overview

Given that the sentence is the largest unit of grammatical analysis, the most basic structural distinction of natural language is the one between the sentence moods, i.e., between *declarative, interrogative*, and *imperative* sentences, whereby some languages have additional moods (cf. Portner 2005), like the *optative* in classical Greek.

10.1.1 CORRELATING THE MAJOR CONSTRUCTIONS

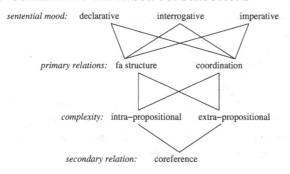

The variants of sentence mood are subject to the primary relations of functor–argument structure and coordination. These primary relations occur both intrapropositionally (cf. Chaps. 6 and 8) and extrapropositionally (cf. Chaps. 7 and 9). The secondary relation of coreference is defined across the primary relations, including extrasentential coordination.

Consider the following examples of coreference:

10.1.2 DIFFERENT KINDS OF COREFERENCE

1. Name-based coreference in an extrasentential coordination

Julia ate an apple. Then Julia took a nap.

⌈noun: Julia⌉	⌈verb: eat ⌉	⌈noun: apple⌉	⌈noun: Julia⌉	⌈verb: take ⌉	⌈noun: nap⌉
fnc: eat	arg: Julia apple	fnc: eat	fnc: take	arg: Julia nap	fnc: take
mdr:	pc:	mdr:	mdr:	pc: < 36 eat	mdr:
idy: 1	nc: > 37 take	idy: 2	idy: 3 (=1)	nc:	idy: 4
⌊prn: 36 ⌋	⌊prn: 36 ⌋	⌊prn: 36 ⌋	⌊prn: 37 ⌋	⌊prn: 37 ⌋	⌊prn: 37 ⌋

The two propositions are coordinated extrapropositionally via the features [nc: > 37 take] of the first verb proplet *eat* and [pc: < 36 eat] of the second verb proplet *take*. The noun proplets *Julia, apple, Julia,* and *nap* receive the default idy values 1, 2, 3, and 4, respectively. It is the job of the coreference inference to set the idy value of the second *Julia* proplet equal to that of the first (cf. [idy: 3 (= 1)]).

2. Pronoun-based coreference in an extrasentential coordination

Julia ate an apple. Then she took a nap.

⌈noun: Julia⌉	⌈verb: eat ⌉	⌈noun: apple⌉	⌈noun: pro_1⌉	⌈verb: take ⌉	⌈noun: nap⌉
fnc: eat	arg: Julia apple	fnc: eat	fnc: take	arg: pro_1 nap	fnc: take
mdr:	pc:	mdr:	mdr:	pc: < 38 eat	mdr:
idy: 5	nc: > 39 take	idy: 6	idy: 7 (=5)	nc:	idy: 8
⌊prn: 38 ⌋	⌊prn: 38 ⌋	⌊prn: 38 ⌋	⌊prn: 39 ⌋	⌊prn: 39 ⌋	⌊prn: 39 ⌋

This coordination of two propositions resembles Example 1, except that the subject of the second proposition is she rather than Julia. Again, the noun proplets *Julia, apple, she,* and *nap* receive default idy values, here 5, 6, 7, and 8, respectively. It is the job of the coreference inference to set the idy value of the *she* proplet equal to that of the first (cf. [idy: 7 (= 5)]).

3. Blocked intrapropositional coreference between two equal names

%John shaved John.

⌈noun: John⌉	⌈verb: shave ⌉	⌈noun: John⌉
fnc: shave	arg: John John	fnc: shave
idy: 9	mdr:	idy: 10
⌊prn: 40 ⌋	⌊prn: 40 ⌋	⌊prn: 40 ⌋

As indicated by the marker %, the example is grammatically well-formed, but no coreference is possible between the subject and the object, even though they are represented by the same name. Thus the different idy values 9 and 10 assigned as defaults must remain, and no coreference inference can apply.

4. Intrapropositional coreference between a name and a reflexive pronoun

John shaved himself.

$$
\begin{bmatrix} \text{noun: John} \\ \text{fnc: shave} \\ \text{idy: 1} \\ \text{prn: 1} \end{bmatrix}
\begin{bmatrix} \text{verb: shave} \\ \text{arg: John rfl\_1} \\ \text{mdr:} \\ \text{prn: 1} \end{bmatrix}
\begin{bmatrix} \text{noun: rfl\_1} \\ \text{fnc: shave} \\ \text{idy: 2} \\ \text{prn: 1} \end{bmatrix}
$$

This semantic representation shows the value [idy: 2] assigned to the reflexive pronoun as a default. The required coreference inference will be explicitly derived in the following section (cf. 10.2.3 for the version after the coreference adjustement). Coreference is obligatory here, in contradistinction to the examples 1 and 2 with nonreflexive pronouns, in which it is optional. That nonreflexive personal pronouns do not require a coreferential interpretation is because they can always have a noncoreferential, indexical interpretation instead.

5. Coreference between a nominal symbol and an intrapropositional coordination

The man washed his hands, clipped his nails, and shaved himself.

$$
\begin{bmatrix} \text{noun: man} \\ \text{fnc: wash} \\ \text{mdr:} \\ \text{idy: 13} \\ \text{prn: 42} \end{bmatrix}
\begin{bmatrix} \text{verb: wash \&} \\ \text{arg: man hand} \\ \text{nc: clip} \\ \text{pc:} \\ \text{prn: 42} \end{bmatrix}
\begin{bmatrix} \text{noun: hand} \\ \text{fnc: wash} \\ \text{mdr:} \\ \text{idy: 14} \\ \text{prn: 42} \end{bmatrix}
\begin{bmatrix} \text{verb: clip} \\ \text{arg: \# nail} \\ \text{nc: shave} \\ \text{pc: wash} \\ \text{prn: 42} \end{bmatrix}
\begin{bmatrix} \text{noun: nail} \\ \text{fnc: clip} \\ \text{mdr:} \\ \text{idy: 15} \\ \text{prn: 42} \end{bmatrix}
\begin{bmatrix} \text{verb: shave} \\ \text{arg: \# rfl\_2} \\ \text{nc:} \\ \text{pc: clip} \\ \text{prn: 42} \end{bmatrix}
\begin{bmatrix} \text{noun: rfl\_2} \\ \text{fnc: shave} \\ \text{mdr:} \\ \text{idy: 16(=13)} \\ \text{prn: 42} \end{bmatrix}
$$

In this example of subject gapping (cf. Sect. 8.4), the reflexive pronoun may occur in any of the verb-object conjuncts, and must be set to be coreferential with the subject (cf. [idy: 16(=13)] in the last proplet).

Given the varieties of coreference, the structures treated in the following sections are limited to the basic cases. These are (i) intrapropositional coreference with a reflexive pronoun (LA-think.pro-1, Sect. 10.2), and (ii) extrapropositional coreference in accordance with the Langacker–Ross Constraint. The latter is shown for sentential arguments (LA-think.pro-2, Sect. 10.3), adnominal sentential modifiers (LA-think.pro-3, Sect. 10.4), and adverbial sentential modifiers (LA-think.pro-4, Sect. 10.5). In Sect. 10.6, the different LA-think.pro grammars are combined, and are applied to a notoriously difficult example, known as the Bach–Peters sentence.

10.2 Intrapropositional Coreference

As an example of intrapropositional coreference consider John shaved himself, a classic example since Lees and Klima (1963). The initial interpretation of this simple functor–argument structure is as in Example 4 of 10.1.2: The noun proplets *John* and *himself* have been assigned the idy values 1 and 2, respectively, as a default.

Resetting these idy values to be equal is handled by an inference, defined here as an LA-think grammar, called **LA-think.pro-1**. The input to this grammar is the sequence of nouns n-1, n-2, n-3, ... surrounding the reflexive pronoun in the proposition. Thus, the noun proplets must have the same prn value as the reflexive pronoun.

10.2.1 DEFINITION OF **LA-think.pro-1**

$ST_S =_{def} \{ (\begin{bmatrix} noun: RFL\_n \end{bmatrix} \{ rfl\text{-}0\ rfl\text{-}1 \}) \}$

$$rfl\text{-}0: \begin{bmatrix} noun: RFL\_n \\ cat: X' \\ idy: j \\ prn: k \end{bmatrix} \begin{bmatrix} noun: \alpha \\ cat: X \\ idy: i \\ prn: k \end{bmatrix} \quad \begin{array}{l} \text{if X is not compatible with X'} \\ \text{set } nw = \text{preceding noun} \end{array} \quad \{rfl\text{-}0, rfl\text{-}1\}$$

$$rfl\text{-}1: \begin{bmatrix} noun: RFL\_n \\ cat: X' \\ idy: j \\ prn: k \end{bmatrix} \begin{bmatrix} noun: \alpha \\ cat: X \\ idy: i \\ prn: k \end{bmatrix} \quad \begin{array}{l} \text{if X is compatible with X'} \\ \text{set } j = i \end{array} \quad \{\}$$

$ST_F =_{def} \{ (\begin{bmatrix} noun: \alpha \end{bmatrix} rp_{rfl-1}) \}$

The variable RFL_n is restricted to the core value of reflexive pronouns. The prn values, represented by the variable k, are specified to be equal.

When LA-think.pro-1 is triggered by a language proplet matching the start state ST_S, the two rules called by ST_S are applied to the relative pronoun and the noun n-1. If rule rfl-1 is successful, the idy number of the pronoun is adjusted to that of the coreferential noun and the inference is completed successfully. However, if rule rfl-0 is successful (i.e., if the inference fails on the noun n-1), both rules are tried on the next noun n-2, and so forth, until rule rfl-1 happens to be successful (or the end of the sequence has been reached and the interpretation fails).

Consider the following application of rfl-1 to the proplets of 10.1.2 (4), whereby the proplet *himself* is the noun n and the proplet *John* is the noun n-1 (see idy values at the language level):

10.2.2 APPLYING THE INFERENCE RULE **rfl-1**

rule level	rfl-1:	$\begin{bmatrix} noun: RFL\_n \\ cat: X' \\ idy: j \\ prn: k \end{bmatrix}$	$\begin{bmatrix} noun: \alpha \\ cat: X \\ idy: i \\ prn: k \end{bmatrix}$	if X is compatible with X' set j = i	{ }
language level		$\begin{bmatrix} noun: rfl\_1 \\ fnc: shave \\ cat: m\ sg \\ idy: 2 \\ prn: 1 \end{bmatrix}$	$\begin{bmatrix} noun: John \\ fnc: shave \\ cat: m\ sg \\ idy: 1 \\ prn: 1 \end{bmatrix}$		

The rule level presents the explicit definition of the rule. Like all LA-grammar rules, the rule consists of a rule name (here rfl-1), a pattern for the sentence start (here for a reflexive pronoun), a pattern for the next word (here for a coreferential noun candidate), a set of operations, and a rule package, here empty.

The input patterns at the rule level are matched with suitable proplets at the language level. Because the candidates fulfill the agreement condition of the operation (i.e., X is compatible with X'), the idy value of the reflexive pronoun is adjusted to that of *John*. As a result, the interpretation of our example is revised as follows:

10.2.3 INTERPRETATION OF John shaved himself AFTER INFERENCE

$$
\begin{bmatrix} \text{noun: John} \\ \text{cat: m sg} \\ \text{fnc: shave} \\ \text{idy: 1} \\ \text{prn: 1} \end{bmatrix}
\begin{bmatrix} \text{verb: shave} \\ \text{arg: John, rfl\_1} \\ \text{prn: 1} \end{bmatrix}
\begin{bmatrix} \text{noun: rfl\_1} \\ \text{cat: m sg} \\ \text{fnc: shave} \\ \text{idy: 2 (=1)} \\ \text{prn: 1} \end{bmatrix}
$$

The requirement of compatibility between the cat values of the reflexive and its antecedent (cf. rule rfl-1) will also provide for the correct interpretation of examples like John showed Mary himself and John showed Mary herself.

The question of whether or not two nouns in the input sequence (hearer mode) can be coreferential is empirically somewhat complex, and different for pronouns, names, and various determiner-noun combinations. For example, in a sentence like John shaved John (cf. 10.1.2, 3), the two names cannot be coreferential. In coordinations like John, Bill, and Ben shaved Bill, Ben, and John, however, coreference is possible, with the same names referring to the same individuals (as long as they are shaving each other, and not themselves).

The *production* of pronouns (speaker mode) is fairly straightforward. In the Word Bank, certain noun proplets have been set to be coreferent by an inference like 10.2.2. When a noun proplet is to be lexicalized, the system checks whether there is another noun proplet with the same idy value recently activated in order to decide whether one of them should be realized as a pronoun or not. The constellations triggering the choice of a pronoun are summarized in Helfenbein (2005).

10.3 Langacker–Ross Constraint for Sentential Arguments

Like intrapropositional coreference (cf. Sect. 10.2), extrapropositional coreference is a secondary relation, based on inferences which adjust default idy values assigned during syntactic–semantic parsing. Like extrapropositional coordination (cf. Chap. 9), extrapropositional coreference occurs intra- and extrasententially.[1]

The most famous restriction on intrasentential coreference is the Langacker–Ross constraint (Langacker 1969; Ross 1969). It applies to sentential arguments serving as subjects (cf. Sect. 7.2) and objects (cf. Sect. 7.3) as well as to sentential modifiers serving as adnominals (cf. Sects. 7.4 and 7.5) and adverbials (cf. Sect. 7.6).

In DBS, the formulation of the constraint is based on the distinction between a higher proposition **H** and a lower proposition **L** in an extrapropositional functor–argument relation (cf. 7.1.3). The two propositions may occur in the order **LH** and **HL**. If one proposition (marked with ') contains a personal pronoun compatible with a noun in the other, there result four possibilities, namely **LH'**, **H'L**, **L'H**, and **HL'**. The constraint says that the **H'L** constellation does not allow coreference between the pronoun in **H'** and any compatible noun in **L**, while the other three constellations do.

---

[1] The linguistic literature on extrapropositional coreference has dealt mostly with intrasentential structures, Grosz and Sidner (1986) being a notable exception.

Using sentential arguments serving as subjects and objects, the constraint may be illustrated as follows:

10.3.1 LANGACKER–ROSS CONSTRAINT IN SENTENTIAL ARGUMENTS

1. **LH':** That *Mary* had found the answer pleased *her*.
2. **H'L:** %*She* knew that *Mary* had found the answer.
3. **L'H:** That *she* had found the answer pleased *Mary*.
4. **HL':** *Mary* knew that *she* had found the answer.

The relevant noun–pronoun pairs are shown in italics. The coreferential noun (cnn) is called *antecedent* or *postcedent* depending on whether it precedes or follows the pronoun. The **H'L** constellation is marked with "%," indicating that the example is grammatically well-formed, but does not permit a coreferential interpretation of *she* and *Mary*.

The inference which resets the idy value of the pronoun to that of the ante- or postcedent is defined as a navigation which starts from the pronoun and searches through all noun candidates within the sentence. The constraint is implemented by preventing the inference from resetting the idy value of the pronoun if the compatible noun is in a lower proposition and follows the pronoun.

As an aid to formulating the inference as a rule of an LA-think grammar, we propose a kind of declarative analysis which resembles the schematic characterization of a rule application, for example, 3.5.1 and 10.2.2. It consists of a two-level structure, characterizing the inference navigation at the upper and the relevant proplets at the lower level. Consider the declarative two-level analysis of the first example in 10.3.1:

10.3.2 **LH':** That *Mary* had found the answer pleased *her*. (n/v-cnn)

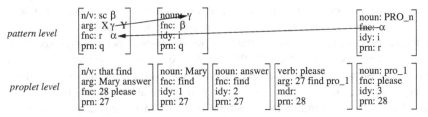

At the pattern level, the inference navigation is indicated by arrows between the patterns. This preliminary analysis does not yet constitute a rule, because there is no rule name, no definition of operations, and no rule package. The analysis will be completed later into the rule of an LA-think grammar, namely 10.3.6, for the relevant extrapropositional coreference inferences. For future reference, the name of the associated rule is indicated in the heading, here (n/v-cnn).

At the proplet level, the five proplets representing the example are shown. Three of them match patterns at the upper level. By binding the variables of the upper level to corresponding values in the language proplets, the inference navigation indicated at the upper level is executed at the lower level. The coreference inference uses a retrieval based on the values of lower attributes, for example, fnc, in contrast to the navigation underlying language production, which uses a retrieval based on core values only.

Starting from the pronoun, the inference in 10.3.2 searches for a compatible noun in a small pool of proplets with a prn value *adjacent* to that of the pronoun.[2] This search consists in two steps. First, the navigation proceeds extrapropositionally from the pronoun to an adjacent n/v proplet which must have the same fnc value as the pronoun (here please). Then, the navigation proceeds intrapropositionally from the n/v proplet to a noun proplet the core value of which must be (i) the same as one of the arg values of the n/v proplet and (ii) be grammatically compatible with the pronoun. This third proplet (here *Mary*) is the coreferential noun candidate.[3]

Using the same patterns, the crucial (noncoreferential) example of the Langacker–Ross constraint is represented as follows:

10.3.3 H'L: %*She* knew that *Mary* had found the answer

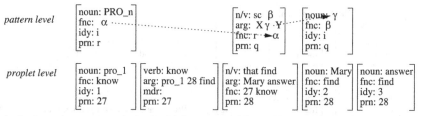

As before, the pronoun is in the higher proposition (**H'**), but the noun candidate does not precede (**H'L**) – as indicated by the prn values of the proplets. Therefore, coreference must be blocked by not resetting the pronoun's idy value.

Next, consider the schematic analysis of the examples **L'H** and **HL'**, in which the pronoun is in the lower proposition:

10.3.4 L'H: That *she* had found the answer pleased *Mary* (n/v-pro)

pattern level	⎡n/v: sc α⎤ arg: X PRO_n Y fnc: r β ⎣prn: r⎦	⎡noun: PRO_n⎤ fnc: α idy: i ⎣prn: r⎦			⎡noun: γ⎤ fnc: β idy: i ⎣prn: q⎦
proplet level	⎡n/v: that find⎤ arg: pro_1 answer fnc: 28 please ⎣prn: 27⎦	⎡noun: pro_1⎤ fnc: find idy: 3 ⎣prn: 27⎦	⎡noun: answer⎤ fnc: find idy: 2 ⎣prn: 27⎦	⎡verb: please⎤ arg: 27 find Mary mdr: ⎣prn: 28⎦	⎡noun: Mary⎤ fnc: please idy: 1 ⎣prn: 28⎦

---

[2] For example, if the prn value of the pronoun is 10, then the adjacent prn values of the coreferential noun candidates are 9 and 11. The prn values, like the idy values, are provided automatically by the Java[TM] implementations of LA-hear during syntactic–semantic parsing.

[3] It is a *candidate* only because the pronouns in question always permit an indexical interpretation as well. Cf. FoCL'99, Sect. 6.3.

10.3.5 **HL':** *Mary* knew that *she* had found the answer(n/v-pro)

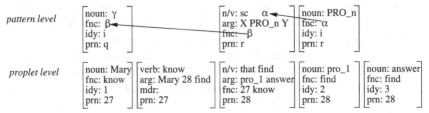

pattern level
$$\begin{bmatrix} \text{noun: } \gamma \\ \text{fnc: } \beta \\ \text{idy: i} \\ \text{prn: q} \end{bmatrix} \quad \begin{bmatrix} \text{n/v: sc} \quad \alpha \\ \text{arg: X PRO\_n Y} \\ \text{fnc: } \beta \\ \text{prn: r} \end{bmatrix} \begin{bmatrix} \text{noun: PRO\_n} \\ \text{fnc: } \alpha \\ \text{idy: i} \\ \text{prn: r} \end{bmatrix}$$

proplet level
$$\begin{bmatrix} \text{noun: Mary} \\ \text{fnc: know} \\ \text{idy: 1} \\ \text{prn: 27} \end{bmatrix} \begin{bmatrix} \text{verb: know} \\ \text{arg: Mary 28 find} \\ \text{mdr:} \\ \text{prn: 27} \end{bmatrix} \begin{bmatrix} \text{n/v: that find} \\ \text{arg: pro\_1 answer} \\ \text{fnc: 27 know} \\ \text{prn: 28} \end{bmatrix} \begin{bmatrix} \text{noun: pro\_1} \\ \text{fnc: find} \\ \text{idy: 2} \\ \text{prn: 28} \end{bmatrix} \begin{bmatrix} \text{noun: answer} \\ \text{fnc: find} \\ \text{idy: 3} \\ \text{prn: 28} \end{bmatrix}$$

Here coreference is possible no matter whether the lower proposition **L'** precedes (cf. 10.3.4) or follows (cf. 10.3.5) the higher proposition **H**.

Having established the patterns, it is only a short step to the rules of an LA-think grammar formalizing the inference. All we have to add to the patterns are the rule names, the rule operations, and the rule packages. In addition, the start states ST_S and the final states ST_F of the LA-grammar have to be defined.

10.3.6 DEFINITION OF **LA-think.pro-2** (SENTENTIAL ARGUMENTS)

$$ST_S =_{def} \{ (\begin{bmatrix} \text{noun: PRO\_n} \end{bmatrix} \{\text{n/v-cnn, n/v-pro}\}) \}$$

n/v-cnn:
$$\begin{bmatrix} \text{noun: PRO\_n} \\ \text{fnc: } \alpha \\ \text{idy: i} \\ \text{prn: r} \end{bmatrix} \begin{bmatrix} \text{n/v: sc } \beta \\ \text{arg: X } \gamma \text{ Y} \\ \text{fnc: r } \alpha \\ \text{prn: q} \end{bmatrix} \begin{bmatrix} \text{noun: } \gamma \\ \text{fnc: } \beta \\ \text{idy: j} \\ \text{prn: q} \end{bmatrix}$$
if q and r are adjacent, q < r, and PRO_n and γ are compatible, set i = j   {}

n/v-pro:
$$\begin{bmatrix} \text{noun: PRO\_n} \\ \text{fnc: } \alpha \\ \text{idy: i} \\ \text{prn: r} \end{bmatrix} \begin{bmatrix} \text{n/v: sc } \alpha \\ \text{arg: X PRO\_n Y} \\ \text{fnc: r } \beta \\ \text{prn: r} \end{bmatrix} \begin{bmatrix} \text{noun: } \gamma \\ \text{fnc: } \beta \\ \text{idy: j} \\ \text{prn: q} \end{bmatrix}$$
if q and r are adjacent and PRO_n and γ are compatible, set i = j   {}

$$ST_F =_{def} \{(\begin{bmatrix} \text{noun: } \alpha \end{bmatrix} \text{rp}_{n/v-cnn}), (\begin{bmatrix} \text{noun: } \alpha \end{bmatrix} \text{rp}_{n/v-pro})\}$$

The first rule, called n/v-cnn, handles the coreferential noun in the sentential argument and the pronoun in the higher proposition, while the second rule, called n/v-pro, handles the pronoun in the sentential argument and the coreferential noun in the higher proposition. Note that the operation of the first, but not the second, rule is restricted by the condition q < r, which means that the proposition with the prn value q must precede the proposition with the prn value r. The rule packages are both empty.

10.4 Langacker–Ross Constraint for Adnominal Sentential Modifiers

The second kind of extrapropositional functor–argument structures are sentential modifiers in adnominal use (relative clauses). Like sentential arguments, they are subject to the Langacker–Ross constraint. We continue to use the **LH', H'L, L'H, HL'** notation to characterize the constellations, even though the subclause **L** may be located in the middle of the higher clause **H**. The **LH HL** distinction is used here to indicate the piece of **H** which contains the part relevant for the pronoun–noun relation (namely either the pronoun or the coreferential noun).

10.4.1 Langacker–Ross constraint in adnominal subclauses

1. **LH'**: The man who loves *the woman* kissed *her*.
2. **H'L**: %*She* was kissed by the man who loves *the woman*.
3. **L'H**: The man who loves *her* kissed *the woman*.
4. **HL'**: *The woman* was kissed by the man who loves *her*.

Because the proplet patterns for adnominal sentential modifiers differ from those for sentential arguments (cf. Sect. 10.3), the implementation of the Langacker–Ross constraints for relative clauses requires another set of inference rules. Based on the time-linear hearer and speaker mode derivations of extrapropositional functor–argument structure in Sects. 7.4 and 7.5, the primary relations for adnominal sentential modifiers are already available.

Of the constellations in 10.4.1, **LH'** (Example 1) has received a great deal of attention in Logical Semantics for natural language. On this approach of truth-conditional Predicate Calculus, pronouns are treated as variables bound by quantifiers. The **LH'** constellation, widely known as the "donkey sentence," raises the problem that the scope of the quantifier postulated in the analysis of the antecedent does not reach to bind the coreferential pronoun.[4] When pronominal coreference is based on inferencing, however, no such problem arises, as shown by the following analysis.

As in the preceding section, we begin the analysis with a two-level representation consisting of the proplets of the relevant example at the lower and the relevant rule patterns at the upper level:

10.4.2 **LH'**: Every farmer who owns *a donkey* beats *it* (adn-cnn)

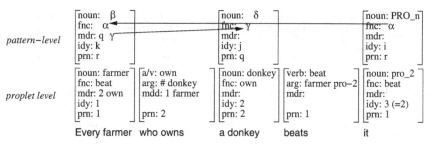

Based on the fnc value of the pronoun, the inference retrieves a second noun with the same fnc value (here beat), the same prn value (here 1), and a propositional mdr value (here 2 own). The mdr value is used to retrieve a pronoun-compatible third noun proplet which has this value in its fnc attribute. It is the coreferential noun candidate.

---

[4] For example, if Every man who loves a woman loses her is represented as $\forall x\ [[man(x)\ \&\ \exists y\ [woman(y)\ \&\ love(x,y)]] \rightarrow lose(x,y)]$, the y in lose(x,y) is not bound by the existential quantifier. First pointed out by Geach (1969), such examples have led to much work on the "donkey sentence" (Kamp and Reyle 1993; Geurts 2002).

Because 10.4.2 is structurally equivalent to Example 1 of 10.4.1, we may turn next to Example 2 in 10.4.1. It illustrates the grammatical structure in which no coreference is possible between a pronoun and a compatible noun:

10.4.3 **H'L:** *%She* was kissed by the man who loves *the woman*

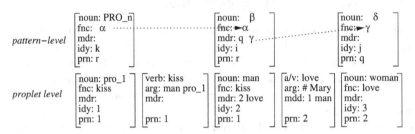

As in 10.4.2, the pronoun is in the higher clause **H'**, but the noun candidate does not precede. Due to the fixed word order of English, passive (cf. Sect. 6.5) had to be used to obtain the **H'L** correlation in this relative clause construction.

Finally, consider the **L'H** (Example 3) and **HL'** (Example 4) constellations, both of which permit a coreferential interpretation of the compatible noun–pronoun pair.

10.4.4 **L'H:** The man who loves *her* kissed *the woman* (adn-pro)

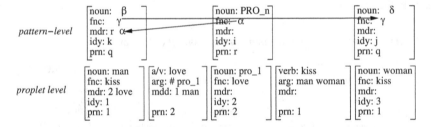

10.4.5 **HL':** *The woman* was kissed by the man who loves *her* (adn-pro)

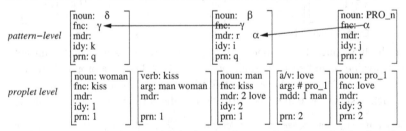

Using the patterns characterizing the coreference inferences in the four examples above, it is only a short step to the LA-grammar handling pronoun–noun relations involving adnominal sentential modifiers (relative clauses):

10.4.6 DEFINITION OF **LA-think.pro-3** (ADNOMINAL SENTENTIAL MODIFIERS)

$ST_S =_{def} \{ (\;[\text{noun: PRO\_n}]\; \{\text{adn-cnn adn-pro}\}) \}$

$$
\begin{array}{c|ccc}
\text{adn-cnn:} &
\begin{bmatrix}\text{noun: PRO\_n}\\ \text{fnc: } \alpha \\ \text{mdr:} \\ \text{idy: i} \\ \text{prn: r}\end{bmatrix} &
\begin{bmatrix}\text{noun: } \beta \\ \text{fnc: } \alpha \\ \text{mdr: q } \gamma \\ \text{idy: k} \\ \text{prn: r}\end{bmatrix} &
\begin{bmatrix}\text{noun: } \delta \\ \text{fnc: } \gamma \\ \text{mdr:} \\ \text{idy: j} \\ \text{prn: q}\end{bmatrix} &
\begin{array}{l}\text{if q and r are adjacent, q < r, and}\\ \text{PRO\_n and } \alpha \text{ are compatible, set i = j}\end{array} & \{\} \\[4ex]
\text{adn-pro:} &
\begin{bmatrix}\text{noun: PRO\_n}\\ \text{fnc: } \alpha \\ \text{mdr:} \\ \text{idy: i} \\ \text{prn: r}\end{bmatrix} &
\begin{bmatrix}\text{noun: } \beta \\ \text{fnc: } \gamma \\ \text{mdr: r } \alpha \\ \text{idy: k} \\ \text{prn: q}\end{bmatrix} &
\begin{bmatrix}\text{noun: } \delta \\ \text{fnc: } \gamma \\ \text{mdr:} \\ \text{idy: j} \\ \text{prn: q}\end{bmatrix} &
\begin{array}{l}\text{if q and r are adjacent and}\\ \text{PRO\_n and } \gamma \text{ are compatible, set i = j}\end{array} & \{\}
\end{array}
$$

$ST_F =_{def} \{(\;[\text{noun: } \alpha]\; \text{rp}_{\text{adn}-\text{fnc}}), (\;[\text{noun: } \alpha]\; \text{rp}_{\text{adn}-\text{mdr}})\}$

The rule adn-cnn of LA-think.pro-3 resembles the rule n/v-cnn of LA-think.pro-2 (cf. 10.3.6) in that the pronoun must follow the coreferential noun, while the rule adn-pro resembles the rule n/v-pro in that the pronoun may either precede or follow.

10.5 Langacker–Ross Constraint for Adverbial Sentential Modifiers

The remaining extrapropositional functor–argument structure is adverbial sentential modifiers.[5] Like sentential arguments (cf. Sect. 10.3) and adnominal sentential modifiers (cf. Sect. 10.4), they are subject to the Langacker–Ross constraint:

10.5.1 LANGACKER–ROSS CONSTRAINT IN ADVERBIAL SUBCLAUSES

1. **LH':** When *Mary* returned *she* kissed John.
2. **H'L:** %*She* kissed John when *Mary* returned.
3. **L'H:** When *she* returned *Mary* kissed John.
4. **HL':** *Mary* kissed John when *she* returned.

Consider the two-level analysis of the first example in 10.5.1:

10.5.2 **LH':** When *Mary* returned *she* kissed John (adv-cnn)

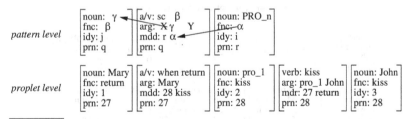

$$
\begin{array}{c|ccccc}
\textit{pattern level} &
\begin{bmatrix}\text{noun: } \gamma \\ \text{fnc: } \beta \\ \text{idy: j} \\ \text{prn: q}\end{bmatrix} &
\begin{bmatrix}\text{a/v: sc } \beta \\ \text{arg: } \cancel{\times}\, \gamma \quad Y \\ \text{mdd: r } \alpha \\ \text{prn: q}\end{bmatrix} &
\begin{bmatrix}\text{noun: PRO\_n}\\ \text{fnc: } \alpha \\ \text{idy: i} \\ \text{prn: r}\end{bmatrix} \\[4ex]
\textit{proplet level} &
\begin{bmatrix}\text{noun: Mary}\\ \text{fnc: return}\\ \text{idy: 1}\\ \text{prn: 27}\end{bmatrix} &
\begin{bmatrix}\text{a/v: when return}\\ \text{arg: Mary}\\ \text{mdd: 28 kiss}\\ \text{prn: 27}\end{bmatrix} &
\begin{bmatrix}\text{noun: pro\_1}\\ \text{fnc: kiss}\\ \text{idy: 2}\\ \text{prn: 28}\end{bmatrix} &
\begin{bmatrix}\text{verb: kiss}\\ \text{arg: pro\_1 John}\\ \text{mdr: 27 return}\\ \text{prn: 28}\end{bmatrix} &
\begin{bmatrix}\text{noun: John}\\ \text{fnc: kiss}\\ \text{idy: 3}\\ \text{prn: 28}\end{bmatrix}
\end{array}
$$

---

[5] Adverbial sentential modifiers are especially suited to illustrate the constraint in English because their order is free. Thus we do not have to resort to using subject versus object sentence (cf. Sect. 10.3) or active versus passive (cf. Sect. 10.4) for obtaining the different orders needed for the relevant constellations. In fact, adverbial subclauses provide for eight constellations because they allow the coreferential noun or pronoun in subject position (cf. 10.5.1) and in object position (cf. 10.5.7).

The pronoun *she* is in the higher clause **H'**. Its fnc value kiss is the same as the mdd value of the a/v proplet *return* with an adjacent prn value. The arg value of the second proplet is the same as the core value of the third proplet *Mary* – which is a legal coreferential noun candidate for *she*.

Using the same patterns, the noncoreferential example of the Langacker–Ross constraint is represented as follows:

10.5.3 **H'L:** %*She* kissed John when *Mary* returned

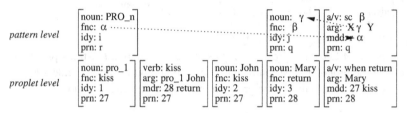

As before the pronoun is in the higher clause (**H'**), but the noun candidate does not precede (**H'L**) – as indicated by the prn values of the proplets. Therefore, coreference must be blocked by not resetting the pronoun's idy value.

The constellations with the pronoun in the lower clause, i.e., **L'H** (Example 3) and **HL'** (Example 4), are illustrated below:

10.5.4 **L'H:** When *she* returned *Mary* kissed John (adv-pro)

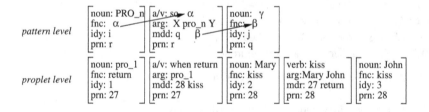

10.5.5 **HL':** *Mary* kissed John when *she* returned (adv-pro)

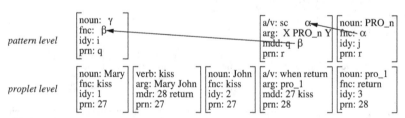

Using the patterns characterizing the coreference inferences in the four examples above, it is only a short step to the LA-grammar for adverbial subclauses with the relevant noun–pronoun pairs in subject position:

10.5.6 DEFINITION OF **LA-think.pro-4** (ADVERBIAL SENTENTIAL MODIFIERS)

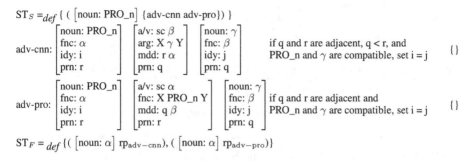

Next, let us show that the corresponding set of sentences with an oblique pronoun or an oblique coreferential noun is handled by this grammar as well:

10.5.7 LANGACKER–ROSS CONSTRAINT FOR OBLIQUE COREFERENTS

1. **LH':** When *Mary* returned John kissed *her*.
2. **H'L:** %John kissed *her* when *Mary* returned.
3. **L'H:** When *she* returned John kissed *Mary*.
4. **HL':** John kissed *Mary* when *she* returned.

Consider the two-level analyses of these examples:

10.5.8 **LH':** When *Mary* returned John kissed *her* (adv-cnn)

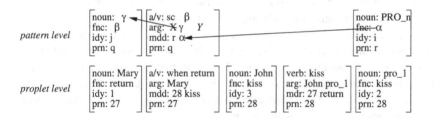

10.5.9 **H'L:** %John kissed *her* when *Mary* returned

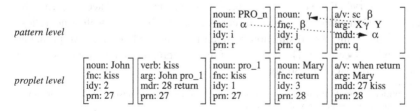

10.5.10 **L'H:** When *she* returned John kissed *Mary* (adv-pro)

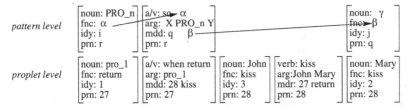

10.5.11 **H'L:** John kissed *Mary* when *she* returned (adv-pro)

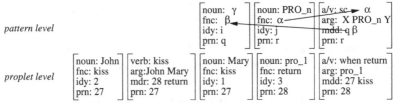

LA-think.pro-4, defined in 10.5.6, applies also to the above examples with oblique coreferents: The difference between the pronoun in subject versus object position, e.g., she kissed John (cf. 10.5.1) versus John kissed her (cf. 10.5.7), is handled in the higher verb proplet which does not participate in the inference navigation; and similarly for the coreferent noun in subject versus object position.

10.6 Handling Pronominal Coreference by Means of Inference

In conclusion, let us combine the LA-grammars for establishing intrapropositional coreference (LA-think.pro-1, cf. 10.2.1), and for establishing extrapropositional coreference in sentential argument constructions (LA-think.pro-2, cf. 10.3.6), adnominal sentential modifier constructions (LA-think.pro-3, cf. 10.4.6), and adverbial sentential modifier constructions (LA-think.pro-4, cf. 10.5.6) into one. Combining these four LA-grammars into the new grammar **LA-think.pro** is based on (i) collecting the rule names of the smaller grammars into the rule package of the new start state ST_S, (ii) listing the rules of the smaller grammars in the new one, and (iii) collecting the specifications of final states under a new ST_F.

In the combined grammar LA-think.pro, the rule rfl-0 for grammatically incompatible constellations of reflexive pronouns and nouns (cf. 10.2.1) is renamed pro-0 and generalized to serve all the coreference rules. Pronouns are represented uniformly by the variable PRO_n, which can match the core values of reflexive as well as nonreflexive personal pronouns. The distinction between reflexive and nonreflexive pronouns is handled in the operations. The prn value of the coreferential noun must be the same as, or adjacent to, that of the pronoun.[6]

---

[6] This simplified assumption will have to be revised for handling extrapropositional functor–argument constructions with several levels of embedding.

10.6.1 DEFINITION OF **LA-think.pro**

$\text{ST}_S =_{def} \{ \, (\, [\text{noun: PRO\_n}] \, \{\text{pro-0 rfl-1 n/v-cnn n/v-pro adn-cnn adn-pro adv-cnn adv-pro}\}) \, \}$

pro-0:
$\begin{bmatrix} \text{noun: PRO\_n} \\ \text{idy: j} \\ \text{prn: r} \end{bmatrix} \begin{bmatrix} \text{noun: } \alpha \\ \text{idy: i} \\ \text{prn: q} \end{bmatrix}$
PRO_n and α are not compatible, set *nw* = preceding noun in the input sequence
$\begin{Bmatrix} \text{pro-0 rfl-1} \\ \text{n/v-cnn n/v-PRO} \\ \text{adn-cnn adn-PRO} \\ \text{adv-cnn adv-PRO} \end{Bmatrix}$

rfl-1:
$\begin{bmatrix} \text{noun: PRO\_n} \\ \text{idy: j} \\ \text{prn: r} \end{bmatrix} \begin{bmatrix} \text{noun: } \alpha \\ \text{idy: i} \\ \text{prn: r} \end{bmatrix}$
if PRO_n is a reflexive pronoun, and PRO_n and α are compatible, set j = i
$\{ \}$

n/v-cnn:
$\begin{bmatrix} \text{noun: PRO\_n} \\ \text{fnc: } \alpha \\ \text{idy: i} \\ \text{prn: r} \end{bmatrix} \begin{bmatrix} \text{n/v: sc } \beta \\ \text{arg: X } \gamma \text{ Y} \\ \text{fnc: r } \alpha \\ \text{prn: q} \end{bmatrix} \begin{bmatrix} \text{noun: } \gamma \\ \text{fnc: } \beta \\ \text{idy: j} \\ \text{prn: q} \end{bmatrix}$
if PRO_n is a nonreflexive personal pronoun, PRO_n and γ are compatible, q and r are adjacent, and q < r, set i = j
$\{ \}$

n/v-pro:
$\begin{bmatrix} \text{noun: PRO\_n} \\ \text{fnc: } \alpha \\ \text{idy: i} \\ \text{prn: r} \end{bmatrix} \begin{bmatrix} \text{n/v: sc } \alpha \\ \text{arg: X PRO\_n Y} \\ \text{fnc: r } \beta \\ \text{prn: r} \end{bmatrix} \begin{bmatrix} \text{noun: } \gamma \\ \text{fnc: } \beta \\ \text{idy: j} \\ \text{prn: q} \end{bmatrix}$
if PRO_n is a nonreflexive personal pronoun, PRO_n and γ are compatible, and q and r are adjacent, set i = j
$\{ \}$

adn-cnn:
$\begin{bmatrix} \text{noun: PRO\_n} \\ \text{fnc: } \alpha \\ \text{mdr:} \\ \text{idy: i} \\ \text{prn: r} \end{bmatrix} \begin{bmatrix} \text{noun: } \beta \\ \text{fnc: } \alpha \\ \text{mdr: q } \gamma \\ \text{idy: k} \\ \text{prn: r} \end{bmatrix} \begin{bmatrix} \text{noun: } \delta \\ \text{fnc: } \gamma \\ \text{mdr:} \\ \text{idy: j} \\ \text{prn: q} \end{bmatrix}$
if PRO_n is a nonreflexive personal pronoun, PRO_n and α are compatible, q and r are adjacent, and q < r, set i = j
$\{ \}$

adn-pro:
$\begin{bmatrix} \text{noun: PRO\_n} \\ \text{fnc: } \alpha \\ \text{mdr:} \\ \text{idy: i} \\ \text{prn: r} \end{bmatrix} \begin{bmatrix} \text{noun: } \beta \\ \text{fnc: } \gamma \\ \text{mdr: r } \alpha \\ \text{idy: k} \\ \text{prn: q} \end{bmatrix} \begin{bmatrix} \text{noun: } \delta \\ \text{fnc: } \gamma \\ \text{mdr:} \\ \text{idy: j} \\ \text{prn: q} \end{bmatrix}$
if PRO_n is a nonreflexive personal pronoun, PRO_n and γ are compatible, and q and r are adjacent, set i = j
$\{ \}$

adv-cnn:
$\begin{bmatrix} \text{noun: PRO\_n} \\ \text{fnc: } \alpha \\ \text{idy: i} \\ \text{prn: r} \end{bmatrix} \begin{bmatrix} \text{a/v: sc } \beta \\ \text{arg: X } \gamma \text{ Y} \\ \text{mdd: r } \alpha \\ \text{prn: q} \end{bmatrix} \begin{bmatrix} \text{noun: } \gamma \\ \text{fnc: } \beta \\ \text{idy: j} \\ \text{prn: q} \end{bmatrix}$
if PRO_n is a nonreflexive personal pronoun, PRO_n and γ are compatible, q and r are adjacent, and q < r, set i = j
$\{ \}$

adv-pro:
$\begin{bmatrix} \text{noun: PRO\_n} \\ \text{fnc: } \alpha \\ \text{idy: i} \\ \text{prn: r} \end{bmatrix} \begin{bmatrix} \text{a/v: sc } \alpha \\ \text{fnc: X PRO\_n Y} \\ \text{mdd: q } \beta \\ \text{prn: r} \end{bmatrix} \begin{bmatrix} \text{noun: } \gamma \\ \text{fnc: } \beta \\ \text{idy: j} \\ \text{prn: q} \end{bmatrix}$
if PRO_n is a nonreflexive personal pronoun, PRO_n and γ are compatible, and q and r are adjacent, set i = j
$\{ \}$

$\text{ST}_F =_{def} \{ (\, [\text{noun: } \alpha] \, \text{rp}_{\text{rfl}-1}), (\, [\text{noun: } \alpha] \, \text{rp}_{\text{n/v}-\text{cnn}}), (\, [\text{noun: } \alpha] \, \text{rp}_{\text{n/v}-\text{pro}}),$
$(\, [\text{noun: } \alpha] \, \text{rp}_{\text{adn}-\text{cnn}}), (\, [\text{noun: } \alpha] \, \text{rp}_{\text{adn}-\text{pro}}), (\, [\text{noun: } \alpha] \, \text{rp}_{\text{adv}-\text{cnn}})$
$(\, [\text{noun: } \alpha] \, \text{rp}_{\text{adn}-\text{pro}}) \}$

LA-think.pro is triggered into action whenever its ST_S pattern [noun: PRO_n] matches an incoming proplet to be stored in the Word Bank. Input to LA-think.pro are all the noun proplets of a sentence containing a pronoun. Whether or not a coreferential interpretation provided by LA-think.pro is to be adopted by the agent as the most likely, however, must be decided by taking the utterance situation into account, including the preceding text or dialog, and the current context.

Having compatible *ss* patterns, the eight rules are equally applicable. Having incompatible *nw* patterns, at most one of them can be successful. Consequently, LA-think.pro is a C1-Lag (cf. FoCL'99, Sect. 11.5) and does coreference adjustment for any given pronoun in linear time. Despite its low mathematical complexity, the handling of coreference by means of inferences is sufficiently powerful descriptively.

This is illustrated below with an analysis of the Bach–Peters sentence (Peters and Ritchie 1973; Jacobson 2000). We begin with the derivation of the primary relations:

10.6.2 HEARER MODE DERIVATION OF THE BACH–PETERS SENTENCE

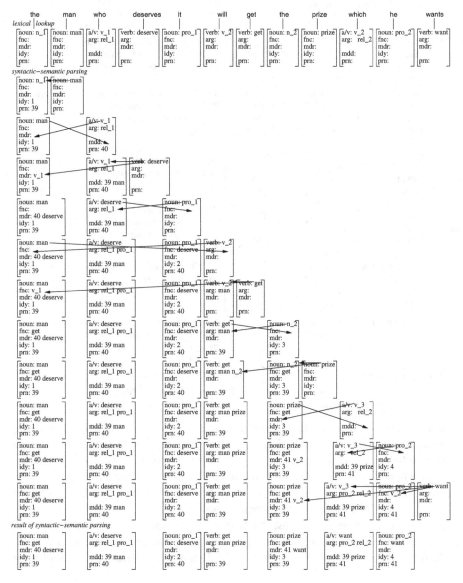

In Transformational Grammar (TG), this example has been used to prove that TG is undecidable.[7] In Database Semantics, in contrast, no complexity problem arises, due to (i) the lexical treatment of pronouns and (ii) the separate derivation of primary and secondary relations. As usual in the DBS analysis of natural language (cf. FoCL'99, 12.5.7 and 21.5.2), the mathematical complexity of the derivation 10.6.2 is linear.

Next, let us turn to the secondary relations, i.e., the inferences for providing proper coreference. The Bach–Peters sentence contains two constellations supporting a coreference inference, namely an **HL'** and an **L'H** constellation of adnominal sentential modifiers (cf. Examples 3 and 4 in 10.4.1):

10.6.3 THE **HL'** CONSTELLATION

> **H:** The *man* will get the prize
> > **L':** which *he* wants

10.6.4 THE **L'H** CONSTELLATION

> The man   **H:** will get the *prize*
> > **L':** who deserves *it*

Using the proplets resulting from the derivation 10.6.2, the assignment of the proper coreferences may be characterized schematically as follows:

10.6.5 THE COREFERENCE INFERENCES

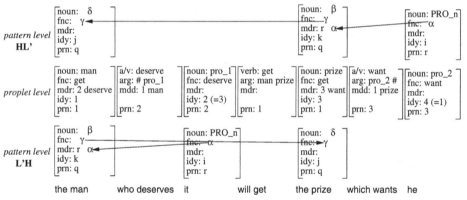

The patterns for the **HL'** constellation are shown above, while the patterns for the **L'H** constellation are shown below the proplet level. Given that in both constellations the pronoun is in the lower clause, the coreference inference of both is handled by the same rule, namely adn-pro of LA-think.pro grammar defined in 10.6.1.

---

[7] Peters and Ritchie (1973). The complexity problem arises because TG derives pronouns from "full noun phrases" in the "deep structure" which are identical with their ante/post/cedent. Therefore, the pronoun *it* is expanded into *the prize he wants*, and the pronoun *he* into *the man who deserves it*, leading to an infinite regress. This phenomenon is a direct consequence of TG's method of deriving pronouns from "underlying full noun phrases."

Remark Concluding Part II

In this part, the major constructions of natural language have been analyzed from a semantic point of view. In accordance to the classic tradition, the elementary semantic relations are (i) functor–argument structure, (ii) coordination, and (iii) coreference. These elementary relations have been treated here first in isolation and have then been systematically combined into grammatical structures of arbitrary complexity.

In free text, however, many additional structures may be found. This variety raises the question of how to complement the grammatical taxonomy motivated by the semantic representations with a maximally complete data coverage of the surface variations. Consider the following proposal:

After building an automatic word form recognition providing full coverage for the natural language at hand,[8] corpora may be turned automatically into n-gram like sequences of categories, ordered according to frequency. Starting at the top of the list, the category sequences are analyzed and used to build a small initial fragment of Database Semantics (DBS). Then more and more of the following category sequences are analyzed and incorporated into the fragment.

Compared to the substitution-based approaches, this is easy due to the time-linear nature of the syntactic–semantic (hearer mode) and semantic–syntactic (speaker mode) analysis in DBS (cf. FoCL'99, Sect. 18.1). Furthermore, if the frequency distribution of the different category sequences turns out to correspond to the frequency distribution of the different word forms in corpora (cf. FoCL'99, 15.4.2, 15.4.3), this method will result in an extremely rapid extension of the data coverage.

How to define and extend a formal fragment of English is shown in the following Part III. The fragments are defined as declarative specifications for LA-hear, LA-think, and LA-speak grammars, which allow their direct implementation as running software in a programming language of choice. Due to the required degree of detail, the scope of the grammatical analyses in Part III will have to be more narrow than in Part II.

---

[8] Given a good traditional dictionary existing online and an off-the-shelf software framework for the allomorph approach (cf. FoCL'99, Chapts. 13–15), this may be achieved in a few month, depending on the natural language.

Part III

The Declarative Specification of Formal Fragments

11. DBS.1: Hearer Mode

The declarative specification (cf. Sect. 1.2) of a system of natural language communication must be defined at a level of detail sufficient for a straightforward implementation in a programming language of choice. Given the large structural variety of natural language expressions, the size of the lexicon, and the complexity of natural language communication, let us begin with a small "fragment."

By a fragment we mean a system of natural language communication which has limited coverage, but is functionally complete in that it models the hearer mode, the think mode (defined as navigating through the content of the database), and the speaker mode. Given the limitation of having to use standard computers rather than robots, the following fragments do not include contextual recognition and action (i.e., they are capable of mediated reference only, cf. 2.5.1). Therefore, the Word Bank may be simplified to store language proplets without a separate context section (cf. 3.3.1).

The first fragment of English defined in Database Semantics is called DBS.1. For simplicity, the coverage of DBS.1 is restricted to the sentence sequence

Julia sleeps. John sings. Susanne dreams.

The focus of DBS.1 is on concatenating propositions, as in a text (extrapropositional coordination, cf. Sect. 9.2). DBS.1 consists of components for automatic word form recognition and production, and three LA-grammars, called LA-hear.1, LA-think.1, and LA-speak.1. In Chaps. 13 and 14, DBS.1 will be extended into DBS.2 without losing any of the previously achieved functionality or coverage.

11.1 Automatic Word Form Recognition

For a cognitive agent with language, the cycle of communication may begin in the speaker mode or in the hearer mode. However, before an agent can produce language, its Word Bank must be filled with content. In order to read content automatically into the system, let us begin the definition of the fragment with the hearer mode.

An LA-hear system consists of two components: (i) a system of word form recognition and (ii) an LA-hear grammar for syntactic–semantic interpretation. Word form recognition takes unanalyzed natural language surfaces as input and produces corresponding lexically analyzed types as output.[1]

---

[1] For a detailed description of automatic word form recognition see FoCL'99, Chaps. 13–15.

The basic functioning of automatic word form recognition may be characterized schematically as a combination of surface recognition and lexical lookup:

11.1.1 SURFACE RECOGNITION AND LEXICAL LOOKUP

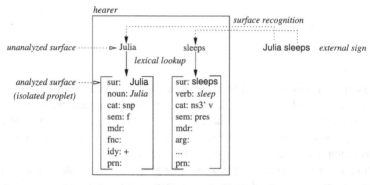

In *surface recognition*, the external sign surfaces (token) are matched with corresponding internal sign surfaces (types) provided by the agent's Word Bank (cf. Sects. 4.3–4.5). This process may be achieved by speech recognition, optical character recognition (OCR), or by simply typing the letters of the external surface into the computer. In the latter procedure, the external surface is converted directly into a digitally coded, modality-independent form – as opposed to speech recognition or OCR, which are modality-dependent (cf. Sect. 2.2).

The internal representation of the unanalyzed surface is submitted to *lexical lookup*. Lexical lookup is based on an electronic lexicon defined as a list of lexical entries. Assuming that each entry is defined as an isolated proplet, lexical lookup compares the unanalyzed surface with the value of the sur attribute of each entry. The proplet with a sur value matching the unanalyzed surface is returned as the result.

Depending on whether lexical lookup is based on full word forms or on morphological analysis, there are different kinds of automatic word form recognition (cf. FoCL'99, Sect. 13.5). The full form method is the simplest, but it can only recognize a finite number of items. An infinite number of word forms can be recognized by systems based on morphologically analyzing the surface into smaller parts called allomorphs, e.g., learn, ing, or ed. Such a compositional approach is especially important for languages with a morphology richer than English.

No matter which method of automatic word form recognition is used, it should work for any language. Changing to another language should require no more than providing another language-specific lexicon and, if present, other rules of morphological analysis. Also, it must be possible at any time to replace the current component of automatic word form recognition by a more advanced one (modularity). For this, the new component must merely be input/output equivalent with the old one: It should take unanalyzed surface tokens as input and render lexically analyzed surface types (e.g., isolated proplets) as output, which are passed to the parser.

11.2 Lexicon of LA-hear.1

In order for an LA-hear grammar to parse a sentence or text, it must be able to lexically recognize all the word forms occurring in it. Let us therefore define the word forms needed for the small fragment of DBS.1. For simplicity, we use full-form lookup.

To facilitate storage and retrieval, the entries in a lexicon are usually ordered alphabetically, using the word form surface as the key. However, to show the structure of the different kinds of words, the following entries are ordered according to the part of speech, i.e., first all the nouns, then all the verbs, and finally the punctuation sign.

11.2.1 THE LEXICAL ENTRIES OF **LA-hear.1**

proper names:

$$
\begin{bmatrix}
\text{sur: Julia} \\
\text{noun: } Julia \\
\text{cat: nm} \\
\text{sem: f} \\
\text{mdr:} \\
\text{fnc:} \\
\text{idy:} \\
\text{prn:}
\end{bmatrix}
\begin{bmatrix}
\text{sur: John} \\
\text{noun: } John \\
\text{cat: nm} \\
\text{sem: m} \\
\text{mdr:} \\
\text{fnc:} \\
\text{idy:} \\
\text{prn:}
\end{bmatrix}
\begin{bmatrix}
\text{sur: Susanne} \\
\text{noun: } Susanne \\
\text{cat: nm} \\
\text{sem: f} \\
\text{mdr:} \\
\text{fnc:} \\
\text{idy:} \\
\text{prn:}
\end{bmatrix}
$$

finite one-place verbs, inflected for third-person singular

$$
\begin{bmatrix}
\text{sur: sleeps} \\
\text{erb: } sleep \\
\text{cat: ns3' v} \\
\text{sem: pres} \\
\text{mdr:} \\
\text{arg:} \\
\text{nc:} \\
\text{pc:} \\
\text{prn:}
\end{bmatrix}
\begin{bmatrix}
\text{sur: sings} \\
\text{verb: } sing \\
\text{cat: ns3' v} \\
\text{sem: pres} \\
\text{mdr:} \\
\text{arg:} \\
\text{nc:} \\
\text{pc:} \\
\text{prn:}
\end{bmatrix}
\begin{bmatrix}
\text{sur: dreams} \\
\text{verb: } dream \\
\text{cat: ns3' v} \\
\text{sem: pres} \\
\text{mdr:} \\
\text{arg:} \\
\text{nc:} \\
\text{pc:} \\
\text{prn:}
\end{bmatrix}
$$

punctuation sign

$$
\begin{bmatrix}
\text{sur: .} \\
\text{cat: v' decl}
\end{bmatrix}
$$

The three kinds of lexical entries have in common that their first attribute, called sur, takes the surface of the word form as its value (cf. 4.1.2, 1). It is printed here in sans serif font. In the hearer mode, it serves as the key to be matched with the unanalyzed input surface (cf. 11.1.1).

The nouns and verbs are examples of content words, while the punctuation sign is an example of a function word. In content words, the second attribute is the core attribute (cf. 4.1.2, 2). It specifies the basic part of speech, i.e., noun, verb, or adj, and may take a concept, a name marker, or an index as its value. For simplicity, concepts are represented by a corresponding English word serving as a placeholder (cf. 4.1.4 ff.) and are printed in italics.

The next two attributes, cat and sem, are called grammatical attributes (cf. 4.1.2, 3). cat specifies the syntactic category of the word form. It retains the notation of category segments familiar from the older syntactic systems of LA-grammar (NEWCAT'84 and CoL'89). In the simple LA-hear.1 grammar defined in 11.4.1, the following *category segments* are used:

11.2.2 VALUES OF THE cat ATTRIBUTE

decl = declarative sentence
nm   = proper name
ns3′ = nominative third-person singular valency position
v   = verb, unmarked for sentence mood
v′   = valency position for verb unmarked for sentence mood

Being constants, the category segments are written in lowercase Roman letters.

The sem attribute specifies semantic properties of the word form. In LA-hear.1, these are the gender values in noun proplets and a tense value in verb proplets:

11.2.3 VALUES OF THE sem ATTRIBUTE

f   = femininum
m   = masculinum

pres = present tense

The remaining attributes of the isolated proplets in the lexicon 11.2.1 do not have values yet, but will receive values during syntactic–semantic parsing. The attributes in question are of three kinds. The first specifies *intrapropositional relations* between content words in terms of traditional valency relations (cf. 4.1.2, 4):

11.2.4 INTRAPROPOSITIONAL CONTINUATION ATTRIBUTES

arg: specifies the arguments of verbs (list)
fnc: specifies the functor of nouns (atom)
mdr: specifies the modifiers of nouns and verbs (list)
mdd: specifies the modified of adnominals and adverbials (atom)

The value restrictions specified above will have to be revised for handling the constructions presented in Part II. For example, the attribute fnc must be able to take nonatomic values, e.g., [fnc: 28 amuse], as in 7.1.2, 1.

The second specifies *extrapropositional relations* (cf. 4.1.2, 5). These are the identity relation between nouns and the coordination relation between verbs.

11.2.5 EXTRAPROPOSITIONAL CONTINUATION ATTRIBUTES

idy: identity between nouns. Takes a number as value.
nc: next conjunct. Takes an optional conjunction, a proposition number, and a verb concept as value.
pc: previous conjunct. Takes values similar to nc.

The attribute idy is restricted to nouns and prepositional phrases (complex adjectives), while the attributes nc and pc are used by DBS-1 only in verbs.

The third kind of attribute with a nonlexical value is a bookkeeping attribute (cf. 4.1.2, 6):

11.2.6 BOOKKEEPING ATTRIBUTE OF **LA-hear.1**

prn: proposition number

This attribute is common to all proplets representing content words. Analyzed content words belonging to the same proposition have a common prn value.

Finally, consider the feature structure of the function word in 11.2.1. The punctuation sign has only two attributes, one for the surface and one for the syntactic category. This is sufficient because the punctuation sign is absorbed into the proplet of the verb (e.g., 11.5.2).

11.3 Preamble of LA-hear.1

The rules of LA-hear.1 are based on patterns defined as flat (nonrecursive) feature structures. The patterns of the rule level differ from their counterparts at the language level by using *variables* rather than constants as the values of some of their attributes. These variables are defined in the preamble of an LA-hear grammar, including the restrictions on their domain and their agreement conditions. In this way, different rules may utilize the same variable definitions provided by the preamble.

The rules of LA-hear.1 use the following binding variables:

11.3.1 LIST OF BINDING VARIABLES

SM	= sentence mood
VT	= verb type filler
VT$'$	= verb type valency position
NP	= noun phrase filler
NP$'$	= noun phrase valency position
α, β, γ, etc.,	= for individual concepts like *Julia, sleep, young,* etc.,
i, j, k	= for number values of the prn and idy attributes

As explained in Sect. 3.2, the matching of a proplet pattern at the rule level with a proplet at the language level requires (i) that all attributes in the rule pattern have counterparts in the language proplet and (ii) that the attribute values of the language proplet satisfy the restrictions of the corresponding variables of corresponding attributes in the rule patterns. The variables of LA-hear.1 have the following restrictions:

11.3.2 RESTRICTION OF BINDING VARIABLES

$SM \epsilon \{decl\}$
$VT \epsilon \{v\}$
$VT' \epsilon \{v'\}$
$NP \epsilon \{nm\}$
$NP' \epsilon \{ns3'\}$

The set of values for these variables will be extended in later versions of the grammar.

The role of variable restrictions may be shown schematically as follows:

11.3.3 MATCHING BETWEEN A VARIABLE AND A CONSTANT

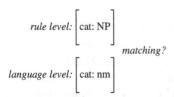

The match is successful because the constant value nm of the attribute cat at the language level is defined in 11.3.2 to be in the restriction set of the variable value NP of the corresponding attribute at the rule level.

The definition of restricted variables may be extended to a simple, general treatment of *agreement*.[2] This is done by defining conditionals of the following form:

If variable X has the values a, b, or c, then the variable Y must have the
values p or q.

Such a conditional relates two variables X and Y at the rule level by further refining their restrictions.

The agreement conditions of LA-hear.1 are very simple and relate valency fillers to suitable valency positions.

11.3.4 AGREEMENT CONDITIONS

if VT ϵ {v}, then VT$'$ ϵ {v$'$}
if NP ϵ {nm}, then NP$'$ ϵ {ns3$'$}

For a more detailed analysis of agreement regarding the restrictions between nominal valency fillers and the verb, between finite auxiliaries and the nonfinite main verb, and between determiners and nouns in English see the preamble of LA-hear.2 defined in Sect. 13.2.

11.4 Definition of LA-hear.1

For parsing simple texts like

Julia sleeps. John dreams. Susanne sings.

LA-hear.1 requires three rules, called NOM+FV (nominative plus finite verb), S+IP (sentence plus interpunctuation), and IP+START (interpunctuation plus start of the new sentence). The states and rules of this input grammar are based on the definition

---

[2] For a complete treatment of agreement in English see FoCL'99, Sect. 16.3, pp. 307–310, and Chap. 17, pp. 331–332.

of attributes and values in Sect. 11.2 and on the definition of variables and agreement in Sect. 11.3.

NOM+FV adds a finite verb to a sentence start consisting of a noun, S+IP adds a full stop to a sentence start ending in a finite verb, and IP+START adds a noun to a sentence start ending in a full stop. Then the cycle starts over again: Treating the noun as the new sentence start, NOM+FV adds a finite verb, etc.

In addition to these three rules, LA-hear.1 defines a start state ST_S which ensures that a derivation begins with the rule NOM+FV, and a final state ST_F which ensures that a derivation ends with an application of the rule S+IP.

11.4.1 FORMAL DEFINITION OF **LA-hear.1**

$ST_S =_{def} \{ \, (\, [\text{cat: X}] \; \{1 \; \text{NOM+FV}\}) \, \}$

NOM+FV $\{2 \; \text{S+IP}\}$

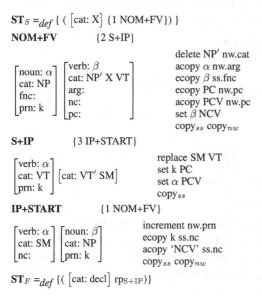

delete NP' nw.cat
acopy α nw.arg
ecopy β ss.fnc
ecopy PC nw.pc
acopy PCV nw.pc
set β NCV
copy_{ss} copy_{nw}

S+IP $\{3 \; \text{IP+START}\}$

$\begin{bmatrix} \text{verb: } \alpha \\ \text{cat: VT} \\ \text{prn: k} \end{bmatrix}$ $[\text{cat: VT' SM}]$

replace SM VT
set k PC
set α PCV
copy_{ss}

IP+START $\{1 \; \text{NOM+FV}\}$

$\begin{bmatrix} \text{verb: } \alpha \\ \text{cat: SM} \\ \text{nc:} \end{bmatrix}$ $\begin{bmatrix} \text{noun: } \beta \\ \text{cat: NP} \\ \text{prn: k} \end{bmatrix}$

increment nw.prn
ecopy k ss.nc
acopy 'NCV' ss.nc
copy_{ss} copy_{nw}

$ST_F =_{def} \{ (\, [\text{cat: decl}] \; \text{rp}_{\text{S+IP}}) \}$

The rules in the rule packages of the grammar are numbered in sequence.[3] These numbers are useful in debugging because a rule may be called from different rule packages.[4]

Each rule consists of a rule name, e.g., NOM+FV, a rule package, e.g., {2 S+IP}, a pattern for the sentence start, a pattern for the next word, and a list of operations, e.g., delete NP' nw.cat.

The operations of the rules have the following interpretation (see also Appendix B.5.2–B.5.5):

---

[3] During grammar development, the contents of the rule packages may frequently change. Therefore the grammar-specific numbering of the rules should be provided automatically by the system. Otherwise, the grammar writer has to adjust the numbering by hand after each revision.

[4] This is not illustrated by LA-hear.1, due to the fact that each of its rule packages has only one rule and each rule is called from only one rule package. See the definition of LA-hear.2 in 13.2.4 instead.

11.4.2 DEFINITIONS OF THE OPERATIONS

delete variable proplet-attr. = delete the value corresponding to the variable in the corresponding attribute of the corresponding proplet at the level of language.

Example: delete NP′ nw.cat (in NOM+FV)

acopy variable proplet-attr. = additively copy value(s) corresponding to the variable into the specified target slot; default position is at the end of the target slot.

Examples: acopy α nw.arg (in NOM+FV)
acopy PCV nw.pc (in NOM+FV)
acopy 'NCV' ss.nc (in IP+START)

ecopy variable proplet-attr. = exclusively copy value(s) corresponding to the variable into the specified proplet attribute.

Examples: ecopy β ss.fnc (in NOM+FV)
ecopy PC nw.pc (in NOM+FV)
ecopy k ss.nc (in IP+START)

set value variable = rule-based (rather than matching-based) binding of a variable to a value.

Examples: set β NCV (in NOM+FV)
set k PC (in S+IP)
set α PCV (in S+IP)

replace variable2 variable1 = replace value of variable1 with value of variable2.

Examples: replace SM VT (in S+IP)

increment proplet-attr. = increment numerical value of corresponding attribute by one.

Example: increment nw.prn (in IP+START)

copy$_{ss}$ = include the proplets of the sentence start in the result.

Examples: NOM+FV, S+IP, IP+START

copy$_{nw}$ = include the proplet of the next word in the result.

Examples: NOM+FV, IP+START

To add a value "additively" with acopy means that the target attribute may already have non-NIL values. To add a value "exclusively" with ecopy means that the target attribute may not have any non-NIL values. Instead of referring to a value by means of a variable, e.g., acopy α nw.arg, the operations may also refer to a value by specifying a proplet attribute, e.g., acopy ss.noun nw.arg.

The set operation allows binding a value to a variable by a rule (rather than binding a value to a variable by matching rule patterns with the language level). The variables NCV (next conjunct verb), PC (previous conjunct prn), and PCV (previous conjunct verb) are a special kind of global variable. They are called *loading variables* because they are assigned values at certain stages of the derivation by certain rules, such that the values can be (i) used or (ii) supplied at other stages. Loading variables occur at the level of language and the level of rules, in contrast to the binding variables, which occur only at the level of rules.

The operations apply in the order of their appearance in the rule. Their functioning will be explained in connection with the detailed sample derivation presented in the following section.

11.5 Interpreting a Sequence of Sentences

An LA-hear derivation is activated by the first word form passed to the grammar by automatic word form recognition. This analyzed word form (lexical proplet) is matched with the pattern(s) of the start state ST_S. If the match is successful, the associated rule package of the start state ST_S is activated, the second word is provided by automatic word form recognition, and the rules of the rule package are applied to the first and second proplet serving as *ss* and *nw* (cf. 3.4.3, Appendix B.1).

Given the definition of LA-hear.1 (cf. 11.4.1) and the first word form of our sample text, this operation is successful: The pattern [cat: X] of the start state trivially matches the lexical type of *Julia*, activating lexical lookup of the second word form *sleep* and the rule package {1 NOM+FV}. The single rule in this rule package is applied to the lexical proplets of the first two words:

11.5.1 COMBINING Julia AND sleeps

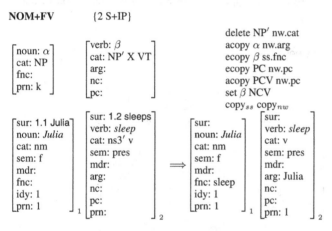

The proplets at the language level have a *word number* as subscript. It refers to the word which the proplet represents, indicating the word's position in the surface.

The precondition for applying the operations is the successful matching between the rule patterns and the language proplets in accordance with the matching conditions 3.2.3. The attribute condition is fulfilled insofar as the attributes of the patterns are a subset of the attributes of the corresponding language proplets. The value condition includes the requirement that the agreement condition between the values of the variables is fullfilled. Given that cat values satisfy the restiction of the variable NP to nm and and the variable NP' to ns3' (cf. 11.3.4), the operations may apply.

The effect of the operations is shown in the proplets to the right of the arrow. The first operation, delete NP' nw.cat, deletes the category segment ns3' in the cat attribute of the verb. The second operation, acopy α nw.arg, copies the value Julia of the noun attribute into the arg attribute of the proplet *sleep*. The third operation, ecopy β ss.fnc, copies the value sleep of the verb attribute into the fnc attribute of the proplet *Julia*. Linguistically, the first operation models the canceling of the nominative valency position, while the second and third operations realize the functor–argument structure holding between the first and the second proplet.

The following three operations ecopy PC nw.pc, acopy PCV nw.pc, and set β NCV are for establishing the extrapropositional relations between the present and the previous proposition. However, given that the current sentence is initial, the three operations apply vacuously in this particular case.[5] A nonvacuous application of the three operations in question is shown in 11.5.4.

The last two operations copy$_{ss}$ and copy$_{nw}$ specify that both input proplets are in the output of the rule. The proplets in the output differ from the input proplet in that the latter have been subjected to the rule operations.

The application of NOM+FV activates its rule package, which contains only one rule: S+IP. The input to S+IP consists of the output of NOM+FV and the new next word "." (punctuation, full stop). The application of S+IP in the derivation of Julia sleeps + . is illustrated below:

11.5.2 COMBINING Julia sleeps AND .

S+IP   {3 IP+START}

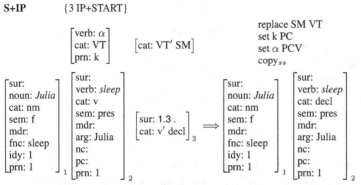

The first operation replaces the cat value v of the verb with decl. The second and the third operations introduce the loading variables PC and PCV and assign values to them. These values, namely PC = 1 and PCV = sleep, are for the pc slot of the verb of the next proposition. Because the proplets of the next proposition are not yet available (and might not come at all), the patterns of the current rule S+IP have no place for the variables PC and PCV. This is why PC and PCV cannot be assigned values via pattern matching with the language level, but by means of the rule operations in question.

---

[5] If there were a previous proposition, the PC and PCV variables would have been bound to values, which would now be copied into the pc slot of the current proposition (forward loading). Also, the NCV variable would have been copied as a name into the nc slot of the previous proposition; it would now be provided with a value (backward loading) .

The last operation copies only the sentence start into the result. This is because punctuation is treated as a function word which is absorbed into the verb.

The application of S+IP activates its rule package, which contains only one rule: IP+START. The input to IP+START consists of the output of S+IP and the new next word, i.e., *John*. The application of IP+START in the derivation of Julia sleeps. + John is illustrated below:

11.5.3 COMBINING Julia sleeps. AND John

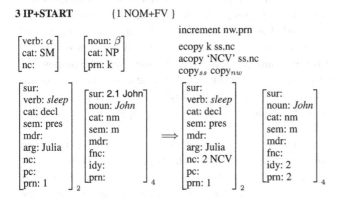

The operation increment nw.prn in IP+START increments the proposition number of the *nw*, which happens to be the first word of the next proposition. The second operation copies the incremented prn value of the *nw* into the nc slot of the *ss*, i.e., the verb proplet *sleep*. The third operation adds the variable name NCV to the nc slot of the *ss*. NCV will be provided with a value in the following proposition (backward loading) by the rule NOM+FV, which applies next.

11.5.4 COMBINING Julia sleeps. John AND sings

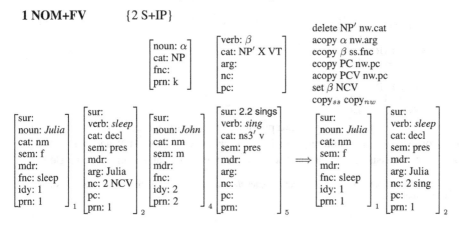

$$
\begin{bmatrix} \text{sur:} \\ \text{noun: } John \\ \text{cat: nm} \\ \text{sem: m} \\ \text{mdr:} \\ \text{fnc: sing} \\ \text{idy: 2} \\ \text{prn: 2} \end{bmatrix}_4
\begin{bmatrix} \text{sur:} \\ \text{verb: } sing \\ \text{cat: v} \\ \text{sem: pres} \\ \text{mdr:} \\ \text{arg: John} \\ \text{nc:} \\ \text{pc: 1 sleep} \\ \text{prn: 2} \end{bmatrix}_5
$$

The proplets of the previous sentence are shown in addition to the current sentence start in order to illustrate the assignment of the nc (next conjunct) and the pc (previous conjunct) values. Reference to the previous proposition is needed because the coordination of two propositions is coded in their respective verbs, and – due to the word order of English – the verb of the current proposition is only now being provided.

Although the ss-pattern fits two input proplets, *Julia* and *John*, only the proposition number of the *John* proplet is in concord with the counter value of the current sentence start. Furthermore, even though the nw-pattern roughly[6] fits the input proplets *sleep* and *sing*, only *sing* is a possible candidate because the *nw* proplet must be provided by lexical lookup.

As in 11.5.2, the first three operations code the functor–argument relations between the two proplets of proposition 2. The fourth and the fifth operation copy the PC and PCV values set in 11.5.2 by S+IP into the pc slot of the current verb proplet (resulting in pc: 1 sleep in the *sing* proplet). The sixth operation assigns a value to the NCV variable of the previous verb proplet (backward loading, resulting in nc: 2 sing in the *sleep* proplet). Now the first two propositions of the test sample are properly concatenated via the nc and pc values of their verb proplets *sleep* and *sing*.

Given that the test sentences all have the same structure, the remainder of the derivation is analogous to the steps shown above, and is therefore omitted. The sequence of word forms in the test sample is added by the following rule applications:

11.5.5 SEQUENCE OF RULE APPLICATIONS IN DERIVING THE SAMPLE OF DBS-1

```
              1.1 Julia
1 NOM+FV     1.2 sleeps
2 S+IP        1.3 .
3 IP+START   2.1 John
1 NOM+FV     2.2 sings
2 S+IP        2.3 .
3 IP+START   3.1 Susanne
1 NOM+FV     3.2 dreams
2 S+IP        3.3 .
```

The first line contains the first word provided by the start state ST_S. Each subsequent line consists of a rule number, e.g., 1, a rule name, e.g., NOM+FV, and a next word. The latter consists of a proposition.word number, e.g., 1.2, and a surface, e.g., sleeps.

---

[6] In fact, the nw-pattern would not fit the proplet *sleep* because of conflicting cat values (see variable restrictions 11.3.2).

The format illustrated in 11.5.5 is suited well to show the transitions through the finite-state backbone of an LA-grammar during a derivation. The rules and rule packages of LA-hear.1 form the following finite-state transition network:

11.5.6 FINITE-STATE TRANSITION NETWORK OF **LA-hear.1**

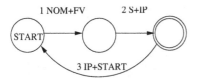

The perplexity of this system is 3 : 3 = 1, that is, only one attempted rule application per composition. The notion of perplexity as applied to an LA-grammar is explained in FoCL'99, p. 339.

With no upper limit on the length, **LA-hear.1** analyzes infinitely many sentence sequences.[7] The simplest way to expand the data coverage of LA-hear.1 is by adding more proper names and more one-place verbs to its lexicon.

11.6 Storing the Output of LA-hear.1 in a Word Bank

The hearer's next step of interpreting a text of natural language consists in sorting the proplets derived into the Word Bank.

11.6.1 SORTING AN **LA-hear** DERIVATION INTO A WORD BANK

owner records   *member records*
(isolated proplets)   (connected proplets)

$$
\begin{bmatrix}
\text{sur:} \\
\text{verb: } dream \\
\text{cat: n-s3' v} \\
\text{sem: pres} \\
\text{mdr:} \\
\text{arg:} \\
\text{nc:} \\
\text{pc:} \\
\text{prn:}
\end{bmatrix}
\quad
\begin{bmatrix}
\text{sur:} \\
\text{verb: } dream \\
\text{cat: decl} \\
\text{sem: pres} \\
\text{mdr:} \\
\text{arg: Susanne} \\
\text{nc:} \\
\text{pc: 2 sing} \\
\text{prn: 3}
\end{bmatrix}
$$

$$
\begin{bmatrix}
\text{sur:} \\
\text{noun: } John \\
\text{cat: nm} \\
\text{sem: m} \\
\text{mdr:} \\
\text{fnc:} \\
\text{idy:} \\
\text{prn:}
\end{bmatrix}
\quad
\begin{bmatrix}
\text{sur:} \\
\text{noun: } John \\
\text{cat: nm} \\
\text{sem: m} \\
\text{mdr:} \\
\text{fnc: sing} \\
\text{idy: 2} \\
\text{prn: 2}
\end{bmatrix}
$$

---

[7] This is illustrated by repetitive sequences like Julia sleeps.
Julia sleeps. Julia sleeps.
Julia sleeps. Julia sleeps. Julia sleeps. Etc.

owner records　　　　*member records*
(isolated proplets)　　(connected proplets)

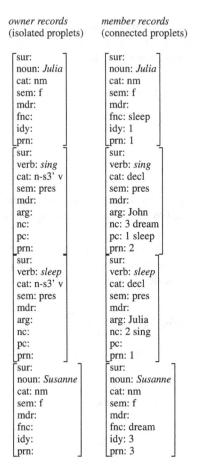

In this Word Bank, complete lexical proplets (rather than just their core values, cf. 3.3.1) are used as the owner records. The owner records of the verbs are represented by the unmarked form of the present tense, e.g., sing, whereby the cat value n-s3' represents a valency position for "nominative minus singular third-person."

The LA-hear.1 interpretation shown in 11.5.1–11.5.4 has resulted in a *set* of proplets the elements of which are sorted into the Word Bank 11.6.1 according to their main key, i.e., the value of their core attribute. Sorting proplets into a Word Bank is completely automatic. It constitutes the first step of the hearer's pragmatic interpretation and corresponds to the down arrow in 2.5.1 (simplified theory of language). Subsequent steps of pragmatic interpretation consist in inferences.

12. DBS.1: Speaker Mode

This chapter completes the definition of DBS.1 by modeling the speaker mode for the test sample derived in the previous chapter in the hearer mode. The fragment's speaker mode is based on two LA-grammars, called **LA-think.1** and **LA-speak.1**.

LA-think navigates through the content of a Word Bank by taking a proplet as input, computing a continuation proplet, and specifying an output position. Navigating through the content of a Word Bank is like moving a focus point from one proplet to the next, highlighting the proplets traversed. The navigation procedure models thought as a temporary *activation* of certain propositions in a potentially vast amount of content.

In language production, the rule patterns of LA-speak match the sequence of proplets activated by LA-think and produce a sequence of corresponding natural language surfaces as output. This process requires adjustment of word order, lexicalization including the precipitation of function words, and the handling of agreement.

12.1 Definition of LA-think.1

The combination of (i) proplets in a Word Bank and (ii) an LA-think grammar constitutes an LA-think system. An LA-think system is designed for the autonomous navigation through the content of a Word Bank. The proplets provided by the Word Bank to LA-think have a similar function as those provided by automatic word form recognition to LA-hear.

The content of the Word Bank and the navigation through this content by means of an LA-think grammar is independent of a particular natural language. The navigation is used for the derivation of inferences (cf. Sect. 5.3) and for conceptualization. For simplicity, we are dealing here only with conceptualization – which is the speaker's process of selecting *what to say*.

Given that the rule patterns of LA-think.1 apply to proplets which have been derived by means of the lexicon and the rules of LA-hear.1, it follows that LA-think.1 must use the same attributes and the same values as the LA-hear.1 system defined in the previous chapter. LA-think.1 is defined as follows:

12.1.1 FORMAL DEFINITION OF **LA-think.1**

LX: proplet tokens in the Word Bank 11.6.1

$\mathbf{ST}_S =\_def \{([\text{verb: } \alpha] \{1 \text{ V\_N\_V}\})\}$

V_N_V   {2 V_V_V}

$\begin{bmatrix} \text{verb: } \alpha \\ \text{arg: } \beta \\ \text{prn: i} \end{bmatrix}$ $\begin{bmatrix} \text{noun: } \beta \\ \text{fnc: } \alpha \\ \text{prn: i} \end{bmatrix}$ output position ss
switch to LA-speak.1 (optional, only in the speaker mode)

V_V_V   {1 V_N_V}

$\begin{bmatrix} \text{verb: } \alpha \\ \text{nc: j } \beta \\ \text{prn: i} \end{bmatrix}$ $\begin{bmatrix} \text{verb: } \beta \\ \text{pc: i } \alpha \\ \text{prn: j} \end{bmatrix}$ output position nw

$\mathbf{ST}_F =\_def \{ ([\text{verb: x}] \text{ rpv\_N\_V})\}$

The start state $\mathbf{ST}_S$ of LA-think.1 is activated when a verb proplet in the Word Bank is activated by an external or internal stimulus. This triggers the application of the rule(s) in the associated rule package, here {1 V_N_V}, to the initial proplet, starting the navigation.

LA-think.1 has only two rules, called V_N_V and V_V_V, whereby V stands for verb and N for noun. The first letter of these rule names represents the sentence start proplet, the second the next word proplet, and the third the output position (serving as the resulting sentence start and the beginning of the next transition).

The rule V_N_V is for intrapropositional navigation; it proceeds from the V to the N back to the V. The rule V_V_V is for extrapropositional navigation; it proceeds from the current V to the next V and stays there.

The rules and rule packages of LA-think.1 constitute the following finite-state transition network:

12.1.2 FINITE-STATE TRANSITION NETWORK OF **LA-think.1**

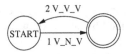

Before explaining the formal details of LA-think.1, such as the proplet patterns and operations of its rules, let us characterize its functioning schematically:

12.1.3 SCHEMATIC DESCRIPTION OF **LA-think.1** NAVIGATION:

rule name	sample navigation	rule package
V_N_V	sleep_Julia_sleep	{V_V_V}
V_V_V	sleep_dream_dream	{V_N_V}

After the successful application of the first rule, the second rule is called (cf. rule package), which adds a second V, which calls the first rule, which adds a second N, etc. This is illustrated by the following schematic derivation of our sample sequence:

12.1.4 DERIVING A VNVNVN SEQUENCE

sleep Julia + sing John + dream Susanne
   VN   VN   VN

rule name	navigation steps	result sequence
V_N_V	sleep_Julia_sleep	VN
V_V_V	sleep_sing_sing	VNV
V_N_V	sing_John_sing	VNVN
V_V_V	sing_dream_dream	VNVNV
V_N_V	dream_Susanne_dream	VNVNVN

The underlying sequence for each proposition is VN (e.g., *sleep Julia*) rather than NV (e.g., *Julia sleep*), because the coordination between two propositions is defined by their verbs' nc and pc values.

In addition to an extrapropositional V_V_V navigation based on the coordination between verb proplets, DBS also supports an extrapropositional N_N_N navigation based on the identity between noun proplets. Just as a coordination-based V_V_V transition must start the next proposition with its V proplet, an identity-based N_N_N transition must start the next proposition with an N proplet. Consequently, the universal navigation cannot be limited to the intrapropositional traversal of VN, VNN, and VNNN sequences, but must also support the intrapropositional traversal of NV, NVN, and NVNN sequences (see Appendix A for a more detailed discussion).

Which of the two kinds of extrapropositional transitions applies depends on whether the coordination-based V_V or an identity-based N_N concatenation from one proposition to the next is chosen by the speaker. For the moment we will concentrate on V_V transitions and the concomitant VN order,[1] leaving the N_N concatenations and the concomitant NV order for later. The intrapropositional VNN and VNNN navigation of propositions with two- and three-place verbs and their correct surface serialization in English is shown in Chap. 14.

12.2 Navigating with LA-think.1

An LA-think navigation begins with the first proplet passed to the grammar by the control structure, reflecting, for example, an external stimulus.[2] This connected proplet (token in a Word Bank) is matched with the pattern(s) of the start state ST_S (cf. 12.1.1). If the match is successful, the proplet constitutes the beginning of an activated sequence and the rule package associated with the start state ST_S is called up.

---

[1] Given that English is a subject–verb–object (SVO) language, production from an underlying VN, VNN, or VNNN order based on the coordination of verbs seems to be more challenging and instructive than from an underlying NV, NVN, or NVNN order based on the identity of nouns.

[2] This is realized in the JSLIM implementation by typing the base form of a verb to the prompt (cf. Appendix B, B.6.3)

12.2.1 PROVIDING AN INITIAL PROPLET FOR THE NAVIGATION

$$
\begin{bmatrix}
\text{sur:} \\
\text{verb: } sleep \\
\text{cat: decl} \\
\text{sem: pres} \\
\text{mdr:} \\
\text{arg: Julia} \\
\text{nc: 2 sing} \\
\text{pc:} \\
\text{prn: 1}
\end{bmatrix}_1
$$

The starting point of the navigation is chosen
by activating an arbitrary proplet in the word bank 11.6.1.

Now the rule(s) in the rule package(s) of the start state(s) ST_S are applied by matching their *ss*-pattern with the initial proplet, binding the variables in the *ss*-pattern to corresponding values of the initial proplet. These bindings hold also in the *nw*-pattern, thus permitting retrieval of a unique continuation proplet, here *Julia*:

12.2.2 TRAVERSING THE FIRST PROPOSITION

1 V_N_V   {2 V_V_V}

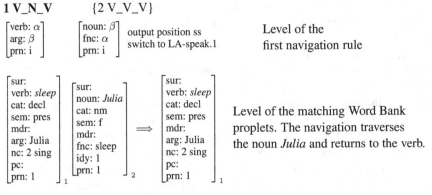

$$
\begin{bmatrix} \text{verb: } \alpha \\ \text{arg: } \beta \\ \text{prn: } i \end{bmatrix}
\begin{bmatrix} \text{noun: } \beta \\ \text{fnc: } \alpha \\ \text{prn: } i \end{bmatrix}
$$
output position ss
switch to LA-speak.1

Level of the
first navigation rule

Level of the matching Word Bank
proplets. The navigation traverses
the noun *Julia* and returns to the verb.

Activated sequence:

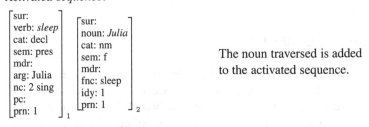

The noun traversed is added
to the activated sequence.

The above navigation from the verb via the noun back to the verb enables a continuation from the current verb to the verb of another proposition, using the rule V_V_V (see rule package of V_N_V). While V_N_V uses the arg feature to find an intrapropositional continuation, V_V_V uses the nc feature to find an extrapropositional continuation.

12.2.3 TRANSITION TO THE SECOND PROPOSITION

2 V_V_V   {1 V_N_V}

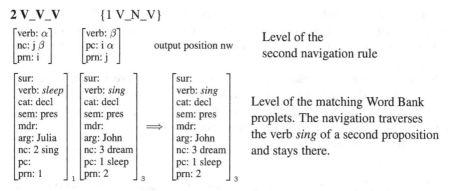

$$\begin{bmatrix} \text{verb: } \alpha \\ \text{nc: } j\ \beta \\ \text{prn: } i \end{bmatrix} \quad \begin{bmatrix} \text{verb: } \beta \\ \text{pc: } i\ \alpha \\ \text{prn: } j \end{bmatrix} \quad \text{output position nw}$$

Level of the
second navigation rule

$$\begin{bmatrix} \text{sur:} \\ \text{verb: } sleep \\ \text{cat: decl} \\ \text{sem: pres} \\ \text{mdr:} \\ \text{arg: Julia} \\ \text{nc: 2 sing} \\ \text{pc:} \\ \text{prn: 1} \end{bmatrix}_1 \begin{bmatrix} \text{sur:} \\ \text{verb: } sing \\ \text{cat: decl} \\ \text{sem: pres} \\ \text{mdr:} \\ \text{arg: John} \\ \text{nc: 3 dream} \\ \text{pc: 1 sleep} \\ \text{prn: 2} \end{bmatrix}_3 \implies \begin{bmatrix} \text{sur:} \\ \text{verb: } sing \\ \text{cat: decl} \\ \text{sem: pres} \\ \text{mdr:} \\ \text{arg: John} \\ \text{nc: 3 dream} \\ \text{pc: 1 sleep} \\ \text{prn: 2} \end{bmatrix}_3$$

Level of the matching Word Bank
proplets. The navigation traverses
the verb *sing* of a second proposition
and stays there.

Activated sequence:

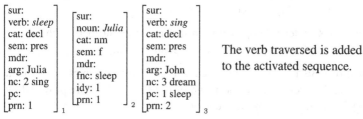

$$\begin{bmatrix} \text{sur:} \\ \text{verb: } sleep \\ \text{cat: decl} \\ \text{sem: pres} \\ \text{mdr:} \\ \text{arg: Julia} \\ \text{nc: 2 sing} \\ \text{pc:} \\ \text{prn: 1} \end{bmatrix}_1 \begin{bmatrix} \text{sur:} \\ \text{noun: } Julia \\ \text{cat: nm} \\ \text{sem: f} \\ \text{mdr:} \\ \text{fnc: sleep} \\ \text{idy: 1} \\ \text{prn: 1} \end{bmatrix}_2 \begin{bmatrix} \text{sur:} \\ \text{verb: } sing \\ \text{cat: decl} \\ \text{sem: pres} \\ \text{mdr:} \\ \text{arg: John} \\ \text{nc: 3 dream} \\ \text{pc: 1 sleep} \\ \text{prn: 2} \end{bmatrix}_3$$

The verb traversed is added
to the activated sequence.

The output of the above rule is the new V, thus matching the *ss*-pattern of the next
rule. Consequently, the derivation is in the same state as in 12.2.2 and continues in
the same way. The rule package recalls V_N_V. The remainder of the derivation is
omitted for reasons of space.

After traversing the three propositions of our test example, the activated sequence is
as follows:

12.2.4 ACTIVATED SEQUENCE AT THE END OF THE NAVIGATION

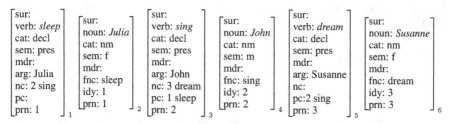

$$\begin{bmatrix} \text{sur:} \\ \text{verb: } sleep \\ \text{cat: decl} \\ \text{sem: pres} \\ \text{mdr:} \\ \text{arg: Julia} \\ \text{nc: 2 sing} \\ \text{pc:} \\ \text{prn: 1} \end{bmatrix}_1 \begin{bmatrix} \text{sur:} \\ \text{noun: } Julia \\ \text{cat: nm} \\ \text{sem: f} \\ \text{mdr:} \\ \text{fnc: sleep} \\ \text{idy: 1} \\ \text{prn: 1} \end{bmatrix}_2 \begin{bmatrix} \text{sur:} \\ \text{verb: } sing \\ \text{cat: decl} \\ \text{sem: pres} \\ \text{mdr:} \\ \text{arg: John} \\ \text{nc: 3 dream} \\ \text{pc: 1 sleep} \\ \text{prn: 2} \end{bmatrix}_3 \begin{bmatrix} \text{sur:} \\ \text{noun: } John \\ \text{cat: nm} \\ \text{sem: m} \\ \text{mdr:} \\ \text{fnc: sing} \\ \text{idy: 2} \\ \text{prn: 2} \end{bmatrix}_4 \begin{bmatrix} \text{sur:} \\ \text{verb: } dream \\ \text{cat: decl} \\ \text{sem: pres} \\ \text{mdr:} \\ \text{arg: Susanne} \\ \text{nc:} \\ \text{pc:2 sing} \\ \text{prn: 3} \end{bmatrix}_5 \begin{bmatrix} \text{sur:} \\ \text{noun: } Susanne \\ \text{cat: nm} \\ \text{sem: f} \\ \text{mdr:} \\ \text{fnc: dream} \\ \text{idy: 3} \\ \text{prn: 3} \end{bmatrix}_6$$

The partial derivation shown in 12.2.2–12.2.3 shows the maximally verbose display format of LA-think.1. This format corresponds to the maximally verbose display
format of LA-hear.1 shown in Sect. 11.5.

12.3 Automatic Word Form Production

The navigation powered by LA-think may either run as pure thought, i.e., without a concomitant language production, or it may serve as the conceptualization of the speaker mode. In the latter case, there is a frequent switching between LA-think and LA-speak.

Just as LA-hear requires automatic word form recognition in order to run, LA-speak requires automatic word form production. In LA-speak.1, word form production is based on *lexicalization functions* which take (i) full-form patterns[3] and (ii) lexicalization tables as input and render word form surfaces as output.

Lexicalization tables have the form

If $\alpha = f$, then $\alpha' = g$,

where α and α' are variables, f is a language-independent concept[4] serving as a proplet value, and g is its language-dependent counterpart.

Full-form patterns are roughly defined as follows:

If proplet pattern X matches proplet p such that p has an attribute with the value α, then α lexicalizes as prefix prefix... α' suffix suffix....

The sample text of DBS.1 requires the lexicalization of proper names, of verbs in the third-person singular present tense form, and of full stops. These are provided by the lexicalization functions lex-n, lex-fv, and lex-p.

12.3.1 THE FUNCTION lex-n FOR THE GENERATION OF PROPER NAMES

If $\begin{bmatrix} \text{noun: } \alpha \\ \text{cat: nm} \end{bmatrix}$ matches an activated N proplet, then lex-n [noun: α] = α'.

If $\alpha =$	then $\alpha' =$
John	John
Julia	Julia
Susanne	Susanne

The full-form pattern is followed here by a lexicalization table for core values. Lexicalization tables provide a simple method to extend lexical coverage in language production.

12.3.2 THE FUNCTION lex-fv FOR THE GENERATION OF VERB FORMS

If $\begin{bmatrix} \text{verb: } \alpha \\ \text{arg: } \beta \text{ z} \\ \text{sem: pres} \end{bmatrix}$ $\begin{bmatrix} \text{noun: } \beta \\ \text{cat: nm} \end{bmatrix}$ match an activated VN sequence, then lex-fv [verb: α] = α'+s.

---

[3] A word form production based on full-form patterns corresponds to a word form recognition based on full-form lookup (cf. Sects. 11.1 and 11.2).

[4] As pointed out in Sect. 11.3, concepts are represented here by corresponding English words. It is for this reason that the lexicalization tables for English appear to be rather trivial. In a nontrivial implementation, the lexicalization table would show the surfaces of different languages for the same concept, e.g., book, livre, buch, etc. This would be most useful for implementing translingual information retrieval systems as described in Frederking, Mitamura, Nyberg, and Carbonell (1997).

If $\alpha =$	then $\alpha' =$
dream	dream
sing	sing
sleep	sleep

Here the input pattern is defined for two proplets, the subject and the verb. The V proplets in the Word Bank (cf. 11.6.1) have the cat value decl. Thus, the information regarding person and number of the nominative, needed to select the proper inflectional form of the verb (agreement), must be obtained by matching the related nominative N proplet, specified by the first value of the arg attribute of the verb. For example, if α' = dream, then α'+s = dreams.

The generation of full stops, finally, is handled by a lexicalization function with a "zero" lexicalization table:

12.3.3 THE FUNCTION lex-p FOR THE GENERATION OF A FULL STOP

If $\begin{bmatrix} \text{verb: } \alpha \\ \text{cat: decl} \\ \text{arg: } \beta \end{bmatrix}$ $\begin{bmatrix} \text{noun: } \beta \\ \text{verb: } \alpha \end{bmatrix}$ match an activated VN sequence, then lex-p [verb: α] = . (full stop).

Items are lexicalized by the full-form pattern alone if they belong to a very small class, and are realized from values other than the core value (here from decl). This applies to function words like pronouns and determiners, which are lexicalized solely by means of full-form patterns (cf. Sect. 14.3), without any lexicalization tables.

The lexicalization functions are called by the rules of LA-speak. A rule application of LA-speak fails if the associated lexicalization function is not successful – either because the input does not match the input condition of the full-form pattern or because the lexicalization table is not defined for the value in question.

12.4 Definition of LA-speak.1

The input to LA-speak.1 consists of the proplets originally derived by LA-hear.1 and then activated in the process of an LA-think.1 navigation. Therefore the states and rules of LA-speak.1 must use the same attributes and values as LA-hear.1 and LA-think.1.

12.4.1 FORMAL DEFINITION OF **LA-speak.1**

LX: proplet tokens in the activated sequence

$ST_S =_{def} \{(\begin{bmatrix} \text{verb: } \alpha \end{bmatrix} \{1 -NoP\}) \}$

–NoP $\{2 -FVERB\}$

$\begin{bmatrix} \text{noun: } \beta \\ \text{cat: nm} \\ \text{prn: i} \end{bmatrix}$ lex-n $\begin{bmatrix} \text{noun: } \beta \end{bmatrix}$

–FVERB   {3 –STOP}

$$\begin{bmatrix} \text{verb: } \alpha \\ \text{cat: decl} \\ \text{arg: } \beta \\ \text{prn: i} \end{bmatrix} \quad \text{lex-fv } \begin{bmatrix} \text{verb: } \alpha \end{bmatrix}$$

–STOP   {1 –NoP}

$$\begin{bmatrix} \text{verb: } \beta \\ \text{cat: decl} \\ \text{arg: } \alpha \\ \text{prn: i} \end{bmatrix} \quad \begin{array}{l} \text{lex-p } \begin{bmatrix} \text{verb: } \beta \end{bmatrix} \\ \text{switch to LA-think.1} \end{array}$$

$\mathbf{ST}_F =_{def} \{(\ \begin{bmatrix} \text{cat:decl} \end{bmatrix} \text{ rp}_{-\text{STOP}})\}$

The arguments of the lexicalization functions, for example, [verb: α], are an abbreviation of the full proplet pattern preceding in the same rule.

Each rule application lexicalizes only one word form, whereby the rule names –NoP (name or pronoun), –FVERB (finite verb), and –STOP (punctuation sign) indicate what kind of word form is lexicalized. The rule names of LA-speak are preceded by a minus (–), indicating that something is given out by the agent, in contradistinction to those of LA-hear, which contain a plus (+), as in NOM+FV, indicating that something is coming into the agent.

The LA-speak.1 grammar handles word order serialization and function word precipitation by means of a simple finite-state transition network, defined by the rules and their rule packages:

12.4.2 FINITE-STATE TRANSITION NETWORK OF **LA-speak.1**

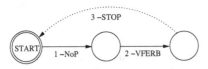

Lexicalization, on the other hand, is handled by the appropriate functions, defined in Sect. 12.3, and called lex-n, lex-fv, and lex-p.

12.5 Producing a Sequence of Sentences

LA-speak.1 is started by the LA-think.1 rule V_N_V, which switches to LA-speak.1 (cf. 12.1.1) after activating the second proplet of a proposition. Once the initial proposition has been realized by LA-speak.1, –STOP switches back to LA-think.1, which adds the proplets of the next proposition to the activated sequence, and so on.

Given that the LA-think aspect of this process has already been shown in Sect. 12.2, the following output derivation of the test sequence is limited to the operations of LA-speak. The incremental switching between LA-think and LA-speak is illustrated in 14.4.1, 14.5.1, and 14.6.1 for DBS.2.

12.5.1 REALIZING Julia OF THE FIRST PROPOSITION

1 –NoP   {2 –FVERB}

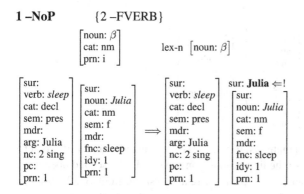

At this point, LA-think has navigated from V to N and back to V, activating the VN proplets shown at the language level and switching to LA-speak. The LA-speak rule –NoP realizes the N proplet as a proper name (cf. ⇐!), ensuring that the sentence begins with a nominal. The rule package of –NoP calls the LA-speak rule –FVERB.

12.5.2 REALIZING sleeps OF THE FIRST PROPOSITION

2 –FVERB   {3 –STOP}

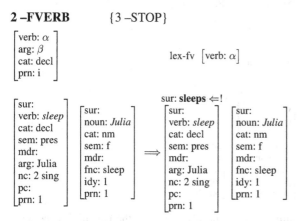

In this rule application, the V proplet is realized as a finite verb form (cf. ⇐!), ensuring that the finite verb is in postnominative position. The verbal ending is supplied by the lexicalization function (cf. 12.3.3). The rule package of –FVERB calls the LA-speak rule –STOP.

12.5.3 REALIZING THE PUNCTUATION SIGN OF THE FIRST PROPOSITION

3 –STOP   {1–NoP}

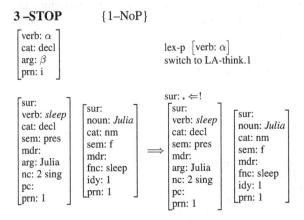

In this rule application, the punctuation sign (cf. ⇐!) is lexicalized from the V proplet. This completes the realization of the first proposition traversed. The second operation of the rule –STOP triggers a switch to LA-think.1 (called a speak-think or ST switch), which results in adding the proplets of the second proposition to the activated sequence (cf. 12.2.3).

Following the subsequent TS (think–speak) switch, the rule –NoP called by the rule package of –STOP is applied to the proplets of the second proposition, realizing the surface John.

12.5.4 REALIZING John OF THE SECOND PROPOSITION

1 –NoP   {2 –FVERB}

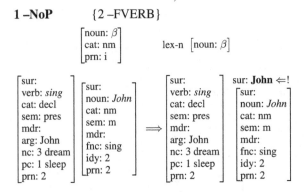

The LA-speak.1 derivation continues in synchronization with the LA-think.1 navigation until the test example, originally interpreted in the hearer mode, is coded back into an English surface in the speaker mode. See 9.2.2 for the corresponding production in the simplified format of Part II.

12.6 Summarizing the DBS.1 System

The DBS.1 system defined in the previous and the present chapter consists of the following components:

1. **Word form recognition** (Sects. 11.1 and 11.2) takes unanalyzed surfaces of natural language as input, and produces corresponding analyzed lexical entries (types, isolated proplets) as output. For simplicity, it is based here on a lookup from a full-form lexicon.
2. **LA-hear.1** (Sects. 11.3 and 11.4) takes the output of automatic word form recognition as input, and produces sets of connected proplets serving as the input sign's semantic representation.
3. **Word Bank** (Sect. 11.6) takes the output of LA-hear.1 as input, and stores it automatically by using the core values of the proplets as the key.
4. **LA-think.1** (Sect. 12.1) takes the proplets of the Word Bank as input, navigates autonomously through the content of the Word Bank, and activates the proplets traversed.
5. **LA-speak.1** (Sect. 12.3) matches the proplets activated by LA-think.1, and produces unanalyzed surfaces of natural language with the help of
6. **Word form production** (Sect. 12.3) which takes proplets as input and renders suitable surfaces as output. For simplicity it is based here on full-form patterns and lexicalization tables.

Once this cycle of communication has been implemented for the purposely simple DBS.1 system defined above, its empirical coverage may be increased as follows: (i) automatic word form recognition and production are extended to handle additional word forms, and (ii) the syntactic–semantic (hearer mode) and semantic–syntactic (speaker mode) parsing of LA-hear, LA-think, and LA-speak are extended to handle additional constructions.

These extensions require no more than revising the input and output lexica, the list of attributes, values, etc., in the preamble of LA-hear, and the rule systems of LA-hear, LA-think, and LA-speak. In other words, the basic software machine underlying DBS.1 is not affected by the process of upscaling from DBS.1 to DBS.2 and beyond.

Compared to a natural cognitive agent, DBS.1 is greatly simplified because (i) LA-think has not yet been extended to inferencing, (ii) the word form recognition of LA-hear and (iii) word form production of LA-speak do not handle modality-dependent signs, (iv) there is no contextual recognition and action, such that the context is limited to interacting with the language level alone, and consequently (v) the control structure of the system cannot be designed to interact with the agent's internal and external environment.

Nevertheless, the system represented by DBS.1 already provides the *interfaces* necessary for adding the missing functionalities. Inferencing can be defined in extended versions of LA-think; the current word form recognition and production can be replaced by morphology-based, modality-dependent variants; contextual input and output can be extended to include nonverbal cognition; and the control structure of the system can be upscaled from fixed schemata[5] to a sensible interaction with the task environment.

---

[5] DBS.1 does not provide for random choices, because its LA-grammars are deterministic. The kind of control structure needed for modeling cognitive agents based on Database Semantics is described in Hausser (2002a).

13. DBS.2: Hearer Mode

In this chapter, LA-hear.1 is extended to complex noun and verb phrases. As examples, we use a small text consisting of the following sentences:

The heavy old car hit a beautiful tree.

The car had been speeding.

A farmer gave the driver a lift.

The extension results in LA-hear.2, which handles the intrapropositional functor–argument structures presented in 6.2.1, 6.3.1, and 6.4.1.

The upscaling from LA-hear.1 to LA-hear.2 is based solely on changes in the linguistic definitions. Compared to LA-hear.1, LA-hear.2 has an extended lexicon, a revised preamble for an extended handling of agreement, and a revised rule system for handling the additional constructions of the test sequence.

13.1 Lexicon of LA-hear.2

The syntactic–semantic parsing of the new test sequence requires that each word form is provided with a lexical analysis. We extend the LA-hear.1 lexicon with complete paradigms of personal pronouns, determiners, nouns, main verbs, auxiliaries, and adjectives. Based on these lexical word forms, a general treatment of agreement between English determiners and nouns, between auxiliaries and nonfinite main verbs, and between the subject and the verb will be defined in 13.2.3.

13.1.1 PROPER NAMES

As in LA-hear.1 (cf. Sect. 11.2)

13.1.2 PERSONAL PRONOUNS[1]

sur: I	sur: you	sur: he	sur: she	sur: it	sur: we
noun: *I*	noun: *you*	noun: *he*	noun: *he*	noun: *he*	noun: *I*
cat: ns1	cat: pro2	cat: ns3	cat: ns3	cat: snp	cat: np-2
sem: sg	sem:	sem: sg m	sem: sg f	sem: sg	sem: pl
mdr:	mdr:	mdr:	mdr:	mdr:	mdr:
fnc:	fnc:	fnc:	fnc:	fnc:	fnc:
idy:	idy:	idy:	idy:	idy:	idy:
prn:	prn:	prn:	prn:	prn:	prn:

---

[1] For an explanation of the category segments of the personal pronouns, see FoCL'99, 17.2.1.

$$
\begin{bmatrix} \text{sur: they} \\ \text{noun: } he \\ \text{cat: np-2} \\ \text{sem: pl} \\ \text{mdr:} \\ \text{fnc:} \\ \text{idy:} \\ \text{prn:} \end{bmatrix}
\begin{bmatrix} \text{sur: me} \\ \text{noun: } I \\ \text{cat: obq} \\ \text{sem: sg} \\ \text{mdr:} \\ \text{fnc:} \\ \text{idy:} \\ \text{prn:} \end{bmatrix}
\begin{bmatrix} \text{sur: him} \\ \text{noun: } he \\ \text{cat: obq} \\ \text{sem: sg m} \\ \text{mdr:} \\ \text{fnc:} \\ \text{idy:} \\ \text{prn:} \end{bmatrix}
\begin{bmatrix} \text{sur: her} \\ \text{noun: } he \\ \text{cat: obq} \\ \text{sem: sg f} \\ \text{mdr:} \\ \text{fnc:} \\ \text{idy:} \\ \text{prn:} \end{bmatrix}
\begin{bmatrix} \text{sur: us} \\ \text{noun: } I \\ \text{cat: obq} \\ \text{sem: pl} \\ \text{mdr:} \\ \text{fnc:} \\ \text{idy:} \\ \text{prn:} \end{bmatrix}
\begin{bmatrix} \text{sur: them} \\ \text{noun: } he \\ \text{cat: obq} \\ \text{sem: pl} \\ \text{mdr:} \\ \text{fnc:} \\ \text{idy:} \\ \text{prn:} \end{bmatrix}
$$

13.1.3 DETERMINERS

$$
\begin{bmatrix} \text{sur: a} \\ \text{noun: n\_1} \\ \text{cat: sn}' \text{ snp} \\ \text{sem: indef sg} \\ \text{mdr:} \\ \text{fnc:} \\ \text{idy:} \\ \text{prn:} \end{bmatrix}
\begin{bmatrix} \text{sur: every} \\ \text{noun: n\_1} \\ \text{cat: sn}' \text{ snp} \\ \text{sem: pl exh} \\ \text{mdr:} \\ \text{fnc:} \\ \text{idy:} \\ \text{prn:} \end{bmatrix}
\begin{bmatrix} \text{sur: some} \\ \text{noun: n\_1} \\ \text{cat: pn}' \text{ pnp} \\ \text{sem: pl sel} \\ \text{mdr:} \\ \text{fnc:} \\ \text{idy:} \\ \text{prn:} \end{bmatrix}
\begin{bmatrix} \text{sur: all} \\ \text{noun: n\_1} \\ \text{cat: pn}' \text{ pnp} \\ \text{sem: pl exh} \\ \text{mdr:} \\ \text{fnc:} \\ \text{idy:} \\ \text{prn:} \end{bmatrix}
\begin{bmatrix} \text{sur: the} \\ \text{noun: n\_1} \\ \text{cat: nn}' \text{ np} \\ \text{sem: def} \\ \text{mdr:} \\ \text{fnc:} \\ \text{idy:} \\ \text{prn:} \end{bmatrix}
$$

13.1.4 NOUNS

$$
\begin{bmatrix} \text{sur: car} \\ \text{noun: } car \\ \text{cat: sn} \\ \text{sem: sg} \\ \text{mdr:} \\ \text{fnc:} \\ \text{idy:} \\ \text{prn:} \end{bmatrix}
\begin{bmatrix} \text{sur: cars} \\ \text{noun: } car \\ \text{cat: pn} \\ \text{sem: pl} \\ \text{mdr:} \\ \text{fnc:} \\ \text{idy:} \\ \text{prn:} \end{bmatrix}
\begin{bmatrix} \text{sur: driver} \\ \text{noun: } driver \\ \text{cat: sn} \\ \text{sem: sg} \\ \text{mdr:} \\ \text{fnc:} \\ \text{idy:} \\ \text{prn:} \end{bmatrix}
\begin{bmatrix} \text{sur: drivers} \\ \text{noun: } driver \\ \text{cat: pn} \\ \text{sem: pl} \\ \text{mdr:} \\ \text{fnc:} \\ \text{idy:} \\ \text{prn:} \end{bmatrix}
\begin{bmatrix} \text{sur: farmer} \\ \text{noun: } farmer \\ \text{cat: sn} \\ \text{sem: sg} \\ \text{mdr:} \\ \text{fnc:} \\ \text{idy:} \\ \text{prn:} \end{bmatrix}
\begin{bmatrix} \text{sur: farmers} \\ \text{noun: } farmer \\ \text{cat: pn} \\ \text{sem: pl} \\ \text{mdr:} \\ \text{fnc:} \\ \text{idy:} \\ \text{prn:} \end{bmatrix}
$$

$$
\begin{bmatrix} \text{sur: lift} \\ \text{noun: } lift \\ \text{cat: sn} \\ \text{sem: sg} \\ \text{mdr:} \\ \text{fnc:} \\ \text{idy:} \\ \text{prn:} \end{bmatrix}
\begin{bmatrix} \text{sur: lifts} \\ \text{noun: } lift \\ \text{cat: pn} \\ \text{sem: pl} \\ \text{mdr:} \\ \text{fnc:} \\ \text{idy:} \\ \text{prn:} \end{bmatrix}
\begin{bmatrix} \text{sur: tree} \\ \text{noun: } tree \\ \text{cat: sn} \\ \text{sem: sg} \\ \text{mdr:} \\ \text{fnc:} \\ \text{idy:} \\ \text{prn:} \end{bmatrix}
\begin{bmatrix} \text{sur: trees} \\ \text{noun: } tree \\ \text{cat: pn} \\ \text{sem: pl} \\ \text{mdr:} \\ \text{fnc:} \\ \text{idy:} \\ \text{prn:} \end{bmatrix}
$$

The feature structures of proper names, personal pronouns, determiners, and nouns share the same attributes. They differ mainly in the value of their core attribute noun. In proper names, the core value is a name marker, in pronouns a pointer,[2] in nouns a concept, and in determiners a substitution value to be replaced by a concept.[3]

The values of the cat attribute specify combinatorial properties of a word form, such as agreement and valency. A list of all cat values, including those of verbs and adjectives, is provided in 13.1.13. The values of the sem attribute characterize semantic properties of a word form, such as natural gender or tense. A list of all sem values is

---

[2] For simplicity, the distinction between the indexicals of first-, second-, and third-person is represented by the core values *I*, *you*, and *he*, regardless of case, number, or gender.

[3] The different kinds of core values correspond to the different kinds of signs, which in turn have different mechanisms of reference (cf. 2.6.4–2.6.7). These are implemented in the pragmatics of Database Semantics. The theory of signs presumed here is presented in FoCL'99, Chap. 6.

provided in 13.1.14. For a detailed analysis of complex nouns and verbs in English, see FoCL'99, Sects. 17.1–17.4.

13.1.5 MAIN VERBS, ONE-PLACE

1 *Third-person singular present tense*: as in LA-hear.1 (cf. Sect. 11.2).

2 *Non-third-person singular present tense*

$$
\begin{bmatrix}
\text{sur: sleep} \\
\text{verb: } sleep \\
\text{cat: n-s3}' \text{ v} \\
\text{sem: pres} \\
\text{mdr:} \\
\text{arg:} \\
\text{nc:} \\
\text{pc:} \\
\text{prn:}
\end{bmatrix}
\begin{bmatrix}
\text{sur: sing} \\
\text{verb: } sing \\
\text{cat: n-s3}' \text{ v} \\
\text{sem: pres} \\
\text{mdr:} \\
\text{arg:} \\
\text{nc:} \\
\text{pc:} \\
\text{prn:}
\end{bmatrix}
\begin{bmatrix}
\text{sur: dream} \\
\text{verb: } dream \\
\text{cat: n-s3}' \text{ v} \\
\text{sem: pres} \\
\text{mdr:} \\
\text{arg:} \\
\text{nc:} \\
\text{pc:} \\
\text{prn:}
\end{bmatrix}
\begin{bmatrix}
\text{sur: speed} \\
\text{verb: } speed \\
\text{cat: n-s3}' \text{ v} \\
\text{sem: pres} \\
\text{mdr:} \\
\text{arg:} \\
\text{nc:} \\
\text{pc:} \\
\text{prn:}
\end{bmatrix}
$$

3 *Past tense – past participle*

$$
\begin{bmatrix}
\text{sur: slept} \\
\text{verb: } sleep \\
\text{cat: n}' \text{ v} \\
\text{sem: past/perf} \\
\text{mdr:} \\
\text{arg:} \\
\text{nc:} \\
\text{pc:} \\
\text{prn:}
\end{bmatrix}
\begin{bmatrix}
\text{sur: sang} \\
\text{verb: } sing \\
\text{cat: n}' \text{ v} \\
\text{sem: past} \\
\text{mdr:} \\
\text{arg:} \\
\text{nc:} \\
\text{pc:} \\
\text{prn:}
\end{bmatrix}
\begin{bmatrix}
\text{sur: dreamt} \\
\text{verb: } dream \\
\text{cat: n}' \text{ v} \\
\text{sem: past/perf} \\
\text{mdr:} \\
\text{arg:} \\
\text{nc:} \\
\text{pc:} \\
\text{prn:}
\end{bmatrix}
\begin{bmatrix}
\text{sur: speeded} \\
\text{verb: } speed \\
\text{cat: n}' \text{ v} \\
\text{sem: past/perf} \\
\text{mdr:} \\
\text{arg:} \\
\text{nc:} \\
\text{pc:} \\
\text{prn:}
\end{bmatrix}
$$

4 *Separate past participle*

$$
\begin{bmatrix}
\text{sur: sung} \\
\text{verb: } sing \\
\text{cat: hv} \\
\text{sem: perf} \\
\text{mdr:} \\
\text{arg:} \\
\text{nc:} \\
\text{pc:} \\
\text{prn:}
\end{bmatrix}
$$

5 *Present participle*

$$
\begin{bmatrix}
\text{sur: sleeping} \\
\text{verb: } sleep \\
\text{cat: be} \\
\text{sem: prog} \\
\text{mdr:} \\
\text{arg:} \\
\text{nc:} \\
\text{pc:} \\
\text{prn:}
\end{bmatrix}
\begin{bmatrix}
\text{sur: singing} \\
\text{verb: } sing \\
\text{cat: be} \\
\text{sem: prog} \\
\text{mdr:} \\
\text{arg:} \\
\text{nc:} \\
\text{pc:} \\
\text{prn:}
\end{bmatrix}
\begin{bmatrix}
\text{sur: dreaming} \\
\text{verb: } dream \\
\text{cat: be} \\
\text{sem: prog} \\
\text{mdr:} \\
\text{arg:} \\
\text{nc:} \\
\text{pc:} \\
\text{prn:}
\end{bmatrix}
\begin{bmatrix}
\text{sur: speeding} \\
\text{verb: } speed \\
\text{cat: be} \\
\text{sem: prog} \\
\text{mdr:} \\
\text{arg:} \\
\text{nc:} \\
\text{pc:} \\
\text{prn:}
\end{bmatrix}
$$

The proplets in 13.1.5, 1–5 differ mainly in the values of their sur and verb attributes. In accordance with Surface Compositionality, homonymous past tense and past participle forms are treated as one lexical entry (cf. 13.1.5, 3). If past tense and past participle have different surfaces, as in sang versus sung, this is reflected in the values of their sem attributes and the cat attribute of the past participle (compare 3 and 4).

With additional valency positions in the cat attribute, the analysis of one-place verbs extends to two- and three-place verbs.

13.1.6 MAIN VERBS, TWO-PLACE

1 *Third-person singular present tense*

$$
\begin{bmatrix}
\text{sur: hits} \\
\text{verb: } hit \\
\text{cat: ns3}' \text{ a}' \text{ v} \\
\text{sem: pres} \\
\text{mdr:} \\
\text{arg:} \\
\text{nc:} \\
\text{pc:} \\
\text{prn:}
\end{bmatrix}
\begin{bmatrix}
\text{sur: knows} \\
\text{verb: } know \\
\text{cat: ns3}' \text{ a}' \text{ v} \\
\text{sem: pres} \\
\text{mdr:} \\
\text{arg:} \\
\text{nc:} \\
\text{pc:} \\
\text{prn:}
\end{bmatrix}
$$

2 *Non-third-person singular present tense*

$$
\begin{bmatrix}
\text{sur: hit} \\
\text{verb: } hit \\
\text{cat: n-s3}' \text{ a}' \text{ v} \\
\text{sem: pres} \\
\text{mdr:} \\
\text{arg:} \\
\text{nc:} \\
\text{pc:} \\
\text{prn:}
\end{bmatrix}
\begin{bmatrix}
\text{sur: know} \\
\text{verb: } know \\
\text{cat: n-s3}' \text{ a}' \text{ v} \\
\text{sem: pres} \\
\text{mdr:} \\
\text{arg:} \\
\text{nc:} \\
\text{pc:} \\
\text{prn:}
\end{bmatrix}
$$

3 *Past tense/past participle*

$$
\begin{bmatrix}
\text{sur: hit} \\
\text{verb: } hit \\
\text{cat: n}' \text{ a}' \text{ v} \\
\text{sem: past/perf} \\
\text{mdr:} \\
\text{arg:} \\
\text{nc:} \\
\text{pc:} \\
\text{prn:}
\end{bmatrix}
\begin{bmatrix}
\text{sur: knew} \\
\text{verb: } know \\
\text{cat: n}' \text{ a}' \text{ v} \\
\text{sem: past} \\
\text{mdr:} \\
\text{arg:} \\
\text{nc:} \\
\text{pc:} \\
\text{prn:}
\end{bmatrix}
$$

4 *Separate past participle*

$$
\begin{bmatrix}
\text{sur: known} \\
\text{verb: } know \\
\text{cat: a}' \text{ hv} \\
\text{sem: perf} \\
\text{mdr:} \\
\text{arg:} \\
\text{nc:} \\
\text{pc:} \\
\text{prn:}
\end{bmatrix}
$$

5 *Present participle*

$$
\begin{bmatrix}
\text{sur: hitting} \\
\text{verb: } hit \\
\text{cat: a}'\text{ be} \\
\text{sem: prog} \\
\text{mdr:} \\
\text{arg:} \\
\text{nc:} \\
\text{pc:} \\
\text{prn:}
\end{bmatrix}
\begin{bmatrix}
\text{sur: knowing} \\
\text{verb: } know \\
\text{cat: a}'\text{ be} \\
\text{sem: prog} \\
\text{mdr:} \\
\text{arg:} \\
\text{nc:} \\
\text{pc:} \\
\text{prn:}
\end{bmatrix}
$$

13.1.7 FORMS OF A THREE-PLACE MAIN VERB

$$
\begin{bmatrix}
\text{sur: give} \\
\text{verb: } give \\
\text{cat: n-s3}'\text{ d}'\text{ a}'\text{ v} \\
\text{sem: pres} \\
\text{mdr:} \\
\text{arg:} \\
\text{nc:} \\
\text{pc:} \\
\text{prn:}
\end{bmatrix}
\begin{bmatrix}
\text{sur: gives} \\
\text{verb: } give \\
\text{cat: ns3}'\text{ d}'\text{ a}'\text{ v} \\
\text{sem: pres} \\
\text{mdr:} \\
\text{arg:} \\
\text{nc:} \\
\text{pc:} \\
\text{prn:}
\end{bmatrix}
\begin{bmatrix}
\text{sur: gave} \\
\text{verb: } give \\
\text{cat: n}'\text{ d}'\text{ a}'\text{ v} \\
\text{sem: past} \\
\text{mdr:} \\
\text{arg:} \\
\text{nc:} \\
\text{pc:} \\
\text{prn:}
\end{bmatrix}
\begin{bmatrix}
\text{sur: given} \\
\text{verb: } give \\
\text{cat: d}'\text{ a}'\text{ hv} \\
\text{sem: perf} \\
\text{mdr:} \\
\text{arg:} \\
\text{nc:} \\
\text{pc:} \\
\text{prn:}
\end{bmatrix}
\begin{bmatrix}
\text{sur: giving} \\
\text{verb: } give \\
\text{cat: d}'\text{ a}'\text{ be} \\
\text{sem: prog} \\
\text{mdr:} \\
\text{arg:} \\
\text{nc:} \\
\text{pc:} \\
\text{prn:}
\end{bmatrix}
$$

Next, consider the lexical definition of the auxiliaries be, have, and do. Their feature structures have the same attributes as the main verbs.

13.1.8 FORMS OF THE AUXILIARY be

$$
\begin{bmatrix}
\text{sur: am} \\
\text{verb: v\_1} \\
\text{cat: ns1}'\text{ be}'\text{ v} \\
\text{sem: be\_pres} \\
\text{mdr:} \\
\text{arg:} \\
\text{nc:} \\
\text{pc:} \\
\text{prn:}
\end{bmatrix}
\begin{bmatrix}
\text{sur: ain't} \\
\text{verb: v\_1} \\
\text{cat: ns13}'\text{ be}'\text{ v} \\
\text{sem: be\_pres neg} \\
\text{mdr:} \\
\text{arg:} \\
\text{nc:} \\
\text{pc:} \\
\text{prn:}
\end{bmatrix}
\begin{bmatrix}
\text{sur: is} \\
\text{verb: v\_1} \\
\text{cat: ns3}'\text{ be}'\text{ v} \\
\text{sem: be\_pres} \\
\text{mdr:} \\
\text{arg:} \\
\text{nc:} \\
\text{pc:} \\
\text{prn:}
\end{bmatrix}
\begin{bmatrix}
\text{sur: isn't} \\
\text{verb: v\_1} \\
\text{cat: ns3}'\text{ be}'\text{ v} \\
\text{sem: be\_pres neg} \\
\text{mdr:} \\
\text{arg:} \\
\text{nc:} \\
\text{pc:} \\
\text{prn:}
\end{bmatrix}
$$

$$
\begin{bmatrix}
\text{sur: are} \\
\text{verb: v\_1} \\
\text{cat: n-s13}'\text{ be}'\text{ v} \\
\text{sem: be\_pres} \\
\text{mdr:} \\
\text{arg:} \\
\text{nc:} \\
\text{pc:} \\
\text{prn:}
\end{bmatrix}
\begin{bmatrix}
\text{sur: aren't} \\
\text{verb: v\_1} \\
\text{cat: n-s13}'\text{ be}'\text{ v} \\
\text{sem: be\_pres neg} \\
\text{mdr:} \\
\text{arg:} \\
\text{nc:} \\
\text{pc:} \\
\text{prn:}
\end{bmatrix}
\begin{bmatrix}
\text{sur: was} \\
\text{verb: v\_1} \\
\text{cat: ns13}'\text{ be}'\text{ v} \\
\text{sem: be\_past} \\
\text{mdr:} \\
\text{arg:} \\
\text{nc:} \\
\text{pc:} \\
\text{prn:}
\end{bmatrix}
\begin{bmatrix}
\text{sur: wasn't} \\
\text{verb: v\_1} \\
\text{cat: ns13}'\text{ be}'\text{ v} \\
\text{sem: be\_past neg} \\
\text{mdr:} \\
\text{arg:} \\
\text{nc:} \\
\text{pc:} \\
\text{prn:}
\end{bmatrix}
$$

$$
\begin{bmatrix}
\text{sur: were} \\
\text{verb: v\_1} \\
\text{cat: n-s13}'\text{ be}'\text{ v} \\
\text{sem: be\_past} \\
\text{mdr:} \\
\text{arg:} \\
\text{nc:} \\
\text{pc:} \\
\text{prn:}
\end{bmatrix}
\begin{bmatrix}
\text{sur: weren't} \\
\text{verb: v\_1} \\
\text{cat: n-s13}'\text{ be}'\text{ v} \\
\text{sem: be\_past neg} \\
\text{mdr:} \\
\text{arg:} \\
\text{nc:} \\
\text{pc:} \\
\text{prn:}
\end{bmatrix}
\begin{bmatrix}
\text{sur: been} \\
\text{verb: v\_1} \\
\text{cat: be}'\text{ hv} \\
\text{sem: be\_perf} \\
\text{mdr:} \\
\text{arg:} \\
\text{nc:} \\
\text{pc:} \\
\text{prn:}
\end{bmatrix}
\begin{bmatrix}
\text{sur: being} \\
\text{verb: v\_1} \\
\text{cat: be}'\text{ be} \\
\text{sem: be\_prog} \\
\text{mdr:} \\
\text{arg:} \\
\text{nc:} \\
\text{pc:} \\
\text{prn:}
\end{bmatrix}
$$

13.1.9 FORMS OF THE AUXILIARY have

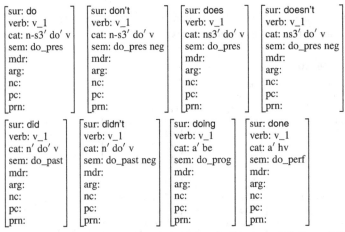

$$
\begin{bmatrix}
\text{sur: have} \\
\text{verb: v\_1} \\
\text{cat: n-s3}' \text{ hv}' \text{ v} \\
\text{sem: hv\_pres} \\
\text{mdr:} \\
\text{arg:} \\
\text{nc:} \\
\text{pc:} \\
\text{prn:}
\end{bmatrix}
\begin{bmatrix}
\text{sur: haven't} \\
\text{verb: v\_1} \\
\text{cat: n-s3}' \text{ hv}' \text{ v} \\
\text{sem: hv\_pres neg} \\
\text{mdr:} \\
\text{arg:} \\
\text{nc:} \\
\text{pc:} \\
\text{prn:}
\end{bmatrix}
\begin{bmatrix}
\text{sur: has} \\
\text{verb: v\_1} \\
\text{cat: s3}' \text{ hv}' \text{ v} \\
\text{sem: hv\_pres} \\
\text{mdr:} \\
\text{arg:} \\
\text{nc:} \\
\text{pc:} \\
\text{prn:}
\end{bmatrix}
\begin{bmatrix}
\text{sur: hasn't} \\
\text{verb: v\_1} \\
\text{cat: s3}' \text{ hv}' \text{ v} \\
\text{sem: hv\_pres neg} \\
\text{mdr:} \\
\text{arg:} \\
\text{nc:} \\
\text{pc:} \\
\text{prn:}
\end{bmatrix}
$$

$$
\begin{bmatrix}
\text{sur: had} \\
\text{verb: v\_1} \\
\text{cat: n}' \text{ hv}' \text{ v} \\
\text{sem: hv\_past} \\
\text{mdr:} \\
\text{arg:} \\
\text{nc:} \\
\text{pc:} \\
\text{prn:}
\end{bmatrix}
\begin{bmatrix}
\text{sur: hadn't} \\
\text{verb: v\_1} \\
\text{cat: n}' \text{ hv}' \text{ v} \\
\text{sem: hv\_past neg} \\
\text{mdr:} \\
\text{arg:} \\
\text{nc:} \\
\text{pc:} \\
\text{prn:}
\end{bmatrix}
\begin{bmatrix}
\text{sur: having} \\
\text{verb: v\_1} \\
\text{cat: be}' \text{ hv} \\
\text{sem: hv\_prog} \\
\text{mdr:} \\
\text{arg:} \\
\text{nc:} \\
\text{pc:} \\
\text{prn:}
\end{bmatrix}
$$

13.1.10 FORMS OF THE AUXILIARY do

$$
\begin{bmatrix}
\text{sur: do} \\
\text{verb: v\_1} \\
\text{cat: n-s3}' \text{ do}' \text{ v} \\
\text{sem: do\_pres} \\
\text{mdr:} \\
\text{arg:} \\
\text{nc:} \\
\text{pc:} \\
\text{prn:}
\end{bmatrix}
\begin{bmatrix}
\text{sur: don't} \\
\text{verb: v\_1} \\
\text{cat: n-s3}' \text{ do}' \text{ v} \\
\text{sem: do\_pres neg} \\
\text{mdr:} \\
\text{arg:} \\
\text{nc:} \\
\text{pc:} \\
\text{prn:}
\end{bmatrix}
\begin{bmatrix}
\text{sur: does} \\
\text{verb: v\_1} \\
\text{cat: ns3}' \text{ do}' \text{ v} \\
\text{sem: do\_pres} \\
\text{mdr:} \\
\text{arg:} \\
\text{nc:} \\
\text{pc:} \\
\text{prn:}
\end{bmatrix}
\begin{bmatrix}
\text{sur: doesn't} \\
\text{verb: v\_1} \\
\text{cat: ns3}' \text{ do}' \text{ v} \\
\text{sem: do\_pres neg} \\
\text{mdr:} \\
\text{arg:} \\
\text{nc:} \\
\text{pc:} \\
\text{prn:}
\end{bmatrix}
$$

$$
\begin{bmatrix}
\text{sur: did} \\
\text{verb: v\_1} \\
\text{cat: n}' \text{ do}' \text{ v} \\
\text{sem: do\_past} \\
\text{mdr:} \\
\text{arg:} \\
\text{nc:} \\
\text{pc:} \\
\text{prn:}
\end{bmatrix}
\begin{bmatrix}
\text{sur: didn't} \\
\text{verb: v\_1} \\
\text{cat: n}' \text{ do}' \text{ v} \\
\text{sem: do\_past neg} \\
\text{mdr:} \\
\text{arg:} \\
\text{nc:} \\
\text{pc:} \\
\text{prn:}
\end{bmatrix}
\begin{bmatrix}
\text{sur: doing} \\
\text{verb: v\_1} \\
\text{cat: a}' \text{ be} \\
\text{sem: do\_prog} \\
\text{mdr:} \\
\text{arg:} \\
\text{nc:} \\
\text{pc:} \\
\text{prn:}
\end{bmatrix}
\begin{bmatrix}
\text{sur: done} \\
\text{verb: v\_1} \\
\text{cat: a}' \text{ hv} \\
\text{sem: do\_perf} \\
\text{mdr:} \\
\text{arg:} \\
\text{nc:} \\
\text{pc:} \\
\text{prn:}
\end{bmatrix}
$$

Finally, consider the lexical definition of adjectives (cf. Sect. 6.3). Adjectives have the cat value adn when used as adnominal modifiers, and adv when used as adverbial modifiers.

13.1.11 FORMS OF ADNOMINALS

$$
\begin{bmatrix}
\text{sur: beautiful} \\
\text{adj: } \textit{beautiful} \\
\text{cat: adn} \\
\text{sem:} \\
\text{mdr: B} \\
\text{mdd:} \\
\text{idy: B} \\
\text{prn:}
\end{bmatrix}
\begin{bmatrix}
\text{sur: heavy} \\
\text{adj: } \textit{heavy} \\
\text{cat: adn} \\
\text{sem:} \\
\text{mdr: B} \\
\text{mdd:} \\
\text{idy: B} \\
\text{prn:}
\end{bmatrix}
\begin{bmatrix}
\text{sur: heavier} \\
\text{adj: } \textit{heavy} \\
\text{cat: adn} \\
\text{sem: comp} \\
\text{mdr: B} \\
\text{mdd:} \\
\text{idy: B} \\
\text{prn:}
\end{bmatrix}
\begin{bmatrix}
\text{sur: heaviest} \\
\text{adj: } \textit{heavy} \\
\text{cat: adn} \\
\text{sem: SUP} \\
\text{mdr: B} \\
\text{mdd:} \\
\text{idy: B} \\
\text{prn:}
\end{bmatrix}
\begin{bmatrix}
\text{sur: old} \\
\text{adj: } \textit{old} \\
\text{cat: adn} \\
\text{sem:} \\
\text{mdr: B} \\
\text{mdd:} \\
\text{idy: B} \\
\text{prn:}
\end{bmatrix}
\begin{bmatrix}
\text{sur: older} \\
\text{adj: } \textit{old} \\
\text{cat: adn} \\
\text{sem: comp} \\
\text{mdr: B} \\
\text{mdd:} \\
\text{idy: B} \\
\text{prn:}
\end{bmatrix}
$$

$$\begin{bmatrix} \text{sur: oldest} \\ \text{adj: } old \\ \text{cat: adn} \\ \text{sem: sup} \\ \text{mdr: B} \\ \text{mdd:} \\ \text{idy: B} \\ \text{prn:} \end{bmatrix}$$

13.1.12 FORMS OF ADVERBIALS

$$\begin{bmatrix} \text{sur: heavily} \\ \text{adj: } heavy \\ \text{cat: adv} \\ \text{sem:} \\ \text{mdr: B} \\ \text{mdd:} \\ \text{idy: B} \\ \text{prn:} \end{bmatrix} \quad \begin{bmatrix} \text{sur: beautifully} \\ \text{adj: } beautiful \\ \text{cat: adv} \\ \text{sem:} \\ \text{mdr: B} \\ \text{mdd:} \\ \text{idy: B} \\ \text{prn:} \end{bmatrix}$$

The present chapter describes adnominal uses of elementary adjectives. Chap. 15 describes adverbial uses and prepositional phrases (complex adjectives). The value B (for "blocked") is explained in 15.1.1 ff.

In LA-hear.2, the attribute cat may take the following category segments as values:

13.1.13 LEXICAL VALUES OF THE cat ATTRIBUTE

decl = declarative sentence
v = verb, unmarked for sentence mood
ns1 = nominative singular first-person filler
pro2 = nominative and oblique second-person singular and plural filler
ns3 = nominative singular third-person filler
np-2 = nominative plural minus second-person filler (i.e. plural first- and third-person)
obq = noun phrase filler in the oblique (nonnominative) case
snp = third-person singular noun phrase filler unmarked for case
pnp = third-person plural noun phrase filler unmarked for case
np = third-person noun phrase filler unmarked for case and number
nm = proper name
sn = singular noun valency filler
pn = plural noun valency filler
nn = noun filler unmarked for number
be = valency filler indicating a present participle
hv = valency filler indicating a past participle
adn = adnominal
n' = valency position for verb unmarked for sentence mood
n' = valency position for nominative of any person or number
$n\text{-}s3'$ = valency position for nominative minus singular third-person
$ns1'$ = valency position for nominative singular first-person
$ns3'$ = valency position for nominative singular third-person
$ns13'$ = valency position for nominative singular first- and third-person
$n\text{-}s13'$ = valency position for nominative minus singular first- and third-person
a' = accusative valency position for oblique noun phrase
d' = dative valency position for oblique noun phrase
sn' = valency position for third-person singular noun
pn' = valency position for third-person plural noun
be' = valency position for a present participle

hv′   = valency position for a past participle
do′   = valency position for an infinitive

The attribute **sem** may take the following values:

13.1.14 LEXICAL VALUES OF THE **sem** ATTRIBUTE

f   = femininum
m   = masculinum
sg   = singular
pl   = plural
def   = definite
indef   = indefinite
sel   = selective
exh   = exhaustive
pres   = present tense
past   = past tense
perf   = past participle
prog   = progressive
be_pres   = present tense of auxiliary be
hv_pres   = present tense of auxiliary have
do_pres   = present tense of auxiliary do, including modals
be_past   = past tense of auxiliary be
hv_past   = past tense of auxiliary have
do_past   = past tense of auxiliary do, including modals
be_perf   = past participle of auxiliary be
hv_perf   = past participle of auxiliary have
do_perf   = past participle of auxiliary do
neg   = negated
comp   = comparative
sup   = superlative

Many attributes of lexical types (isolated proplets) which currently have the value NIL (represented by space) will be filled during syntactic–semantic parsing (hearer mode).

13.2 Preamble and Definition of LA-hear.2

The rules of LA-hear.2 define patterns which are based on restricted variables. As in LA-hear.1, these variables, their restrictions, and their agreement relations are defined in the preamble of LA-hear.2.

13.2.1 LIST OF VARIABLES

α, β, γ = for a core value
SM   = sentence mood
VT   = verb type filler
VT′   = verb type valency position
NP   = noun phrase filler
NP′   = noun phrase valency position
OBQ   = oblique noun phrase filler
OBQ′   = oblique noun phrase valency position
N   = noun filler
N′   = noun valency position
AUX   = auxiliary filler
AUX′   = auxiliary valency position

X, Y, Z = .?.?.?.? (arbitrary sequence up to length 4)
N_*n*   = simultaneous substitution variable for a noun
V_*n*   = simultaneous substitution variable for a verb

13.2.2 RESTRICTIONS OF VARIABLES

SM ϵ {decl}
VT ϵ {v}
VT$'$ ϵ {v$'$}
NP ϵ {pro2, nm, ns1, ns3, np-2, snp, pnp, pn, np, obq}
NP$'$ ϵ {n$'$, n-s3$'$, ns1$'$, ns3$'$, ns13$'$, n-s13$'$, d$'$, a$'$}
OBQ ϵ {snp, pnp, pn, obq}
OBQ$'$ ϵ {d$'$, a$'$}
N ϵ {sn, pn}
N$'$ ϵ {nn$'$, sn$'$, pn$'$}
AUX ϵ {do, hv, be}
AUX$'$ ϵ {do$'$, hv$'$, be$'$}
N_*n* ϵ {n_1, n_2, n_3, ... }
V_*n* ϵ {v_1, v_2, v_3, ... }

13.2.3 AGREEMENT CONDITIONS

if NP = ns1,   then NP$'$ ϵ {n$'$, n-s3$'$, ns1$'$, ns13$'$}
if NP = pro2,   then NP$'$ ϵ {n$'$, n-s3$'$, n-s13$'$, d$'$, a$'$}
if NP = ns3,   then NP$'$ ϵ {n$'$, ns3$'$, ns13$'$}
if NP = np-2,   then NP$'$ ϵ {n$'$, n-s3$'$, n-s13$'$}
if NP ϵ {nm, snp}, then NP$'$ ϵ {n$'$, ns3$'$, ns13$'$, d$'$, a$'$}
if NP = pnp,   then NP$'$ ϵ {n$'$, n-s3$'$, n-s13$'$, d$'$, a$'$}
if NP = np,   then NP$'$ ϵ {n$'$, ns3$'$, ns13$'$, n-s3$'$, n-s13$'$, d$'$, a$'$}
if NP = obq,   then NP$'$ ϵ {d$'$, a$'$}
if AUX$'$ = do$'$, then AUX = n-s3$'$
if AUX$'$ = hv$'$, then AUX ϵ {hv, n$'$}
if AUX$'$ = be$'$, then AUX = be
if N$'$ = nn$'$, then N ϵ {nn, sn, pn}
if N$'$= sn$'$,   then N ϵ {nn, sn}
if N$'$= pn$'$,   then N ϵ {nn, pn}

Note that the agreement conditions for verbal valency specify the positions for a filler, while those for auxiliaries and determiners specify the fillers for a position.

The infinitive form of the verb equals that of the non-third-person singular present tense, e.g. give as in I, you, we, they give, John wanted to give, and John didn't give. To avoid a lexical ambiguity, agreement between the auxiliary do and its nonfinite verb uses the non-third-person singular present tense form as the infinitive. Similarly, to avoid an ambiguity between the past tense and the past participle of most verbs, e.g. learned (regular) and slept (irregular), agreement between the auxiliary have and its nonfinite verb is specified for hv (separate past participle form), or if not available – as indicated by the sem-value past/perf (e.g. 13.1.5, 3) – for n$'$.

The states and rules of LA-hear.2 extend LA-hear.1 by (i) revising the start state, (ii) adding the new rules DET+ADN (determiner plus adnominal), DET+NN (determiner plus noun), FV+NP (finite verb plus noun phrase), and AUX+NFV (auxiliary plus nonfinite verb), and (iii) modifying the existing rules NOM+FV and IP+START by extending their rule packages and loosening the *nw* pattern of IP+START. The rule S+IP and the final state ST_F remain unchanged. The LA-hear.1 sample continues to be parsed by LA-hear.2.

13.2.4 FORMAL DEFINITION OF LA-HEAR.2

$ST_S =_{def} \{ \ (\ [\text{cat: X}] \ \{1 \text{ DET+ADN, 2 DET+NN, 3 NOM+FV}\}) \ \}$

DET+ADN   {4 DET+ADN, 5 DET+NN}

$$\begin{bmatrix} \text{noun: N\_}n \\ \text{cat: N' X} \\ \text{mdr:} \\ \text{idy:} \end{bmatrix} \begin{bmatrix} \text{adj: } \alpha \\ \text{cat: adn} \\ \text{mdd:} \end{bmatrix} \quad \begin{array}{l} \text{acopy } \alpha \text{ ss.mdr} \\ \text{ecopy ss.noun nw.mdd} \\ \text{acopy ss.idy nw.mdd} \\ \text{copy}_{ss} \text{ copy}_{nw} \end{array}$$

DET+NN   {6 NOM+FV, 7 FV+NP, 8 S+IP}

$$\begin{bmatrix} \text{noun: N\_}n \\ \text{cat: N' X} \\ \text{sem: Y} \end{bmatrix} \begin{bmatrix} \text{noun: } \alpha \\ \text{cat: N} \\ \text{sem: Z} \end{bmatrix} \quad \begin{array}{l} \text{delete N' ss.cat} \\ \text{acopy nw.sem ss.sem} \\ \text{replace } \alpha \text{ N\_}n \\ \text{copy}_{ss} \end{array}$$

NOM+FV   {9 FV+NP, 10 AUX+NFV, 11 S+IP}

$$\begin{bmatrix} \text{noun: } \alpha \\ \text{cat: NP} \\ \text{fnc:} \\ \text{prn: k} \end{bmatrix} \begin{bmatrix} \text{verb: } \beta \\ \text{cat: NP' X VT} \\ \text{arg:} \\ \text{nc:} \\ \text{pc:} \end{bmatrix} \quad \begin{array}{l} \text{delete NP' nw.cat} \\ \text{acopy } \alpha \text{ nw.arg} \\ \text{ecopy } \beta \text{ ss.fnc} \\ \text{ecopy PC nw.pc} \\ \text{acopy PCV nw.pc} \\ \text{set } \beta \text{ NCV} \\ \text{copy}_{ss} \text{ copy}_{nw} \end{array}$$

FV+NP   {12 DET+ADN, 13 DET+NN, 14 FV+NP, 15 S+IP}

$$\begin{bmatrix} \text{verb: } \beta \\ \text{cat: NP' X VT} \\ \text{arg:} \end{bmatrix} \begin{bmatrix} \text{noun: } \alpha \\ \text{cat: Y NP} \\ \text{fnc:} \end{bmatrix} \quad \begin{array}{l} \text{delete NP' ss.cat} \\ \text{acopy } \alpha \text{ ss.arg} \\ \text{ecopy } \beta \text{ nw.fnc} \\ \text{copy}_{ss} \text{copy}_{nw} \end{array}$$

AUX+NFV   {16 AUX+NFV, 17 FV+NP 18 S+IP}

$$\begin{bmatrix} \text{verb: V\_}n \\ \text{cat: AUX' V} \\ \text{sem: X} \end{bmatrix} \begin{bmatrix} \text{verb: } \alpha \\ \text{cat: Y AUX} \\ \text{sem: Z} \end{bmatrix} \quad \begin{array}{l} \text{replace Y AUX'} \\ \text{acopy nw.sem ss.sem} \\ \text{replace } \alpha \text{ V\_}n \\ \text{copy}_{ss} \end{array}$$

S+IP   { 19 IP+START}

$$\begin{bmatrix} \text{verb: } \alpha \\ \text{cat: VT} \\ \text{prn: k} \end{bmatrix} [\text{cat: VT' SM}] \quad \begin{array}{l} \text{replace SM VT} \\ \text{set k ss.PC} \\ \text{set } \alpha \text{ PCV} \\ \text{copy}_{ss} \end{array}$$

IP+START   {1 DET+ADN, 2 DET+NN, 3 NOM+FV}

$$\begin{bmatrix} \text{verb: } \alpha \\ \text{cat: SM} \\ \text{nc:} \end{bmatrix} \begin{bmatrix} \text{noun: } \beta \\ \text{cat: X NP} \\ \text{prn: k} \end{bmatrix} \quad \begin{array}{l} \text{increment nw.prn} \\ \text{ecopy k ss.nc} \\ \text{acopy 'NCV' ss.nc} \\ \text{copy}_{ss} \text{ copy}_{nw} \end{array}$$

$ST_F =_{def} \{ \ (\ [\text{cat: decl}] \ \text{rp } _{S+IP})\}$

LA-hear.2 defines the following finite-state transition network (cf. FoCL'99, p. 333):

13.2.5 FINITE-STATE TRANSITION NETWORK OF LA-HEAR.2

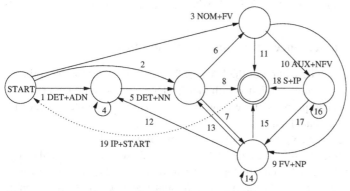

Almost every rule is called from several different rule packages. For example, DET+ADN is called from the start state, from DET+ADN itself, as well as from FV+NP and from IP+START. It is for this reason that the numbering of rule names in rule packages was introduced in LA-hear.1 (cf. 11.5.5 following). The grammatical perplexity (cf. FoCL'99, p. 339) of LA-hear.2 is 19 : 7 = 2.71, that is, 2.71 attempted rule applications on average per composition.

The sequence of word forms in the test sample of LA-hear.2 is added by the following rule applications:

13.2.6 SEQUENCE OF RULE APPLICATIONS IN DERIVATIONS 5.4, 5.5, AND 5.6

	1.1 The
1 DET+ADN	1.2 heavy
4 DET+ADN	1.3 old
5 DET+NN	1.4 car
6 NOM+FV	1.5 hit
9 FV+NP	1.6 a
12 DET+ADN	1.7 beautiful
5 DET+NN	1.8 tree
8 S+IP	1.9 .
19 IP+START	2.1 The
2 DET+NN	2.2 car
6 NOM+FV	2.3 had
10 AUX+NFV	2.4 been
16 AUX+NFV	2.5 speeding
18 S+IP	2.6 .
19 IP+START	3.1 The
2 DET+NN	3.2 farmer
6 NOM+FV	3.3 gave
9 FV+NP	3.5 the
13 DET+NN	3.6 driver
7 FV+NP	3.7 a
13 DET+NN	3.8 lift
8 S+IP	3.4 .

This way of characterizing a derivation is similar to 11.5.5, but the transitions through the finite-state transition network 13.2.5 of LA-hear.2 are much more varied.

13.3 Interpreting a Sentence with Complex Noun Phrases

Next, let us analyze each derivation of the LA-hear.2 test examples using the verbose format, which shows the rules explicitly with their patterns and operations in combination with the associated proplets at the language level. The first sample sentence is The heavy old car hit a beautiful tree.

The start state pattern [cat: X] trivially matches the lexical type of the first word form, here the, thus activating the rule package {1 DET+ADN, 2 DET+NN, 3 NOM+FV} of ST_S of LA-hear.2. After lexical lookup of the next word heavy, the three rules of the start package are applied to the proplets *the* and *heavy*. Of these rules, only DET+ADN matches the input:

13.3.1 COMBINING The AND heavy

1 DET+ADN   {4 DET+ADN, 5 DET+NN}

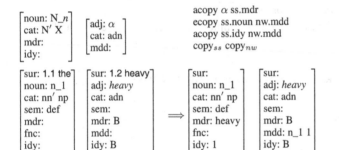

Prior to the application of the operations, proposition and identity numbers are supplied by the control structure. The first operation copies the value *heavy* of the variable α into the ss.mdr attribute. The second operation copies the value n_1 of the ss.noun attribute into the nw.mdd attribute. The third operation adds the identity number of the *ss* to the nw.mdd attribute. Both input proplets are retained in the output.

After the application of DET+ADN, the category of the determiner proplet *the* remains unchanged: it is nn' np.[4] The mdd slot of the adnominal proplet *heavy* now contains the substitution value n_1. The rule package of DET+ADN differs from the previous rule package of the start state.

The rule package {4 DET+ADN, 5 DET+NN} is applied to the resulting sentence start and the new next word old. Of the rules in this rule package, only DET+ADN matches the input. In other words, the same rule applies again (modifier recursion):

---

[4] The definite article of English can be singular or a plural, depending on the noun. The resulting complication in the handling of agreement is easily programmed, but not formalized here for simplicity.

13.3.2 COMBINING The heavy AND old

4 DET+ADN   {4 DET+ADN, 5 DET+NN}

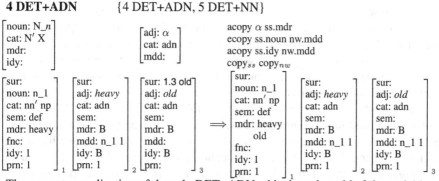

The current reapplication of the rule DET+ADN adds the value *old* of the variable α to the value of the ss.mdr attribute and copies the substitution value n_1 of the ss.noun attribute into the nw.mdd attribute. All three input proplets are copied into the output.

After the application of DET+ADN, its rule package {4 DET+ADN, 5 DET+NN} is applied to the resulting sentence start and the new next word *car*. Of the rules in this rule package, this time DET+NN matches the input.

13.3.3 COMBINING The heavy old AND car

5 DET+NN   { 6 NOM+FV, 7 FV+NP, 8 S+IP}

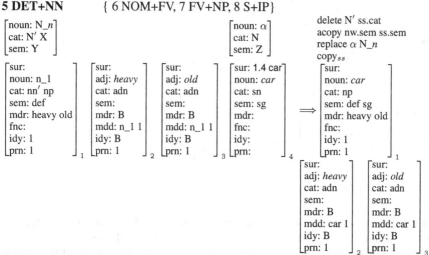

The first operation, delete N′ ss.cat, cancels the nominal valency in the determiner. The second operation, acopy nw.sem ss.sem, adds the value sg to the sem attribute of the determiner. The third operation, replace α N_*n*, replaces all occurrences of the substitution value n_1 by the value of the noun attribute of the next word. In this way all the relevant values of the next word are copied into the sentence start proplets and the next word proplet is discarded ($copy_{ss}$, but not $copy_{nw}$).

In other words, the noun proplet (content word) is *absorbed* into the determiner (function word), which becomes the nominal proplet in the sense of representing a content word. This is different from the handling of punctuation signs (cf. 11.4.2), where the full stop proplet (function word) is absorbed into the verb (content word). During language production, determiners and full stops are *precipitated* from nominal and verbal proplets, respectively.[5]

After the application of the rule DET+NN, its rule package {6 NOM+FV, 7 FV+NP, 8 S+IP} is applied to the resulting sentence start and the next word hit. Of the rules in this package, only the patterns of NOM+FV match the input. This rule has been inherited unchanged from LA-hear.1. Its application here resembles 11.5.1: Because the current input sentence is at the beginning of the sample text, the operations for establishing extrapropositional relations with a preceding sentence apply vacuously. The operations in question are ecopy PC nw.pc, acopy PCV nw.pc (use of a previous forward loading) and set β NCV (current backward loading). See 11.5.4, 13.4.3, and 13.5.3 for noninitial, nonvacuous applications of these operations.

13.3.4 COMBINING The heavy old car AND hit

6 NOM+FV   {9 FV+NP, 10 AUX+NFV, 11 S+IP}

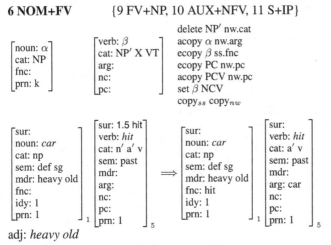

adj: *heavy old*

For reasons of space, only the relevant sentence start proplet is shown. The proplets omitted are listed underneath the sentence start proplet (here adj: *heavy old*).

The next derivation step is the application of the rule package {9 FV+NP, 10 AUX+NFV, 11 S+IP} of NOM+FV to the resulting sentence start and the next word, the determiner a. Of the rules in this rule package, only the patterns of the rule FV+NP

---

[5] The precipitation of determiners is illustrated in 14.4.2, 14.4.7, 14.5.2, 14.6.2, 14.6.5, and 14.6.7. The precipitation of full stops is shown in 12.5.3, 14.4.10, 14.5.7, and 14.6.9.

match the input. Note that the cat pattern Y NP′ of the *nw* matches determiners as well as names and pronouns (because the variable Y does not require a non-NIL value).

13.3.5 COMBINING The heavy old car hit AND a

9 FV+NP   {12 DET+ADN, 13 DET+NN, 14 FV+NP, 15 S+IP}

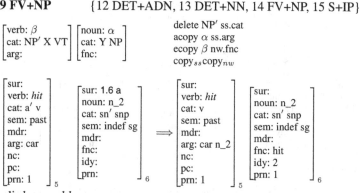

adj: *heavy old*, noun: *car*

The interesting point of this and the following two rule applications is the handling of a complex noun phrase in postverbal position. Whereas a complex noun in preverbal position is put together first and then combined with the verb, a complex noun in postverbal position is added to the verb incrementally, as required by a strictly time-linear derivation order.[6]

Despite the apparent asymmetry in the derivation of complex noun phrases in pre- versus postverbal position, the rule DET+ADN applies alike in either case, and similarly for DET+NN. This is due to the use of the substitution variable N_*n* in these rules and the corresponding value n_1/n_2/...,[7] which serves as a placeholder in the noun attribute of the determiner (e.g. 13.3.1), the arg attribute of the verb (e.g. 13.3.5), and the mdd attribute of adnominal adjectives (e.g. 13.3.2). When the content word is finally added, all occurences of the value n_*n* are substituted globally.[8]

After the application of FV+NP, its rule package {12 DET+ADN, 13 DET+NN, 14 FV+NP, 15 S+IP} is applied to the set of proplets comprising the resulting sentence start and the next word beautiful. Of these rules, only the patterns of the rule DET+ADN match the input.

---

[6] See FoCL'99, Sect. 17.1, pp. 321–326, for further discussion from a syntactic point of view. The analogous case for pre- and postverbal noun coordination is discussed above in connection with 8.2.3.

[7] Each time a lexical placeholder value is introduced into a derivation, it is automatically incremented (e.g. n_1 in 13.3.1 and n_2 in 13.3.5).

[8] The case of determiner–adnominal–noun combinations is illustrated in 13.3.1–13.3.3 (preverbal) and 13.3.5–13.3.7 (postverbal), that of determiner–noun combinations in 13.4.2 (preverbal), 13.5.2 (preverbal), 13.5.5 (postverbal), and 13.5.7 (postverbal). The same technique is used in auxiliary-verb combinations, as illustrated in 13.4.5.

13.3.6 COMBINING The heavy old car hit a AND beautiful

12 DET+ADN   {4 DET+ADN, 5 DET+NN}

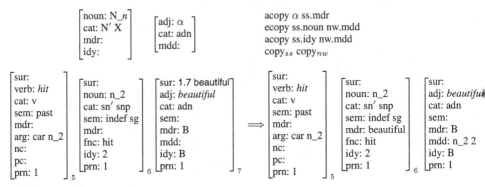

adj: *heavy old*, noun: *car*

Given that there are several adjective proplets in the input, namely *heavy, old*, and *beautiful*, there seems to be a choice as to which adjective proplet should be matched by the nw-pattern. However, because the matching proplet of an nw-pattern must be provided by lexical lookup, the only candidate for matching the nw-pattern is the adn proplet *beautiful*.

A similar choice seems to arise when applying the ss-pattern, due to the presence of two noun proplets, namely *car* and the indefinite article. However, because the ss-pattern of DET+ADN explicitly specifies the variable N_n as the *ss* core value, it can only match the definite article (cf. variable restrictions 13.2.2).

The next step in the derivation is the application of the rule package {4 DET+ADN, 5 DET+NN} of DET+ADN to the resulting sentence start and the next word tree. Of the rules in this rule package, only the patterns of the rule DET+NN match the input.

13.3.7 COMBINING The heavy old car hit a beautiful AND tree

5 DET+NN   {6 NOM+FV, 7 FV+NP, 8 S+IP}

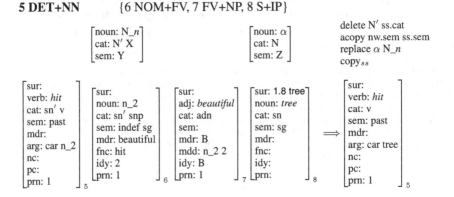

$$
\begin{bmatrix}
\text{adj: } heavy\ old \\
\text{noun: } car
\end{bmatrix}
\quad
\begin{bmatrix}
\text{sur:} \\
\text{noun: } tree \\
\text{cat: snp} \\
\text{sem: indef sg} \\
\text{mdr: beautiful} \\
\text{fnc: hit} \\
\text{idy: 2} \\
\text{prn: 1}
\end{bmatrix}_6
\quad
\begin{bmatrix}
\text{sur:} \\
\text{adj: } beautiful \\
\text{cat: adn} \\
\text{sem:} \\
\text{mdr: B} \\
\text{mdd: tree 2} \\
\text{idy: B} \\
\text{prn: 1}
\end{bmatrix}_7
$$

The substitution value n_2 in the verb proplet *hit*, the determiner proplet *a*, and the adjective proplet *beautiful* is globally replaced by the value tree (replace α N_n). As in 13.3.3, the noun proplet is absorbed into the determiner. The postverbal noun proplet *tree* has the same kind of structure as the preverbal proplet *car*, and the postverbal adjective proplet *beautiful* has the same structure as the preverbal proplets *heavy* and *old*.

Finally, the "." (punctuation) is added by the rule S+IP (cf. rule package of DET+NN).

13.3.8 COMBINING The heavy old car hit a beautiful tree AND .

8 S+IP   { 19 IP+START }

$$
\begin{bmatrix}
\text{verb: } \alpha \\
\text{cat: VT} \\
\text{prn: k}
\end{bmatrix}
\qquad
\begin{bmatrix}
\text{cat: VT}'\ \text{SM}
\end{bmatrix}
\qquad
\begin{array}{l}
\text{replace SM VT} \\
\text{set k PC} \\
\text{set } \alpha \text{ PCV} \\
\text{copy}_{ss}
\end{array}
$$

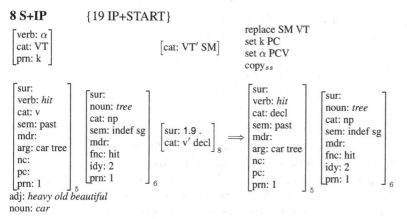

$$
\begin{bmatrix}
\text{sur:} \\
\text{verb: } hit \\
\text{cat: v} \\
\text{sem: past} \\
\text{mdr:} \\
\text{arg: car tree} \\
\text{nc:} \\
\text{pc:} \\
\text{prn: 1}
\end{bmatrix}_5
\begin{bmatrix}
\text{sur:} \\
\text{noun: } tree \\
\text{cat: np} \\
\text{sem: indef sg} \\
\text{mdr:} \\
\text{fnc: hit} \\
\text{idy: 2} \\
\text{prn: 1}
\end{bmatrix}_6
\begin{bmatrix}
\text{sur: 1.9 .} \\
\text{cat: v}'\ \text{decl}
\end{bmatrix}_8
\Longrightarrow
\begin{bmatrix}
\text{sur:} \\
\text{verb: } hit \\
\text{cat: decl} \\
\text{sem: past} \\
\text{mdr:} \\
\text{arg: car tree} \\
\text{nc:} \\
\text{pc:} \\
\text{prn: 1}
\end{bmatrix}_5
\begin{bmatrix}
\text{sur:} \\
\text{noun: } tree \\
\text{cat: np} \\
\text{sem: indef sg} \\
\text{mdr:} \\
\text{fnc: hit} \\
\text{idy: 2} \\
\text{prn: 1}
\end{bmatrix}_6
$$

$$
\begin{bmatrix}
\text{adj: } heavy\ old\ beautiful \\
\text{noun: } car
\end{bmatrix}
$$

As in 11.5.2, the loading variables PC and PCV are assigned values, here PC = 1 and PCV = hit. The punctuation proplet is absorbed into the verb proplet (copy$_{ss}$).

The result of this derivation is the following set of proplets:

13.3.9 RESULT OF PARSING The heavy old car hit a beautiful tree.

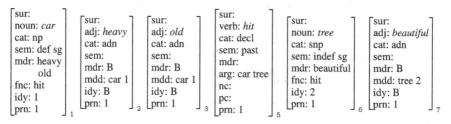

$$
\begin{bmatrix}
\text{sur:} \\
\text{noun: } car \\
\text{cat: np} \\
\text{sem: def sg} \\
\text{mdr: heavy} \\
\quad\quad\ old \\
\text{fnc: hit} \\
\text{idy: 1} \\
\text{prn: 1}
\end{bmatrix}_1
\begin{bmatrix}
\text{sur:} \\
\text{adj: } heavy \\
\text{cat: adn} \\
\text{sem:} \\
\text{mdr: B} \\
\text{mdd: car 1} \\
\text{idy: B} \\
\text{prn: 1}
\end{bmatrix}_2
\begin{bmatrix}
\text{sur:} \\
\text{adj: } old \\
\text{cat: adn} \\
\text{sem:} \\
\text{mdr: B} \\
\text{mdd: car 1} \\
\text{idy: B} \\
\text{prn: 1}
\end{bmatrix}_3
\begin{bmatrix}
\text{sur:} \\
\text{verb: } hit \\
\text{cat: decl} \\
\text{sem: past} \\
\text{mdr:} \\
\text{arg: car tree} \\
\text{nc:} \\
\text{pc:} \\
\text{prn: 1}
\end{bmatrix}_5
\begin{bmatrix}
\text{sur:} \\
\text{noun: } tree \\
\text{cat: snp} \\
\text{sem: indef sg} \\
\text{mdr: beautiful} \\
\text{fnc: hit} \\
\text{idy: 2} \\
\text{prn: 1}
\end{bmatrix}_6
\begin{bmatrix}
\text{sur:} \\
\text{adj: } beautiful \\
\text{cat: adn} \\
\text{sem:} \\
\text{mdr: B} \\
\text{mdd: tree 2} \\
\text{idy: B} \\
\text{prn: 1}
\end{bmatrix}_7
$$

These proplets are almost ready to be sorted into the hearer's Word Bank. It merely remains to be seen whether there follows another sentence. If this is the case, the verb proplet of the current sentence will have to be supplied with the proper nc values.

13.4 Interpreting a Sentence with a Complex Verb Phrase

The next sample sentence is The car had been speeding. It is connected to the first sample sentence by applying IP+START, which is called by S+IP (13.3.8). After lexical lookup of the next word the, IP+START applies as follows:

13.4.1 COMBINING The heavy old car hit a beautiful tree. AND The

19 IP+START   {1 DET+ADN, 2 DET+NN, 3 NOM+FV}

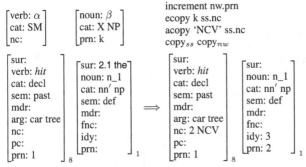

$$
\begin{bmatrix} \text{verb: } \alpha \\ \text{cat: SM} \\ \text{nc:} \end{bmatrix}
\begin{bmatrix} \text{noun: } \beta \\ \text{cat: X NP} \\ \text{prn: k} \end{bmatrix}
\begin{array}{l} \text{increment nw.prn} \\ \text{ecopy k ss.nc} \\ \text{acopy 'NCV' ss.nc} \\ \text{copy}_{ss}\ \text{copy}_{nw} \end{array}
$$

$$
\begin{bmatrix} \text{sur:} \\ \text{verb: } hit \\ \text{cat: decl} \\ \text{sem: past} \\ \text{mdr:} \\ \text{arg: car tree} \\ \text{nc:} \\ \text{pc:} \\ \text{prn: 1} \end{bmatrix}_8
\begin{bmatrix} \text{sur: 2.1 the} \\ \text{noun: n\_1} \\ \text{cat: nn}'\ \text{np} \\ \text{sem: def} \\ \text{mdr:} \\ \text{fnc:} \\ \text{idy:} \\ \text{prn:} \end{bmatrix}_1
\Longrightarrow
\begin{bmatrix} \text{sur:} \\ \text{verb: } hit \\ \text{cat: decl} \\ \text{sem: past} \\ \text{mdr:} \\ \text{arg: car tree} \\ \text{nc: 2 NCV} \\ \text{pc:} \\ \text{prn: 1} \end{bmatrix}_8
\begin{bmatrix} \text{sur:} \\ \text{noun: n\_1} \\ \text{cat: nn}'\ \text{np} \\ \text{sem: def} \\ \text{mdr:} \\ \text{fnc:} \\ \text{idy: 3} \\ \text{prn: 2} \end{bmatrix}_1
$$

This step is analogous to 11.5.3. The first operation increments the prn value of the nw. The second operation copies the prn value k = 2 of the *nw* into the nc slot of the ss. The third operation adds the variable name NCV to the nc slot of the *ss*.

After the application of IP+START, its rule package {1 DET+ADN, 2 DET+NN, 3 NOM+FV} is applied to the resulting sentence start and the next word car. Of these rules, only the patterns of the rule DET+NN match the input.

13.4.2 COMBINING The AND car

2 DET+NN   {6 NOM+FV, 7 FV+NP, 8 S+IP}

$$
\begin{bmatrix} \text{noun: N\_}n \\ \text{cat: N}'\ \text{X} \\ \text{sem: Y} \end{bmatrix}
\begin{bmatrix} \text{noun: } \alpha \\ \text{cat: N} \\ \text{sem: Z} \end{bmatrix}
\begin{array}{l} \text{delete N}'\ \text{ss.cat} \\ \text{acopy nw.sem ss.sem} \\ \text{replace } \alpha\ \text{N\_}n \\ \text{copy}_{ss} \end{array}
$$

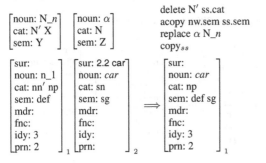

$$
\begin{bmatrix} \text{sur:} \\ \text{noun: n\_1} \\ \text{cat: nn}'\ \text{np} \\ \text{sem: def} \\ \text{mdr:} \\ \text{fnc:} \\ \text{idy: 3} \\ \text{prn: 2} \end{bmatrix}_1
\begin{bmatrix} \text{sur: 2.2 car} \\ \text{noun: } car \\ \text{cat: sn} \\ \text{sem: sg} \\ \text{mdr:} \\ \text{fnc:} \\ \text{idy:} \\ \text{prn:} \end{bmatrix}_2
\Longrightarrow
\begin{bmatrix} \text{sur:} \\ \text{noun: } car \\ \text{cat: np} \\ \text{sem: def sg} \\ \text{mdr:} \\ \text{fnc:} \\ \text{idy: 3} \\ \text{prn: 2} \end{bmatrix}_1
$$

This rule application shows the combination of the definite article and a noun without intervening adnominal adjectives (in contradistinction to the previous sample derivation). The noun proplet is absorbed into the determiner, including the sem value sg.[9]

After the application of DET+NN, its rule package {6 NOM+FV, 7 FV+NP, 8 S+IP} is applied to the resulting sentence start and the next word had. Of these rules, only the patterns of the rule NOM+FV match the input.

13.4.3 COMBINING The car AND had

6 NOM+FV   {9 FV+NP, 10 AUX+NFV, 11 S+IP}

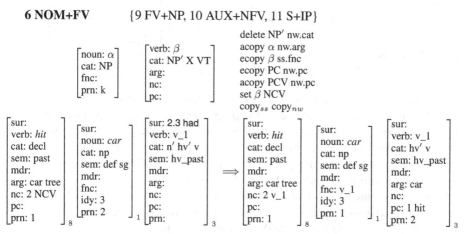

In this application of NOM+FV, the extrapropositional relations between the verbs of the first and second sentence are established. This involves the proplet *hit* of the previous sentence, which is why it is shown here at the language level.

Let us consider the rule operations one by one. The first, delete NP′ nw.cat, cancels the nominative valency position in had. The second, acopy α nw.arg, copies the value car of the *ss* attribute noun into the arg attribute of the *nw* proplet had. The third, ecopy β ss.fnc, copies the substitution value v_1 exclusively into the fnc attribute of the *ss* proplet *car*. The fourth, ecopy PC nw.pc copies the value 1, assigned in 13.3.8 to the loading variable PC, into the pc attribute of the auxiliary. The fifth, acopy PCV nw.pc, adds the value hit, assigned in 13.3.8 to the loading variable PCV (forward loading), in the pc attribute of the auxiliary. The sixth, set β NCV, provides the value v_1 to the loading variable NCV of the previous verb (backward loading). The last operations, copy$_{ss}$ and copy$_{nw}$, retain the *ss* and *nw* proplets in the output.

After the application of NOM+FV, its rule package {9 FV+NP, 10 AUX+NFV, 11 S+IP} is applied to the resulting sentence start and the next word been. Of these rules, only the patterns of the rule AUX+NFV match the input.

---

[9] To handle the agreement between a definite noun phrase subject and a present tense finite verb, either the agreement condition associated with the rule NOM+FV must refer to the sem slot of the definite noun phrase, or the rule DET+NN must modify the determiner cat value np into snp or pnp, depending on the cat value of the noun.

13.4.4 Combining The car had AND been

10 AUX+NFV   { 16 AUX+NFV, 17 FV+NP 18 S+IP }

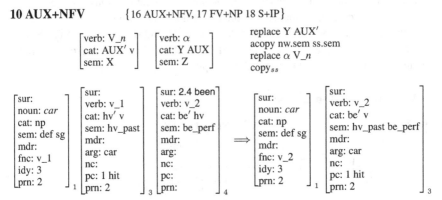

In this rule application, the finite auxiliary had absorbs the nonfinite auxiliary been. Thereby the substitution value v_2 of the proplet been replaces all occurrences of the substitution value v_1 (including that in the nc slot of the previous verb *hit*, cf. 13.4.3). The syntactic category of the auxiliary verb proplet is changed from hv′ v to be′ v, preparing the addition of a progressive form. The semantic effect is the addition of the value be_perf to the sem attribute of the auxiliary.

After the application of AUX+NFV, its rule package { 16 AUX+NFV, 17 FV+NP 18 S+IP} is applied to the resulting sentence start and the next word speeding. Of these rules, only the patterns of the rule AUX+NFV match the input.

13.4.5 Combining The car had been AND speeding

16 AUX+NFV   { 16 AUX+NFV, 17 FV+NP 18 S+IP }

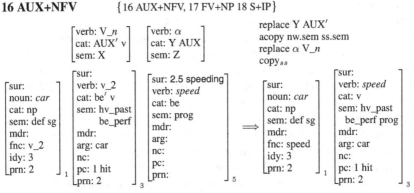

In the application of AUX+NFV, the nonfinite main verb speeding is absorbed into the proplet representing the complex auxiliary had been: The operation replace α V_n replaces all instances of the substitution value v_2 with the value speed – including the v_2 value in the nc slot of *hit* (cf. 13.4.3). In the previous two derivation steps, the values of the arg and pc attributes have been supplied incrementally to the auxiliary proplet and are already in place.

After the application of AUX+NFV, its rule package {16 AUX+NFV, 17 FV+NP 18 S+IP} is applied to the resulting sentence start and the next word "." (punctuation, full stop). Of these rules, only the patterns of the rule S+IP match the input.

13.4.6 COMBINING The car had been speeding AND .

18 S+IP   {19 IP+START}

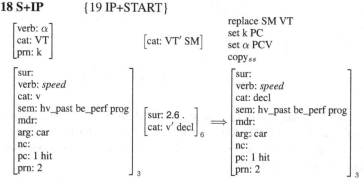

As in 11.5.2 and 13.3.8, the loading variables PC and PCV are assigned values, here PC = 2 and PCV = speed. The punctuation proplet is absorbed into the verb proplet (copy$_{ss}$). The derivation results in the following set of proplets:

13.4.7 RESULT OF PARSING The car had been speeding.

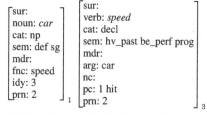

All function words, i.e. the, had, been, and . (full stop), have been absorbed into content word proplets, where they are reflected as sem and cat values. Extrapropositional pc relations to the previous sentence have been established. Also, values for the pc slot of the following verb have been assigned (forward loading).

13.5 Interpreting a Sentence with a Three-Place Verb

The third sample sentence is A farmer gave the driver a lift, illustrating the handling of a three-place verb. The continuation from the previous to the current sample sentence is again provided by the rule IP+START, which is the only rule in the rule package of S+IP (cf. 13.4.6):

13.5.1 COMBINING The car had been speeding. AND A

19 IP+START   { 1 DET+ADN, 2 DET+NN, 3 NOM+FV}

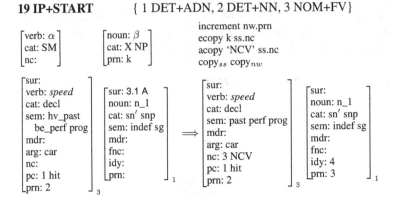

This rule application is analogous to that shown in 13.4.1. After the application of IP+START, its rule package {1 DET+ADN, 2 DET+NN, 3 NOM+FV} is applied to the resulting sentence start and the next word car. Of these rules, only the patterns of the rule DET+NN match the input.

13.5.2 COMBINING A AND farmer

2 DET+NN   {6 NOM+FV, 7 FV+NP, 8 S+IP}

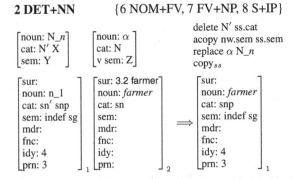

This rule application is analogous to 13.4.2. The difference between the definite article used in 13.4.2 and the indefinite article used here appears in the values def vs. indef in the respective sem attributes. For further discussion of the handling of determiners ("quantifiers") in Database Semantics, see Sect. 6.2.

After the application of DET+NN, its rule package {6 NOM+FV, 7 FV+NP, 8 S+IP} is applied to the resulting sentence start and the next word gave. Of these rules, only the patterns of the rule NOM+FV match the input.

13.5.3 COMBINING A farmer AND gave

6 NOM+FV   {9 FV+NP, 10 AUX+NFV, 11 S+IP}

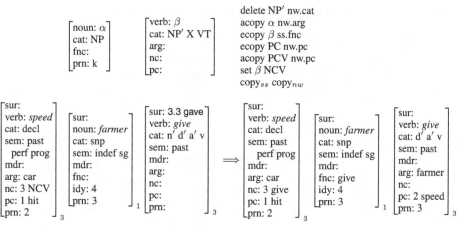

$$
\begin{bmatrix} \text{noun: } \alpha \\ \text{cat: NP} \\ \text{fnc:} \\ \text{prn: k} \end{bmatrix}
\begin{bmatrix} \text{verb: } \beta \\ \text{cat: NP}' \text{ X VT} \\ \text{arg:} \\ \text{nc:} \\ \text{pc:} \end{bmatrix}
\begin{array}{l} \text{delete NP}' \text{ nw.cat} \\ \text{acopy } \alpha \text{ nw.arg} \\ \text{ecopy } \beta \text{ ss.fnc} \\ \text{ecopy PC nw.pc} \\ \text{acopy PCV nw.pc} \\ \text{set } \beta \text{ NCV} \\ \text{copy}_{ss} \text{ copy}_{nw} \end{array}
$$

$$
\begin{bmatrix} \text{sur:} \\ \text{verb: } speed \\ \text{cat: decl} \\ \text{sem: past} \\ \quad \text{perf prog} \\ \text{mdr:} \\ \text{arg: car} \\ \text{nc: 3 NCV} \\ \text{pc: 1 hit} \\ \text{prn: 2} \end{bmatrix}_3
\begin{bmatrix} \text{sur:} \\ \text{noun: } farmer \\ \text{cat: snp} \\ \text{sem: indef sg} \\ \text{mdr:} \\ \text{fnc:} \\ \text{idy: 4} \\ \text{prn: 3} \end{bmatrix}_1
\begin{bmatrix} \text{sur: 3.3 gave} \\ \text{verb: } give \\ \text{cat: n}' \text{ d}' \text{ a}' \text{ v} \\ \text{sem: past} \\ \text{mdr:} \\ \text{arg:} \\ \text{nc:} \\ \text{pc:} \\ \text{prn:} \end{bmatrix}_3
\Longrightarrow
\begin{bmatrix} \text{sur:} \\ \text{verb: } speed \\ \text{cat: decl} \\ \text{sem: past} \\ \quad \text{perf prog} \\ \text{mdr:} \\ \text{arg: car} \\ \text{nc: 3 give} \\ \text{pc: 1 hit} \\ \text{prn: 2} \end{bmatrix}_3
\begin{bmatrix} \text{sur:} \\ \text{noun: } farmer \\ \text{cat: snp} \\ \text{sem: indef sg} \\ \text{mdr:} \\ \text{fnc: give} \\ \text{idy: 4} \\ \text{prn: 3} \end{bmatrix}_1
\begin{bmatrix} \text{sur:} \\ \text{verb: } give \\ \text{cat: d}' \text{ a}' \text{ v} \\ \text{sem: past} \\ \text{mdr:} \\ \text{arg: farmer} \\ \text{nc:} \\ \text{pc: 2 speed} \\ \text{prn: 3} \end{bmatrix}_3
$$

This rule application is analogous to 13.3.2, except that here the finite verb is a main verb rather than an auxiliary. The NCV variable of the previous verb proplet *speed* is supplied with the value give. Also, the pc slot of the current verb proplet *give* is supplied with the values of PC and PCV set in 13.4.6, i.e. 2 speed.

After the application of FV+NP, its rule package {9 FV+NP, 10 AUX+NFV, 11 S+IP} is applied to the resulting sentence start and the next word the. Of these rules, only the patterns of the rule FV+NP match the input.

13.5.4 COMBINING A farmer gave AND the

9 FV+NP   { 12 DET+ADN, 13 DET+NN, 14 FV+NP, 15 S+IP }

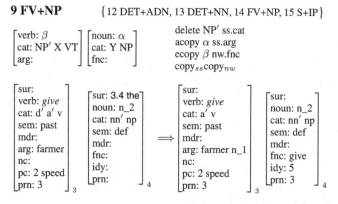

$$
\begin{bmatrix} \text{verb: } \beta \\ \text{cat: NP}' \text{ X VT} \\ \text{arg:} \end{bmatrix}
\begin{bmatrix} \text{noun: } \alpha \\ \text{cat: Y NP} \\ \text{fnc:} \end{bmatrix}
\begin{array}{l} \text{delete NP}' \text{ ss.cat} \\ \text{acopy } \alpha \text{ ss.arg} \\ \text{ecopy } \beta \text{ nw.fnc} \\ \text{copy}_{ss} \text{copy}_{nw} \end{array}
$$

$$
\begin{bmatrix} \text{sur:} \\ \text{verb: } give \\ \text{cat: d}' \text{ a}' \text{ v} \\ \text{sem: past} \\ \text{mdr:} \\ \text{arg: farmer} \\ \text{nc:} \\ \text{pc: 2 speed} \\ \text{prn: 3} \end{bmatrix}_3
\begin{bmatrix} \text{sur: 3.4 the} \\ \text{noun: n\_2} \\ \text{cat: nn}' \text{ np} \\ \text{sem: def} \\ \text{mdr:} \\ \text{fnc:} \\ \text{idy:} \\ \text{prn:} \end{bmatrix}_4
\Longrightarrow
\begin{bmatrix} \text{sur:} \\ \text{verb: } give \\ \text{cat: a}' \text{ v} \\ \text{sem: past} \\ \text{mdr:} \\ \text{arg: farmer n\_1} \\ \text{nc:} \\ \text{pc: 2 speed} \\ \text{prn: 3} \end{bmatrix}_3
\begin{bmatrix} \text{sur:} \\ \text{noun: n\_2} \\ \text{cat: nn}' \text{ np} \\ \text{sem: def} \\ \text{mdr:} \\ \text{fnc: give} \\ \text{idy: 5} \\ \text{prn: 3} \end{bmatrix}_4
$$

noun: *farmer*

In this rule application, the first oblique argument position d' is canceled in the cat attribute of the verb.

After the application of FV+NP, its rule package { 12 DET+ADN, 13 DET+NN, 14 FV+NP, 15 S+IP} is applied to the resulting sentence start and the next word driver. Of these rules, only the patterns of the rule DET+NN match the input.

13.5.5 COMBINING A farmer gave the AND driver

13 DET+NN   {6 NOM+FV, 7 FV+NP, 8 S+IP}

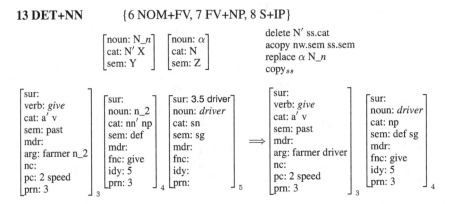

After the application of DET+NN, its rule package {6 NOM+FV, 7 FV+NP, 8 S+IP} is applied to the resulting sentence start and the next word **a**. Of these rules, only the patterns of the rule FV+NP match the input.

13.5.6 COMBINING A farmer gave the driver AND a

7 FV+NP   {12 DET+ADN, 13 DET+NN, 14 FV+NP, 15 S+IP}

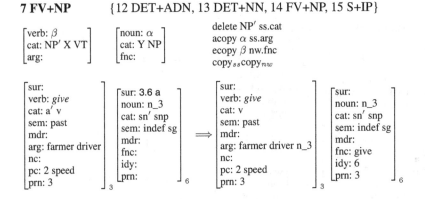

After the application of FV+NP, its rule package {12 DET+ADN, 13 DET+NN, 14 FV+NP, 15 S+IP} is applied to the resulting sentence start and the next word **lift**. Of these rules, only the patterns of the rule DET+NN match the input.

13.5.7 COMBINING A farmer gave the driver a AND lift

13 DET+NN   {6 NOM+FV, 7 FV+NP, 8 S+IP}

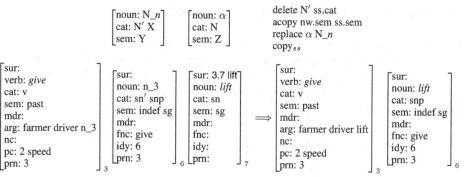

The derivation concludes with an application of S+IP, adding the punctuation sign:

13.5.8 COMBINING A farmer gave the driver a lift AND .

8 S+IP   { 19 IP+START}

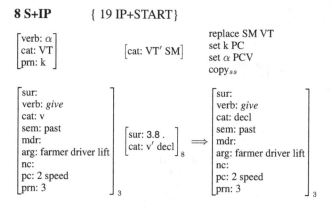

The derivation of the third test sentence results in the following set of proplets:

13.5.9 RESULT OF PARSING A farmer gave the driver a lift.

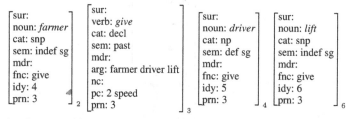

As the semantic representation of the last sentence in the sample text, the nc slot of the verb proplet *give* is empty. If the text were continued, the next rule to apply would be IP+START. It would fill the nc slot of the verb with the values 4 NCV.

13.6 Storing the Output of LA-hear.2 in a Word Bank

The hearer's final step of interpreting a text of natural language is the pragmatic interpretation. It begins quite simply by sorting the proplets derived into a Word Bank. This step uses the concepts of the proplets as the primary key and is completely automatic. The proplets of the sample sequence of LA-hear.2 derived above result in the following Word Bank.

13.6.1 SORTING PROPLETS OF LA-HEAR.2 SAMPLE INTO WORD BANK

owner records   *member records*
(isolated proplets)   (connected proplets)

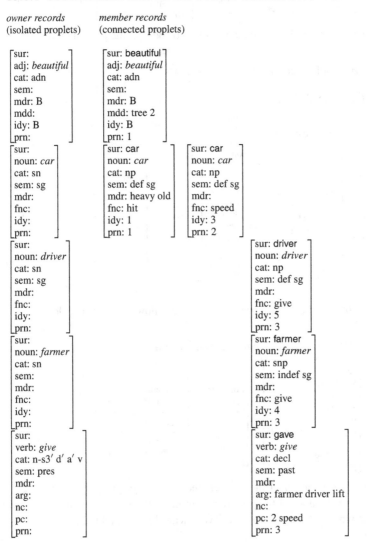

owner records   *member records*

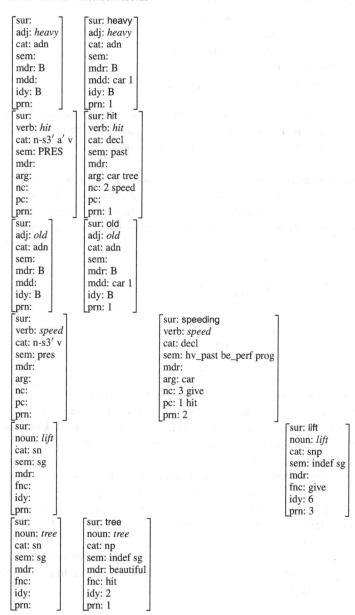

Once the proplets have been sorted into the Word Bank, the main task of language pragmatics is inferencing. Given the sample sequence of LA-hear.2, a human interpreter would readily agree:

that the occurrences of car in the first and the second sentence are *coreferential*,
that speeding probably *caused* the car to hit the tree,
that hitting the tree *damaged* the car,
that the event *attracted* the attention of the farmer,
that the driver *belonged* to the car,
that the farmer *helped* the driver,
etc.

These pragmatic inferences lead from the literal meaning of the sign (meaning$_1$), illustrated by the semantic representations 13.3.7, 13.4.7, and 13.5.9, to the utterance meaning[10] of the speaker (meaning$_2$). They constitute a major part of language understanding.[11]

Some pragmatic inferences could be easily implemented and are thus quite tempting. For example, in accordance with the treatment of coference in Chap. 10, the LA-hear.2 system has assigned different idy values to the two occurrences of car by default, as shown by the following token line, repeated from 13.6.1 for convenience:

isolated proplet   *connected proplets*

$$
\begin{bmatrix}
\text{sur: car} \\
\text{noun: } car \\
\text{cat: sn} \\
\text{sem: sg} \\
\text{mdr:} \\
\text{fnc:} \\
\text{idy:} \\
\text{prn:}
\end{bmatrix}
\begin{bmatrix}
\text{sur:} \\
\text{noun: } car \\
\text{cat: np} \\
\text{sem: def sg} \\
\text{mdr: heavy old} \\
\text{fnc: hit} \\
\text{idy: 1} \\
\text{prn: 1}
\end{bmatrix}
\begin{bmatrix}
\text{sur:} \\
\text{noun: } car \\
\text{cat: np} \\
\text{sem: def sg} \\
\text{mdr:} \\
\text{fnc: speed} \\
\text{idy: 3} \\
\text{prn: 2}
\end{bmatrix}
$$

It would be easy enough to extend the LA-think.pro grammar defined in 10.6.1 to assign extrasentential coreference by adjusting the idy numbers to be equal. This, however, would lead beyond the limits of the present chapter, which has the task of illustrating the establishment of the primary relations in terms of a surface compositional, time-linear syntactic–semantic derivation.

Extending the present system to a systematic pragmatic interpretation would require (i) that the episodic propositions in a Word Bank are complemented by absolute propositions coding world knowledge, (ii) that the episodic propositions are related to the spatio-temporal orientation system of the cognitive agent (robot), (iii) that the different sign kinds of symbol, indexical, and name are implemented as different reference mechanisms, etc. Database Semantics has been designed to include these structures, but for present purposes, hearer mode pragmatics is limited to sorting the proplets into the Word Bank.

---

[10] The distinction between meaning$_1$ and meaning$_2$ is defined in 2.6.1, and is discussed in FoCL'99, pp. 76, 77, 86, 108, and 500–503.

[11] In addition to inferencing, understanding – and not just language understanding – is based on *depictive* and *enactive imagery* (cf. MacWhinney 2005b). In Database Semantics, these aspects are handled in terms of the core values (cf. Sect. 5.6).

14. DBS.2: Speaker Mode

The production of coherent language presupposes coherent content in the speaker's database. The most reliable manner of acquiring content is direct observation. Thereby, the coherence of the content follows from the coherence of the external world.[1]

Another possibility to acquire content is the interpretation of natural language signs. Because such signs are produced by authors who may reorder and reconnect elements that are familiar from observation, content coded by the signs of a language may be incoherent.

Only agents capable of direct observation have the means to evaluate whether or not a given language-coded content is coherent, and to label it accordingly. This, however, requires autonomous context recognition and action, which are not yet available to us for technical reasons. It is therefore our responsibility as users to provide the current DBS.2 system with coherent content as a precondition for coherent language production.

14.1 Definition of LA-think.2

In the previous chapter, the test sequence The heavy old car hit a beautiful tree. The car had been speeding. A farmer gave the driver a lift., regarded as a coherent content, was automatically read into the Word Bank by LA-hear.2. Given this content, the construction of a complete cycle of communication next requires the definition of a navigation parser for its activation. This navigation parser is **LA-think.2**.

LA-think.2 is based on the same software mechanism as LA-think.1. LA-think.2 inherits the rules V_N_V and V_V_V from LA-think.1, though in modified form, and adds three more, namely V_N_N, N_A_N, and N_A_V. The additional rules are needed for traversing adnominal modifier proplets, abbreviated as A.

14.1.1 FORMAL DEFINITION OF **LA-think.2**

LX: episodic proplets in the Word Bank 13.6.1

$$ST_S =_{def} \{([verb: \alpha] \{1 \ V\_N\_V, 2 \ V\_N\_N \})\}$$

---

[1] See FoCL'99, Sect. 23.4, pp. 464–466, for further discussion.

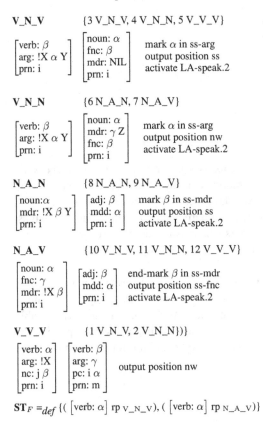

V_N_V   {3 V_N_V, 4 V_N_N, 5 V_V_V}

$$\begin{bmatrix} \text{verb: } \beta \\ \text{arg: } !X \ \alpha \ Y \\ \text{prn: } i \end{bmatrix} \quad \begin{bmatrix} \text{noun: } \alpha \\ \text{fnc: } \beta \\ \text{mdr: NIL} \\ \text{prn: } i \end{bmatrix} \quad \begin{array}{l} \text{mark } \alpha \text{ in ss-arg} \\ \text{output position ss} \\ \text{activate LA-speak.2} \end{array}$$

V_N_N   {6 N_A_N, 7 N_A_V}

$$\begin{bmatrix} \text{verb: } \beta \\ \text{arg: } !X \ \alpha \ Y \\ \text{prn: } i \end{bmatrix} \quad \begin{bmatrix} \text{noun: } \alpha \\ \text{mdr: } \gamma \ Z \\ \text{fnc: } \beta \\ \text{prn: } i \end{bmatrix} \quad \begin{array}{l} \text{mark } \alpha \text{ in ss-arg} \\ \text{output position nw} \\ \text{activate LA-speak.2} \end{array}$$

N_A_N   {8 N_A_N, 9 N_A_V}

$$\begin{bmatrix} \text{noun:} \alpha \\ \text{mdr: } !X \ \beta \ Y \\ \text{prn: } i \end{bmatrix} \quad \begin{bmatrix} \text{adj: } \beta \\ \text{mdd: } \alpha \\ \text{prn: } i \end{bmatrix} \quad \begin{array}{l} \text{mark } \beta \text{ in ss-mdr} \\ \text{output position ss} \\ \text{activate LA-speak.2} \end{array}$$

N_A_V   {10 V_N_V, 11 V_N_N, 12 V_V_V}

$$\begin{bmatrix} \text{noun: } \alpha \\ \text{fnc: } \gamma \\ \text{mdr: } !X \ \beta \\ \text{prn: } i \end{bmatrix} \quad \begin{bmatrix} \text{adj: } \beta \\ \text{mdd: } \alpha \\ \text{prn: } i \end{bmatrix} \quad \begin{array}{l} \text{end-mark } \beta \text{ in ss-mdr} \\ \text{output position ss-fnc} \\ \text{activate LA-speak.2} \end{array}$$

V_V_V   {1 V_N_V, 2 V_N_N})}

$$\begin{bmatrix} \text{verb: } \alpha \\ \text{arg: } !X \\ \text{nc: } j \ \beta \\ \text{prn: } i \end{bmatrix} \quad \begin{bmatrix} \text{verb: } \beta \\ \text{arg: } \gamma \\ \text{pc: } i \ \alpha \\ \text{prn: } m \end{bmatrix} \quad \text{output position nw}$$

$\mathbf{ST}_F =_{def} \{(\begin{bmatrix} \text{verb: } \alpha \end{bmatrix} \text{ rp } _{\text{V\_N\_v}}), (\begin{bmatrix} \text{verb: } \alpha \end{bmatrix} \text{ rp } _{\text{N\_A\_v}})\}$

LA-think.2 adds to the operations introduced by LA-think.1 two more, called mark and end-mark. Mark adds the sign ! before a value (e.g., !β in N_A_N), while end-mark adds it behind (e.g., β! in N_A_V). The mark operations prevent repeated intrapropositional traversal of the same argument (cf. FoCL'99, p. 464, Tracking Principles). In V_N_V and V_N_N, the traversed nominal filler is marked in the V proplet. In N_A_N and N_A_V the traversed adnominal modifier is marked in the N proplet.

The rule V_N_V traverses a noun without modifiers (mdr: NIL) and returns to the V of the current proposition. By letting V_N_V call itself (see rule package), the original LA-think.1 rule is expanded to verbs with more than one argument, for example, *see* (two-place) and *give* (three-place).

The new rules V_N_N, N_A_N, and N_A_V are for adding an unlimited number of intraphrasal adnominals (modifier recursion), such as *girl_hot_cool_beautiful_young _honest_rich_modest_intelligent_charming_witty_sweet_erudite_endearing*, etc. The rule V_N_N traverses nouns with at least one adnominal modifier (mdr: γ Z). From its output position N, the navigation continues with the rules N_A_N or N_A_V.

The rule N_A_N is used for nouns with several adnominal modifiers. The application traverses the A and returns to the N, whereby the modifier traversed is marked in the mdr attribute of the N. The rule N_A_V is for traversing the last adnominal modifier: The application traverses the A and returns to the V of the current proposition, whereby the modifier traversed is end-marked in the mdr attribute of the N.

The rule V_V_V provides an extrapropositional continuation, based on the nc or pc values of the current V proplet. The LA-think.2 version of this rule requires that all arguments of the current verb have been traversed, as indicated by the value !X of its arg attribute.

The rules and rule packages form the following finite-state transition network:

14.1.2 FINITE-STATE TRANSITION NETWORK OF **LA-think.2**

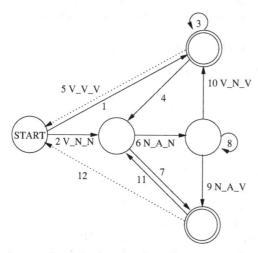

This schema reflects the fact that the rule packages of LA-think.2 each contain several rules – in contradistinction to LA-think.1, where each rule package contains only a single rule (cf. 12.1.1 and 12.1.2).

Furthermore, the rule packages of LA-think.2 contain potentially *input-compatible rules*,[2] for example, V_N_V and V_N_N. This results in the possibility of alternative continuations. For example, with a slight loosening of the rule patterns, the system could traverse the content of the first sample sentence only partially as in The car hit the tree, omitting the adnominal modifiers heavy, old, and beautiful. For present purposes, however, it is most instructive to illustrate a complete traversal of the Word Bank content.

Before explaining the formal details of LA-think.2, let us characterize its functioning schematically. As in Sect. 12.1, we proceed in two steps. First, the rule names, a sample navigation illustrating an application of each rule, and the rule packages for

---

[2] For further discussion of this notion see FoCL'99, Sect. 11.3, pp. 209–212.

the continuations are shown (cf. 14.1.3). Then the proplet sequence underlying the DBS.2 test sentences is derived by giving the rule name, the associated navigation, and the resulting sequence of activated V, N, and A proplets (cf. 14.1.4).

14.1.3 SCHEMATIC DESCRIPTION OF **LA-think.2**:

rule name	sample navigation	rule package
V_N_V	give_girl_give	{V_N_V, V_N_N, V_V_V}
V_N_N	give_girl_girl	{N_A_N, N_A_V}
N_A_N	girl_beautiful_girl	{N_A_N, N_A_V}
N_A_V	girl_young_give	{V_N_V, V_N_N, V_V_V}
V_V_V	give_ read_read	{V_N_V, V_N_N}

The above examples show the operations of rules in isolation. Next consider the operations applying in the sequence which underlies the DBS.2 test sentences:

14.1.4 DERIVING A VNAANA VN VNNN SEQUENCE

rule name	navigation steps	result sequence
V_N_N	hit_car_car	VN
N_A_N	car_heavy_car	VNA
N_A_V	car_old_hit	VNAA
V_N_N	hit_tree_tree	VNAAN
N_A_V	tree_beautiful_hit	VNAANA
V_V_V	hit_speed_speed	VNAANA V
V_N_V	speed_car_speed	VNAANA VN
V_V_V	speed_give_give	VNAANA VN V
V_N_V	give_farmer_give	VNAANA VN VN
V_N_V	give_driver_give	VNAANA VN VNN
V_N_V	give_lift_give	VNAANA VN VNNN

Starting at *hit*, LA-think.2 retrieves the first arg value car. From *car*, LA-think.2 retrieves the first mdr value heavy and returns to *car*. From there, LA-think.2 retrieves the second mdr value old and proceeds to the fnc value of *car*, i.e., hit. From *hit*, the second arg value tree is retrieved. From *tree*, LA-think.2 retrieves the mdr value beautiful and returns to *hit*.

From *hit*, LA-think.2 retrieves the nc value speed, proceeding to the second proposition. From *speed*, LA-think.2 retrieves the arg value car and returns to *speed*. From *speed*, LA-think.2 retrieves the nc value give, proceeding to the third proposition, etc.

14.2 Definition of LA-speak.2

Based on the navigation patterns of LA-think, LA-speak.2 (re)produces the intrapropositional functor–argument structures which are presented in 6.2.1, 6.3.1, and 6.4.1 in the hearer mode. Given the intricate patterns of the lexicalization functions defined in the following Sect. 14.3, the rules of LA-speak.2 can handle function word precipitation and word order in a rather simple fashion.

14.2.1 FORMAL DEFINITION OF **LA-speak.2**

$$ST_S =_{def} \{(\; [\text{noun: } \alpha] \; \{1 -DET, 2 -NoP\})\}$$

–DET $\{3 -ADN, 4 -NOUN\}$

$\begin{bmatrix} \text{noun: } \alpha \\ \text{mdr: X} \\ \text{prn: i} \end{bmatrix}$ lex-d $[\text{noun: } \alpha]$
if X $\neq$ NIL activate LA-think.2

–NoP $\{5 -FVERB, 6 -AUX, 7 -DET, 8 -NoP, 9 -STOP\}$

$\begin{bmatrix} \text{verb: } \beta \\ \text{arg: !X !}\alpha\text{ Y} \\ \text{prn: i} \end{bmatrix}$ $\begin{bmatrix} \text{noun: } \alpha \\ \text{fnc: } \beta \\ \text{cat: nm} \\ \text{prn: i} \end{bmatrix}$ lex-n $[\text{noun: } \alpha]$
mark β in $[\text{noun: } \alpha]$
if !X $\neq$ NIL and Y $\neq$ NIL activate LA-think.2

–ADN $\{10 -ADN, 11 -NOUN\}$

$\begin{bmatrix} \text{noun: } \alpha \\ \text{mdr: !X }\beta\text{+ Y} \\ \text{prn: i} \end{bmatrix}$ $\begin{bmatrix} \text{adj: } \beta \\ \text{cat: adn} \\ \text{mdd: } \alpha \\ \text{prn: i} \end{bmatrix}$ where $\beta+ = !\beta$ or $\beta+ = \beta!$
lex-an $[\text{adj: } \beta]$
if $\beta+ = !\beta$, activate LA-think.2
if $\beta+ = \beta!$, end-mark $\beta+$ again

–NOUN $\{12 -FVERB, 13 -AUX, 14 -DET, 15 -NoP, 16 -STOP\}$

$\begin{bmatrix} \text{verb: } \beta \\ \text{arg: !X !}\alpha\text{ Y} \\ \text{prn: i} \end{bmatrix}$ $\begin{bmatrix} \text{noun: } \alpha \\ \text{mdr: Z }\gamma \\ \text{prn: i} \end{bmatrix}$ where Z γ = NIL or $\gamma = \delta$!!
lex-nn $[\text{noun: } \alpha]$
mark α in $[\text{noun: } \alpha]$
if !X $\neq$ NIL and Y $\neq$ NIL activate LA-think.2

–FVERB $\{17 -DET, 18 -NoP, 19 -STOP\}$

$\begin{bmatrix} \text{verb: } \beta \\ \text{cat: decl} \\ \text{arg: !}\alpha\text{ X} \\ \text{prn: i} \end{bmatrix}$ lex-fv $[\text{verb: } \beta]$
mark decl in $[\text{verb: } \beta]$
if X $\neq$ NIL activate LA-think.2

–AUX $\{20 -AUX, 21 -NVERB\}$

$\begin{bmatrix} \text{verb: } \beta \\ \text{cat: decl} \\ \text{sem: !X AUX Y} \\ \text{arg: !}\alpha\text{ Z} \\ \text{prn: i} \end{bmatrix}$ lex-ax $[\text{verb: } \beta]$
mark ax in $[\text{verb: } \beta]$

–NVERB $\{22 -DET, 23 -NoP, 24 -STOP\}$

$\begin{bmatrix} \text{verb: } \beta \\ \text{cat: decl} \\ \text{sem: !X Y} \\ \text{arg: !}\alpha\text{ Z} \\ \text{prn: i} \end{bmatrix}$ lex-nv $[\text{verb: } \beta]$
mark decl in $[\text{verb: } \beta]$
Z $\neq$ NIL activate LA-think.2

–STOP   {1 –DET, 2 N}

$$\begin{bmatrix} \text{verb: } \beta \\ \text{cat: !decl} \\ \text{arg: !X !}\alpha \\ \text{prn: i} \end{bmatrix} \begin{bmatrix} \text{noun: !}\alpha \\ \text{fnc: } \beta \\ \text{prn: i} \end{bmatrix} \begin{array}{l} \text{lex-p} \begin{bmatrix} \text{verb: } \beta \end{bmatrix} \\ \text{activate LA-think.2} \end{array}$$

$ST_F =_{def} \{(\begin{bmatrix} \text{cat:decl} \end{bmatrix} \text{ rp-STOP})\}$

The rules –NoP and –NOUN are distinguished because only –NOUN is called by –DET.

LA-speak.2 resembles LA-speak.1 in that each rule application lexicalizes one word form. The variable !X is matched either by NIL or by a sequence of one or more values each marked by !. The ! markings are either introduced by the rules of LA-think.2 (see, for example, V_N_V) or by the rules of LA-speak.2 (see, for example, –FVERB). These markings are of a temporary nature. They serve to prevent the system from using a value more than once during navigation and language production, and are removed from the Word Bank when they are no longer needed for the navigation or production in question.

The rules and rule-packages of LA-speak.2 define the following FSN:

14.2.2 FINITE-STATE TRANSITION NETWORK OF **LA-speak.2**

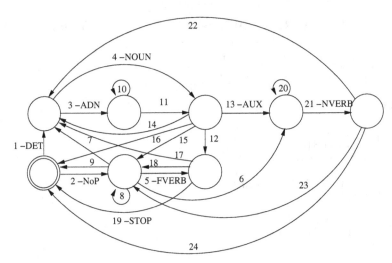

The grammatical perplexity of LA-speak.2 is 24 : 8 = 3, that is, 3 attempted rule applications on average per realization.[3]

---

[3] There is the additional computational cost of automatic word form production (cf. Sect. 14.3), but given a suitable implementation, based, for example, on a trie structure for access to the lexicalization tables, the cost will be no more than a constant.

14.3 Automatic Word Form Production

The rules of LA-speak.2 apply to activated proplets which must be realized as language-dependent external surfaces. As in LA-speak.1, this step is handled by the function *lexicalize*, which matches one or more proplets with patterns and renders a surface as output.

In LA-speak.2, the realization of proper names and pronouns is handled by the same lexicalization function, called lex-n. The realization of different verb forms, in contrast, is handled by three different lexicalization functions. They are lex-fv for finite main verbs, lex-ax for auxiliaries, and lex-nv for nonfinite main verbs. In other words, the classification of word forms in language production is orthogonal to the *paradigms* of traditional morphology, which seem to be motivated mainly in the context of language interpretation.[4]

In addition to the lexicalization of n, fv, ax, and nv, LA-speak.2 requires the lexicalization of nn, d, an, and p, for nouns, determiners, adnominal adjectives, and punctuation signs, respectively. These word forms are realized by the lexicalization functions lex-nn , lex-d, lex-an, and lex-p.

The lexicalization functions of LA-speak.2 resemble those of LA-speak.1 (cf. Sect. 12.3) in that they consist of (i) a full-form pattern defined as a conditional and (ii) a lexicalization table. In order to handle the complexity of LA-speak.2 lexicalization, however, the following functions combine several full-form patterns and the associated tables. Such a sequence of full-form patterns with tables is interpreted by first trying the first pattern, then the second and so on, until a successful match has been found.

The patterns of the lexicalization functions ignore the ! markings introduced by the rule operations of LA-think.2 (cf. 14.1.1).

14.3.1 THE FUNCTION lex-n FOR REALIZING NAMES OR PRONOUNS

If $\begin{bmatrix} \text{noun: } \alpha \\ \text{cat: nm} \end{bmatrix}$ matches an activated N proplet, then lex-n [noun: α] = α'.

---

[4] The distinction between language interpretation and language production may help to explain a long-standing contradiction in morphological classification. According to the standard view, word forms are classified as *inflectional* if they do not change grammatical function, represented by the the part of speech, and as *derivational* if they do. For example, learn and learns have the same part of speech and therefore belong to the same inflectional paradigm, while learn and learner have different parts of speech, for which reason learner is treated as a derivational form.

The apparent contradiction arises with past participles. For example, written clearly belongs into the verbal paradigm write, writes, writing, wrote, written. Yet written changes grammatical function: It works like an adnominal adjective, as in the written letter (in other languages such as Latin or German, it even inflects to agree with the noun or the determiner).

The contradiction disappears if we take a rather liberal view of inflectional paradigms in language interpretation, and a rather strict view of grammatical function during language production. In language interpretation, the goal is to sort all possible word forms, including derivational ones, around the same semantic core. In language production, in contrast, the goal is to select the correct grammatical function for a given semantic core.

If α =	then α' =
John	John
Julia	Julia
Susanne	Susanne

If one of the following patterns matches an activated N proplet, then lex-n applied to this proplet produces the associated surface:

pattern	surface	pattern	surface
$\begin{bmatrix} \text{noun: } I \\ \text{cat: ns1} \end{bmatrix}$	I	$\begin{bmatrix} \text{noun:} you \\ \text{cat: pro2} \end{bmatrix}$	you
$\begin{bmatrix} \text{noun:} he \\ \text{cat: ns3} \\ \text{sem: sg m} \end{bmatrix}$	he	$\begin{bmatrix} \text{noun:} he \\ \text{cat: ns3} \\ \text{sem: sg f} \end{bmatrix}$	she
$\begin{bmatrix} \text{noun:} he \\ \text{cat: snp} \\ \text{sem: sg} \end{bmatrix}$	it	$\begin{bmatrix} \text{noun:} I \\ \text{cat: np1} \end{bmatrix}$	we
$\begin{bmatrix} \text{noun:} he \\ \text{cat: np3} \end{bmatrix}$	they	$\begin{bmatrix} \text{noun:} I \\ \text{cat: obq} \\ \text{sem: sg} \end{bmatrix}$	me
$\begin{bmatrix} \text{noun:} he \\ \text{cat: obq} \\ \text{sem: sg m} \end{bmatrix}$	him	$\begin{bmatrix} \text{noun:} he \\ \text{cat: obq} \\ \text{sem: sg f} \end{bmatrix}$	her
$\begin{bmatrix} \text{noun:} I \\ \text{cat: obq} \\ \text{sem: pl} \end{bmatrix}$	us	$\begin{bmatrix} \text{noun:} he \\ \text{cat: obq} \\ \text{sem: pl} \end{bmatrix}$	them

14.3.2 THE FUNCTION lex-d FOR REALIZING DETERMINERS

If one of the following patterns matches an activated N proplet (cf. 6.2.9), then lex-d applied to this proplet produces the associated surface:

pattern	surface	pattern	surface
$[\text{sem: indef sg}]$	a(n)	$\begin{bmatrix} \text{cat: snp} \\ \text{sem: pl exh} \end{bmatrix}$	every
$[\text{sem: sel}]$	some	$\begin{bmatrix} \text{cat: pnp} \\ \text{sem: pl exh} \end{bmatrix}$	all
$[\text{sem: def}]^5$	the		

14.3.3 THE FUNCTION lex-nn FOR REALIZING NOUNS

If $\begin{bmatrix} \text{noun: } \alpha \\ \text{sem: sg} \end{bmatrix}$ matches an activated N proplet, then lex-nn[noun: α] = α'.

If $\begin{bmatrix} \text{noun: } \alpha \\ \text{sem: pl} \end{bmatrix}$ matches an activated N proplet, then lex-nn[noun: α] = α'+s.

---

[5] Technically, the value patterns require additional variables, for example, $[\text{sem: X def Y}]$, to indicate that def may be preceded or followed by other values. When not required for relevant distinctions, this aspect is omitted for the sake of simplicity and perspicuity.

If   α = *car*   then α' =   car
        driver   driver
        farmer   farmer
        lift   lift

14.3.4 THE FUNCTION lex-fv FOR REALIZING FINITE VERB FORMS

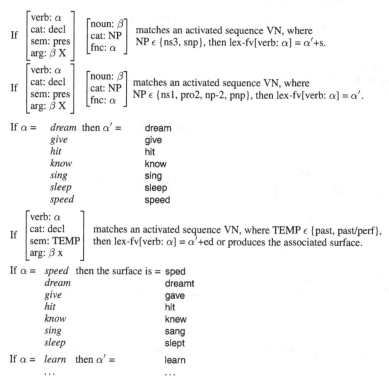

If
$\begin{bmatrix} \text{verb: } \alpha \\ \text{cat: decl} \\ \text{sem: pres} \\ \text{arg: } \beta\ X \end{bmatrix}$
$\begin{bmatrix} \text{noun: } \beta \\ \text{cat: NP} \\ \text{fnc: } \alpha \end{bmatrix}$
matches an activated sequence VN, where
NP ∈ {ns3, snp}, then lex-fv[verb: α] = α'+s.

If
$\begin{bmatrix} \text{verb: } \alpha \\ \text{cat: decl} \\ \text{sem: pres} \\ \text{arg: } \beta\ X \end{bmatrix}$
$\begin{bmatrix} \text{noun: } \beta \\ \text{cat: NP} \\ \text{fnc: } \alpha \end{bmatrix}$
matches an activated sequence VN, where
NP ∈ {ns1, pro2, np-2, pnp}, then lex-fv[verb: α] = α'.

If α =   *dream* then α' =   dream
        give   give
        hit   hit
        know   know
        sing   sing
        sleep   sleep
        speed   speed

If
$\begin{bmatrix} \text{verb: } \alpha \\ \text{cat: decl} \\ \text{sem: TEMP} \\ \text{arg: } \beta\ x \end{bmatrix}$
matches an activated sequence VN, where TEMP ∈ {past, past/perf},
then lex-fv[verb: α] = α'+ed or produces the associated surface.

If α = *speed* then the surface is = sped
      dream   dreamt
      give   gave
      hit   hit
      know   knew
      sing   sang
      sleep   slept

If α = *learn* then α' =   learn
        ...   ...

14.3.5 THE FUNCTION lex-ax FOR REALIZING AUXILIARIES

If one of the following patterns matches an activated V proplet, then lex-ax applied to this proplet produces the associated surface:

pattern   *surface*

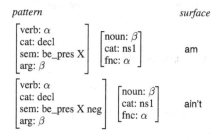

$\begin{bmatrix} \text{verb: } \alpha \\ \text{cat: decl} \\ \text{sem: be\_pres } X \\ \text{arg: } \beta \end{bmatrix}$
$\begin{bmatrix} \text{noun: } \beta \\ \text{cat: ns1} \\ \text{fnc: } \alpha \end{bmatrix}$
am

$\begin{bmatrix} \text{verb: } \alpha \\ \text{cat: decl} \\ \text{sem: be\_pres } X \text{ neg} \\ \text{arg: } \beta \end{bmatrix}$
$\begin{bmatrix} \text{noun: } \beta \\ \text{cat: ns1} \\ \text{fnc: } \alpha \end{bmatrix}$
ain't

pattern   *surface*

$$\begin{bmatrix} \text{verb: } \alpha \\ \text{cat: decl} \\ \text{sem: be\_pres X} \\ \text{arg: } \beta \end{bmatrix} \begin{bmatrix} \text{noun: } \beta \\ \text{cat: NP} \\ \text{fnc: } \alpha \end{bmatrix}$$

are, where NP ϵ {pro2, np-2, pnp}

$$\begin{bmatrix} \text{verb: } \alpha \\ \text{cat: decl} \\ \text{sem: be\_pres X neg} \\ \text{arg: } \beta \end{bmatrix} \begin{bmatrix} \text{noun: } \beta \\ \text{cat: NP} \\ \text{fnc: } \alpha \end{bmatrix}$$

aren't, where NP ϵ {pro2, np-2, pnp}

$$\begin{bmatrix} \text{verb: } \alpha \\ \text{cat: decl} \\ \text{sem: be\_pres X} \\ \text{arg: } \beta \end{bmatrix} \begin{bmatrix} \text{noun: } \beta \\ \text{cat: NP} \\ \text{fnc: } \alpha \end{bmatrix}$$

is, where NP ϵ {np3, nm, snp}

$$\begin{bmatrix} \text{verb: } \alpha \\ \text{cat: decl} \\ \text{sem: be\_pres X neg} \\ \text{arg: } \beta \end{bmatrix} \begin{bmatrix} \text{noun: } \beta \\ \text{cat: NP} \\ \text{fnc: } \alpha \end{bmatrix}$$

isn't, where NP ϵ {np3, nm, snp}

$$\begin{bmatrix} \text{verb: } \alpha \\ \text{cat: decl} \\ \text{sem: be\_past X} \\ \text{arg: } \beta \end{bmatrix} \begin{bmatrix} \text{noun: } \beta \\ \text{cat: NP} \\ \text{fnc: } \alpha \end{bmatrix}$$

was, where NP ϵ {ns1, np3, nm, snp}

$$\begin{bmatrix} \text{verb: } \alpha \\ \text{cat: decl} \\ \text{sem: be\_past X neg} \\ \text{arg: } \beta \end{bmatrix} \begin{bmatrix} \text{noun: } \beta \\ \text{cat: NP} \\ \text{fnc: } \alpha \end{bmatrix}$$

wasn't, where NP ϵ {ns1, np3, nm, snp}

$$\begin{bmatrix} \text{verb: } \alpha \\ \text{cat: decl} \\ \text{sem: be\_past X} \\ \text{arg: } \beta \end{bmatrix} \begin{bmatrix} \text{noun: } \beta \\ \text{cat: NP} \\ \text{fnc: } \alpha \end{bmatrix}$$

were, where NP ϵ {pro2, np-2, pnp}

$$\begin{bmatrix} \text{verb: } \alpha \\ \text{cat: decl} \\ \text{sem: be\_past X neg} \\ \text{arg: } \beta \end{bmatrix} \begin{bmatrix} \text{noun: } \beta \\ \text{cat: NP} \\ \text{fnc: } \alpha \end{bmatrix}$$

weren't, where NP ϵ {pro2, np-2, pnp}

$$\begin{bmatrix} \text{verb: } \alpha \\ \text{cat: decl} \\ \text{sem: be\_perf X} \\ \text{arg: } \beta \end{bmatrix}$$

been

$$\begin{bmatrix} \text{verb: } \alpha \\ \text{cat: decl} \\ \text{sem: hv\_pres X} \\ \text{arg: } \beta \end{bmatrix} \begin{bmatrix} \text{noun: } \beta \\ \text{cat: NP} \\ \text{fnc: } \alpha \end{bmatrix}$$

have, where NP ϵ {np1, pro2, np-2, pnp}

$$\begin{bmatrix} \text{verb: } \alpha \\ \text{cat: decl} \\ \text{sem: hv\_pres X neg} \\ \text{arg: } \beta \end{bmatrix} \begin{bmatrix} \text{noun: } \beta \\ \text{cat: NP} \\ \text{fnc: } \alpha \end{bmatrix}$$

haven't, where NP ϵ {np1, pro2, np-2, pnp}

$$\begin{bmatrix} \text{verb: } \alpha \\ \text{cat: decl} \\ \text{sem: hv\_pres X} \\ \text{arg: } \beta \end{bmatrix} \begin{bmatrix} \text{noun: } \beta \\ \text{cat: NP} \\ \text{fnc: } \alpha \end{bmatrix}$$

has, where NP ϵ {np3, nm, snp}

pattern   surface

$$\begin{bmatrix} \text{verb: } \alpha \\ \text{cat: decl} \\ \text{sem: hv\_pres X neg} \\ \text{arg: } \beta \end{bmatrix} \begin{bmatrix} \text{noun: } \beta \\ \text{cat: NP} \\ \text{fnc: } \alpha \end{bmatrix}$$ hasn't, where NP ϵ {np3, nm, snp}

$$\begin{bmatrix} \text{verb: } \alpha \\ \text{cat: decl} \\ \text{sem: hv\_past X} \\ \text{arg: } \beta \end{bmatrix} \begin{bmatrix} \text{noun: } \beta \\ \text{cat: NP} \\ \text{fnc: } \alpha \end{bmatrix}$$ had, where NP ϵ {np1, pro2, np-2, nm, snp, pnp, np3}

$$\begin{bmatrix} \text{verb: } \alpha \\ \text{cat: decl} \\ \text{sem: hv\_past X neg} \\ \text{arg: } \beta \end{bmatrix} \begin{bmatrix} \text{noun: } \beta \\ \text{cat: NP} \\ \text{fnc: } \alpha \end{bmatrix}$$ hadn't, where NP ϵ {np1, pro2, np-2, nm, snp, pnp, np3}

$$\begin{bmatrix} \text{verb: } \alpha \\ \text{cat: decl} \\ \text{sem: do\_pres X} \\ \text{arg: } \beta \end{bmatrix} \begin{bmatrix} \text{noun: } \beta \\ \text{cat: NP} \\ \text{fnc: } \alpha \end{bmatrix}$$ do, where NP ϵ {np1, pro2, np-2, pnp}

$$\begin{bmatrix} \text{verb: } \alpha \\ \text{cat: decl} \\ \text{sem: do\_pres X neg} \\ \text{arg: } \beta \end{bmatrix} \begin{bmatrix} \text{noun: } \beta \\ \text{cat: NP} \\ \text{fnc: } \alpha \end{bmatrix}$$ don't, where NP ϵ {np1, pro2, np-2, pnp}

$$\begin{bmatrix} \text{verb: } \alpha \\ \text{cat: decl} \\ \text{sem: do\_pres X} \\ \text{arg: } \beta \end{bmatrix} \begin{bmatrix} \text{noun: } \beta \\ \text{cat: NP} \\ \text{fnc: } \alpha \end{bmatrix}$$ does, where NP ϵ {np3, nm, snp}

$$\begin{bmatrix} \text{verb: } \alpha \\ \text{cat: decl} \\ \text{sem: do\_pres X neg} \\ \text{arg: } \beta \end{bmatrix} \begin{bmatrix} \text{noun: } \beta \\ \text{cat: NP} \\ \text{fnc: } \alpha \end{bmatrix}$$ doesn't, where NP ϵ {np3, nm, snp}

$$\begin{bmatrix} \text{verb: } \alpha \\ \text{cat: decl} \\ \text{sem: do\_past X} \\ \text{arg: } \beta \end{bmatrix} \begin{bmatrix} \text{noun: } \beta \\ \text{cat: NP} \\ \text{fnc: } \alpha \end{bmatrix}$$ did, where NP ϵ {np1, pro2, np-2, nm, snp, pnp, np3}

$$\begin{bmatrix} \text{verb: } \alpha \\ \text{cat: decl} \\ \text{sem: do\_past X neg} \\ \text{arg: } \beta \end{bmatrix} \begin{bmatrix} \text{noun: } \beta \\ \text{cat: NP} \\ \text{fnc: } \alpha \end{bmatrix}$$ didn't, where NP ϵ {np1, pro2, np-2, nm, snp, pnp, np3}

14.3.6 THE FUNCTION lex-nv FOR REALIZING NONFINITE VERB FORMS

If $\begin{bmatrix} \text{verb: } \alpha \\ \text{cat: decl} \\ \text{sem: prog} \end{bmatrix}$ matches an activated proplet V, then lex-nv[verb: α] = α'+ing, whereby α and α' are related as follows:[6]

If α =	then α' =
dream	dream
give	giv

---

[6] This is for treating simple allomorph phenomena as in giv+ing and hit+t+ing. The allomorphy in semiregular paradigms is discussed in FoCL'99, pp. 263 ff.

hit	hitt
know	know
sing	sing
sleep	sleep
speed	speed

If $\begin{bmatrix} \text{verb: } \alpha \\ \text{cat: decl} \\ \text{sem: perf} \end{bmatrix}$ matches an activated proplet V, then lex-fv[verb: α] produces the surface α':[7]

$\alpha =$	$\alpha' =$
give	given
know	known
sing	sung

14.3.7 THE FUNCTION lex-adn FOR REALIZING ELEMENTARY ADNOMINALS

If $\begin{bmatrix} \text{adj: } \alpha \\ \text{cat: adn} \\ \text{sem:} \end{bmatrix}$ matches an activated proplet a, then lex-adn[adj: α] = α'.

If $\alpha =$	then $\alpha' =$
beautiful	beautiful
heavy	heavy
old	old

If $\begin{bmatrix} \text{adj: } \alpha \\ \text{cat: adn} \\ \text{sem: comp} \end{bmatrix}$ matches an activated proplet a, then lex-adn[adj: α] = α'+er.

If $\begin{bmatrix} \text{adj: } \alpha \\ \text{cat: adn} \\ \text{sem: sup} \end{bmatrix}$ matches an activated proplet a, then lex-adn[adj: α] = α'+est.

If $\alpha =$	then $\alpha' =$
heavy	heavy[8]
old	old

14.3.8 THE FUNCTION lex-p FOR REALIZING A FULL STOP

If $\begin{bmatrix} \text{cat: decl} \end{bmatrix}$ matches an activated V proplet, then lex-p applied to this proplet produces the surface . (full stop).

The functions lex-n, lex-d, lex-nn, lex-fv, lex-nv, lex-ax, lex-an, and lex-p are called by the rules of LA-speak.2, defined in the preceding section.

---

[7] Past participles are treated here as regular if their surface equals that of the past tense (cf. 14.3.4). In this case, the sem attribute of the V proplet has the value past/perf. This value originates in the lexical definitions of LA-hear.2 (cf. 13.1.5, 13.1.6, and 13.1.7). Examples are *learn+ed*, but also *hit, dreamt,* and *slept*.

[8] The allographic variation of heavy in the comparative and superlative is disregarded here for simplicity. A completely accurate treatment can be provided in either case by specifying the surface directly, as illustrated in 14.3.4.

14.4 Producing a Sentence with Complex Noun Phrases

The derivations in this and the following two sections are based on the rule patterns of LA-speak.2 which match sequences of proplets activated by LA-think.2. The LA-speak rules realize word forms based on the lexicalization functions defined in Sect. 14.3.

Before we proceed with the verbose derivation of the first sample sentence of DBS.2, however, let us summarize the interchanging LA-think and LA-speak applications with their different mark operations. The sequence of activated proplets in the Word Bank 13.6.1 underlying the sample sentence The heavy old car hit the beautiful tree. is initially VN and then extended step by step to VNAANA.

14.4.1 LA-THINK AND LA-SPEAK RULE APPLICATIONS WITH MARKINGS

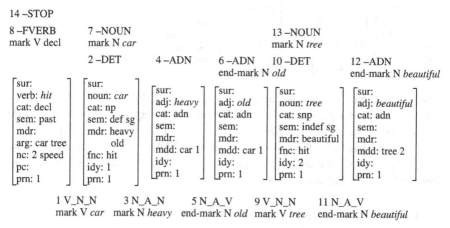

The rule names and markings below the six proplets indicate the operations of LA-think; those above indicate the operations of LA-speak. The time-linear order of the derivation, frequently switching between LA-think and LA-speak, is indicated by the consecutive numbering 1,2, 3, ..., 14 in 14.4.1. These numbers will be used in the explanations of the following verbose LA-speak derivation to indicate the sequence position of each rule application.[9] To make them more conspicuous, the sequencing numbers will be surrounded by cornered brackets, e.g., <1>.

To start the derivation, the V proplet *hit* in the Word Bank 13.6.1 has been activated, either by a previous LA-think operation or by an external stimulus. Based on <1> V_N_N, LA-think adds the initial N proplet to the activated sequence. It !-marks the first value car of the attribute arg in the V proplet, and switches to LA-speak.

---

[9] The numbers indicating sequence positions are distinct from those preceding the LA-speak rule names, which refer to the numbering of rules in the rule packages of the grammar, for example 1 –DET in 14.4.2.

The rule package of the start state of LA-speak contains −DET and −NoP. When these rules are applied to the activated VN proplets, −NoP fails to lexicalize because the cat value of the N proplet *car* is not nm (cf. 14.3.1). Lexicalization of <2> −DET, however, succeeds, resulting in the realization of the.

14.4.2 REALIZING The

1 −DET   {3 −ADN, 4 −NOUN}

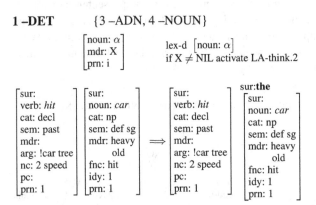

The non-NIL mdr value heavy triggers a switch to LA-think. <3> N_A_N applies, adds the A proplet representing *heavy* to the underlying sequence, now VNA, !-marks the first mdr value in the N proplet (cf. 14.4.3), and switches back to LA-speak.

The rule package of −DET contains −ADN and −NOUN. −NOUN fails because the value of the noun's mdr attribute is not NIL and the currently relevant value has not been end-marked, but <4> −ADN is successful:

14.4.3 REALIZING heavy

3 −ADN   {10 −ADN, 11 −NOUN}

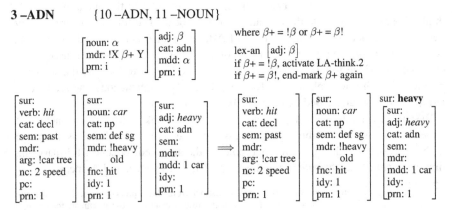

Because $\beta+ = !\beta$, the system switches to LA-think. <5> N_A_V applies, extending the underlying sequence to VNAA, !-end-marking the second mdr value old in the N proplet, and switching back to LA-speak. The rules –ADN and –NOUN are tried; –NOUN fails, but <6> –ADN succeeds again.

14.4.4 REALIZING old

10 –ADN   {10 –ADN, 11 –NOUN}

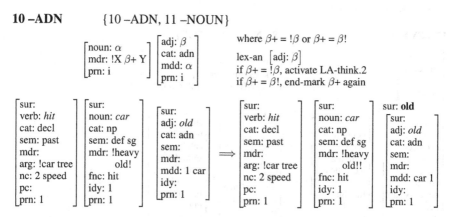

Because $\beta+ = \beta!$, there is no switch to LA-think. Instead, old! is end-marked again, resulting in old!!. This allows LA-speak to continue, now with the realization of the surface car from the corresponding noun proplet. It was originally activated for the realization of the phrase-initial determiner the in 14.4.2 and has provided the continuation proplets *heavy* and *old* at the level of the navigation.

The rule package of –ADN in 14.4.4 contains –ADN and –NOUN. This time, –ADN fails, blocked by the !! end-marker, whereas <7> –NOUN succeeds:

14.4.5 REALIZING car

11 –NOUN   {12 –FVERB, 13 –AUX, 14 –DET, 15 –NoP, 16 –STOP}

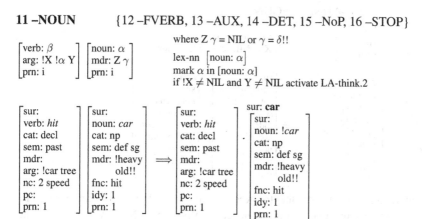

Because !X has no assigned value, i.e., X = NIL, there is no switch to LA-think

Next, the rules −FVERB, −DET, −NoP, and −STOP are tried. −DET and −NoP fail because of the !-marked value of the noun attribute. −STOP fails because the arg value tree of the V proplet is still unmarked. Remains <8> −FVERB:

14.4.6 REALIZING hit

12 −FVERB   {17 −DET, 18 −NoP, 19 −STOP}

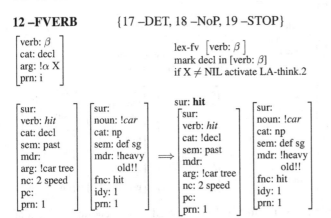

Because X ≠ NIL, there is a switch to LA-think. LA-think extends the underlying sequence to VNAAN using <9> V_N_N, !-marks the second value in the arg attribute of the V proplet, and switches to LA-speak. The rules −DET, −NoP, and −STOP are tried. −NoP fails lexicalization, and −STOP fails because the noun value *tree* of the just activated N proplet has not yet been !-marked. <10> −DET, however, succeeds:

14.4.7 REALIZING a

17 −DET   {3 −ADN, 4 −NOUN}

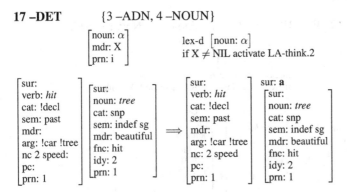

The unmarked mdr value *beautiful* triggers a switch to LA-think. LA-think uses <11> N_A_V to extend the underlying sequence to VNAANA. N_A_V end-marks the

mdr value beautiful (cf. 14.1.1) and switches back to LA-speak, which applies <12> −ADN.

14.4.8 REALIZING beautiful

3 −ADN   { 10 −ADN, 11 −NOUN}

$$\begin{bmatrix} \text{noun: } \alpha \\ \text{mdr: } !X \; \beta + Y \\ \text{prn: } i \end{bmatrix} \begin{bmatrix} \text{adj: } \beta \\ \text{cat: adn} \\ \text{mdd: } \alpha \\ \text{prn: } i \end{bmatrix}$$

where $\beta+ = !\beta$ or $\beta+ = \beta!$

lex-an $\begin{bmatrix} \text{adj: } \beta \end{bmatrix}$

if $\beta+ = !\beta$, activate LA-think.2

if $\beta+ = \beta!$, end-mark $\beta+$ again

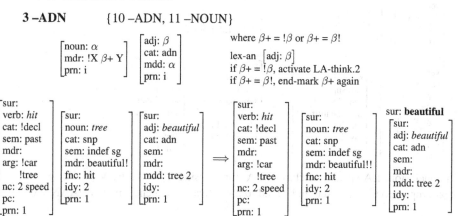

Because the mdr value beautiful is end-marked, it gets end-marked again, and there is no switch to LA-think.

Now the rules −ADN and −NOUN are applied once more, −ADN fails, blocked by the !! end-marker, whereas <13> −NOUN succeeds.

14.4.9 REALIZING tree

11 −NOUN   { 12 −FVERB, 13 −AUX, 14 −DET, 15 −NoP, 16 −STOP}

$$\begin{bmatrix} \text{verb: } \beta \\ \text{arg: } !X \; !\alpha \; Y \\ \text{prn: } i \end{bmatrix} \begin{bmatrix} \text{noun: } \alpha \\ \text{mdr: } Z \; \gamma \\ \text{prn: } i \end{bmatrix}$$

where $Z \; \gamma = $ NIL or $\gamma = \delta!!$

lex-nn $\begin{bmatrix} \text{noun: } \alpha \end{bmatrix}$

mark α in [noun: α]

if $!X \neq$ NIL and $Y \neq$ NIL activate LA-think.2

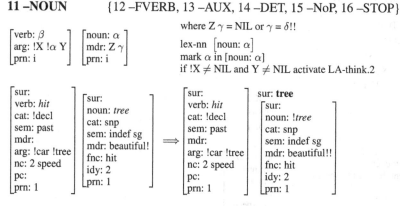

Because Y=NIL, no switch to LA-think is triggered. Application of −FVERB fails because of !decl, introduced in 14.4.6; −AUX fails because its lexicalization fails; −DET and −NoP fail because *tree* in the N proplet is !-marked. <14> −STOP, however, applies successfully, adding punctuation:

14.4.10 REALIZING . (FULL STOP)

16 –STOP   {1 –DET, 2 –NoP}

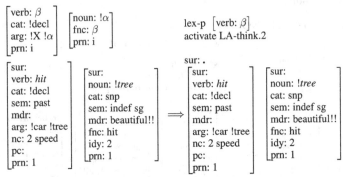

In conclusion, LA-speak switches to LA-think. Using V_V_V, the V proplet of the next proposition is traversed and added to the activated sequence, now VNAANA V.

14.5 Producing a Sentence with a Complex Verb Phrase

Before we proceed with the verbose LA-speak derivation of the second sample sentence let us summarize the interchanging LA-think and LA-speak applications with their different !-mark operations. The proplet sequence underlying the sentence The car had been speeding. is VN.

14.5.1 LA-THINK AND LA-SPEAK RULE APPLICATION WITH MARKINGS

7 –STOP

6 –NFVERB
mark V decl

5 –AUX
mark V be_past

4 –AUX   3 –NOUN
mark V hv_past   mark N car

                                2 –DET

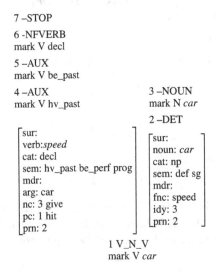

1 V_N_V
mark V car

The realization of the previous sentence in Sect. 14.4 has ended with the LA-speak rule –STOP and an obligatory switch to LA-think. Application of V_V_V has provided the transition to the V proplet of the current proposition. After activation of the V proplet *speed*, based on V_V_V, and the N proplet *car*, based on <1> V_N_V, LA-think switches to LA-speak.

The rule package of the LA-speak start state contains the rules –DET and –NoP, which are applied to the activated VN proplets. Lexicalization of –NoP fails, but that of <2> –DET succeeds:

14.5.2 REALIZING The

1 –DET   {3 –ADN, 4 –NOUN}

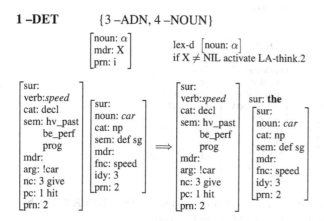

Because the mdr value X = NIL, there is no switch LA-think. Of the rules in the current package, –ADN fails, but <3> –NOUN succeeds:

14.5.3 REALIZING car

4 –NOUN   {12 –FVERB, 13 –AUX, 14 –DET, 15 –NoP, 16 –STOP}

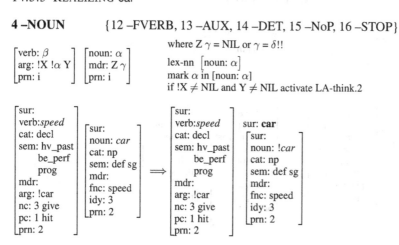

Because !X=NIL, there is no switch to LA-think. Of the rules now activated, –FVERB fails lexicalization; –DET and –NoP fail because of the !-marked noun value; –STOP fails because decl has not been !-marked yet; but <4> –AUX succeeds.

14.5.4 REALIZING had

sectionRealizing had

13 –AUX   {20 –AUX, 21 –NVERB}

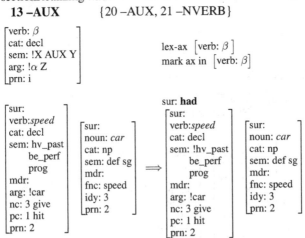

This rule has no switch to LA-think. Of the now activated rules, –NVERB fails because of failing lexicalization, but <5> –AUX applies again:

14.5.5 REALIZING been

20 –AUX   {20 –AUX, 21 –NVERB}

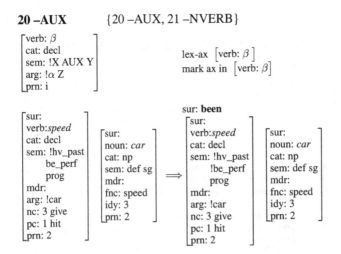

Of the now activated rules, –AUX fails lexicalization, but <6> –NVERB succeeds.

14.5.6 REALIZING speeding

21 –NVERB   {22 –DET, 23 –NoP, 24 –STOP}

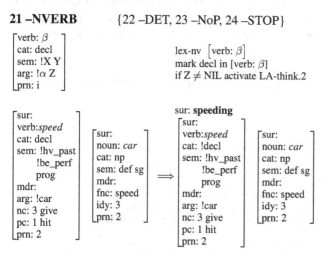

Because Z=NIL, there is no switch to LA-think. Of the rules now activated, –DET and –NoP fail because all noun values are !-marked in the V proplet, but <7> –STOP succeeds:

14.5.7 REALIZING . (FULL STOP)

24 –STOP   {1 –DET, 2 –NoP}

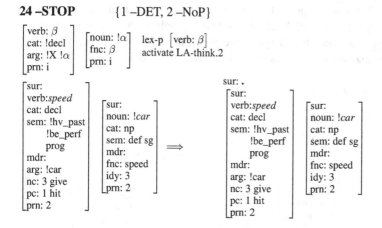

This rule has an unconditional switch to LA-think. LA-think applies the rule V_V_V to traverse the V proplet *give* of the next proposition, extending the activated underlying sequence to VNAANA VN V.

14.6 Producing a Sentence with a Three-Place Verb

As in 14.4.1 and 14.5.1, let us begin the production analysis of the third sample sentence A farmer gave the driver a lift. by summarizing the interchanging LA-think and LA-speak applications with their different !-mark operations. The proplet sequence underlying the sample sentence is initially VN and is then extended step by step to VNNN.

14.6.1 LA-THINK AND LA-SPEAK RULE APPLICATIONS WITH MARKINGS

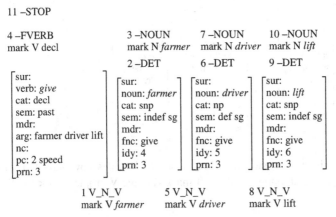

11 –STOP

4 –FVERB   3 –NOUN   7 –NOUN   10 –NOUN
mark V decl   mark N farmer   mark N driver   mark N lift
                2 –DET   6 –DET   9 –DET

$$\begin{bmatrix} \text{sur:} \\ \text{verb: } give \\ \text{cat: decl} \\ \text{sem: past} \\ \text{mdr:} \\ \text{arg: farmer driver lift} \\ \text{nc:} \\ \text{pc: 2 speed} \\ \text{prn: 3} \end{bmatrix} \begin{bmatrix} \text{sur:} \\ \text{noun: } farmer \\ \text{cat: snp} \\ \text{sem: indef sg} \\ \text{mdr:} \\ \text{fnc: give} \\ \text{idy: 4} \\ \text{prn: 3} \end{bmatrix} \begin{bmatrix} \text{sur:} \\ \text{noun: } driver \\ \text{cat: np} \\ \text{sem: def sg} \\ \text{mdr:} \\ \text{fnc: give} \\ \text{idy: 5} \\ \text{prn: 3} \end{bmatrix} \begin{bmatrix} \text{sur:} \\ \text{noun: } lift \\ \text{cat: snp} \\ \text{sem: indef sg} \\ \text{mdr:} \\ \text{fnc: give} \\ \text{idy: 6} \\ \text{prn: 3} \end{bmatrix}$$

1 V_N_V   5 V_N_V   8 V_N_V
mark V farmer   mark V driver   mark V lift

The realization of the previous sentence in Sect. 14.5 has ended with the LA-speak rule –STOP and an obligatory switch to LA-think. Application of V_V_V has provided the transition to the V proplet of the current proposition. From there LA-think proceeds by applying <1> V_N_V, adding the first N proplet to the activated sequence.

This rule triggers a switch to LA-speak, the start state of which activates –DET and –NoP. The lexicalization of –NoP fails, but <2> –DET succeeds:

14.6.2 REALIZING A

1 –DET   {3 –ADN, 4 –NOUN}

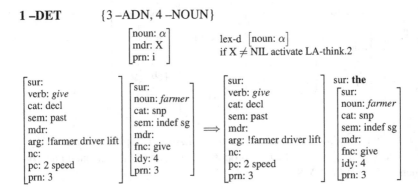

$$\begin{bmatrix} \text{noun: } \alpha \\ \text{mdr: X} \\ \text{prn: i} \end{bmatrix}$$

lex-d $\begin{bmatrix} \text{noun: } \alpha \end{bmatrix}$
if X $\neq$ NIL activate LA-think.2

$$\begin{bmatrix} \text{sur:} \\ \text{verb: } give \\ \text{cat: decl} \\ \text{sem: past} \\ \text{mdr:} \\ \text{arg: !farmer driver lift} \\ \text{nc:} \\ \text{pc: 2 speed} \\ \text{prn: 3} \end{bmatrix} \begin{bmatrix} \text{sur:} \\ \text{noun: } farmer \\ \text{cat: snp} \\ \text{sem: indef sg} \\ \text{mdr:} \\ \text{fnc: give} \\ \text{idy: 4} \\ \text{prn: 3} \end{bmatrix} \implies \begin{bmatrix} \text{sur:} \\ \text{verb: } give \\ \text{cat: decl} \\ \text{sem: past} \\ \text{mdr:} \\ \text{arg: !farmer driver lift} \\ \text{nc:} \\ \text{pc: 2 speed} \\ \text{prn: 3} \end{bmatrix} \begin{matrix} \text{sur: \textbf{the}} \\ \begin{bmatrix} \text{sur:} \\ \text{noun: } farmer \\ \text{cat: snp} \\ \text{sem: indef sg} \\ \text{mdr:} \\ \text{fnc: give} \\ \text{idy: 4} \\ \text{prn: 3} \end{bmatrix} \end{matrix}$$

Because the mdr value X = NIL, no switch to LA-think is triggered. Of the two LA-speak rules now active, –ADN fails (no mdr value in the N proplet), but <3> –NOUN succeeds:

14.6.3 REALIZING farmer

4 –NOUN   {12 –FVERB, 13 –AUX, 14 –DET, 15 –NoP, 16 –STOP}

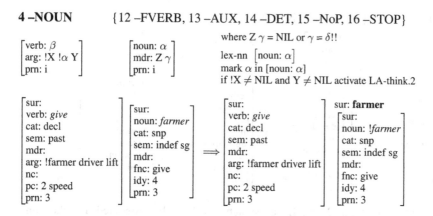

where Z γ = NIL or $\gamma = \delta$!!

lex-nn $[\text{noun: } \alpha]$
mark α in [noun: α]
if !X $\neq$ NIL and Y $\neq$ NIL activate LA-think.2

Because !X=NIL, no switch to LA-think is triggered. The activated LA-speak rules are –FVERB, –AUX, –DET, –NoP, and –STOP. –DET and –NoP fail because !*farmer* has been !-marked; –AUX fails lexicalization; –STOP fails because decl is still unmarked, but <4> –FVERB succeeds.

14.6.4 REALIZING gave

12 –FVERB   {17 –DET, 18 –NoP, 19 –STOP}

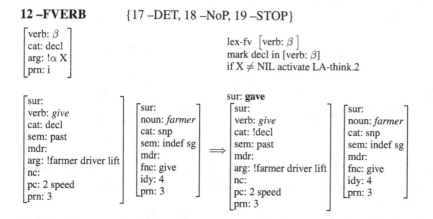

lex-fv $[\text{verb: } \beta]$
mark decl in [verb: β]
if X $\neq$ NIL activate LA-think.2

Because X $\neq$ NIL, a switch to LA-think is triggered. LA-think traverses *driver* by using <5> V_N_V, !-marks the second arg value in the V proplet, and switches to LA-speak. It tries the rules –DET, –NoP, and –STOP. –NoP fails lexicalization; –STOP fails because the V proplet still has unmarked arg values; but <6> –DET succeeds:

14.6.5 REALIZING the

17 –DET   {3 –ADN, 4 –NOUN}

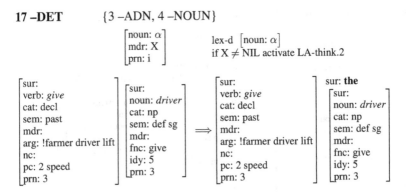

Because the mdr value X = NIL, no switch to LA-think is triggered. For the same reason –ADN fails and <7> –NOUN succeeds:

14.6.6 REALIZING driver

4 –NOUN   {12 –FVERB, 13 –AUX, 14 –DET, 15 –NoP, 16 –STOP}

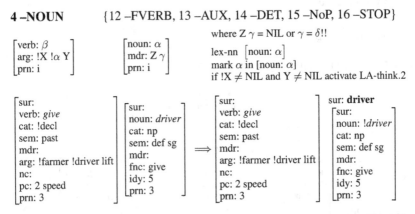

!X and Y $\neq$ NIL trigger a switch to LA-think. LA-think traverses the third N proplet with <8> V_N_V, !-marks the third value in the arg attribute of the V proplet and switches back to LA-speak.

Of the activated LA-speak rules, –FVERB and –AUX fail because of the !-marked decl value; –NoP fails lexicalization; –STOP fails because the value of the noun attribute of the last N proplet has not been !-marked; but <9> –DET succeeds.

14.6.7 REALIZING a

14 –DET   {3 –ADN, 4 –NOUN}

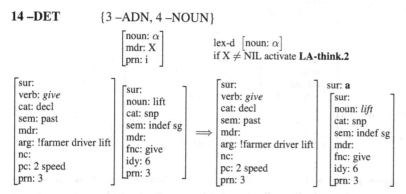

Because the mdr value Z = NIL, no switch to LA-think is triggered. For the same reason –ADN fails and <10> –NOUN succeeds:

14.6.8 REALIZING lift

4 –NOUN   {12 –FVERB, 13 –AUX, 14 –DET, 15 –NoP, 16 –STOP}

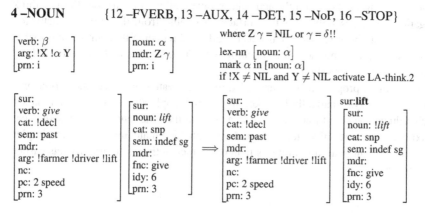

Because Y=NIL, no switch to LA-think is triggered. Of the LA-speak rules now activated, –FVERB and –AUX fail because decl is !-marked; –DET and –NoP fail because the noun value of the last N is !-marked; but <11> –STOP succeeds:

14.6.9 REALIZING . (FULL STOP)

16 –STOP   {1 –DET, 2 –NoP}

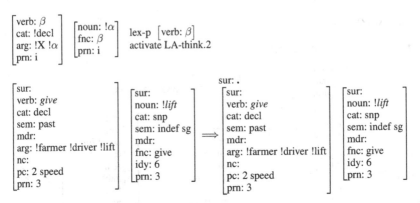

−STOP triggers an unconditional switch to LA-think. However, LA-think cannot find a continuation proplet in the Word Bank 13.6.1 because the nc attribute of *give* has the value NIL. Therefore the ST_F definition of LA-think applies, checks whether the last state derived is a legal final state, and ends the process in a well-formed completion.

The interaction between LA-think and LA-speak in Sects. 14.4, 14.5, and the current section is maximally incremental in the sense (i) that LA-speak continues to realize surfaces as long as the currently activated proplets allow and (ii) that the LA-think navigation continues only after the surfaces derivable from the currently activated proplets have all been realized. This has the effect of reducing the number of possible proplets serving as candidates for matching with the LA-speak patterns, especially at the beginning of a derivation.

Later, as more proplets have been added to the activated sequence, the earlier proplets have been systematically !-marked in past rule applications of both grammars – which reduces the set of matching candidates from the other end. As a consequence, a maximally incremental system can guide the intended matching with much simpler and more efficient pattern definitions than one which activates future proplets earlier than necessary.

15. DBS.3: Adnominal and Adverbial Modifiers

This chapter deals with "prepositional phrase attachment" in the hearer mode. It extends LA-hear.2 into **LA-hear.3** by adding elementary adverbs like quickly, prepositional phrases like on the table, and intensifiers like very, as in very quickly, the very big table, and on the very big table. Apart from their variety of position and interpretation, prepositional phrases present a challenge because when used in sequence they result in a kind of ambiguity which must be treated with great care to avoid exponential complexity in the worst case.

15.1 Interpreting Elementary and Complex Modifiers

Prepositional phrases are complex adjectives (cf. Sect. 6.3). They consist of (i) a preposition like in, on, under, above, below, before, behind, etc., and (ii) a noun phrase which may be elementary (consisting of a name or pronoun) or complex (consisting of a determiner, an open number of adjectives, and a noun).

A prepositional phrase has nominal as well as adjectival qualities. The nominal quality derives from the fact that a prepositional phrase like on the big table contains a noun, for which reason its proplet requires an idy and an mdr attribute – in contradistinction to elementary adjectives like fast, which do not. The adjectival quality derives from the fact that a prepositional phrase functions as an adjective, for which reason its proplet should have the same attributes as an elementary adjective.

One way to resolve the dilemma is to define different kinds of proplets for elementary adjectives and prepositions (similar to the definition of n/v and a/v proplets, cf. 7.1.1). The other way is to define the proplets of elementary adjectives with dummy idy and mdr attributes, as illustrated below:

15.1.1 PREPOSITION, COMPLEX ADJECTIVE, AND ELEMENTARY ADJECTIVE

on   on the big table   fast

$$
\begin{bmatrix}
\text{sur: on} \\
\text{adj: } on\ \text{n\_2} \\
\text{cat: adj} \\
\text{sem:} \\
\text{mdr:} \\
\text{mdd:} \\
\text{idy:} \\
\text{prn:}
\end{bmatrix}
\quad
\begin{bmatrix}
\text{sur: on} \\
\text{adj: } on\ table \\
\text{cat: adj} \\
\text{sem: def sg} \\
\text{mdr: big} \\
\text{mdd: apple 1} \\
\text{idy: 2} \\
\text{prn: 1}
\end{bmatrix}
\quad
\begin{bmatrix}
\text{sur: fast} \\
\text{adj: } fast \\
\text{cat: adj} \\
\text{sem:} \\
\text{mdr: B} \\
\text{mdd: car 4} \\
\text{idy: B} \\
\text{prn: 3}
\end{bmatrix}
$$

While the mdr attribute of the prepositional phrase may take zero or more adnominals as values, this attribute has the value B (for "blocked") in elementary adjectives. Similarly, while the idy (identity) attribute in prepositional phrases specifies the idy number of the noun contained, this attribute has the value B in elementary adjectives.

In this way, the current fragment continues to be based on only three major kinds of proplets[1] with the core attributes noun (for arguments or objects), verb (for functors or relations), and adj (for properties or modifiers), plus two minor kinds with the core attributes n/v and a/v for sentential arguments and sentential modifiers, respectively. Having a small and stable number of feature structures is important for the definition and continuous update of the standard relational database underlying the implementation of LA-hear, LA-think, and LA-speak, implemented by Fischer (2004).

Whether an adjective is used adnominally or adverbially is reflected by the value of its mdd (modified) attribute: in adnominal use, the mdd attribute contains a noun; in adverbial use, it contains a verb. In adnominally used adjectives, the noun value of the mdd attribute is followed by the idy-number of the modified noun (for example, apple 1 in the prepositional phrase and car 4 in the elementary adjective of 15.1.1).[2]

The distinction between adnominal and adverbial use is illustrated below:

15.1.2 REPRESENTING (eat) the apple on the table (ADNOMINAL)

```
┌noun: apple  ┐  ┌adj: on table ┐
│cat: np      │  │cat: adn      │
│sem: def sg  │  │sem: def sg   │
│fnc: eat     │  │mdr:          │
│mdr: on table│  │mdd: apple 1  │
│idy: 1       │  │idy: 2        │
└prn: 1       ┘  └prn: 1        ┘
```

15.1.3 REPRESENTING eat (the apple) on the table (ADVERBIAL)

```
┌sur:             ┐
│verb: eat        │  ┌adj: on table┐
│cat: v           │  │cat: adv     │
│sem: past        │  │sem: def sg  │
│mdr: on table    │  │mdr:         │
│arg: Julia apple │  │mdd: eat     │
│nc:              │  │idy: 2       │
│pc:              │  └prn: 1       ┘
└prn: 1           ┘
```

The mdd attribute of an adjective has a unique value because it can modify only a single verb or a single noun. The mdr attribute of nouns or verbs, in contrast, can have

---

[1] These three kinds of feature structures are differentiated into (i) language and context proplets, (ii) symbol, indexical, and name proplets, and (iii) isolated, episodic, and absolute proplets solely in terms of various characteristic values.

[2] The idy number is placed behind the noun value in order to avoid confusion with the prn numbers, which are written before extrapropositional values (see Chaps. 7 and 9). Happily, mdd attributes take at most one value, making the conventions unambiguous.

several values. For example, the mdr values of the proplet *apple* in the small red apple on the table would be [mdr: small red on table], while that of the proplet *eat* in Julia ate the apple quickly on the table would be [mdr: quickly on table].

Adjectives differ in the positions they can take in a sentence depending on whether they are used adnominally or adverbially, and whether they are elementary or complex. In preparation of our formal treatment let us survey the different possibilities.

The positioning of elementary adnominals is the simplest. They occur noun-phrase internally between the determiner and the noun, as in the following examples:

15.1.4 Positions of Elementary Adnominals

(i)   The + *young* + girl ate an apple   (modifying the subject)
(ii) Julia gave the + *young* + girl an apple   (modifying the indirect object)
(iii) Julia gave the girl a + *red* + apple   (modifying the direct object)

These cases have already been treated in LA-hear.2.[3] The "+" signs indicate the compositions required (i) to add the modifier and (ii) to continue after the modifier.

Next, consider complex adnominals (i.e., prepositional phrases in adnominal use). Like elementary adnominals, their position is fixed relative to the noun they modify. However, while elementary adnominals are positioned prenominally, complex adnominals are positioned postnominally:

15.1.5 Positions of Complex Adnominals (Prepositional Phrases)

(i)   the apple + *on the table* + pleased Julia   (modifying the subject)
(ii) Julia ate the apple + *on the table*   (modifying the direct object)
(iii) Julia gave John the apple + *on the table*   (modifying the direct object)

The relevant composition in all three examples adds the preposition on to a sentence start ending in the noun apple. The subsequent handling of different internal structures of prepositional phrases is the same for all three positions. Different internal structures of complex adnominals are exemplified by on Fido, on the dog, on the big dog, and on the very big dog. Example (ii) is explicitly derived in 15.2.1–15.2.7 below.

In contradistinction to adnominals, the position of adverbials need not be adjacent to the word they modify. Consider elementary adverbials:

15.1.6 Positions of Elementary Adverbials

(i)   *quickly* + Julia ate the apple
(ii) Julia + *quickly* + ate the apple
(iii) Julia slept + *soundly*
(iv) Julia ate the apple + *quickly*

---

[3] For explicit derivations see 13.3.1–13.3.3 (preverbal) and 13.3.6–13.3.7 (postverbal).

The relevant composition of Example (i) is between a sentence initial elementary adverbial and the nominative, and is shown explicitly in 15.3.7. The relevant composition of Example (ii) is between the nominative and an elementary adverbial, and is shown explicitly in 15.3.9. In both examples, the continuation adding the verb is handled by the same rule ADVNOM+FV, illustrated in 15.3.10. The relevant composition of (iii) and (iv) is between the verb and an elementary adverbial, and is shown explicitly in 15.3.3.

Complex adjectives in adverbial use have a more restricted distribution than the corresponding elementary adverbs, as shown below:

15.1.7 POSITIONS OF PREPOSITIONAL PHRASES USED AS ADVERBS

(i)   *on the table* + Julia ate an apple
(ii) *Julia + *on the table* + ate the apple
(iii) Julia slept + *on the table*
(iv) Julia ate the apple + *on the table*

As indicated by the asterisk *, Example (ii) is ungrammatical – even though the corresponding sentence with an elementary adverb is not (cf. 15.1.6, ii). The prevention of the ungrammatical construction (ii) is explained in 15.3.5. The relevant composition of Example (i) in 15.1.7 is analogous to (i) in 15.1.6, and is shown explicitly in 15.3.8. The relevant composition of Examples (iii) and (iv) is between the verb and the preposition, and is shown explicitly in 15.3.1.

An important and interesting detail common to noun phrases, prepositional phrases, and elementary adverbs is the use of intensifiers like very and detensifiers like rather.[4] In Database Semantics, intensifiers are treated as function words which absorb the modified elementary adjective (cf. Sect. 15.4). Thus, intensifiers are not treated as modifiers of the adjective, represented by separate (connected, i.e., nonlexical) proplets, but rather as values of the sem attribute (cf. 15.4.5).

The possible positions of intensifiers are illustrated in the following examples:

15.1.8 POSITIONS OF INTENSIFIERS

(i)   the + *very* big + table   (noun phrase)
(ii) on the + *very* big + table   (prepositional phrase)
(iii) *very* quickly + Julia ate an apple   (elementary adverbial)
(iv) Julia + *very* quickly + ate an apple (elementary adverbial)
(v)   Julia ate the apple + *very* quickly   (elementary adverbial)

The relevant compositions of these constructions are shown explicitly in 15.4.4–15.5.6.

---

[4] For simplicity, and following wider practice, we use the term "intensifier" to include detensifiers unless specified otherwise.

Let us turn now to the ambiguities introduced systematically by prepositional phrases.[5] One kind of ambiguity arises between the adnominal and the adverbial use, as in Julia ate the apple + on the table. On one reading on the table modifies *apple* (adnominal or ADN), but on the other it modifies *eat* (adverbial or ADV).

A second kind of ambiguity arises when prepositional phrases are used in sequence. In that case, the later phrases may modify either (a) the noun or (b) the verb preceding the sequence, or (c) the prepositional phrase preceding within the sequence:

15.1.9 INTERPRETATIONS OF SEQUENCES OF PREPOSITIONAL PHRASES

(i) the car + in the garage + with the broken window
(ii) Julia walked + into the garden + with John's shoes

In (i), with the broken window may either modify *car* (adnominal reading) or *garage* (ad-adjectival reading). In (ii), with John's shoes may either modify *walk* (adverbial reading) or *garden* (ad-adjectival reading).

The ad-adjectival (or ADA) reading may combine with the adnominal (or ADN) and the adverbial (or ADV) reading, as in the following example, which shows the different readings of Julia ate the apple + on the table + behind the tree + in the garden:

15.1.10 READINGS CREATED BY A SEQUENCE PREPOSITIONAL PHRASES

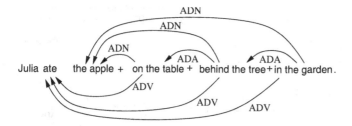

The first prepositional phrase, on the table, may modify *apple* (ADN) or *eat* (ADV). The second prepositional phrase, behind the tree, may modify *apple* (ADN), *eat* (ADV), or *on the table* (ADA). The third prepositional phrase, in the garden, may modify *apple* (ADN), *eat* (ADV), or *behind the tree* (ADA).

In Nativist linguistics, it is general practice to represent each reading and each combination of readings in a sentence by a separate tree. The trees resulting from all the combinations of readings in Example 15.1.10 may be summarized abstractly as follows:

---

[5] These kinds of systematic ambiguity do not arise with elementary adjectives. This is because in adnominal use they are alway positioned before the modified noun, as in the fast car. Also, the distinction between adnominal and adverbial use is often marked morphologically, as in beautiful vs. beautifully.

15.1.11 NATIVIST TREATMENT OF PREPOSITIONAL PHRASE AMBIGUITIES

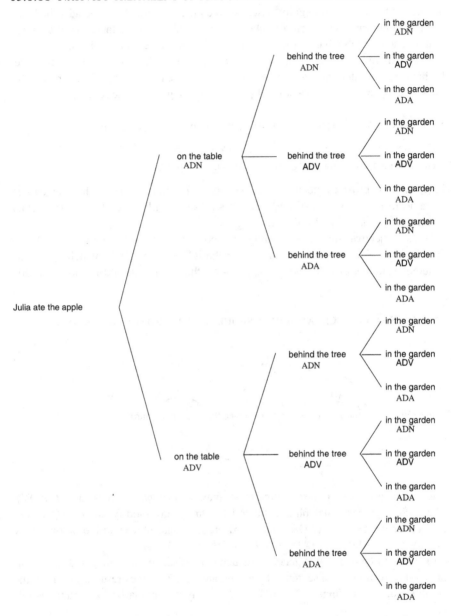

Given that there is no grammatical limit on the length of a sequence of prepositional phrases, the approach illustrated above results in an exponential increase of readings. More precisely, the general formula for the Nativist method results in $2 \cdot 3^{n-1}$ readings in the worst case, where n is the number of prepositional phrases, for $n > 2$. In Example 15.1.11, n equals 3; therefore there are $2 \cdot 3^2 = 18$ different readings.

From the viewpoint of Database Semantics, however, such a multiplying out of all combinations of readings serves no purpose in communication. In production, the speaker has only one combination of readings in mind anyway. In interpretation, the hearer has to determine which of the possible combinations is the appropriate one. This can by done much better if the possible readings are represented individually for each prepositional phrase in the sentence – without the additional step of computing and representing all their possible combinations in the form of separate tree structures.

As shown in 6.6.1, our alternative approach is based on *semantic doubling*. This applies to ambiguities which are strictly semantic. For example, the word perch is lexically ambiguous between *place to roost* and *kind of fish*, whereby both meanings have the same syntactic category, namely noun. Therefore, a sentence containing the word perch may be treated as syntactically unambiguous, though with two meanings$_1$ attached to it:

15.1.12 EXAMPLE OF LEXICALLY-BASED SEMANTIC DOUBLING

The osprey is looking for a   perch

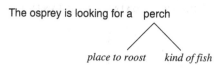

place to roost   kind of fish

The choice between the two meanings is determined by the pragmatics, i.e., the principle of the best match between the meaning$_1$ alternatives and the context of use.

Because prepositional phrases are the same syntactically regardless of whether their interpretation is ADN, ADV, or ADA, semantic doubling may also be used for sequences of prepositional phrases, resulting in the following reanalysis of Example 15.1.11:

15.1.13 PREPOSITIONAL PHRASE AMBIGUITY AS SEMANTIC DOUBLING

Julia ate the apple   +   on the table   +   behind the tree   +   in the garden

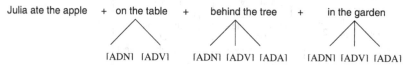

[ADN] [ADV]   [ADN] [ADV] [ADA]   [ADN] [ADV] [ADA]

The analysis is syntactically unambiguous in the sense that only one representation is derived. It is ambiguous semantically,[6] however, in that the first prepositional phrase has an ADN and an ADV meaning, while the second and third have an ADN, ADV, and ADA meaning attached to them.

This way of indicating the alternative interpretations for each prepositional phrase is sufficient for all purposes of semantic and pragmatic interpretation. For example,

---

[6] The distinction between syntactic, semantic, and pragmatic ambiguity is explained in FoCL'99, pp. 232 ff.

if the hearer picks the ADN interpretation of the first prepositional phrase, the ADV interpretation is discarded. If the hearer picks the ADA interpretation of the second prepositional phrase, the ADN and ADV interpretations of the second prepositional phrase are discarded, and similarly for the other prepositional phrases. The procedure of choosing between the interpretations provided by semantic doubling is defined in LA-think as part of the hearer's inferencing (analogous to the inferencing for handling indirect uses, cf. Sect. 5.4).

In terms of computational complexity, semantic doubling is much more efficient than the Nativist method. Instead of *multiplying* the local ambiguities in a sentence, as illustrated in 15.1.11, semantic doubling only *adds* the local ambiguities, resulting in linear complexity. More precisely, the formula for semantic doubling in sequences of prepositional phrases is $2 + [3 \cdot (n - 1)]$ readings in the worst case. In Example 15.1.13, n equals 3; therefore there are only $2 + [3 \cdot (3 - 1)] = 8$ readings – contained in a single syntactic–semantic analysis.

The intuitive representation of the readings presented in 15.1.13 in terms of semantic doubling is formalized in Database Semantics as the following set of proplets:

15.1.14 FORMALIZING SEMANTIC DOUBLING IN DATABASE SEMANTICS

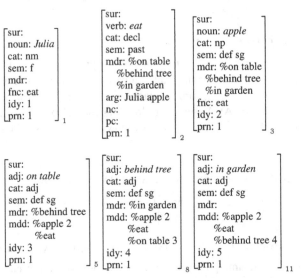

Note that the mdr attributes of *eat* and *apple* each have three values, namely %on table, %behind tree and %in garden. Also, the mdr attribute of *on table* has the value %behind tree and the mdr attribute of *behind tree* has the value %in garden. The % marker characterizes these values as possible mdr values; which of these values constitute the correct interpretation must be determined via inferences.

Furthermore, the mdd attribute of *on table* has two values, namely %apple 2 and %eat. The mdd attributes of *behind tree* and *in garden* each have three values, namely

%apple 2 and %eat, as well as %on table 3 and %behind tree 4, respectively. In the mdd attributes, the % marker indicates that only one of several values can be selected, thus maintaining the general rule that modifiers have a unique modified.

In summary, there are altogether eight modifiers distributed over the proplets *eat, apple, on table,* and *behind tree,* and eight modified distributed over the proplets *on table, behind tree,* and *in garden.* In this way, the intuitive idea of semantic doubling shown in 15.1.13 has a straightforward formal realization in Database Semantics.

The names of the rules producing semantic doubling are preceded by %, for example, %+ADV, %+ADN, and %+ADA. Accordingly, these rules are called "percentage rules" because (i) their simultaneous application derives a single output (in contrast to syntactic ambiguities in LA-grammar, in which each successful application starts a separate branch of possible continuations), and (ii) they introduce *possible* semantic relations, i.e., with a likelihood of holding which is less than a 100%.

The simultaneous application of percentage rules may be illustrated as follows:

15.1.15 ADDING PREPOSITION. PHRASE WITH ADV AND ADN INTERPRETATION

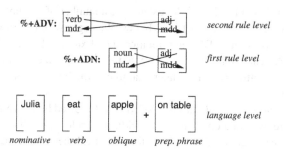

At the language level, there is the sentence start *Julia eat apple,* consisting of a set of proplets, and the next word *on table.* For simplicity, the latter is treated as a single proplet representing the prepositional phrase on the table and is added as a whole.[7] The rules %+ADN and %+ADV apply simultaneously to combine the *ss* and the *nw.*

%+ADN (first rule level) has a pattern for a noun and an adjective; it copies the adj value of the next word into the mdr slot of the noun and the noun value of the *ss* into the mdd slot of the *nw.* %+ADV (second rule level) has a pattern for a verb and an adjective; it copies the adj value of the next word into the mdr slot of the verb and the verb value of the *ss* into the mdd slot of the *nw.* The arrows indicating the copying operations at the two rule levels are executed at the language level.

Next consider the addition of a second prepositional phrase, behind the tree. This time there is not only an ADV and an ADN interpretation, but also an ADA interpretation relative to the preceding prepositional phrase on the table:

---

[7] The incremental addition of the prepositional phrase is shown in 15.2.4–15.2.6 for the ADN interpretation, the addition of the preposition for the ADV interpretation in 15.3.1, and the addition of the preposition for the ADA interpretation in 15.2.4.

15.1.16 PREPOSITIONAL PHRASE WITH ADV, ADN, AND ADA INTERPRETATION

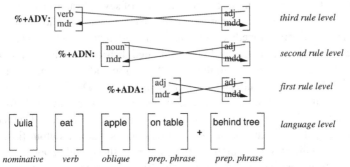

After adding the third prepositional phrase *in the garden* in the same way, there will be eight mdr and eight mdd values marked with %, corresponding to 15.1.14.

15.2 ADN and ADA Interpretations of Prepositional Phrases

Before we extend LA-hear.2 into LA-hear.3, let us analyze a number of examples anticipating the rules of LA-hear.3 defined in 15.6.2 below. We begin with the sentence *Julia ate the apple on the table* in its ADN interpretation, i.e., Example 15.1.5 (ii). As the first example of an LA-hear.3 analysis, it is presented as a complete derivation, in contrast to the syntactic–semantic analysis of later examples, which will be limited to the relevant composition(s).

The step by step derivation begins with familiar NOM+FV, followed by FV+NP and DET+NN. These rules are extended only insofar as additional rule names have been added to their rule packages, in concord with the definition of LA-hear.3 in 15.6.2.

15.2.1 COMBINING Julia AND ate WITH NOM+FV

NOM+FV   {22 FV+NP, 23 AUX+NFV, 24 S+IP}

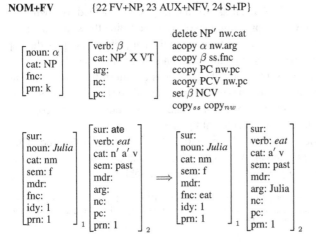

15.2.2 COMBINING Julia ate AND the WITH FV+NP

FV+NP   {DET+NN, DET+ADN, DET+INT, FV+NP, %NP+PREP, %V+ADV, V+INT, S+IP}

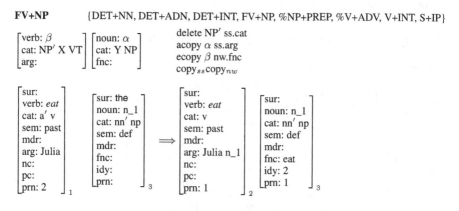

15.2.3 COMBINING Julia ate the AND apple WITH DET+NN

DET+NN   {NOM+FV, ADVNOM+FV, FV+NP, %NP+PREP, %V+ADV, V+INT, S+IP}

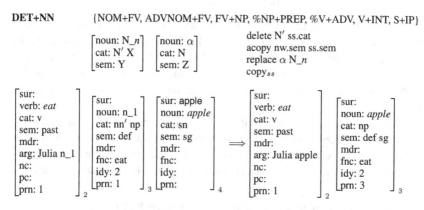

The rule package of DET+NN contains two new rules, %NP+PREP and %V+ADV. Both apply in the derivation of Julia ate the apple + on the table, one for the adnominal and the other for the adverbial interpretation of the prepositional phrase.

The concurrent application of the percentage rules %NP+PREP and %V+ADV will result in only one output. In this single output, however, the adnominal relation between the preposition *on* and the noun *apple*, and the adverbial relation between this preposition and the verb *eat* will be in place. Subsequently, the derivation will be continued by PREP+NP in 15.2.5 and by PREP+NN in 15.2.6, whereby the sequence %NP+PREP, PREP+NP, PREP+NN is the incremental counterpart to simplified %+ADN in 15.1.15, while the sequence %V+ADV, PREP+NP, PREP+NN is the incremental counterpart to simplified %+ADV of that same example.

Dealing here with the ADN interpretation first, let us consider the application of %NP+PREP, adding the preposition on in its adnominal interpretation to the sentence start Julia ate the apple. (The relevant composition of the corresponding adverbial interpretation based on %V+ADV is shown in 15.3.1.)

15.2.4 COMBINING Julia ate the apple AND on WITH %NP+PREP

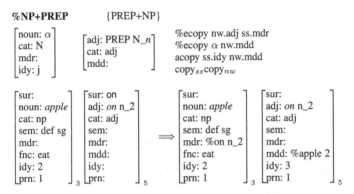

%NP+PREP   {PREP+NP}

$$
\begin{bmatrix} \text{noun: } \alpha \\ \text{cat: N} \\ \text{mdr:} \\ \text{idy: } j \end{bmatrix}
\begin{bmatrix} \text{adj: PREP N\_}n \\ \text{cat: adj} \\ \text{mdd:} \end{bmatrix}
$$

%ecopy nw.adj ss.mdr
%ecopy α nw.mdd
acopy ss.idy nw.mdd
copy$_{ss}$copy$_{nw}$

$$
\begin{bmatrix} \text{sur:} \\ \text{noun: } apple \\ \text{cat: np} \\ \text{sem: def sg} \\ \text{mdr:} \\ \text{fnc: eat} \\ \text{idy: 2} \\ \text{prn: 1} \end{bmatrix}_3
\begin{bmatrix} \text{sur: on} \\ \text{adj: } on \text{ n\_2} \\ \text{cat: adj} \\ \text{sem:} \\ \text{mdr:} \\ \text{mdd:} \\ \text{idy:} \\ \text{prn:} \end{bmatrix}_5
\Longrightarrow
\begin{bmatrix} \text{sur:} \\ \text{noun: } apple \\ \text{cat: np} \\ \text{sem: def sg} \\ \text{mdr: \%on n\_2} \\ \text{fnc: eat} \\ \text{idy: 2} \\ \text{prn: 1} \end{bmatrix}_3
\begin{bmatrix} \text{sur:} \\ \text{adj: } on \text{ n\_2} \\ \text{cat: adj} \\ \text{sem:} \\ \text{mdr:} \\ \text{mdd: \%apple 2} \\ \text{idy: 3} \\ \text{prn: 1} \end{bmatrix}_5
$$

Copying operations preceded by % add this marker to the copied value. The first operation, %ecopy nw.adj ss.mdr, copies the value %on n_2 of the adj attribute into the mdr attribute of the modified noun *apple*. The second and third operations copy the noun value (%acopy α nw.mdd) and the idy value (ecopy ss.idy nw.mdd) of the modified into the mdd slot of the preposition. Both input proplets are retained in the result.

PREP+NP, currently the only rule in the rule package of %NP+PREP, applies next. PREP+NP adds the noun phrase after a preposition, regardless of whether it is used as an ADN, ADV, or ADA, and regardless of whether the noun phrase is elementary (as in book for + Julia) or complex (as in book for + the very pretty young woman).

15.2.5 COMBINING Julia ate the apple on AND the WITH PREP+NP

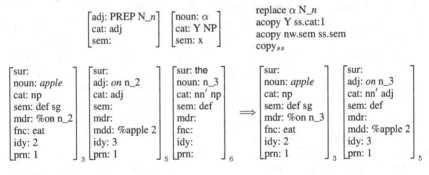

PREP+NP {PREP+NN,PREP+ADN,PREP+INT,%NP+PREP,%V+ADV,%PREP+PREP,ADV+NOM,S+IP}

$$
\begin{bmatrix} \text{adj: PREP N\_}n \\ \text{cat: adj} \\ \text{sem:} \end{bmatrix}
\begin{bmatrix} \text{noun: } \alpha \\ \text{cat: Y NP} \\ \text{sem: } x \end{bmatrix}
$$

replace α N_n
acopy Y ss.cat:1
acopy nw.sem ss.sem
copy$_{ss}$

$$
\begin{bmatrix} \text{sur:} \\ \text{noun: } apple \\ \text{cat: np} \\ \text{sem: def sg} \\ \text{mdr: \%on n\_2} \\ \text{fnc: eat} \\ \text{idy: 2} \\ \text{prn: 1} \end{bmatrix}_3
\begin{bmatrix} \text{sur:} \\ \text{adj: } on \text{ n\_2} \\ \text{cat: adj} \\ \text{sem:} \\ \text{mdr:} \\ \text{mdd: \%apple 2} \\ \text{idy: 3} \\ \text{prn: 1} \end{bmatrix}_5
\begin{bmatrix} \text{sur: the} \\ \text{noun: n\_3} \\ \text{cat: nn' np} \\ \text{sem: def} \\ \text{mdr:} \\ \text{fnc:} \\ \text{idy:} \\ \text{prn:} \end{bmatrix}_6
\Longrightarrow
\begin{bmatrix} \text{sur:} \\ \text{noun: } apple \\ \text{cat: np} \\ \text{sem: def sg} \\ \text{mdr: \%on n\_3} \\ \text{fnc: eat} \\ \text{idy: 2} \\ \text{prn: 1} \end{bmatrix}_3
\begin{bmatrix} \text{sur:} \\ \text{adj: } on \text{ n\_3} \\ \text{cat: nn' adj} \\ \text{sem: def} \\ \text{mdr:} \\ \text{mdd: \%apple 2} \\ \text{idy: 3} \\ \text{prn: 1} \end{bmatrix}_5
$$

In this example, two function words, on and the, are combined. More specifically, the determiner the is absorbed by the preposition on. In the next step, the noun table will be absorbed by the combination of the two function words.[8]

The first operation of PREP+NP, replace α N_n, replaces the substitution value n_2 of the preposition by the noun value of the nw, which happens to be another substitution value, namely n_3.[9] As a result, the adj slot of the preposition and the mdr slot of the modified *apple* continue to contain the same simultaneous substitution values, as desired. The second operation, acopy Y ss.cat:1, adds the category segment sn′ to the left of the cat value adj of the *ss*, resulting in sn′ adj. The third operation, acopy nw.sem ss.sem, copies the sem value of the nw into the sem slot of the *ss*. Having copied all relevant details of the nw into the *ss*, the rule retains only the *ss* in the output (copy$_{ss}$, but not copy$_{nw}$).

Next applies the new rule PREP+NN. It resembles DET+NN, except that the sentence start is an adjective rather than a noun.

15.2.6 COMBINING Julia ate the apple on the AND table WITH PREP+NN

PREP+NN {ADV+NOM, NOM+FV, FV+NP, %NP+PREP, %V+ADV, %PREPP+PREP, V+INT, S+IP}

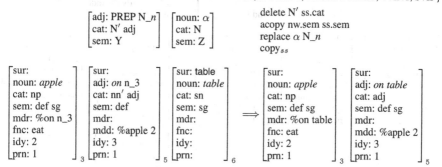

Skipping the application of S+IP, the result of this derivation is as follows:

15.2.7 THE ADN-INTERPRETATION OF Julia ate the apple on the table

$$
\begin{bmatrix}
\text{sur:} \\
\text{noun: } Julia \\
\text{cat: nm} \\
\text{sem: f} \\
\text{mdr:} \\
\text{fnc: eat} \\
\text{idy: 1} \\
\text{prn: 1}
\end{bmatrix}_1
\begin{bmatrix}
\text{sur:} \\
\text{verb: } eat \\
\text{cat: v} \\
\text{sem: past} \\
\text{mdr:} \\
\text{arg: Julia apple} \\
\text{nc:} \\
\text{pc:} \\
\text{prn: 1}
\end{bmatrix}_2
\begin{bmatrix}
\text{sur:} \\
\text{noun: } apple \\
\text{cat: np} \\
\text{sem: def sg} \\
\text{mdr: %on table} \\
\text{fnc: eat} \\
\text{idy: 2} \\
\text{prn: 1}
\end{bmatrix}_3
\begin{bmatrix}
\text{sur:} \\
\text{adj: } on\ table \\
\text{cat: adj} \\
\text{sem: def sg} \\
\text{mdr:} \\
\text{mdd: %apple 2} \\
\text{idy: 3} \\
\text{prn: 1}
\end{bmatrix}_5
$$

---

[8] If the next word had been a proper name, for example, Fido as in on + Fido, the noun would have been absorbed by the preposition directly. In this case, the mdr slot of the modified would contain *%on Fido*.

[9] Remember that a substitution value introduced by a lexical item gets automatically incremented by the control structure of the parser (cf. 6.2.1).

The adj proplet *on table* is characterized as an adnominal by the value of its mdd attribute, %apple 2, and by the value of the mdr attribute %on table of *apple*.

Next consider continuing Julia ate the apple on the table with behind the tree. As noted in 15.1.9 and 15.1.10, this additional prepositional phrase can have three readings, namely ADN, ADV, and ADA. The ADN reading is handled by %NP+PREP already illustrated in 15.2.4: The rule simply selects the first noun phrase preceding the preposition, regardless of intervening prepositional phrases. The ADV reading will be discussed in the following section 15.3. It remains the ADA reading, according to which behind the tree modifies *on table*.[10]

The relevant composition for continuing Julia ate the apple on the table with the preposition behind in its ADA interpretation is based on the new rule %PREPP+PREP (for %PREPositional Phrase + PREPosition), which is illustrated below:

15.2.8 COMBINING the apple on the table AND behind WITH %PREPP+PREP

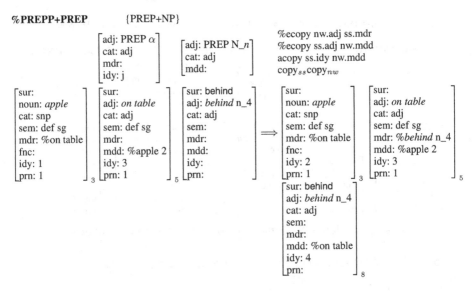

%PREPP+PREP is the initial incremental counterpart to nonincremental (elementary) %+ADA in 15.1.16. Like %NP+PREP and %V+ADV, %PREPP+PREP is continued with PREP+NP.

The composition shown in 15.2.8 is simplified insofar as the rule package of PREP+NN (cf. 15.2.6) simultaneously calls %NP+PREP, %V+ADV, and %PREPP+PREP (cf. 15.1.16). Therefore, the proplets shown at the language level of 15.2.8 would normally show the semantic relations introduced by %NP+PREP and %V+ADV as well. In other words, the effects of the concurrent instances of semantic doubling have been omitted here for the sake of transparency.

---

[10] In other words, the apple is on the table and the table is behind the tree.

15.3 ADV Interpretation of Prepositional Phrases

Having derived the ADN interpretation of the prepositional phrase in Julia ate the
apple + on the table in the previous section, let us turn to the adverbial interpretation
of this example. The initial derivation steps are identical to 15.2.1–15.2.3.

Next comes the relevant composition of adding the preposition on in its ADV interpretation. This step is handled by the new rule %V+ADV, called by DET+NN:

15.3.1 COMBINING Julia ate the apple AND on WITH %V+ADV

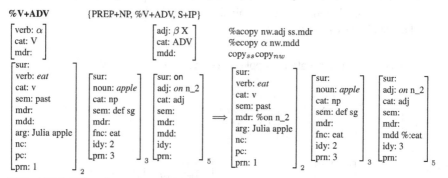

%V+ADV differs from %NP+PREP in that the *ss*-pattern of %V+ADV matches a
verb, while the *ss*-pattern of %NP+PREP matches a noun. %V+ADV adds elementary
adverbs as well as prepositions (as the beginning of a complex adjective, due to the
nw pattern [adj: β X]), while %NP+PREP (cf. 15.2.4) adds only prepositions. A third
difference is the use of the variable ADV, which is restricted to the values adj and
adv (cf. the preamble of LA-hear.3 defined in 15.6.1, 2). Serving as the value of the
cat attribute, it can match prepopositions with the cat value adj as well as elementary
adverbs like slowly with the cat value adv.

The first operation of %V+ADV, %acopy nw.adj ss.mdr, copies the value *on table*
of the adj attribute of the *nw* into the mdr attribute of the *ss*. The second operation,
%ecopy α nw.mdd, copies the value *eat* of the verb attribute of the *ss* into the mdd
attribute of the *nw*. Both input proplets are retained in the output.

The derivation continues with PREP+NP and PREP+NN in analogy to 15.2.5 and
15.2.6, respectively. The result is:

15.3.2 THE ADV-INTERPRETATION OF Julia ate the apple on the table

$$
\begin{bmatrix}
\text{sur:} \\
\text{noun: } Julia \\
\text{cat: nm} \\
\text{sem: f} \\
\text{mdr:} \\
\text{fnc: eat} \\
\text{idy: 1} \\
\text{prn: 1}
\end{bmatrix}_1
\begin{bmatrix}
\text{sur:} \\
\text{verb: } eat \\
\text{cat: v} \\
\text{sem: past} \\
\text{mdr: \%on table} \\
\text{arg: Julia apple} \\
\text{nc:} \\
\text{pc:} \\
\text{prn: 1}
\end{bmatrix}_2
\begin{bmatrix}
\text{sur:} \\
\text{noun: } apple \\
\text{cat: np} \\
\text{sem: def sg} \\
\text{mdr:} \\
\text{fnc: eat} \\
\text{idy: 2} \\
\text{prn: 1}
\end{bmatrix}_3
\begin{bmatrix}
\text{sur:} \\
\text{adj: } on\ table \\
\text{cat: adj} \\
\text{sem: def sg} \\
\text{mdr:} \\
\text{mdd: \%eat} \\
\text{idy: 3} \\
\text{prn: 1}
\end{bmatrix}_5
$$

The adjective proplet *on table* is characterized as an adverbial modifier by the value eat of its mdd attribute, and the value on table of the mdr attribute of the proplet *eat*.

As in 15.2.4, the composition shown in 15.3.2 is simplified insofar as the rule package of PREP+NN (cf. 15.2.6) simultaneously calls %NP+PREP and %V+ADV. Therefore, the proplets shown at the language level of 15.3.2 would normally show the semantic relations introduced by %NP+PREP as well.

Next, consider the adverbial interpretation of the elementary adjective fast in Julia ate the apple fast (cf. 15.1.6, iv). Even though fast is not excluded from adnominal use, as in the fast car, an adnominal interpretation is not permitted here because elementary adnominals require a prenominal position.[11] The relevant composition is again handled by %V+ADV:

15.3.3 COMBINING Julia ate the apple AND fast WITH %V+ADV

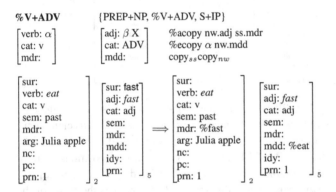

The result of the overall derivation is as follows:

15.3.4 RESULT OF INTERPRETING Julia ate the apple fast

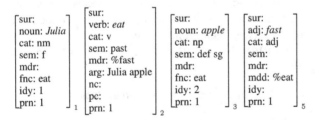

Note that adjectives following an elementary adverbial can have only an adverbial interpretation. For example, while the prepositional phrase on the table in

---

[11] An elementary adverbial like quickly, as in Julia at the apple quickly, would be prevented from an adnominal interpretation also by its morphological marking. See Dauses (1997) et seq. for a critical discussion of this kind of redundancy, which is common in many natural languages.

Julia ate the apple on the table quickly.

can have an adnominal as well as an adverbial interpretation, it can be interpreted only adverbially in

Julia ate the apple quickly on the table.

This observation is implemented by excluding the rule name %NP+PREP from the rule package of %V+ADV. Consider the following schematic analysis:

15.3.5 INTERPRETATION OF POSTADVERBIAL PREPOSITIONAL PHRASES

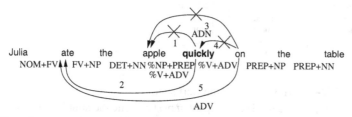

The rules are written underneath – and into the spaces between – the words. The first occurrence of DET+NN, combining Julia ate the and apple, calls both %NP+PREP (adnominal) and %V+ADV (adverbial). However, given the nature of the next word quickly (crossed out arrow 1), only %V+ADV can fire (arrow 2). Next, %V+ADV applies again to add the preposition on. Because %V+ADV contains neither %NP+PREP (crossed out arrow 3) nor %PREPP+NP (crossed out arrow 4) in its rule package, the only interpretation possible is the adverbial one (arrow 5).

15.3.6 RESULT OF INTERPRETING Julia ate the apple quickly on the table

$$
\begin{bmatrix}
\text{sur:} \\
\text{noun: } \textit{Julia} \\
\text{cat: nm} \\
\text{sem: f} \\
\text{mdr:} \\
\text{fnc: eat} \\
\text{idy: 1} \\
\text{prn: 1}
\end{bmatrix}_1
\begin{bmatrix}
\text{sur:} \\
\text{verb: } \textit{eat} \\
\text{cat: v} \\
\text{sem: past} \\
\text{mdr: \%quick} \\
\qquad \text{\%on table} \\
\text{arg: Julia apple} \\
\text{nc:} \\
\text{pc:} \\
\text{prn: 1}
\end{bmatrix}_2
\begin{bmatrix}
\text{sur:} \\
\text{noun: } \textit{apple} \\
\text{cat: np} \\
\text{sem: def sg} \\
\text{mdr:} \\
\text{fnc: eat} \\
\text{idy: 2} \\
\text{prn: 1}
\end{bmatrix}_3
\begin{bmatrix}
\text{sur:} \\
\text{adj: } \textit{quick} \\
\text{cat: adj} \\
\text{sem:} \\
\text{mdr:} \\
\text{mdd: \%eat} \\
\text{idy:} \\
\text{prn: 1}
\end{bmatrix}_6
\begin{bmatrix}
\text{sur:} \\
\text{adj: } \textit{on table} \\
\text{cat: adj} \\
\text{sem: def sg} \\
\text{mdr:} \\
\text{mdd: \%eat} \\
\text{idy: 3} \\
\text{prn: 1}
\end{bmatrix}_5
$$

Even though the mdr values of the verb are marked by the % sign, they may be inferred to each hold completely, i.e., a 100%, because the corresponding mdd attributes in the proplets *quick* and *on table* contain only a single value each (compare 15.1.14).

Next let us consider adverbials in preverbal position. They are a challenge insofar as, for example, in quickly + Julia ate an apple the adverbial quickly combines with the nominative Julia, providing no immediate opportunity to code the mdd–mdr relation between the adverb quickly and the verb ate (suspension). The solution is based on using the simultaneous substitution value v_1 to serve as a value of the nominative's fnc attribute and of the adverbial's mdd attribute.

An initial adverb and the nominative are combined with the new rule ADV+NOM:

15.3.7 COMBINING Quickly AND Julia WITH ADV+NOM

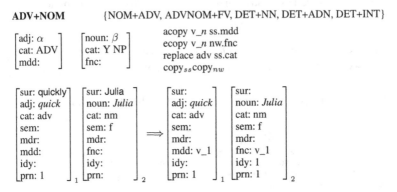

In this example, ADV+NOM is called by the start state.

The operations acopy v_*n* ss.mdd and ecopy v_*n* nw.fnc write the simultaneous substitution value v_1 into the mdd slot of the adverb and into the fnc slot of the nominative. The operation replace adv ss.cat ensures that the category of the modifier is adv (here vacuous; 15.3.8 shows a nonvacuous application of this operation).

The rule ADV+NOM is also used to combine a prepositional phrase with the nominative, in which case it is called by PREP+NP (for example, in for Mary + John bought a dog) or PREP+NN (for example, On the table + Julia ate an apple). The relevant composition of the latter example is shown below:

15.3.8 COMBINING On the table AND Julia WITH ADV+NOM

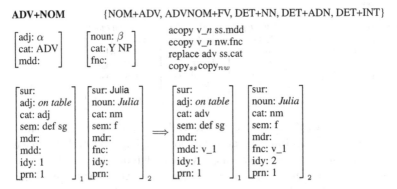

While adverbs occurring initially in the order adverb+nominative can be elementary or complex, as shown by 15.3.7 and 15.3.8, respectively, the inverse order nominative+adverb is restricted to elementary adverbs. For example, Julia + quickly ate the apple is grammatical, while *Julia + on the table ate the apple is not.[12]

---

[12] At least not in the ADV interpretation of the prepositional phrase.

This is accounted for by the new rule NOM+ADV. It restricts the cat value of the next word to adv and does not include the names of rules for continuing a prepositional phrase, such as PREP+NP, PREP+NN, and DET+ADN, in its rule package:

15.3.9 COMBINING Julia AND quickly WITH NOM+ADV

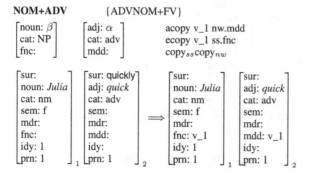

NOM+ADV may be called not only by the start state, but also by ADV+NOM, as in On the table + Julia + quickly (ate an apple).

Sentence starts containing preverbal adverbials, as derived in 15.3.7, 15.3.8, and 15.3.9 as well as the ADV+NOM – NOM+ADV combination mentioned above, are all continued with ADVNOM+FV. It resembles NOM+FV (cf. 15.2.1) except that it also handles the mdr–mdd relation between prenominative adverbials and the post-nominative verb. In the following example, ADVNOM+FV is called by ADV+NOM:

15.3.10 COMBINING Quickly Julia AND ate WITH ADVNOM+FV

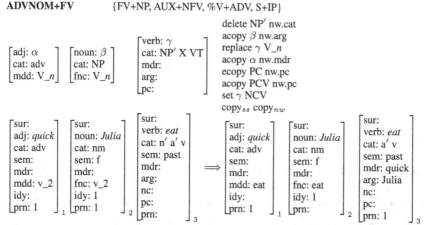

In conclusion, consider the syntactic–semantic analysis of On the table Julia quickly ate the apple. The result, based on the rule sequence PREP+NP, PREP+NN, ADV+NOM,

NOM+ADV, ADVNOM+FV, FV+NP, DET+NN, IP, is represented as the following set of proplets:

15.3.11 RESULT OF PARSING On the table Julia quickly ate the apple

$$
\begin{bmatrix}
\text{sur:} \\
\text{adj: } \textit{on table} \\
\text{cat: adj} \\
\text{sem: def sg} \\
\text{mdr:} \\
\text{mdd: eat} \\
\text{idy: 1} \\
\text{prn: 1}
\end{bmatrix}_1
\begin{bmatrix}
\text{sur:} \\
\text{noun: } \textit{Julia} \\
\text{cat: nm} \\
\text{sem: f} \\
\text{mdr:} \\
\text{fnc: eat} \\
\text{idy: 2} \\
\text{prn: 1}
\end{bmatrix}_4
\begin{bmatrix}
\text{sur:} \\
\text{adj: } \textit{quick} \\
\text{cat: adv} \\
\text{sem:} \\
\text{mdr:} \\
\text{mdd: eat} \\
\text{idy:} \\
\text{prn: 1}
\end{bmatrix}_5
\begin{bmatrix}
\text{sur:} \\
\text{verb: } \textit{eat} \\
\text{cat: decl} \\
\text{sem: past} \\
\text{mdr: on table quick} \\
\text{arg: Julia apple} \\
\text{nc: pc:} \\
\text{prn: 1}
\end{bmatrix}_6
\begin{bmatrix}
\text{sur:} \\
\text{noun: } \textit{apple} \\
\text{cat: np} \\
\text{sem: def sg} \\
\text{mdr:} \\
\text{fnc: eat} \\
\text{idy: 3} \\
\text{prn: 1}
\end{bmatrix}_7
$$

The mdd values, i.e., *eat*, and corresponding mdr values, i.e., *on table* and *quick*, are not marked with % because PREP+NP and NOM+ADV are not percentage rules.

15.4 Intensifiers in Noun Phrases and Prepositional Phrases

Intensifiers like very and rather (cf. 15.1.8) are function words which absorb their adjective, just as determiners are function words which absorb their noun. In Database Semantics, function words are viewed as *wrappers* which are filled with associated content words. Consider the following example of three increasingly complex noun phrases, whereby the determiner and the intensifier are treated as wrappers:

15.4.1 WRAPPERS IN NOUN PHRASES

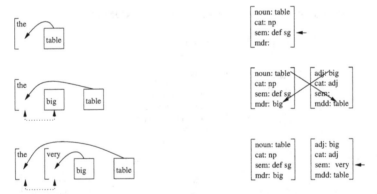

On the left, wrappers[13] are represented as "[", and their content words (or "heads") as "□". The time-linear filling of the wrappers is indicated by the solid left arrows. The dotted double arrows indicate the bidirectional relations between the content words.

---

[13] In Nativism, wrappers are called "modifiers," as in "head and modifier." This deviates from the proper use of the term modifier in logic, which describes the semantic role of adjectives and is unsuitable to express the intuitive analysis of the function words we call wrappers.

The resulting proplets are shown on the right in simplified form, whereby the arrows are intended to draw attention to relevant relations and locations.

In the first example, the wrapper the is filled with the content word table. Such a combination is shown explicitly in 13.4.2. In the second example, the content word big intervenes between the wrapper the and the content word table. The bidirectional relation is between wrapped table and unwrapped big. An explicit derivation is shown in 13.3.1–13.3.3 and in 13.3.6–13.3.7. In the third example, the content word big is put into the wrapper very. The bidirectional relation is between wrapped table and wrapped big. This construction will be modeled in 15.4.4–15.4.6 below.

In prepositional phrases with a complex noun phrase (i.e., excepting prepositional phrases with a proper name, e.g., on Fido), two wrappers are combined:

15.4.2 WRAPPERS IN PREPOSITIONAL PHRASES

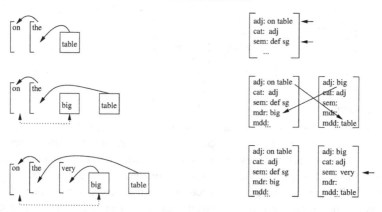

The examples are analogous to those in 15.4.1, except that the initial wrapper on is is filled with the wrapper the, resulting in the combined wrapper on the. The first example has been derived explicitly in 15.2.4–15.2.6. The second example will be derived below in 15.4.7, 15.4.8, and the third in 15.4.10.

Before we turn to prepositional phrases with adjectives and intensifiers, however, let us treat the third example in 15.4.1, i.e., the use of an intensifier in the noun phrase the very big table (see also 15.1.8, i), beginning with the lexical analysis of intensifiers:

15.4.3 LEXICAL ANALYSIS OF INTENSIFIER very AND DETENSIFIER rather

$$
\begin{bmatrix}
\text{sur: very} \\
\text{adj: a\_1} \\
\text{cat: int} \\
\text{sem: very} \\
\text{mdr: B} \\
\text{mdd:} \\
\text{idy: B} \\
\text{prn:}
\end{bmatrix}
\quad
\begin{bmatrix}
\text{sur: rather} \\
\text{adj: a\_1} \\
\text{cat: int} \\
\text{sem: rather} \\
\text{mdr: B} \\
\text{mdd:} \\
\text{idy: B} \\
\text{prn:}
\end{bmatrix}
$$

Intensifiers are wrappers of adjectives and therefore have the feature structure of adjectives, just as determiners (cf. 13.1.3) are wrappers of nouns and therefore have the feature structure of nouns. As wrappers, intensifiers and determiners have in common that the value of their core attributes is a simultaneous substitution value.

The derivation of the very big table begins with the combination of the and very. This requires the new rule DET+INT, illustrated below.

15.4.4 COMBINING The AND very WITH DET+INT

DET+INT   {INT+ADJ}

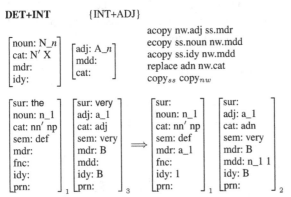

The first operation, acopy nw.adj ss.mdr, copies the value a_1 of the intensifier into the mdr slot of the determiner. The second operation, acopy ss.noun nw.mdd, copies the value n_1 of the determiner into the mdd slot of the intensifier. The third operation, ecopy ss.idy nw.mdd, copies the identity number of the noun into the mdd slot of the intensifier. The fourth operation, replace adn nw.cat, replaces the value of the cat attribute of the intensifier with adn. Given that the article and the intensifier are wrappers for two different content words, here the for table and very for big, both proplets are retained in the output.

The next step is the combination of the very and big. It has the grammatical function of embedding the adjective into the intensifier, based on the new rule INT+ADJ:

15.4.5 COMBINING The very AND big WITH INT+ADJ

INT+ADJ   {DET+NN,DET+ADN,DET+INT,ADV+NOM,ADVNOM+FV,%V+ADV,S+IP}

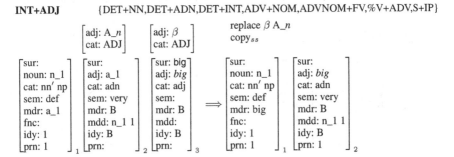

The first operation, replace β A_n, globally replaces the value a_1 with *big*. In this way, the adjective is absorbed by the intensifier and the determiner is supplied with the correct modifier (mdr). The *nw* proplet is not retained in the output.

Finally, the noun is added, using familiar DET+NN. Because it globally replaces the value n_1, the proplet representing *very big* obtains the correct modified (mdd).

15.4.6 COMBINING The very big AND table WITH DET+NN

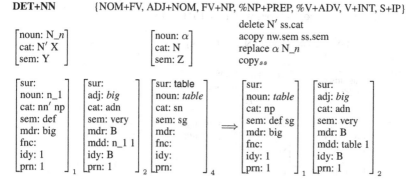

The first operation, delete N′ ss.cat, cancels the valency position of the noun in the cat attribute of the determiner. The second operation, acopy nw.sem ss.sem, adds the segment sg (for singular) to the sem slot of the determiner. The third operation, replace α N_n, globally replaces the value n_1 with *table*. Having been absorbed into the determiner, the *nw* proplet is not retained in the output.

Let us return to prepositional phrases. Having derived on the table in postverbal position in 15.2.4 – 15.2.6, we will now derive the examples on the big table and on the very big table in initial position. Both examples begin with familiar PREP+NP (cf. 15.2.5), which combines the wrappers on (preposition) and the (determiner). The result is a preposition with additional values in the cat and the sem slot.

15.4.7 COMBINING THE PREPOSITION On AND the WITH PREP+NP

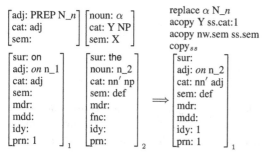

The first operation, replace α N_n, replaces the substitution value n_1 with n_2. The second operation, acopy N′ ss.cat:1, fronts the nn′ segment of the cat attribute of the determiner to the adj segment of the cat attribute of the preposition. The third operation, acopy nw.sem ss.sem, copies the def segment of the sem attribute of the determiner into the sem slot of the preposition. Having absorbed the determiner into the preposition, the proplet of the next word is discarded.

Deriving the example On the big table first, the new rule PREP+ADN applies next:

15.4.8 COMBINING On the AND big WITH PREP+ADN

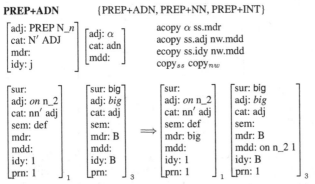

This rule is the counterpart to DET+ADN (cf. 13.3.1, 13.3.2, 13.3.6). The first operation, acopy α ss.mdr, copies the value big into the modifier slot of the ss, i.e., the proplet representing on the. The second operation, acopy ss.adj nw.mdd, adds on n_2 to the mdd slot of the adnominal. The third operation, ecopy ss.idy nw.mdd copies the idy number of the ss into the mdd slot of the nw, thus identifying the *table* in question as the modified of *big*. Both input proplets are retained in the output.

Next applies the familiar rule PREP+NN (see 15.2.6 above and 15.4.12 below). The result is as follows:

15.4.9 RESULT OF PARSING On the big table

$$
\begin{bmatrix}
\text{sur:} \\
\text{adj: } \textit{on table} \\
\text{cat: adj} \\
\text{sem: def sg} \\
\text{mdr: big} \\
\text{mdd:} \\
\text{idy: 1} \\
\text{prn: 1}
\end{bmatrix}_1
\begin{bmatrix}
\text{sur: big} \\
\text{adj: } \textit{big} \\
\text{cat: adj} \\
\text{sem:} \\
\text{mdr: B} \\
\text{mdd: on table 1} \\
\text{idy: B} \\
\text{prn: 1}
\end{bmatrix}_3
$$

It remains to derive the example On the very big table, i.e., a prepositional phrase with an intensifier preceding an adnominal (here big, cf. 15.1.8, ii). The first composition of on and the is shown above in 15.4.7. Next applies the new rule PREP+INT. It is like DET+INT (cf. 15.4.4), except that the sentence start is an adjective rather than a noun. Both rules have the same rule package containing only one rule.

15.4.10 COMBINING On the AND very WITH PREP+INT

PREP+INT   {INT+ADJ}

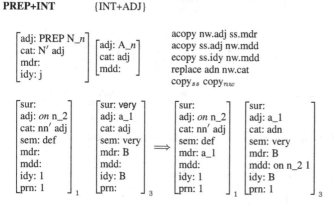

The first operation, acopy nw.adj ss.mdr, copies the value a_1 of the intensifier into the mdr slot of the proplet representing on the, thus ensuring that it will have the modifier *big* (cf. 15.4.5). The second operation, acopy ss.adj nw.mdd, adds the value *on* n_2 to the mdd slot of the intensifier. The third operation, ecopy ss.idy nw.mdd, copies the idy value of the *ss* into the mdd of the intensifier, thus ensuring that the modifier very big will identify the correct table. The fourth operation, replace adn nw.cat, replaces the cat value of the intensifier with adn. Both input proplets are retained in the output. The derivation continues with INT+ADJ (compare 15.4.5):

15.4.11 COMBINING On the very AND big WITH INT+ADJ

INT+ADJ   {DET+NN, DET+ADN, DET+INT, ADV+NOM, ADVNOM+FV, %V+ADV, S+IP}

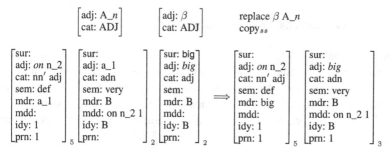

The derivation concludes with familiar PREP+NN (cf. 15.2.6), which resembles DET+NN except that the *ss* is an adjective rather than a noun:

15.4.12 COMBINING On the very big AND table WITH PREP+NN

PREP+NN {ADV+NOM, NOM+FV, FV+NP, %NP+PREP, %V+ADV, %PREPP+PREP, S+IP}

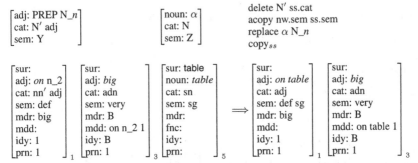

The output of this rule is also the result of parsing the phrase in question:

15.4.13 RESULT OF PARSING On the very big table

$$
\begin{bmatrix}
\text{sur:} \\
\text{adj: } on\ table \\
\text{cat: adj} \\
\text{sem: def sg} \\
\text{mdr: big} \\
\text{mdd:} \\
\text{idy: 1} \\
\text{prn: 1}
\end{bmatrix}_1
\begin{bmatrix}
\text{sur:} \\
\text{adj: } big \\
\text{cat: adn} \\
\text{sem: very} \\
\text{mdr: B} \\
\text{mdd: on table 1} \\
\text{idy: B} \\
\text{prn: 1}
\end{bmatrix}_3
$$

Given that the input phrase contains only two content words, the output consists of only two proplets. All function words, i.e., the preposition *on*, the determiner *the*, and the intensifier *very*, have been reduced to certain values in certain attributes of these two proplets. Given that intensifiers in prepositional phrases are phrase-internal, their handling is the same for prepositional phrases in different positions and grammatical functions (see Sect. 15.2), and requires no further demonstration.

15.5 Elementary Adverbs with Intensifiers

Intensifiers of elementary adverbs, as in *very quickly*, are a challenge insofar as they occur in various positions. Because elementary adverbs are not phrase-internal, transitions must be built for preverbal prenominative adverbs (cf. 15.1.8, iii), preverbal postnominative adverbs (cf. 15.1.8, iv), and postverbal adverbs (cf. 15.1.8, v).

The derivation of the preverbal prenominative example *very quickly Julia ate an apple* begins with familiar INT+ADJ (cf. 15.4.5 and 15.4.11):

15.5.1 COMBINING Very AND quickly WITH INT+ADJ

INT+ADJ   {DET+NN, DET+ADN, DET+INT, ADV+NOM, ADVNOM+FV, %V+ADV, S+IP}

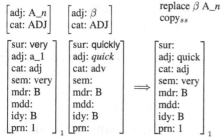

$$\begin{bmatrix} \text{adj: A\_}n \\ \text{cat: ADJ} \end{bmatrix} \begin{bmatrix} \text{adj: }\beta \\ \text{cat: ADJ} \end{bmatrix} \qquad \begin{array}{l} \text{replace }\beta\text{ A\_}n \\ \text{copy}_{ss} \end{array}$$

$$\begin{bmatrix} \text{sur: very} \\ \text{adj: a\_1} \\ \text{cat: adj} \\ \text{sem: very} \\ \text{mdr: B} \\ \text{mdd:} \\ \text{idy: B} \\ \text{prn: 1} \end{bmatrix}_1 \begin{bmatrix} \text{sur: quickly} \\ \text{adj: }quick \\ \text{cat: adv} \\ \text{sem:} \\ \text{mdr: B} \\ \text{mdd:} \\ \text{idy: B} \\ \text{prn:} \end{bmatrix} \implies \begin{bmatrix} \text{sur:} \\ \text{adj: quick} \\ \text{cat: adj} \\ \text{sem: very} \\ \text{mdr: B} \\ \text{mdd:} \\ \text{idy: B} \\ \text{prn: 1} \end{bmatrix}_1$$

The operation replace β A_n replaces the value a_1 in the *ss* with the value *quick* of the next word. The proplet of the next word is not retained in the output.

The above composition has the effect of the intensifier absorbing the adjective. From then on, the derivation runs just as Quickly Julia ate the apple, as shown in 15.3.7 and 15.3.10. The result of parsing our current example is shown below:

15.5.2 RESULT OF PARSING Very quickly Julia ate the apple

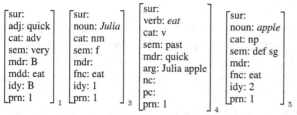

$$\begin{bmatrix} \text{sur:} \\ \text{adj: quick} \\ \text{cat: adv} \\ \text{sem: very} \\ \text{mdr: B} \\ \text{mdd: eat} \\ \text{idy: B} \\ \text{prn: 1} \end{bmatrix}_1 \begin{bmatrix} \text{sur:} \\ \text{noun: }Julia \\ \text{cat: nm} \\ \text{sem: f} \\ \text{mdr:} \\ \text{fnc: eat} \\ \text{idy: 1} \\ \text{prn: 1} \end{bmatrix}_1 \begin{bmatrix} \text{sur:} \\ \text{verb: }eat \\ \text{cat: v} \\ \text{sem: past} \\ \text{mdr: quick} \\ \text{arg: Julia apple} \\ \text{nc:} \\ \text{pc:} \\ \text{prn: 1} \end{bmatrix}_4 \begin{bmatrix} \text{sur:} \\ \text{noun: }apple \\ \text{cat: np} \\ \text{sem: def sg} \\ \text{mdr:} \\ \text{fnc: eat} \\ \text{idy: 2} \\ \text{prn: 1} \end{bmatrix}_5$$

Next, consider the derivation of Julia very quickly ate the apple, showing the combination of an intensifier and an elementary adverb in preverbal position. It begins with the new rule NOM+INT, called by the start state.

15.5.3 COMBINING Julia AND very WITH NOM+INT

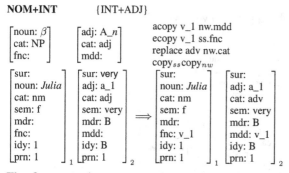

NOM+INT   {INT+ADJ}

$$\begin{bmatrix} \text{noun: }\beta \\ \text{cat: NP} \\ \text{fnc:} \end{bmatrix} \begin{bmatrix} \text{adj: A\_}n \\ \text{cat: adj} \\ \text{mdd:} \end{bmatrix} \qquad \begin{array}{l} \text{acopy v\_1 nw.mdd} \\ \text{ecopy v\_1 ss.fnc} \\ \text{replace adv nw.cat} \\ \text{copy}_{ss}\text{copy}_{nw} \end{array}$$

$$\begin{bmatrix} \text{sur:} \\ \text{noun: }Julia \\ \text{cat: nm} \\ \text{sem: f} \\ \text{mdr:} \\ \text{fnc:} \\ \text{idy: 1} \\ \text{prn: 1} \end{bmatrix}_1 \begin{bmatrix} \text{sur: very} \\ \text{adj: a\_1} \\ \text{cat: adj} \\ \text{sem: very} \\ \text{mdr: B} \\ \text{mdd:} \\ \text{idy: B} \\ \text{prn: 1} \end{bmatrix}_2 \implies \begin{bmatrix} \text{sur:} \\ \text{noun: }Julia \\ \text{cat: nm} \\ \text{sem: f} \\ \text{mdr:} \\ \text{fnc: v\_1} \\ \text{idy: 1} \\ \text{prn: 1} \end{bmatrix}_1 \begin{bmatrix} \text{sur:} \\ \text{adj: a\_1} \\ \text{cat: adv} \\ \text{sem: very} \\ \text{mdr: B} \\ \text{mdd: v\_1} \\ \text{idy: B} \\ \text{prn: 1} \end{bmatrix}_2$$

The first operation, acopy v_1 nw.mdd, copies the value v_1 into the mdd slot of the intensifier, while the second operation, ecopy v_1 ss.fnc, copies it into the fnc slot of the nominative. These occurrences of the value v_1 will be replaced by eat, thus providing the nominative and the intensifier with the same fnc and mdd values, respectively. The third operation, replace adv nw.cat, replaces the cat value of the intensifier with adv. Both input proplets are retained in the output.

The derivation continues with familiar INT+ADJ (cf. 15.5.1), this time in postnominative position.

15.5.4 COMBINING Julia very AND quickly WITH INT+ADJ

INT+ADJ   {DET+NN, DET+ADN, DET+INT, ADV+NOM, ADVNOM+FV, %V+ADV, S+IP}

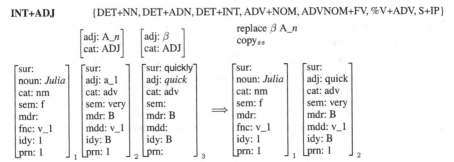

The derivation continues with familiar ADVNOM+FV (cf. 15.3.10). Keep in mind that, for purposes of pattern matching with the rule level, proplets are regarded as unordered sets, for which reason the *Julia quick* output of INT+ADJ in 15.5.4 is equivalent to the *quick Julia* input of ADVNOM+FV in 15.3.10. Based on the rule sequence NOM+INT, INT+ADJ, ADVNOM+FV, FV+NP, DET+NN, and S+IP, the derivation has the same result as that of the previous sentence, shown in 15.5.2 above (excepting the word number subscripts).

Finally, consider the derivation of Julia ate the apple very quickly, showing the combination of an intensifier and an elementary adverb in postverbal position (cf. 15.1.8, v). The initial part of the sentence, i.e., Julia ate the apple, is as shown in 15.2.1–15.2.3. At this point, DET+NN calls the new rule V+INT:

15.5.5 COMBINING Julia ate the apple AND very WITH V+INT

V+INT   {INT+ADJ}

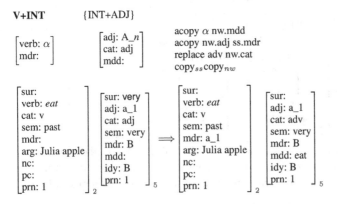

The first operation, acopy α nw.mdd, copies the verb value of *eat* into the mdd slot of *very*. The second operation, acopy nw.adj ss.mdr, copies the adj value a_1 of *very* into the mdr slot of *eat*. The third operation, replace adv nw.cat, changes the cat value of *very* to adv. Next applies familiar INT+ADJ (cf. 15.4.5, 15.4.11, 15.5.1, 15.5.4), called by V+INT:

15.5.6 COMBINING Julia ate the apple very AND quickly WITH INT+ADJ

INT+ADJ　　　　{DET+NN, DET+ADN, DET+INT, ADV+NOM, ADVNOM+FV, %V+ADV, S+IP}

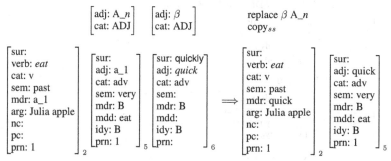

The derivation concludes with S+IP (cf. 11.5.1 and 13.3.8). Based on the rule sequence NOM+FV, FV+NP, DET+NN, V+INT, INT+ADJ, S+IP, the derivation has the same result as that shown in 15.5.2 above (excepting the word number subscripts).

15.6 Definition of LA-hear.3

The analysis of various kinds of modifiers developed in the preceding sections will now be summarized as the formal grammar LA-hear.3. Compared to LA-hear.2, LA-hear.3 has 14 new rules,[14] which are temporarily marked here with "$".

15.6.1 LEXICON AND PREAMBLE OF LA-HEAR3

1. Lexicon of LA-hear.3:
   lexicon of LA-hear.1 and LA-hear.2 plus first entry of 15.1.1 and entries of 15.4.3.

2. Preamble of LA-hear3:
   variable definitions, restrictions, and agreement conditions of LA-hear.1 (cf. 11.2.2) and LA-hear.2 (cf. 13.2.1) plus

   PREP ϵ {*on, in, above, below, ...*}
   ADJ ϵ {adj, adn, adv}
   ADV ϵ {adj, adv}
   ADN ϵ {adj, adn}
   A_n = simultaneous substitution variable for an adjective

---

[14] Because of its complexity, the finite-state transition network of LA-hear.3 is omitted.

15.6.2 FORMAL DEFINITION OF LA-HEAR.3

$\mathbf{ST}_S =_{def}$ { ($\begin{bmatrix} \text{cat: X} \end{bmatrix}$ {1 DET+NN, 2 DET+ADN, 3 DET+INT, 4 NOM+ADV, 5 NOM+INT, 6 NOM+FV, 7 INT+ADJ, 8 PREP+NP, 9 ADV+NOM}) }

DET+NN   {10 NOM+FV, 11 FV+NP, 12 S+IP, 13 %NP+PREP, 14 %V+ADV, 15 V+INT}

$\begin{bmatrix} \text{noun: N\_}n \\ \text{cat: N}' \text{ X} \\ \text{sem: Y} \end{bmatrix}$ $\begin{bmatrix} \text{noun: } \alpha \\ \text{cat: N} \\ \text{sem: Z} \end{bmatrix}$ delete N′ ss.cat
acopy nw.sem ss.sem
replace α N_n
copy$_{ss}$

DET+ADN   {16 DET+NN, 17 DET+ADN, 18 DET+INT}

$\begin{bmatrix} \text{noun: N\_}n \\ \text{cat: N}' \text{ X} \\ \text{mdr:} \\ \text{idy:} \end{bmatrix}$ $\begin{bmatrix} \text{adj: } \alpha \\ \text{cat: adn} \\ \text{mdd:} \end{bmatrix}$ acopy α ss.mdr
ecopy ss.noun nw.mdd
acopy ss.idy nw.mdd
copy$_{ss}$ copy$_{nw}$

$ DET+INT   {19 INT+ADJ}

$\begin{bmatrix} \text{noun: N\_}n \\ \text{cat: N}' \text{ X} \\ \text{mdr:} \\ \text{idy:} \end{bmatrix}$ $\begin{bmatrix} \text{adj: A\_}n \\ \text{mdd:} \end{bmatrix}$ acopy nw.adj ss.mdr
ecopy ss.noun nw.mdd
acopy ss.idy nw.mdd
copy$_{ss}$ copy$_{nw}$

$ NOM+ADV   {20 ADVNOM+FV}

$\begin{bmatrix} \text{noun: } \beta \\ \text{cat: NP} \\ \text{fnc:} \end{bmatrix}$ $\begin{bmatrix} \text{adj: } \alpha \\ \text{cat: adv} \\ \text{mdd:} \end{bmatrix}$ acopy v_1 nw.mdd
acopy v_1 ss.fnc
copy$_{ss}$copy$_{nw}$

$ NOM+INT   {21 INT+ADJ}

$\begin{bmatrix} \text{noun: } \beta \\ \text{cat: NP} \\ \text{fnc:} \end{bmatrix}$ $\begin{bmatrix} \text{adj: A\_}n \\ \text{cat: adj} \\ \text{mdd:} \end{bmatrix}$ acopy v_1 nw.mdd
acopy v_1 ss.fnc
replace adv nw.cat
copy$_{ss}$copy$_{nw}$

NOM+FV   {22 FV+NP, 23 AUX+NFV, 24 S+IP}

delete NP′ nw.cat

$\begin{bmatrix} \text{noun: } \alpha \\ \text{cat: NP} \\ \text{fnc:} \\ \text{prn: k} \end{bmatrix}$ $\begin{bmatrix} \text{verb: } \beta \\ \text{cat: NP}' \text{ X VT} \\ \text{arg:} \\ \text{nc:} \\ \text{pc:} \end{bmatrix}$ acopy α nw.arg
ecopy β ss.fnc
ecopy PC nw.pc
acopy PCV nw.pc
set β NCV
copy$_{ss}$ copy$_{nw}$

$ INT+ADJ   {25 DET+NN, 26 DET+ADN, 27 DET+INT, 28 ADV+NOM, 29 ADVNOM+FV, 30 %V+ADV, 31 S+IP}

$\begin{bmatrix} \text{adj: A\_}n \\ \text{cat: ADJ} \end{bmatrix}$ $\begin{bmatrix} \text{adj: } \beta \\ \text{cat: ADJ} \end{bmatrix}$ replace β A_n
copy$_{ss}$

$ PREP+NP {32 PREP+NN, 33 PREP+ADN, 34 PREP+INT, 35 %NP+PREP, 36 %V+ADV, 37 %PREPP+PREP, 38 ADV+NOM, 39 S+IP}

$\begin{bmatrix} \text{adj: PREP N\_}n \\ \text{cat: adj} \\ \text{sem:} \end{bmatrix}$ $\begin{bmatrix} \text{noun: } \alpha \\ \text{cat: Y NP} \\ \text{sem: X} \end{bmatrix}$ replace α N_n
acopy Y ss.cat:1
acopy nw.sem ss.sem
copy$_{ss}$

\$ ADV+NOM   {40 NOM+ADV, 41 ADVNOM+FV, 42 DET+NN, 43 DET+ADN, 44 DET+INT}

$$\begin{bmatrix} \text{adj: } \alpha \\ \text{cat: ADV} \\ \text{mdd:} \end{bmatrix} \begin{bmatrix} \text{noun: } \beta \\ \text{cat: Y NP} \\ \text{fnc:} \end{bmatrix}$$ acopy v_n ss.mdd
acopy v_n nw.fnc
replace adv ss.cat
$copy_{ss} copy_{nw}$

FV+NP   {45 DET+NN, 46 DET+ADN, 47 DET+INT, 48 FV+NP, 49 %NP+PREP, 50 %V+ADV,
51 V+INT, 52 S+IP}

$$\begin{bmatrix} \text{verb: } \beta \\ \text{cat: NP' X VT} \\ \text{arg:} \end{bmatrix} \begin{bmatrix} \text{noun: } \alpha \\ \text{cat: Y NP} \\ \text{fnc:} \end{bmatrix}$$ delete NP' ss.cat
acopy α ss.arg
ecopy β nw.fnc
$copy_{ss} copy_{nw}$

S+IP   {53 IP+START}

$$\begin{bmatrix} \text{verb: } \alpha \\ \text{cat: VT} \\ \text{prn: k} \end{bmatrix} \begin{bmatrix} \text{cat: VT' SM} \end{bmatrix}$$ replace SM VT
set k PC
set α PCV
$copy_{ss}$

\$ %NP+PREP   {54 PREP+NP}

$$\begin{bmatrix} \text{noun: } \alpha \\ \text{cat: N} \\ \text{mdr:} \\ \text{idy: j} \end{bmatrix} \begin{bmatrix} \text{adj: PREP N\_}n \\ \text{cat: adj} \\ \text{mdd:} \end{bmatrix}$$ ecopy nw.adj ss.mdr
%ecopy α nw.mdd
acopy ss.idy nw.mdd
$copy_{ss} copy_{nw}$

\$ %V+ADV   {55 PREP+NP, 56 %V+ADV, 57 S+IP}

$$\begin{bmatrix} \text{verb: } \alpha \\ \text{cat: v} \\ \text{mdr:} \end{bmatrix} \begin{bmatrix} \text{adj: } \beta \text{ X} \\ \text{cat: ADV} \\ \text{mdd:} \end{bmatrix}$$ acopy nw.adj ss.mdr
ecopy α nw.mdd
$copy_{ss} copy_{nw}$

\$ V+INT   {58 INT+ADJ}

$$\begin{bmatrix} \text{verb: } \alpha \\ \text{mdr:} \end{bmatrix} \begin{bmatrix} \text{adj: A\_}n \\ \text{cat: adj} \\ \text{mdd:} \end{bmatrix}$$ acopy α nw.mdd
acopy nw.adj ss.mdr
$copy_{ss} copy_{nw}$

\$ PREP+NN   {59 ADV+NOM, 60 NOM+FV, 62 FV+NP, 62 %NP+PREP,
63 %V+ADV, 64 % PREPP+PREP, 65 S+IP}

$$\begin{bmatrix} \text{adj: PREP N\_}n \\ \text{cat: N' adj} \\ \text{sem: Y} \end{bmatrix} \begin{bmatrix} \text{noun: } \alpha \\ \text{cat: N} \\ \text{sem: Z} \end{bmatrix}$$ delete N' ss.cat
acopy nw.sem ss.sem
replace α N_n
$copy_{ss}$

\$ PREP+ADN   {66 PREP+ADN, 67 PREP+NN, 68 PREP+INT}

$$\begin{bmatrix} \text{adj: PREP N\_}n \\ \text{cat: N' ADJ} \\ \text{mdr:} \\ \text{idy: j} \end{bmatrix} \begin{bmatrix} \text{adj: } \alpha \\ \text{cat: adn} \\ \text{mdd:} \end{bmatrix}$$ acopy α ss.mdr
acopy ss.adj nw.mdd
ecopy ss.idy nw.mdd
$copy_{ss} copy_{nw}$

\$ PREP+INT   {69 INT+ADJ}

$$\begin{bmatrix} \text{adj: PREP N\_}n \\ \text{cat: N' adj} \\ \text{mdr:} \\ \text{idy: j} \end{bmatrix} \begin{bmatrix} \text{adj: A\_}n \\ \text{cat: adj} \\ \text{mdd:} \end{bmatrix}$$ acopy nw.adj ss.mdr
acopy ss.adj nw.mdd
ecopy ss.idy nw.mdd
replace adn nw.cat
$copy_{ss} copy_{nw}$

$ %PREPP+PREP   {70 PREP+NP}

$$
\begin{bmatrix} \text{adj: PREP } \alpha \\ \text{cat: adj} \\ \text{mdr:} \\ \text{idy: j} \end{bmatrix}
\begin{bmatrix} \text{adj: PREP } N\_n \\ \text{cat: adj} \\ \text{mdd:} \end{bmatrix}
\begin{array}{l} \text{\%ecopy nw.adj ss.mdr} \\ \text{\%ecopy ss.adj nw.mdd} \\ \text{acopy ss.idy nw.mdd} \\ \text{copy}_{ss}\text{copy}_{nw} \end{array}
$$

$ ADVNOM+FV   {71 FV+NP, 72 AUX+NFV, 73 %V+ADV, 74 S+IP}

$$
\begin{bmatrix} \text{adj: } \alpha \\ \text{cat: adv} \\ \text{mdd: } V\_n \end{bmatrix}
\begin{bmatrix} \text{noun: } \beta \\ \text{cat: NP} \\ \text{fnc: } V\_n \end{bmatrix}
\begin{bmatrix} \text{verb: } \gamma \\ \text{cat: } NP' \text{ X VT} \\ \text{mdr:} \\ \text{arg:} \\ \text{pc:} \end{bmatrix}
\begin{array}{l} \text{delete } NP' \text{ nw.cat} \\ \text{acopy } \beta \text{ nw.arg} \\ \text{replace } \gamma \ V\_n \\ \text{acopy } \alpha \text{ nw.mdr} \\ \text{ecopy PC nw.pc} \\ \text{acopy PCV nw.pc} \\ \text{set } \gamma \text{ NCV} \\ \text{copy}_{ss} \text{ copy}_{nw} \end{array}
$$

AUX+NFV   {75 AUX+NFV, 76 FV+NP, 77 S+IP}

$$
\begin{bmatrix} \text{verb: } V\_n \\ \text{cat: } AUX' \text{ V} \\ \text{sem: X} \end{bmatrix}
\begin{bmatrix} \text{verb: } \alpha \\ \text{cat: Y AUX} \\ \text{sem: Z} \end{bmatrix}
\begin{array}{l} \text{replace Y } AUX' \\ \text{acopy nw.sem ss.sem} \\ \text{replace } \alpha \ V\_n \\ \text{copy}_{ss} \end{array}
$$

IP+START   {1 DET+NN, 2 DET+ADN, 3 DET+INT, 4 NOM+ADV, 5 NOM+INT, 6 NOM+FV, 7 INT+ADJ, 8 PREP+NP, 9 ADV+NOM}

$$
\begin{bmatrix} \text{verb: } \alpha \\ \text{cat: SM} \\ \text{nc:} \end{bmatrix}
\begin{bmatrix} \text{noun: } \beta \\ \text{cat: NP} \\ \text{prn:} \end{bmatrix}
\begin{array}{l} \text{increment nw.prn} \\ \text{ecopy k ss.nc} \\ \text{acopy 'NCV' ss.nc} \\ \text{copy}_{ss} \text{ copy}_{nw} \end{array}
$$

$$
ST_F =_{def} \{ \ (\ [\text{cat: decl}] \ \text{rp}_{S+IP}) \}
$$

The extension of LA-hear.2 to LA-hear.3 has increased the number of rules from 7 to 21, and the total number of different transitions (i.e., the sum of all rule names in all rule packages) from 19 to 77. Thus, the perplexity of 2.71 of LA-hear.2 (cf. 13.2.5 ff.) has increased to 3.66 in LA-hear.3 (77:21 = 3.66).[15]

Even more important than grammatical perplexity, however, is the degree of ambiguity. Leaving lexical ambiguities aside, the only possible source of ambiguity are rule packages with *input-compatible* rules.[16] Incompatible input conditions are easiest to spot in rules which specify different categories for the next word. In rules which specify different sentence starts, however, matters may be more complicated – due to the possibility of selecting different proplets in the same sentence start.

To simplify matters, consider the following list of all LA-hear.3 rules with their associated rule packages, whereby each rule in a rule package is provided with an example. This is to provide a rough idea of whether rule packages contain input-compatible rules by looking at the examples rather than the formal *ss* and *nw* patterns.

---

[15] In other words, the average size of a rule package is 3.66 rules; therefore there is an average of 3.66 rules to choose from in each combination of each path of the derivation.

[16] See FoCL'99, Sect. 11.3.

15.6.3 TRANSITIONS HANDLED BY RULE PACKAGES

Rule name	*Rule package*	*Applications of rules in rule package*
IP+START: (= ST$_S$)	DET+NN	The + table
	DET+ADN	The + beautiful (table)
	DET+INT	The + very (beautiful table)
	NOM+ADV	Julia + quickly (ate an apple)
	NOM+INT	Julia + very (quickly ate an apple)
	NOM+FV	Julia + read (the book)
	INT+ADJ	Very + quickly (Julia ate an apple)
	PREP+NP	On + the (table)
	ADV+NOM	Quickly + Julia (ate an apple)
DET+NN:	NOM+FV	the book + pleased (Julia)
	FV+NP	Julia gave the man + a (book)
	S+IP	Julia read the book + .
	%NP+PREP	the book + on (the table pleased Julia)
	%V+ADV	Julia read the book + on (the table)
	V+INT	Julia ate the apple + very (quickly)
DET+ADN:	DET+NN	the big + table
	DET+ADN	the big + beautiful (table)
	DET+INT	the big + very (beautiful table)
DET+INT:	INT+ADJ	the very + beautiful (table)
NOM+ADV:	ADVNOM+FV	Julia quickly + ate (an apple)
NOM+INT:	INT+ADJ	The young woman + very (quickly ate an apple)
NOM+FV:	FV+NP	Julia ate + the (apple)
	AUX+NFV	Julia has + eaten (an apple)
	S+IP	Julia slept + .
INT+ADJ:	DET+NN	the very beautiful + table
	DET+ADN	the very beautiful + big (table)
	DET+INT	the very beautiful + very (big table)
	ADV+NOM	very quickly + Julia
	ADVNOM+FV	Julia very quickly + ate (an apple)
	%V+ADV	Julia slept very soundly + on (the table)
	S+IP	Julia slept very soundly + .

Rule name	Rule package	Applications of rules in rule package
PREP+NP:	PREP+NN	on the + table
	PREP+ADN	on the + big (table)
	PREP+INT	on the + very (big table)
	%NP+PREP	the letter for Julia + on (the table)
	%V+ADV	John read the letter for Julia + quickly
	%PREPP+PREP	the letter for Julia + from Hamburg
	ADV+NOM	for Mary + John bought a book
	S+IP	John read the letter for Julia + .
ADV+NOM	NOM+ADV	On the table Julia + quickly (ate an apple)
	ADVNOM+FV	Quickly Julia + ate (an apple)
	DET+NN	Quickly the + girl (ate an apple)
	DET+ADN	Quickly the + pretty (girl ate an apple)
	DET+INT	Quickly the + very (pretty girl ate an apple)
FV+NP:	DET+NN	John saw the + table
	DET+ADN	John saw the + beautiful (table)
	DET+INT	John saw the + very (beautiful table)
	FV+NP	John gave Julia + the (book)
	%NP+PREP	John saw Julia + from (Hamburg)
	%V+ADV	John saw Julia + from (Hamburg)
	V+INT	John saw Julia + very (often).
	S+IP	John saw Julia + .
S+IP:	IP+START	Julia was sleeping. + The (dog barked)
%NP+PREP:	PREP+NP	the book on + the (table)
%V+ADV:	PREP+NP	Julia ate the apple on + the (table)
	%V+ADV	Julia ate the apple quickly + on (the table)
	S+IP	Julia ate the apple quickly + .
V+INT:	INT+ADJ	Julia slept very + soundly
PREP+NN:	ADV+NOM	on the table + Julia (ate an apple)
	NOM+FV	the book on the table + pleased (Julia)
	FV+NP	Julia gave the man in the corner + a (book)
	%NP+PREP	Julia ate the apple on the table + behind (the tree)
	%V+ADV	Julia ate the apple on the table + behind (the tree)
	%PREPP+PREP	Julia ate the apple on the table + behind (the tree)
	S+IP	Julia ate the apple on the table + .

Rule name	Rule package	Applications of rules in rule package
PREP+ADN	PREP+ADN	on the big + beautiful (table)
	PREP+NN	on the big + table
	PREP+INT	on the big + very (beautiful table)
PREP+INT	INT+ADJ	on the very + beautiful (table)
%PREPP+PREP	PREP+NP	Julia ate the apple on the table + behind (the tree)
ADVNOM+FV:	FV+NP	Julia quickly ate + an (apple)
	AUX+NFV	In this bed Julia will + sleep
	%V+ADV	Quickly Julia slipped + under (the covers)
	S+IP	In this bed Julia slept + .
AUX+NFV:	AUX+NFV	the car had been + speeding
	FV+NP	Julia had read + the (book)
	S+IP	Julia was sleeping + .
IP+START:	DET+NN	The + table
	DET+ADN	The + beautiful (table)
	DET+INT	The + very (beautiful table)
	NOM+ADV	Julia + quickly (ate an apple)
	NOM+INT	Julia + very (quickly ate an apple)
	NOM+FV	Julia + read (the book)
	INT+ADJ	Very + quickly (Julia ate an apple)
	PREP+NP	On + the (table)
	ADV+NOM	Quickly + Julia (ate an apple)

It turns out that in each rule package almost all the rules have incompatible next word patterns and are therefore not input-compatible. In those cases where the next word patterns happen to be compatible, it can usually be shown fairly easily that the rules are input-incompatible nevertheless due to their different sentence starts (consider, for example, DET+INT and NOM+INT in the IP+START package).

The only critical cases remaining are the rule packages of DET+NN, FV+NP, PREP+NN, and PREP+NP, each of which has more than one percentage rule in its rule package. This kind of rule is special, however, in that different percentage rules in the same rule package jointly produce a single output (rather than each starting a separate branch, as in syntactic ambiguities). In this way, the potentially recursive ADN–ADV–ADA ambiguity of prepositional phrase sequences is handled instead by means of semantic doubling – which is of linear complexity. We conclude therefore that the complexity of LA-hear.3 is linear.

In order to complete DBS.3, it remains to define the grammars LA-think.3 and LA-speak.3. We have shown in Chaps. 12 and 14 how LA-think and LA-speak grammars are to be designed for an existing LA-hear grammar. Thus it is fairly routine to define LA-think.3 and LA-speak.3 for existing LA-hear.3 in an analogous manner.

Remark Concluding Part III

This part has presented formal fragments of English. They are specified as definitions of LA-hear, LA-think, and LA-speak grammars, including word form interpretation and production. In future work, these fragments may be extended in several directions.

First, they should be upscaled to the coverage of Part II and beyond. This may be done (i) by first writing the running software and then extracting the declarative specification from it, (ii) by writing the declarative specification first and then implementing it as running software, or (iii) by developing the declarative specification and the running software hand in hand. Whichever method is chosen, at the end there must be both: the declarative specification as the description of the necessary properties and the running software as the verification.

Second, the fragments of English should be complemented by corresponding fragments of other languages. This is important for determining the degree of variation in the mapping between the language-dependent surfaces and the (relatively?) language-independent semantic representations. After all, it is not clear whether or not typologically different kinds of natural language can all be supplied with the same semantic representations; it might well be that the universal basis is limited to the context level (pace Chomsky) such that there may be some fundamental differences in the semantic representations of typologically different languages,[17] buffered by the pragmatics.

Third, the fragments must be integrated into robots with external interfaces for recognition and action at the language and the context level. Here, the primary focus is not on the upscaling to a maximal data coverage, but rather on solving the basic task of developing a control structure with a suitable pragmatics. The solution will have considerable impact on how to answer the question of the preceding paragraph.

Of the following Appendices A, B, and C, two deal with general aspects of Database Semantics: Appendix A discusses the relation between the navigation order and the resulting surface in typologically different natural languages. Appendix B discusses the relation between the general software framework of Database Semantics and its language-dependent applications in the hearer, the think, and the speaker mode.

Appendix C, finally, is a glossary. It provides lists of the attributes, the values, the variable restrictions, the agreement conditions, the rule names, and the examples analyzed in this book, including brief explanations and references to corresponding locations in the preceding pages.

---

[17] Nichols (1992) argues that the surface form of certain natural languages may limit function and content.

Appendices

A. Universal Basis of Word Order Variation

This appendix investigates (i) the possible navigations through one-, two-, and three-place propositions, and (ii) the possible variations of surface order for a given navigation. The latter depend on the type of language and the syntactic construction. The languages compared are English (SVO, fixed word order), German (SVO, free word order), and Korean (SOV, free word order[1]). The constructions are different sentence moods (declarative versus yes/no interrogative) and different voices of the verb (active versus passive).

A.1 Overview of the Basic Railroad System

The interpretation of natural language is based on an ordered sequence of word forms in a sentence and of sentences in a text or dialogue. The result of the interpretation, however, is an unordered set of proplets, whereby the grammatical relations between them are coded solely in terms of features, defined as attribute–value pairs. During thought, a sequential order is reintroduced into this set by a navigation which follows the intra- and extrapropositional relations between the proplets (cf. 3.5.4). This navigation order is the basis of word order in language production.

For simplicity, let us represent the functor–argument relations between nouns and verbs in one-, two-, and three-place propositions in the following standard format:

A.1.1 ONE-PLACE, TWO-PLACE, AND THREE-PLACE PROPOSITIONS

one–place proposition: $\quad$ V ——— N

two–place proposition: $\quad$ V ——— N ——— N

three–place proposition: $\quad$ V ——— N ——— N ——— N

The first N is regarded as the agent or underlying subject, and the second N as the patient or underlying object. In three-place propositions, the second N is the indirect and the third N the direct object. One-, two- and three-place propositions are also written as VN, VNN, or VNNN, respectively.

---

[1] Cf. Chang (1996); Choi and Kim (1986).

In addition to intrapropositional relations, there are also two kinds of extrapropositional relations, namely the coordination between verbs and the identity between nouns. During a navigation, the extrapropositional relations are distinguished as to whether they lead into or out of the current proposition (cf. 9.6.1).

One-place propositions may have the following extrapropositional relations:

A.1.2 EXTRAPROPOSITIONAL RELATIONS OF ONE-PLACE PROPOSITIONS

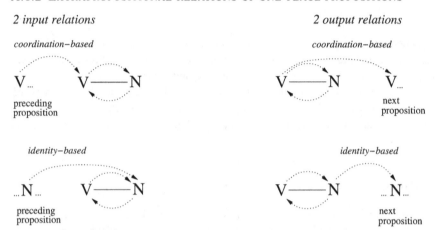

2 input relations   *2 output relations*

coordination–based   *coordination–based*

preceding
proposition

next
proposition

identity–based   *identity–based*

preceding
proposition

next
proposition

The two upper relations are coordination-based; those below are identity-based. The left pair are in-going relations, the right pair out-going.

As an example of two propositions related by a coordination-based relation between their verbs consider:

Julia sang. Then Susanne slept.

Here the relation based on the conjunction then (cf. 9.1.1) is out-going for the first sentence and in-going for the second.

At the level of the database, the direction of the navigation may be inverted (cf. 9.6.1), as represented by the surface:

Susanne slept. Before that Julia sang.

Coordination-based relations may also be established by one proposition simply following another, without a conjunction (cf. 9.2.1), as in:

Julia worked. Susanne slept.

As an example of two propositions related by an identity-based relation between (one of) their nouns consider:

Susanne slept. She dreamed.

Here the identity-based relation (cf. 10.1.2, 2) between Susanne and she is out-going for the first proposition and in-going for the second.

If two propositions are connected by more than one extrapropositional relation, there arises a choice as to which relation should be used for the navigation. For example, in:

Julia worked. Then she sang.

the navigation uses the coordination relation, whereas in:

Julia worked. She then sang.

it uses the identity relation.

Any proposition in a Word Bank normally has a coordination-based relation to a preceding and a following proposition, simply because the time-linear order of the propositions' arrival is automatically interpreted as a primary relation. Identity-based relations, in contrast, are a secondary relation which must be established on the basis of inferences (cf. Chap. 10), utilizing equality of names, definiteness, pronouns, etc.

In one-place propositions, the combination of two in-going and two out-going relations (cf. A.1.2) results in four possible constellations of extrapropositional relations:

$$V...\quad VN_i\quad V...\qquad\qquad ...N_i...\quad VN_i\quad V...$$
$$V...\quad VN_i\quad ...N_i...\qquad\qquad ...N_i...\quad VN_i\quad ...N_i....$$

In the extrapropositional ante- or postcedent $...N_i...$, the subscript is used to indicate coreference with the subject of the current proposition.

Next let us turn to two-place propositions. They have three possible kinds of in-going and three possible kinds of out-going relations:

A.1.3 EXTRAPROPOSITIONAL RELATIONS OF TWO-PLACE PROPOSITIONS

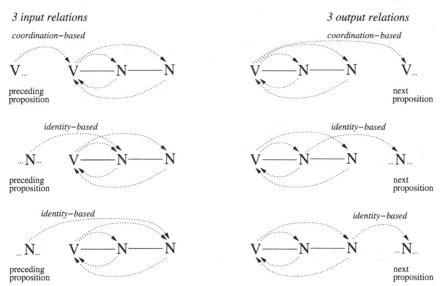

Of the three in-going relations on the left, one is coordination-based and two are identity-based. The first and second correspond to those in A.1.2, while the third is between the noun of a preceding proposition and the object of the current two-place proposition. The analogous situation holds for the three out-going relations in A.1.3.

The combination of three in-going and three out-going relations in two-place propositions results in nine possible constellations of extrapropositional relations:

$$
\begin{array}{lll}
\text{V...} & \text{VN}_i\text{N}_j & \text{V...} \\
\text{V...} & \text{VN}_i\text{N}_j & \text{...N}_i\text{...} \\
\text{V...} & \text{VN}_i\text{N}_j & \text{...N}_j\text{...}
\end{array}
\quad\bigg|\quad
\begin{array}{lll}
\text{...N}_i\text{...} & \text{VN}_i\text{N}_j & \text{V...} \\
\text{...N}_i\text{...} & \text{VN}_i\text{N}_j & \text{...N}_i\text{...} \\
\text{...N}_i\text{...} & \text{VN}_i\text{N}_j & \text{...N}_j\text{...}
\end{array}
\quad\bigg|\quad
\begin{array}{lll}
\text{...N}_j\text{...} & \text{VN}_i\text{N}_j & \text{V...} \\
\text{...N}_j\text{...} & \text{VN}_i\text{N}_j & \text{...N}_i\text{...} \\
\text{..N}_j\text{...} & \text{VN}_i\text{N}_j & \text{...N}_j\text{...}
\end{array}
\quad\bigg|
$$

The subscripts '$_i$' and '$_j$' indicate coreference of extrapropositional antecedents and postcedents with the subject and the object, respectively.

Finally consider three-place propositions. They have four possible kinds of in-going and four possible kinds of out-going relations:

A.1.4 EXTRAPROPOSITIONAL RELATIONS OF THREE-PLACE PROPOSITIONS

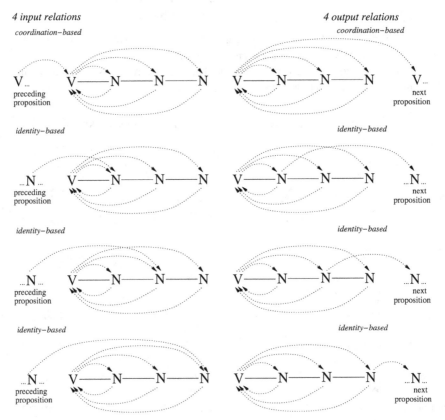

Of the four in-going relations on the left, the first is coordination-based and the others are identity-based, and similarly for the out-going relations. Their combination results in sixteen possible constellations of extrapropositional relations. Using the subscript

'$_i$', '$_j$', and '$_k$' for coreference with the subject, indirect object, and direct object, respectively, they may be written as the following sequence patterns:

$$
\begin{array}{|llll|}
\text{V.. VN}_i\text{N}_j\text{N}_k \text{ V..} & \text{..N}_i\text{.. VN}_i\text{N}_j\text{N}_k \text{ V..} & \text{..N}_j\text{.. VN}_i\text{N}_j\text{N}_k \text{ V..} & \text{..N}_k\text{.. VN}_i\text{N}_j\text{N}_k \text{ V..} \\
\text{V.. VN}_i\text{N}_j\text{N}_k \text{ ..N}_i\text{..} & \text{..N}_i\text{.. VN}_i\text{N}_j\text{N}_i \text{ ..N}_i\text{..} & \text{..N}_j\text{.. VN}_i\text{N}_j\text{N}_k \text{ ..N}_i\text{..} & \text{..N}_k\text{.. VN}_i\text{N}_j\text{N}_k \text{ ..N}_i\text{..} \\
\text{V.. VN}_i\text{N}_j\text{N}_k \text{ ..N}_j\text{..} & \text{..N}_i\text{.. VN}_i\text{N}_j\text{N}_k \text{ ..N}_j\text{..} & \text{..N}_j\text{.. VN}_i\text{N}_j\text{N}_k \text{ ..N}_j\text{..} & \text{..N}_k\text{.. VN}_i\text{N}_j\text{N}_k \text{ ..N}_j\text{..} \\
\text{V.. VN}_i\text{N}_j\text{N}_k \text{ ..N}_k\text{..} & \text{..N}_i\text{.. VN}_i\text{N}_j\text{N}_k \text{ ..N}_k\text{..} & \text{..N}_j\text{.. VN}_i\text{N}_j\text{N}_k \text{ ..N}_k\text{..} & \text{..N}_k\text{.. VN}_i\text{N}_j\text{N}_k \text{ ..N}_k\text{..}
\end{array}
$$

We note with relief that three places seem to be the maximum for propositions. Nevertheless, there are many more possible railroad patterns to be considered. First, there are the adjectives which may be added as adnominal, adverbial, and ad-adjectival modifiers to elementary propositions (cf. 15.1.10). Second, the treatment of extrapropositional relations so far has been limited to *coordination* and must be complemented with a treatment of *subordination* (cf. Chaps. 7 and 9).

However, rather than getting too far ahead in exploring all the relations possible in a Word Bank, let us turn next to the production of natural language surfaces. This procedure is based on navigating along the extra- and intrapropositional relations. Thereby, each of the 29 railroad systems discussed above (namely $4 + 9 + 16$) permits a multitude of different navigation *orders*. For example, a VNN proposition may be traversed by going from the V to the first N and then the second, or by going from the V to the second N and then the first.

These different navigation steps are powered by an LA-think grammar. Currently, LA-think merely executes legal continuations, leaving the important task of choosing between the several possibilities given at each step to a still primitive control structure, consisting of random selection or fixed schemata. Ideally, the control structure should provide the agent with short-, mid-, and long-term *purposes* relative to which different choices are evaluated.

In addition to the railroad system and the choice of the navigation, the surface order depends on the word order regularities of the target language, which are handled by a language-dependent LA-speak grammar. As illustrated in 14.4.1, 14.5.1, and 14.6.1, during language production the system switches frequently between LA-think and LA-speak. The language-dependent aspect of the LA-think rules specifies whether the system should continue to navigate or switch to LA-speak. The LA-speak rules specify whether the system should continue to realize surfaces or switch to LA-think (cf. Chaps. 12 and 14).

A.2 Incremental Language Production Based on Navigation

As an example of the incremental interaction between LA-think and LA-speak consider the following schematic derivation of the sentence The girl could have eaten an apple. This sentence is based on an underlying VNN proposition. For simplicity, the navigation is viewed in isolation, disregarding the in-going and out-going extrapropositional relations. We are thus dealing with the following railroad system:

A.2.1 RAILROAD SYSTEM OF AN ISOLATED TWO-PLACE PROPOSITION

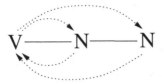

This railroad system may be traversed in two alternative orders, indicated below by numbers 1, 2, 3, and 4 on the transitions:

A.2.2 ALTERNATIVE NAVIGATION ORDERS

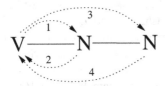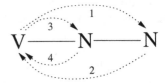

The navigation on the left activates the proplets in the order VSO (verb subject object) while that on the right activates the proplets in the order VOS. In English declaratives, a VSO navigation is reflected by active, e.g., The girl ate the apple, while a VOS navigation is reflected by passive, e.g., The apple was eaten by the girl (cf. 6.5.2).

Next, the language-independent navigation orders shown in A.2.2 must be adapted to the language-dependent word order of the language at hand, for example, the SVO surface order of English. This is based on the distinction between transitions with and without surface realization. Surface realization is implemented as a switch from LA-think (navigation) to LA-speak (realization). Navigations which switch the system to LA-speak have their numbers marked with @. Consider the following example:

A.2.3 NAVIGATION WITH ACTIVATION OF SURFACE REALIZATION

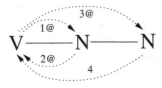

Here, a basic SVO surface order is derived via the activation sequence 1@ 2@ 3@. Transition 4 returns to the verb without any surface realization and readies the system for a coordination-based extrapropositional navigation to the verb of the next proposition. A basic SOV surface order, as for Korean, would be derived from the same railroad system and the same navigation order via the alternative activation sequence 1@ 3@ 4@.

It remains to show how the function words, originally absorbed into the proplets during language interpretation with LA-hear, are precipitated from these proplets by

LA-speak during language production. As an example, consider the production of the sentence The girl could have eaten an apple based on the navigation A.2.3 (see also Sects. 6.4 and 14.5).

The production must precipitate the determiners the and an from the N proplets, and the auxiliaries could and have from the V proplet. As in previous examples (e.g., 3.5.3), the derivation uses abstract surfaces: determiners are represented as d, nouns as nn, auxiliaries as ax, nonfinite verbs as nv, and punctuation signs as p.

Let us assume that the proplets underlying our sample derivation share the proposition number i ([prn: i]). Each word form surface produced in the derivation is numbered, from i.1 to i.8:

A.2.4 SCHEMATIC PRODUCTION OF The girl could have eaten an apple

	activated sequence			*realization*
i				
	... V			
	V	N		
i.1		d		d
	V	N		
i.2		d nn		d nn
	V	N		
i.3	ax	d nn		d nn ax
	V	N		
i.4	ax ax	d nn		d nn ax ax
	V	N		
i.5	ax ax nv	d nn		d nn ax ax nv
	V	N		
i.6	ax ax nv	d nn	d	d nn ax ax nv d
	V	N	N	
i.7	ax ax nv	d nn	d nn	d nn ax ax nv d nn
	V	N	N	
i.8	ax ax nv p	d nn	d nn	d nn ax ax nv d nn p
	V	N	N	

After activating the initial V, LA-think traverses and activates the first N, resulting in the proplet sequence VN. The navigation (cf. A.2.2) consists of two steps, namely from the V to the first N (1) and back to the V (2). After the navigation, the system switches to LA-speak to realize the surface sequence d nn (i.1–i.2) from the N proplet. corresponding to 1@, and the sequence ax ax nv from the V proplet (i.3–i.5), corresponding to 2@ (cf. A.2.3). In i.5, the system switches back to LA-think to traverse and activate the second N, resulting in the proplet sequence VNN. Again, the navigation consists of two steps, namely from the V to the second N (3) and back to the V (4). Then the system switches to LA-speak to realize the surface sequence d nn from the second N proplet (i.6–i.7), corresponding to 3@, and the p from the V proplet, resulting in the overall surface sequence d nn ax ax nv d nn p. The application of the last LA-speak rule switches the system to LA-think, enabling it to proceed to the next proposition.

The time-linear derivation of a d nn ax ax nv d nn p surface sequence from a VNN proplet sequence shown in A.2.4 is based on two factors:

A.2.5 PRODUCTION PRINCIPLES OF SURFACE ORDERING

Earlier surfaces may be produced from later proplets.
Example: The initial d nn surface sequence is achieved by realizing the second proplet in the activated VN sequence first (cf. line i.1–i.2 in A.2.4).
Later surfaces may be produced from earlier proplets.
Example: The final punctuation p (full stop) is realized from the first proplet in the VNN sequence (cf. line i.8 in A.2.4).

These possibilities are based on the patterns of the LA-speak rules: they may match any of the proplets traversed so far in order to produce certain surfaces.

The basic strategy is to realize as many surfaces as possible from the activated proplet sequence. The navigation stops as soon as a newly activated proplet can provide additional surfaces. The navigation resumes when the currently activated proplet sequence can produce no more surfaces.

This maximally incremental interaction between LA-think and LA-speak is motivated not only by psychological considerations,[2] but also by computational efficiency. The reason is that an incremental activation of proplets results in a more restricted set of candidates for matching by the LA-speak rules than an activated proplet sequence which is complete from the start. Chaps. 12 and 14 have shown the production of various constructions from underlying proplet sequences in explicit detail.

A.3 Realizing Alternative Word Orders from One-Place Propositions

By controlling the moment of *when* a particular surface is realized from a sequence of activated proplets, the characteristic word orders of different natural languages can be realized from the same navigation. As examples, let us consider three different natural languages, namely English, German, and Korean. After a brief summary of the basic word order of these languages, we will present the derivation of simple[3] declarative sentences and the corresponding yes/no interrogatives.

The basic word order of English declarative sentences is subject–verb–object (SVO), whereby the verb is *postnominative*. This means that in a sentence with an initial adverb, for example, Suddenly John left, the adverb and the nominative share the place

---

[2] For corresponding evidence from language interpretation see footnote 13 on page 31.
[3] As illustrated by Example A.2.4, i.e., sentences without subclauses.

before the verb. In sentences with two- or three-place verbs, the order of the arguments is interpreted as nominative-accusative or nominative-dative-accusative, respectively.

The basic word order of German declarative sentences is also SVO, but with the verb in *second* position. This means that in a sentence with an initial adverb, for example, Plötzlich ging John (Suddenly left John), the subject appears third following the verb. Also, in sentences with two- or three-place verbs, the position of the nominative, dative, and accusative is free, as long as the verb is in second position.

The basic word order of Korean is subject–object–verb (SOV); arguments are case-marked with suffixes and their order is free. The SOV order holds even in yes/no interrogatives, whereby interrogatives and declaratives are distinguished morphologically by the suffixes ta (declarative) and kka (interrogative) on the verb.

In old English and contemporary German, in contrast, yes/no interrogatives have the verb in initial position, for example, Ging John? (Left John?). Modern English uses a complex verb construction with a sentence-initial auxiliary or modal, followed by the nominative and the nonfinite main verb, as in Did John leave?

The simplest constellation is a one-place proposition, represented by the VN notation introduced in A.1.1. In coordination-based extrapropositional concatenation, the proplets of the current proposition are preceded and followed by the Vs of the preceding and the following proposition. Thus, the underlying proplet sequence is V...VN...V. The following two examples use the same navigation order, but differ in when the system switches to LA-speak, indicated by '@':

A.3.1 ONE-PLACE DECLARATIVE AND YES/NO INTERROGATIVE NAVIGATION

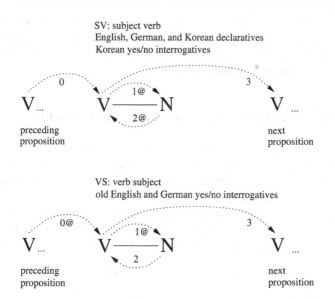

SV: subject verb
English, German, and Korean declaratives
Korean yes/no interrogatives

VS: verb subject
old English and German yes/no interrogatives

The arrows between the proplets indicate the relations between the proplets and con-stitute the railroad system for the navigation. The numbers indicate the order of the navigation steps through the railroad system.

The navigation is driven by two rules of an LA-think grammar (cf. Sect. 14.1), called V_V_V and V_N_V. The rule V_V_V moves from the V of the preceding proposition to the V of the present proposition (0), with the present V as output position. The rule V_N_V moves from the V of the present proposition to the N (1) and back to the V (2), with the present V as output position. A second application of the rule V_V_V moves from the V of the present proposition to the V of the next proposition (3), with the next V as output position. These moves are common to both graphs.

Now consider the surface realizations of the two navigations. In the upper graph, transition 0 proceeds from the V of the previous proposition to the V of the present proposition without realizing a surface. Transitions 1@ and 2@ proceed from the V to the N and back to the V of current proposition, first realizing the N and then the V. Transition 3 proceeds from the current to the next V.

In the lower graph, in contrast, transition 0@ realizes the V of the current proposi-tion and transition 1@ realizes the N. The following transitions 2 and 3 proceed from the N back to the V and then to the next V.[4]

The results are the alternative surface orders noun–verb (upper graph) and verb–noun (lower graph) from a common proplet network and a common navigation. These alternative orders constitute the *basic* surface serializations of the syntactic mood and the genus verbi (voice) of the languages in question. In the case of one-place propo-sitions, the basic word order of declarative sentences is subject–verb in English, Ger-man, and Korean. The interrogative serialization, in contrast, is verb-subject in old English and German, but subject–verb in Korean. In addition to the basic surface order handled by the LA-think navigation, production requires function word precipitation, as shown schematically in A.2.4, and the selection of the proper morpho-syntactic properties, including agreement (cf. Sects. 14.2–14.6).

A.4 Realizing Basic SO Word Orders from Two-Place Propositions

The surface orders derivable from two-place propositions are more varied than those derivable from one-place propositions. In addition to the alternative between the subject–verb and the verb–subject order, two-place propositions provide the alterna-tive between the subject–object and the object–subject order.

As a result, two-place propositions provide six basic surface orders, namely the three SO orders SVO, VSO, and SOV, and the three OS orders OVS, VOS, and OSV – as compared to the two basic surface orders VS and SV of one-place propositions

---

[4] In dialog-initial interrogatives (i.e., in the absence of a preceding proposition), the verb is realized in the process of activating the proposition-initial V proplet. Whether or not transition 3 to the next V realizes a surface depends on the sentence mood of the next sentence.

(cf. A.3.1). Let us begin with the three SO orders of two-place propositions, while the corresponding OS orders are presented in Sect. A.5 of this appendix.

The following examples show the proplet network and the navigation resulting in the SVO declaratives of English and German, the VSO yes/no interrogatives of modern English and German, and the SOV declaratives and yes/no interrogatives of Korean:

A.4.1 TWO-PLACE SO NAVIGATION FOR SVO AND SOV LANGUAGES

SVO: subject verb object
English and German declaratives

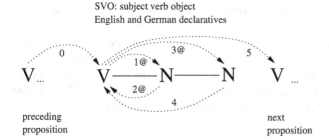

VSO: verb subject object
modern English and German yes/no interrogatives

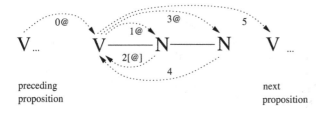

SOV: subject object verb
Korean declaratives and yes/no interrogatives

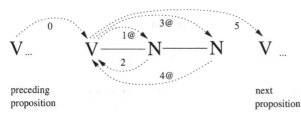

All three examples are based on the same navigation order through the same V...VNN...V proplet network. Based on the rule V_V_V, the navigation proceeds from the V of the preceding proposition to the V of the current proposition (0). Then the rule V_N_V navigates from the current V to the first N (1) and back to the current V (2). Then the rule V_N_V applies again, navigating from the current V to the second

N (3) and back to the current V (4). Finally, the rule V_V_V applies once more to proceed to the V of the following proposition (5).

The language- and mood-specific difference between the three examples consists solely in when certain navigation steps switch to surface realization. The SVO surface of the first example is realized by the steps 1@, 2@, and 3@. The VSO surface of the second example is realized by the steps 0@, 1@, 3@, whereby the parentheses in 2[@] indicate the complex verb construction of English yes/no interrogatives, for example, *Did* Julia *eat* the apple? as opposed to German *Aß* Julia den Apfel? (Ate Julia the apple?). The SOV surface of the third example is realized by the steps 1@, 3@, 4@.

Again, the alternative SVO, VSO, and SOV surface serializations, derived from a common navigation through a common proplet network, constitute only the most basic language- and mood-dependent surface orders from which the sequence of concrete surfaces, including function word precipitation, must be realized. Consider the interrogative counterpart to A.2.4: Could the girl have eaten an apple?

A.4.2 SCHEMATIC PRODUCTION OF Could the girl have eaten an apple?

i	*activated sequence*			*realization*
	... V			
i.1	ax			ax
	V	N		
i.2	ax	d		ax d
	V	N		
i.3	ax	d nn		ax d nn
	V	N		
i.4	ax ax	d nn		ax d nn ax
	V	N		
i.5	ax ax nv	d nn		ax d nn ax nv
	·V	N		
i.6	ax ax nv	d nn	d	ax d nn ax nv d
	V	N	N	
i.7	ax ax nv	d nn	d nn	ax d nn ax nv d nn
	V	N	N	
i.8	ax ax nv p	d nn	d nn	ax d nn ax nv d nn p
	V	N	N	

The transition 2[@] of the second example in A.4.1 is reflected above in the transition from i.3 to i.5: after realizing the surface of the first N proplet, i.e., d nn or the girl, the navigation returns to the initial V and realizes the remainder of the complex verb, namely ax nv, representing have eaten.

As an example of a VSO yes/no interrogative without a complex verb construction and a 2 rather than a 2[@] transition consider the following schematic derivation of German Aß das Mädchen den Apfel? (Ate the girl the apple?).

A.4.3 SCHEMATIC PRODUCTION OF Aß das Mädchen den Apfel?

activated sequence			realization
i			
... V			
i.1 v			v
V			
i.2 v d			v d
V N			
i.3 v d nn			v d nn
V N			
i.4 v d nn d			v d nn d
V N N			
i.5 v d nn d nn			v d nn d nn
V N N			
i.6 v p d nn d nn			v d nn d nn p
V N N			

The absence of a 2[@] transition is shown in i.4: after realizing the first N with LA-speak, the system switches to LA-think, navigates back to the V, and gathers the information for retrieving the second N proplet. Unlike English, no additional surfaces are yielded from the V proplet. After activating the second N, the system switches to LA-speak to realize the surfaces d nn yielded by the second N proplet.

While German yes/no interrogatives with an elementary verb form have a 2 rather than a 2[@] transition, corresponding sentences with a complex verb have a 2[@] transition just like English. Consider the following schematic derivation of Könnte das Mädchen einen Apfel gegessen haben? (Could the girl an apple eaten have?), which is the counterpart to the English example derived in A.4.2.

A.4.4 GERMAN Könnte das Mädchen einen Apfel gegessen haben?

activated sequence		realization
i		
... V		
i.1 ax		ax
V		
i.2 ax d		ax d
V N		

i.3	ax	d nn		ax d nn
	V	N		
i.4	ax	d nn	d	ax d nn d
	V	N	N	
i.5	ax	d nn	d nn	ax d nn d nn
	V	N	N	
i.6	ax nv	d nn	d nn	ax d nn d nn nv
	V	N	N	
i.7	ax nv ax	d nn	d nn	ax d nn d nn nv ax
	V	N	N	
i.8	ax nv ax p	d nn	d nn	ax d nn d nn nv ax p
	V	N	N	

Note that the activation of the second N proplet is in line i.6 of A.4.2 (English) and in line i.4 of A.4.4 (German) – despite the fact that both sentences use corresponding complex verbs and nouns. This is due to the different language-dependent LA-speak grammars. They realize different amounts of surface yielded from the currently activated proplets, thus creating different needs to activate a new proplet.

A.5 Realizing OS Word Orders from Alternative Navigations

In addition to the standard SO (subject object) order, natural languages also use the nonstandard OS (object subject) order. The communicative purpose is topicalization of the object. An OS order is based on an alternative navigation which moves from the V to the second N (object), returns to the V, and then moves to the first N (subject).

English being a fixed word order language can realize such an OVS surface order only by means of the *passive*,[5] as opposed to the *active*. In free word order languages like German and Korean, in contrast, the order of the nouns in declarative clauses may be simply reversed, as in German Den Apfel aß das Mädchen, which transliterates as The apple$_{acc}$ ate the girl$_{nom}$.[6] In addition, German can realize an OS surface also by means of the passive construction, analogous to English.

The derivation of OVS, VOS, and OSV surface orders from a standard VNN proplet network is based on the following navigations:

---

[5] The inversion of the subject–object order characteristic of passive in English is not the case generally. This is shown by German, where the free word order permits passive sentences with an SVO order, like *Von dem Mädchen wurde der Apfel gegessen* (By the girl was the apple eaten).

   According to Givòn (1997), the universal function of passive is the possibility to suppress the (deep) subject or agent, as in The apple was eaten. In Korean, passives which do not suppress the agent are considered unnatural (Prof. Jae-Woong Choe, Korea University, Seoul, 2005, personal communication).

[6] The case marking is frequently deficient in German, as in Das Kind füttert die Mutter, which transliterates as The child$_{nom/acc}$ feeds the mother$_{acc/nom}$, and results in syntactic ambiguity.

A.5.1 TWO-PLACE OS NAVIGATION FOR SVO AND SOV LANGUAGES

OVS: object verb subject
declarative English and German passive, and German OS active

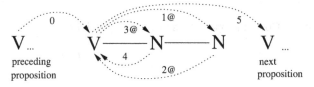

preceding
proposition

next
proposition

VOS: verb object subject
yes/no interrogative of English passive and German active/passive

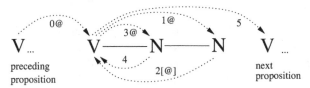

preceding
proposition

next
proposition

OSV: object subject verb
Korean declaratives and interrogatives with topicalized object

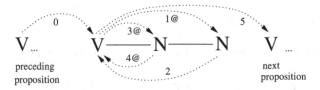

preceding
proposition

next
proposition

These graphs constitute the same railroad system as the SO representation in A.4.1 and show the relations between proplets as a conventional VNN network. The difference is in the navigation *order*, represented by the numbers associated with the dotted arrows: In the OS navigation the transitions 1 and 2 are between the V and the second N, while they are between the V and the first N in the SO navigation. Accordingly, in the OS navigation the transitions 3 and 4 are between the V and the first N, while they are between the V and the second N in SO navigation. Due to the different traversal orders, the activation numbers are the same in the SO and the OS navigation (compare A.4.1 and A.5.1): For OVS surfaces, they are 1@ 2@ 3@; for VOS surfaces, they are 0@ 1@ 2[@] 3@; and for OSV surfaces they are 1@3@4@.

Examples of declarative OSV surfaces in English are the apple was eaten by the girl and The apple could have been eaten by the girl. Examples of yes/no interrogative VOS surfaces in English are Was the apple eaten by the girl? and Could the apple have been eaten by the girl?.

Consider the following schematic derivation of the latter example, whereby d, nn, ax, nv, and p stand for determiner, noun, auxiliary, nonfinite verb, and punctuation as before, and pp stands for preposition. The nonstandard activation order of the N proplets is indicated by realizing the second N before the first (cf. 6.5.2).

A.5.2 PRODUCTION OF Could the apple have been eaten by the girl?

	activated sequence			*realization*
i				
...	V			
i.1	ax			ax
	V			
i.2	ax		d	ax d
	V			
i.3	ax		d nn	ax d nn
	V		N	
i.4	ax ax		d nn	ax d nn ax
	V		N	
i.5	ax ax ax		d nn	ax d nn ax ax
	V		N	
i.6	ax ax ax nv		d nn	ax d nn ax ax nv
	V		N	
i.7	ax ax ax nv	pp	d nn	ax d nn ax ax nv pp
	V	N	N	
i.8	ax ax ax nv	pp d	d nn	ax d nn ax ax nv pp d
	V	N	N	
i.9	ax ax ax nv	pp d nn	d nn	ax d nn ax ax nv pp d nn
	V	N	N	
i.10	ax ax ax nv p	pp d nn	d nn	ax d nn ax ax nv pp d nn p
	V	N	N	

Our derivation of a two-place passive in English as a OVS (declarative) or VOS (yes/no interrogative) realization treats the prepositional phrase by the girl as an N proplet (noun), in contradistinction to prepositional phrases used as modifiers, which are treated as A proplets (complex adjectives, cf. Chap. 15).

A.6 Realizing Basic Word Orders from Three-Place Propositions

While two-place propositions allow two different navigation orders, namely SO and OS, three-place propositions allow six, namely SDI, SID, DSI, DIS, ISD, and IDS. Thereby S stands for subject (or 'deep' nominative), D for direct object (or 'deep' accusative), and I for indirect object (or 'deep' dative). For brevity, we show only SID, SDI, and DSI of the six navigation orders for three-place propositions:

A.6.1 THREE OF THE SIX NAVIGATION GRAPHS

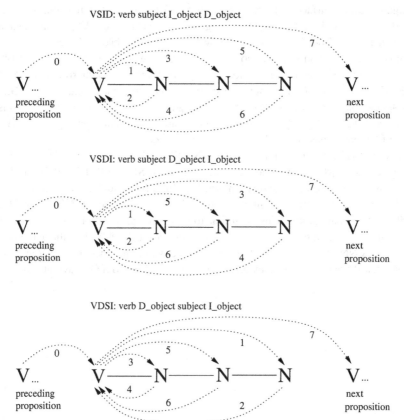

In contradistinction to A.3.1 (one-place propositions) and to A.4.1 and A.5.1 (two-place propositions), the above graphs have no @ markers. Thus, each of the graphs illustrated in A.6.1 must still be specialized to an NVNN, a VNNN, or an NNNV surface order by adding the @ sign to certain transitions. The result are 18 different surfaces, namely SVDI, VSDI, SDIV, SVID, VSID, SIDV, DVSI, VDSI, DSIV, DVIS, VDIS, DISV, IVSD, VISD, ISDV, IVDS, VIDS, and IDSV.

For example, the first graph represents an SID navigation. A declarative SVID surface, such as English The man gave the child an apple (cf. 6.2.1, 6.2.2, Sect.13.5, and Sect. 14.6) and similarly German, is based on a 1@ 2@ 3@ 5@ realization. A corresponding yes/no interrogative VSID surface of old English and German is based on a 0@ 1@ 3@ 5@ realization. A declarative or a yes/no interrogative SIDV surface of Korean is based on a 1@ 3@ 5@ 6@ realization.

The second graph is based on an SDI navigation. A declarative SVDI surface, such as English The man gave the apple to a child and similarly German[7] is based on a 1@ 2@ 3@ 5@ realization. A corresponding yes/no interrogative VSDI surface of English and German is based on a 0@ 1@ 3@ 5@ realization. A declarative or yes/no interrogative SDIV surface of Korean is based on a 1@ 3@ 5@ 6@ realization.

The third graph is based on an DSI navigation. A declarative DVSI surface, such as English passive The apple was given by the man to a child and German active Den Apfel gab der Mann einem Kind (The apple gave the man a child) is based on a 1@ 2@ 3@ 5@ realization. A corresponding yes/no interrogative VSDI surface of English, i.e., Was the apple given by the man to a child? and German Gab den Apfel der Mann einem Kind? (Gave the apple the man a child?) is based on a 0@ 1@ 3@ 5@ realization. A declarative or yes/no interrogative DSIV surface of Korean is based on a 1@ 3@ 5@ 6@ realization.

It turns out that the activation numbers for NVNN surfaces are always 1@ 2@ 3@ 5@, regardless of whether they are derived from SDI, SID, DSI, DIS, ISD, or IDS navigations. Furthermore, the activation numbers for VNNN surfaces are always 0@ 1@ 3@ 5@, and the activation numbers for NNNV surfaces are 1@ 3@ 5@ 6@, regardless of the navigation. This is similar to two-place propositions (cf. A.4.1 and A.5.1), where the activation numbers for NVN surfaces are 1@2@3@, the activation numbers for VNN are 0@ 1@ 2[@] 3@, and the activation numbers for NNV are 1@ 3@ 4@, regardless of whether they are derived from SO or from OS navigations.

---

[7] The corresponding realization for German is Der Mann gab den Apfel einem Kind (The man gave the apple a child). In other words, it is realized without a preposition corresponding to English to.

B. Declarative Description of the Motor Procedure

In a DBS system, two aspects are to be distinguished: one is the definitions provided by the linguist, the other the software which will run with any such definitions as long as they maintain the general format of the overall system. The definitions required include the lexicon; the start state; the number, names, and content of the rules; the content of the rule packages; the number and names of the proplet attributes; the constants and variables; the rule patterns; the final states; and the choice of the operations.

The software for running the linguist-provided definitions during natural language communication includes a general system of word form recognition and production, a database for the storage and retrieval of proplets, and LA-grammars for the hearer, the think, and the speaker mode. The engine driving these components is called the **motor**. This appendix describes the motor procedure of LA-hear in Sects. B.1–B.5, and the motor procedures of LA-think and LA-speak in Sect. B.6.

B.1 Start State Application

In LA-grammar, a derivation proceeds simultaneously at two levels: (i) the grammar level and (ii) the object level. During a derivation, the specifications of the grammar level are applied to proplets at the object level, based on pattern matching and vertical variable binding. In LA-hear derivations, the object level is the *language level*.

The first step of an LA-hear derivation is the application of the start state definition ST_S (grammar level) to each reading of the first word (language level). The application of ST_S to a first word reading may be characterized schematically as follows:

B.1.1 APPLYING ST_S TO A FIRST WORD READING

> *grammar level*: $ST_S =_{def}$ (<ss-pattern> rp_0)
> *language level*:   <first word>

If the first word proplet (provided by lexical lookup) matches the *ss*-pattern of ST_S, the application is successful and results in a *start state*.

A state is generally defined as an ordered pair consisting of a rule package (grammar level) and a sentence start (language level). A sentence start *ss* is a sequence of proplets. In the case of a start state, the sequence of *ss*-proplets is a *unit sequence* because the *ss*-pattern can match at most one proplet, i.e., a reading of the first word.

B.1.2 START STATE RESULTING FROM APPLYING LA-HEAR ST_S DEFINITION

     grammar level: (rp_0

     language level: <first word>)

If the first word is lexically ambiguous, represented by the proplets w1-a, w1-b, and w1-c, for example, application of a start state definition may result in several states:

B.1.3 APPLYING START STATE DEFINITION ST_S TO AMBIGUOUS FIRST WORD

	application of start state definition	*resulting start states*
grammar level	(<ss-pattern> rp_0)	⇒ (rp_0
language level	<w1-a proplet>	<w1-a proplet>)
grammar level	(<ss-pattern> rp_0)	⇒ (rp_0
language level	<w1-b proplet>	<w1-b proplet>)
grammar level	(<ss-pattern> rp_0)	⇒ (rp_0
language level	<w1-c proplet>	<w1-c proplet>)

For the motor, the application of a start state definition is based on an input and an output which are defined simultaneously at the grammar and the language level. At the grammar level, the input is the start state definition, consisting of an *ss*-pattern and a rule package; the output is the rule package. At the language level, the input and output is a unit sequence of a language proplet representing a first word reading, here <w1-a proplet>, <w1-b proplet>, and <w1-c proplet>.

The matching between the *ss*-pattern of a start state definition and a lexical proplet is shown explicitly in the derivation displayed by the JSLIM implementation:

B.1.4 JSLIM DISPLAY OF A START STATE APPLICATION (INPUT)

```
1.
Start state:              [cat: X     ]  rp:{NOM+FV, DET+NN, DET+ADN}

                          [sur: Julia ]
                          [noun: Julia]
                          [cat: nm    ]
                          [sem: f     ]
                          [mdr:       ]
                          [fnc:       ]
                          [idy: +1    ]
                          [prn:       ]
```

The first line specifies the number of the word being consumed by the derivation, here 1. The second line represents the grammar level. It indicates the derivation step, `Start state`, the *ss*-pattern `[cat: X]`, and the rule package `rp`. Directly below the *ss*-pattern of the rule, the matching language proplet (representing a reading of the first word) is displayed.

During a successful pattern matching, the variables at the grammar level are vertically bound to corresponding constants at the language level. The number and names of the attributes, variables, and constants are free and are defined in the grammar. The vertical binding of grammar-level variables to language-level constants is the means for executing grammar-level operations at the language level.

The output of the application B.1.4 is not shown separately in the JSLIM derivation, because it appears in the sentence start of the next composition. Conceptually, such an output may be reconstructed as follows:

B.1.5 OUTPUT OF THE APPLICATION OF A START STATE DEFINITION

```
rp:{NOM+FV, DET+NN, DET+ADN}

[sur:  Julia ]
[noun: Julia]
[cat:  nm    ]
[sem:  f     ]
[mdr:        ]
[fnc:        ]
[idy:  1     ]
[prn:  1     ]
```

The control structure of the motor provides a resulting start state with a prn value, and in the case of a noun proplet with an idy value.

The application of a start state definition with an unrestricted *ss*-pattern (e.g., [cat: X] as in B.1.4) cannot fail.[1] Instead, the possibility of rejecting a first word reading is postponed to the rule applications of the first combination (because rules check not only the next word but also the sentence start by means of pattern matching).

Let us assume, for example, that the rule package rp_0 of the start state definition ST_S contains the rules r-1, r-2, and r-3, and that the first word has the lexical readings w1-a, w1-b, and w1-c. Then the choice between these lexical readings can be decided as follows by the respective *ss*-patterns of these rules:

B.1.6 CONTROLLING THE CHOICE OF THE FIRST WORD READING

grammar level	r-1:	<ss-a pattern>	nw-pattern	operations	rp_1
language level		<w1-a proplet>			

grammar level	r-2:	<ss-b pattern>	nw-pattern	operations	rp_2
language level		<w1-b proplet>			

grammar level	r-3:	<ss-c pattern>	nw-pattern	operations	rp_3
language level		<w1-c proplet>			

---

[1] In some languages, for example, the formal language $a^k b^k c^k$ (cf. FoCL p. 188, 10.2.3), the *ss*-pattern of the start state definition may be restricted to a certain word or kind of word.

In this example, the rules are represented in their usual standard form, consisting of a rule name, e.g., r-1, a sentence start pattern, e.g., <ss-a pattern>, a next word pattern, a set of operations, and a rule package.

Rule r-1 will accept only the w1-a reading, r-2 only the w1-b reading, and r-3 only the w1-c reading of the first word – due to the different *ss*-patterns of the three rules. Thus, even though each lexical proplet is associated with the same rule package rp_0 in B.1.3, only one of its rules will be successful with each of the lexical readings. It is up to the grammar writer to provide the rules with sufficiently specific *ss*-patterns.

B.2 Matching between Proplet Patterns and Language Proplets

The matching of proplet patterns at the grammar level and proplets at the language level has two functions: (i) *limiting* the acceptance of certain language proplets by the grammar (as illustrated in B.1.6), and (ii) *assigning* language-level values to grammar-level variables (required to execute the operations of LA-grammar rules, cf. Sect. B.4). Both functions are based on the use of variables.

Database Semantics uses three kinds of variables: binding variables, replacement variables, and loading variables. These variables differ from those used in Predicate Calculus because there are no quantifiers in DBS (cf. Sects. 5.3 and 6.2).

The *binding variables* are of four kinds: (i) unrestricted binding variables for sequences of zero or more segments, written in uppercase, e.g., X; (ii) binding variables restricted to certain sets of individual grammar constants, written in uppercase, e.g., NP; (iii) binding variables restricted to individual core values[2] written in lowercase Greek letters, e.g., α; and (iv) simultaneous substitution variables, written as N_n, V_n, and A_n, and restricted to the substitution values n_1, n_2, n_3, etc., for nouns, v_1, v_2, v_3, etc., for verbs, and a_1, a_2, a_3, etc., for adjectives, respectively.[3]

The *replacement variables* are not bound to a value, but are replaced by it (cf. 4.1.3, 4.1.4). In the LA-grammars 5.1.2, 5.1.8, 5.1.9, replacement variables occur only at the grammar level, like binding variables. The replacement variables RA.1, RA.2, etc., are restricted to attributes, while the replacement variables RV.1, RV.2, etc., are restricted to values.

The *loading variables* PC, PCV, and NCV (cf. p. 186, 188)[4] occur at the grammar and the object level, and serve to provide the extra-propositional connections. PC, for previous conjunct, is restricted to the proposition number of the previous sentence, PCV to the verb of the previous sentence, and NCV to the verb of the next sentence.

---

[2] i.e., concepts (cf. 2.6.4), indexical pointers (cf. 2.6.5), and name markers (cf. 2.6.7).

[3] Examples illustrating the use of substitution variables at the grammar level and the corresponding substitution values at the language level in complex nouns are 13.3.1, 13.3.2, 13.3.3, 13.3.6, and 13.3.7, in complex verbs 13.4.4 and 13.4.5, and in complex adjectives 15.4.4, 15.4.5, 15.4.10, 15.4.11, 15.5.1, 15.5.3, 15.5.4, 15.5.5, and 15.5.6.

[4] Examples illustrating the use of loading variables at various stages of a derivation are 11.5.2, 11.5.3, 13.4.6, 13.5.3, and 13.5.8.

Successful matching is based on the attribute condition and the value condition, defined in 3.2.3. These two conditions are completely general and must be implemented as part of the motor. The proplet patterns and language proplets used in the conditions, in contrast, are defined in the grammar: The proplet patterns are provided to the motor by the grammar rules, while the language proplets are provided to the motor by the previous state (sentence start) and the lexicon of the grammar (next word).

While the attribute condition is straightforward, the value condition requires a definition of the notion of *compatibility*. The compatibility between the variable of a proplet pattern and a corresponding constant of a language proplet is based on *variable restrictions* defined in the preamble of the grammar (e.g., 13.2.2). For example, if the variable VAR-i is restricted as

VAR-i ϵ {const-1, const-2, const-3}

then the feature

[attribute-k: VAR-i]

of a proplet pattern will be compatible with the features

[attribute-k: const-1]

or

[attribute-k: const-2]

or

[attribute-k: const-3]

of a language proplet – but not, for example, with the feature

[attribute-k: const-4].

The definition of variable restrictions in the grammar is similar in effect to the typing of attributes, but is more flexible and more differentiated. For example, instead of restricting an attribute, e.g., attribute-k, to a certain type of value, e.g., positive integers, we define the value of the attribute as a variable, e.g.,

attribute-k: VAR-num

and then define VAR-num by restricting it to positive integers, e.g.,

VAR-num ϵ {1, 2, 3, ..., n}

Should it turn out later that attribute-k may also take characters as value, we redefine the restriction of its variable. We can specify the kind of value, e.g., integer or character, or explicitly list specific items.

It is possible to define a restricted variable in terms of other variables. For example, VAR-top may be defined as

VAR-top $\subseteq$ {VAR-sub1 VAR-sub3 VAR-sub5}

where

VAR-sub1 ϵ {a2, a4, a5},

VAR-sub3 ϵ {b1,b2, b3}, and

VAR-sub5 ϵ {d4, d5, d8}.

The set-theoretic relations between variable restrictions are defined in the grammar and built bottom up from the elementary constants.

B.3 Time-Linear Breadth-First Derivation Order

In a rule application, the patterns of the grammar level and the proplets of the language level are aligned as follows:

B.3.1 LEVEL ALIGNMENT IN A RULE APPLICATION

grammar level   r-1: <ss-pattern 1   ss-pattern 2 ... > nw-pattern operations rp_1
language level   <w1-a proplet   w2-a proplet ... > nw proplet

For a sentence start pattern to apply successfully to the language level, all patterns of the sequence at the grammar level must find matching proplets at the language level (as in B.3.1), but not vice versa. Thus, the number of *ss*-patterns may be smaller than the number of proplets in the sentence start. The next word pattern, in contrast, must match exactly one proplet. The successful application of a rule results in a state:

B.3.2 STATE RESULTING FROM A RULE APPLICATION

(rp-1
<w1-a' w2-a' w3-a'>)

The output proplets in B.3.2, e.g., w1-a', will normally differ from the input proplets in B.3.1, e.g., w1-a, due to the application of certain rule operations.

If the input provides another next word, the state resulting from a rule application will trigger another left-associative composition. For this, the next word is lexically analyzed as a set of readings which is positioned at the language level next to the sentence start (*nw*-addition). For example, if the next word has the lexical readings w4-a, w4-b, and w4-c, the following expression results from B.3.2:

B.3.3 *nw*-ADDITION

rp-1
<w1-a' w2-a' w3-a'> {w4-a
                      w4-b
                      w4-c}

Next, the rule package is expanded into a set of rules. For example, if rp-1 = {r-i r-j r-k}, then B.3.3 is turned into the following expression:

B.3.4 EXPANSION OF THE RULE PACKAGE

{r-i r-j r-k}
<w1-a' w2-a' w3-a'> {w4-a
                      w4-b
                      w4-c}

Then, the Cartesian product of all rules of the rule package and all readings of the next word are formed, whereby sentence starts and next words are turned into input pairs at the language level. In this way, Example B.3.4 results in the following set of ordered pairs, each consisting of (i) a rule name (grammar level) and (ii) an input pair (language level) of an *ss* and an *nw*:

B.3.5 CARTESIAN PRODUCT OF RP CONTENT AND *nw* READINGS

r-i
<w1-a' w2-a' w3-a'> w4-a

r-i
<w1-a' w2-a' w3-a'> w4-b

r-i
<w1-a' w2-a' w3-a'> w4-c

r-j
<w1-a' w2-a' w3-a'> w4-a

r-j
<w1-a' w2-a' w3-a'> w4-b

r-j
<w1-a' w2-a' w3-a'> w4-c

r-k
<w1-a' w2-a' w3-a'> w4-a

r-k
<w1-a' w2-a' w3-a'> w4-b

r-k
<w1-a' w2-a' w3-a'> w4-c

Finally, all rule names at the grammar level are expanded into the corresponding explicit rule definitions. Thereby, each element of the Cartesian product B.3.5 is turned into a structure like B.3.1. By applying the rules, a new set of states like B.3.2 results.

Now the combination cycle starts over again. As before, the steps are (i) *nw*-addition by calling up the readings of the next word (cf. B.3.3), (ii) expanding the rule package (cf. B.3.4), (iii) formation of the Cartesian product (cf. B.3.5), (iv) replacing the rule names by the actual definitions (cf. B.4.1), and (v) rule application (cf. B.3.1).

B.4 Rule Application and the Basic Structure of the LA-Hear Motor

The first step of a rule application is matching the rule patterns at the grammar level with the correlated proplets at the language level. If matching fails, the rule application is discarded. Matching fails whenever the attribute condition or the value condition, defined in 3.2.3, are not satisfied.

If matching succeeds, the variables at the grammar level are bound to the corresponding values of the language level (vertical variable binding), and the operations of the rule are executed. The correlation between rule patterns and proplets is automatically displayed by the JSLIM derivation, illustrated below using the implementation of Kycia (2004).

B.4.1 JSLIM DISPLAY OF A RULE APPLICATION

```
2.1
NOM+FV: [noun: alpha]   [verb: beta   ]   ecopy nw_verb ss_fnc    rp:{AUX+NFV,
        [cat: NP    ]   [cat: NP' X VT]   delete_NP'_nw-cat        S+IP, FV+NP}
        [fnc: nil   ]   [arg: nil     ]   acopy ss_noun nw_arg
                        [ctn: nil     ]   acopy ps_verb nw_ctp
                                          acopy ps_prn  nw_ctp
                                          acopy nw_verb ps_ctn
                                          increase IDY
                                          copy_nw


        [sur: Julia ]   [sur: ate     ]
        [noun: Julia]   [verb: eat    ]
        [cat: nm    ]   [cat: n' a' v ]
        [sem: f     ]   [sem: past    ]
        [mdr:       ]   [mdr:         ]
        [fnc:       ]   [arg:         ]
        [idy: +1    ]   [ctn:         ]
        [prn:       ]   [ctp:         ]
                        [prn:         ]
```

The *ss-* and the *nw*-pattern are positioned above the *ss-* and the *nw*-proplets (level alignment, cf. B.3.1). Matching is successful. The variable `alpha` is bound to the value `Julia`, the restricted variable NP is bound to the value nm (for name), etc.

This binding of variables at the grammar level to values at the language level is the precondition for performing the *operations* of the rule. For example, the operation `acopy ss_noun nw_arg` specifies that the value of the noun attribute in the *ss* should be copied into the arg attribute of the *nw*. By binding the variable `alpha` at the grammar level to the constant value `Julia` at the language level, the copying operation defined at the grammar level can be performed at the language level. The result of the rule operations is shown in the sentence start of the next composition:

B.4.2 JSLIM DISPLAY OF A RULE APPLICATION

```
3.13
FV+NP: [verb: beta   ]   [noun: alpha ]   delete_NP'_ss-cat       rp:{DET+NN,
       [cat: NP' X VT]   [cat: Y Np   ]   ecopy ss_verb nw_fnc    DET+ADN,
       [arg:         ]   [fnc: nil    ]   acopy nw_noun ss_arg    FV+NP, S+IP}
                                          increase IDY
                                          copy_nw
                                          copy_ss
```

```
[sur:          ]  [sur: a      ]
[verb: eat     ]  [noun: n_1   ]
[cat: a' v     ]  [cat: sn' snp]
[sem: past     ]  [sem: indef  ]
[mdr:          ]  [mdr:        ]
[arg: Julia    ]  [fnc:        ]
[ctn:          ]  [idy: +1     ]
[ctp:          ]  [prn:        ]
[prn: 7        ]
[wrn: 2        ]
```

The prn value and the wrn attribute are added by the control structure of the motor. The *nw* proplet *eat* of the previous composition B.4.1 now serves as the *ss*. The operations of the previous composition have (i) canceled the nominative valency in the cat attribute and (ii) added the value Julia to the arg attribute.

The interaction of the input, the motor, and the LA-hear grammar may shown schematically as follows:

B.4.3 STEPPING THROUGH THE OPERATIONS OF THE LA-HEAR MOTOR

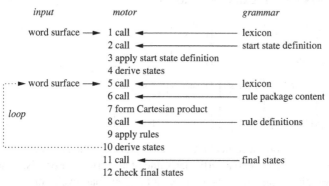

In line 1, the initial word surface is fed into the system. This starts the LA-hear motor by triggering lexical lookup, resulting in a set of initial proplets (analyzed word readings). In line 2, the start state definition is called from the grammar. In line 3, it is applied to each element in the set of initial proplets (cf. B.1.1). In line 4, this results in a set of states, whereby each state is an ordered pair consisting of a rule package name and a proplet representing a reading of the initial word form (cf. B.1.3). In line 5, the next word arrives, triggering lexical lookup (cf. B.3.3); this results in a set of proplets representing lexical readings. In line 6, the rule packages are unpacked (cf. B.3.4). In line 7, the Cartesian product is formed (cf. B.3.5); each of its elements consists of a rule name, a sentence start (set of proplets), and a next word (single proplet). In line 8, the rule names are replaced by the actual rule definitions. In line 9, each rule in the Cartesian product is applied to its sentence start and its next word. In line 10, this results in a set of states and causes the intake of another next word (line 5). The loop between lines 5 and 10 continues until there is no next word available. When this happens, the final state definition is called from the grammar (line 11). In line 12, the final state definition is applied to the current set of states, distinguishing between complete and incomplete well-formed expressions.

B.5 Operations

The operations of a rule interact closely with the specification of its patterns. Assume, for example, that the sentence start of a composition consists of a sequence of five noun proplets at the language level and a sequence of two noun patterns at the grammar level. Then the correlation between patterns and proplets can be controlled via the agreement of the attributes and the compatibility of their values.

For example, the following two patterns each fit only one of the five proplets at the language level, assuming that the constant m is in the restriction set of the binding variable M and the constant n is in the restriction set of binding variable N.

B.5.1 CORRELATION OF PATTERNS AND PROPLETS

$$
\text{r-i:} \quad
\begin{bmatrix} \text{noun: } \alpha \\ \text{cat: M} \\ ... \\ \text{prn: i} \end{bmatrix}
\qquad
\begin{bmatrix} \text{noun: } \beta \\ \text{cat: N} \\ ... \\ \text{prn: i} \end{bmatrix}
$$

$$
\begin{bmatrix} \text{noun: k1} \\ \text{cat: a} \\ ... \\ \text{prn: 23} \end{bmatrix}
\begin{bmatrix} \text{noun: k2} \\ \text{cat: m} \\ ... \\ \text{prn: 23} \end{bmatrix}
\begin{bmatrix} \text{noun: k3} \\ \text{cat: b} \\ ... \\ \text{prn: 23} \end{bmatrix}
\begin{bmatrix} \text{noun: k4} \\ \text{cat: n} \\ ... \\ \text{prn: 23} \end{bmatrix}
\begin{bmatrix} \text{noun: k5} \\ \text{cat: c} \\ ... \\ \text{prn: 23} \end{bmatrix}
$$

In addition to an unambiguous specification of the proplets and the attributes, operations sometimes require reference to a particular value of an attribute. For this, regular expressions with variables and constants are used at the grammar level. For example, if an attribute at the language level has the values a b c d, the value d may be referred to at the grammar level with the expression X D (last value), with X D Y (in any position), or X d Y (using the constant d instead of the restricted variable D).

The following descriptions of the operations (see also 11.4.2) present (i) the ss-pattern, the nw-pattern, and the operation at the grammar level, and (ii) the corresponding attribute–value pairs at the language level. The result of the operation is shown at the language level to the right of the '⇒', directly below the formulation of the operation.

B.5.2 CANCELING OF VALENCY POSITIONS

	ss	*nw*	*operation*
grammar level:	[cat: X NP' Y]	[cat: NP]	delete NP' ss.cat
language level:	[cat: a b np' c]	[cat: np]	⇒[cat: a b c] [cat: np]

	ss	*nw*	*operation*
grammar level:	[cat: NP]	[cat: X NP' Y]	delete NP' nw.cat
language level:	[cat: np]	[cat: a b np' c]	⇒[cat: np] [cat: a b c]

Based on the restriction sets and agreement conditions of the binding variables NP and NP' (cf. preamble of LA-hear.2, 13.2.2 and 13.2.3), proper agreement between the values corresponding to NP and NP' at the language level is checked automatically as an essential part of matching and thus as a precondition for executing the operation.

B.5.3 ADDITIVE COPYING (*acopy*)

	ss	*nw*	*operation*
grammar level:	[noun: α]	[arg: X]	acopy ss.noun nw.arg
language level:	[noun: John][arg: Julia]	⇒[noun: John] [arg: Julia John]	

	ss	*nw*	*operation*
grammar level:	[arg: X]	[noun: α]	acopy α ss.arg:1
language level:	[arg: Julia]	[noun: John]	⇒[arg: John Julia] [noun: John]

As a default, the operation *acopy* adds the copied value at the end of the target slot. It is also possible to specify the position, using the numbers 1, 2, 3, etc., and –1, –2, –3, etc., in the target attribute, whereby 1 stands for the first position from the left, while –1 stands for the first position from the right, and accordingly for 2, –2, 3, –3, etc.

B.5.4 EXCLUSIVE COPYING (*ecopy*)

	ss	*nw*	*operation*
grammar level:	[verb: α]	[fnc:]	ecopy α nw.fnc
language level:	[verb: know][fnc:]	⇒[verb: know] [fnc: know]	

	ss	*nw*	*operation*
grammar level:	[fnc:]	[verb: α]	acopy nw.verb ss.fnc
language level:	[fnc:]	[verb: know]	⇒[fnc: know] [verb: know]

ecopy has no target position (in contradistinction to *acopy*) because the target attribute must have the value NIL by definition. Note that the value to be copied may be specified as a variable, e.g., α, or by means of a proplet.attribute, e.g., nw.verb.

B.5.5 RAISING OR LOWERING NUMERICAL VALUES (*increment – decrement*))

	ss	*operation*
grammar level:	[idy: N]	increment ss.idy
language level:	[idy: 11]	⇒[idy: 12]

The operations *increment* and *decrement* each refer to a single proplet only, like *delete*. If the sentence start at the grammar level consists of several patterns, the proplet in question is specified using the word number (wrn: d), for example, acopy ss-d.noun nw.arg instead of acopy ss.noun nw.arg (cf. B.5.1).

The automatic representation of the derivation by JSLIM does not explicitly show the results of the operations (in contradistinction to B.5.2–B.5.5). They are specified implicitly, however, in the *ss*.proplets of the next composition (cf. B.4.2), and at the end of the derivation in the presentation of the resulting proplets.

B.6 Basic Structure of the LA-Think and the LA-Think–Speak Motor

As in all LA-grammars, **LA-think** derivations are defined at two levels, (i) the grammar level and (ii) the object level, whereby the connection between the two levels is based on pattern matching and vertical variable binding. The object level of an LA-think derivation is the *context level*.

The start state definition of an LA-think grammar applies to a context proplet in the Word Bank – in contradistinction to an LA-hear grammar, in which the start state definition applies to a language proplet provided by the lexicon.

B.6.1 APPLYING THE START STATE DEFINITION OF **LA-think**

> *grammar level*: $ST_S =_{def}$ (<ss-pattern> rp_1)
> *context level*:   <initial proplet>

The initial context proplet starting an LA-think derivation is selected by the agent's control structure. In JSLIM, where no autonomous control structure is available yet, the initial proplet is chosen by the user by typing a verb-name at the prompt.

The successful application of the start state definition results in a state.

B.6.2 START STATE RESULTING FROM APPLYING LA-THINK ST_S DEFINITION

> *grammar level*:   (rp_1
> *context level*:   <initial proplet>)

In JSLIM, the application of a start state is displayed as follows:

B.6.3 JSLIM DISPLAY OF AN LA-THINK START STATE APPLICATION (INPUT)

```
dbs2.DBS2-THINK> know
# Think mode #

1.
Start state:            [verb: alpha    ]                    rp:{V_N_N}

                        [sur:           ]
```

```
[verb: know      ]
[cat: DECL       ]
[sem: pres       ]
[mdr:            ]
[arg: Julia John]
[ctn:            ]
[ctp:            ]
[prn: 8          ]
[wrdn: 4         ]
```

After the successful application of the start state definition, a proplet corresponding to the next word must be selected. This is done by applying the rule(s) contained in the rp to the initial proplet provided by the Word Bank, here the rule V_N_N. As explained in Sect. 3.5, the proplet of an LA-think sentence start provides information which is sufficient to retrieve (activate) one or more semantically related successor proplet(s). For example, possible successors in B.6.3 are the proplets *Julia* and *John*.

To prevent the derivation from splitting into more and more parallel paths, the control structure must choose among the continuation alternatives arising at each point of the navigation. For example, choosing the proplet *Julia* as the successor in B.6.3 constitutes a forward navigation (underlying an active sentence), while choosing the proplet *John* constitutes a backward navigation (underlying a passive sentence).

The interaction between the input, the motor, and the LA-think grammar may be summarized schematically as follows:

B.6.4 STEPPING THROUGH THE OPERATIONS OF THE LA-THINK MOTOR

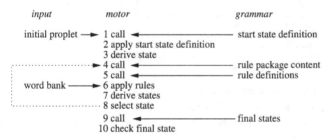

In line 1, the initial proplet is activated, starting the LA-think motor. It calls the start state definition from the grammar and applies it to the initial proplet (line 2). In line 3, the start state is derived, consisting of a rule package and the initial proplet. In line 4, the content of the rule package is called from the grammar. In line 5, the rule names in the rule package are replaced by their actual definitions. In line 6, the rules are applied to the input proplet, resulting in several successor states (line 7). In line 8, one of the successor states is chosen, while the others are discarded. This constellation is equivalent to that of line 3, such that the derivation loops back to line 4, continuing the navigation. In the current implementation, the procedure stops in a state in which no un-traversed successor proplets are available and accessible in the Word Bank. At this point, the motor calls the definition of final states from the grammar (line 9) to determine whether or not the navigation ended in a legal final state (line 10).

The LA-think motor is simpler than the LA-hear motor (cf. B.4.3). This is because (i) the beginning of an LA-think derivation starts with a single proplet, while that of an LA-hear derivation may start with several first word readings, (ii) LA-think finds the successor proplets directly in the Word Bank, while LA-hear requires lexical lookup of the next word, and (iii) LA-think applies the rules in a rule package to a single proplet, while LA-hear applies the rules in a rule package to a set of ordered pairs.

If the agent is in the speaker mode, the LA-think navigation is combined with the LA-speak realization. Thereby, the contextual input, the motor, and the LA-think and LA-speak grammars interact as follows:

B.6.5 STEPPING THROUGH THE OPERATIONS OF THE LA-THINK–SPEAK MOTOR

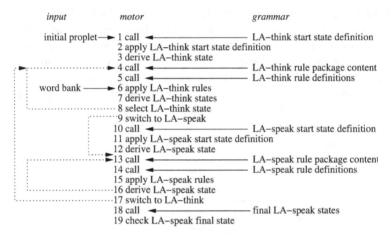

Up to line 8, the LA-think–speak motor is the same as the LA-think motor. However, while the LA-think motor provides an alternative between (i) looping back to line 4 and (ii) exiting, the LA-think–speak motor provides an alternative between (i) looping back to line 4 and (ii) switching to LA-speak (line 9).

If LA-speak has not been used before, the LA-speak start state definition is called from the grammar (line 10) and applied to one of the proplets activated by LA-think (line 11). The derivation of an LA-speak start state in line 12 does not yet result in the utterance of a surface. This happens in lines 13, 14, and 15.

If LA-speak has been used before, the derivation jumps from line 9 to line 13. Either way, after deriving an LA-speak state in line 16, there is an alternative between (i) looping back to line 13 to produce another surface, (ii) switching to LA-think to continue the navigation (return to line 4), and (iii) exiting (lines 18 and 19).

C. Glossary

C.1 Proplet Attributes

Cf. 4.1.2, 11.2.4, 11.2.5, and B.4.2.

attribute:	full name:	value(s):
adj	adjective	modifiers in adnominal and adverbial use
arg	argument	the nouns belonging to a verb
cat	category	category segments specifying combinatorial properties
fnc	functor	the verb belonging to a noun
idy	identity	integer indicating whether two nouns are distinct or not
mdd	modified	noun, verb, or adjective which a modifier modifies
mdr	modifier	adjective modifying a noun, a verb, or an adjective
nc	next conjunct	proposition number and verb of the next proposition
noun	noun	symbols, indexicals, names, and substitution variables
pc	previous conjunct	proposition number and verb of the previous proposition
pcn	punctuation	punctuation signs '.', '?', and '!'
prn	proposition number	integer holding the proplets of a proposition together
sem	semantics	semantic segments specifying noncombinatorial properties
sur	surface	surface of a word form
trc	transition counter	sequence of integers for keeping track of how often a proplet in the Word Bank has been traversed
verb	verb	finite and nonfinite verbs, auxiliaries, and modals
wrn	word number	integer for numbering next word proplets

C.2 Proplet Values

Cf. 11.2.2, 11.2.3, 13.1.13, and 13.1.14.

value:	explanation:	attribute:
a_1, a_2, etc.	substitution value for adjectives	adj
a'	accusative valency position	cat of a verb
adn	adnominal	cat of an adjective
adv	adverbial	cat of an adjective

value:	explanation:	attribute:
be	be, valency filler in nonfinite verb	cat of a nonfinite verb
be′	be, valency position in auxiliary	cat of an auxiliary
be-past	past tense of auxiliary be	sem of a verb
be-perf	past participle of auxiliary be	sem of a verb
be-pres	present tense of auxiliary be	sem of a verb
comp	comparative	sem of a adjective
d′	dative valency position	cat of a verb
def	definite	sem of a determiner
decl	declarative sentence	cat of a verb
do′	do, valency position in auxiliary	cat of an auxiliary
do-past	past tense of auxiliary do	sem of a verb
do-perf	past participle of auxiliary do	sem of a verb
do-pres	pres tense of auxiliary do	sem of a verb
exh	exhaustive	sem of a determiner
f	femininum	sem of a noun
hv	have	cat of an nonfinite verb
hv′	have, valency position in auxiliary	cat of auxiliary
hv-past	past tense of auxiliary have	sem of a verb
hv-perf	past participle of auxiliary have	sem of a verb
hv-pres	present tense of auxiliary have	sem of a verb
imp	imperative	cat of a verb
indef	indefinite	sem of a noun
interrog	interrogative	cat of a verb
m	masculinum	sem of a noun
n_1, n_2, etc.	substitution value for nouns	noun of a determiner
n′	unrestricted nominative valency position	cat of a verb
neg	negated	sem of a verb
ns1′	nominative singular first-person	cat of a verb
n-s3′	nominative except singular third-person	cat of a verb
nm	proper name	cat of a noun
nn	noun filler unmarked for number	cat of a noun
nn′	noun valency position unmarked for number	cat of a determiner
np	3rd pers. noun phrase unmarked for case and number	cat of a determiner
np-2	nominative plural first- and third-person	cat of a pronoun
ns1	nominative singular first-person	cat of a pronoun
ns13′	nominative singular first- and third-person	cat of a verb
ns3	nominative singular third-person	cat of a noun
ns3′	singular third-person	cat of a verb

value:	explanation:	attribute:
n-s13$'$	nominative except singular first- and third-person	cat of a verb
obq	oblique (nonnominative)	cat of a pronoun
past	past tense	sem of a verb
perf	past participle	sem of a verb
pl	plural	sem of a noun
pn	plural noun	cat of a noun
pn$'$	plural noun	cat of a determiner
pnp	third-person plural noun phrase	cat of a determiner
pres	present tense	sem of a verb
pro_1, pro_2, etc.	indexical of a nonreflexive pronoun	noun
pro2	second-person unmarked for number and case	cat of a pronoun
prog	progressive	sem of a verb
rfl_1, rfl_2, etc.	indexical of a reflexive pronoun	noun
sg	singular	sem of a noun
sel	selective	sem of a determiner
sn	singular noun	cat of a noun
sn$'$	singular noun	cat of a determiner
snp	third-person singular noun phrase	cat of a determiner
sup	superlative	sem of a adjective
v	verb, unmarked for sentence mood	cat of a verb
v$'$	verb unmarked for sentence mood	cat of a punctuation mark
v_1, v_2, etc.	substitution value for verbs	verb
vi	verb, marked for interrogative	cat of a verb
vimp	verb, marked for imperative	cat of a verb

C.3 Variables, Restrictions, and Agreement Conditions

C.3.1 BINDING VARIABLES, cf. 4.1.2, 11.2.4, 11.2.5, and 15.6.1.

variables:	explanation:	restriction set:
α, β, etc.	for representing individual concepts	*Julia, sleep, young,* etc.
A_n	simultaneous substitution variable for adj.	a_1, a_2, a_3, ...
ADJ	adjective	adj, adn, adv
ADV	adverbial	adj, adv
ADN	adnominal	adj, adn
AUX	auxiliary valency filler	do, hv, be
AUX$'$	auxiliary valency position	do$'$, hv$'$, be$'$
i, j, k	integer values of the prn and idy attributes	1, 2, 3, ...

variables:	explanation:	restriction set:
N	noun filler	nn, sn, pn
N′	noun valency position nn′, sn′, pn′	
N_n	simultaneous substitution variable for noun	n_1, n_2, n_3, ...
NP	noun phrase filler	pro2, nm, ns1, ns3, np-2, snp, pnp, np, obq
NP′	noun phrase valency position	n′, n-s3′, ns1′, ns3′, ns13′, n-s13′, d′, a′
OBQ	oblique noun phrase filler	snp, pnp, np, obq
OBQ′	oblique noun phrase valency position	D', A'
PREP	preposition	*on, in, above, below, ...*
PRO_n	variable for nonreflexive pronoun	pro_1, pro_2, etc.
RFL_n	variable for a reflexive pronoun	rfl_1, rfl_2, etc.
SM	sentence mood	decl, interrog, imp
TEMP	tempus	past, past/perf
V_n	simultaneous substitution variable for verb	v_1, v_2, v_3, ...
VT	verb type filler	v, vi, vimp
VT′	verb type valency position	v', vi', vimp'
X, Y, Z	.?.?.?.? (arbitrary sequence up to length 4)	none

C.3.2 REPLACEMENT VARIABLES, cf. 4.1.4, 5.1.2, 5.1.8, and 5.1.9.

variables:	explanation:	restriction set:
RA.n	replace-attribute variable	noun, adj, verb
RV.n	replace-value variable	core values of lexical items

C.3.3 LOADING VARIABLES, cf. 11.5.2, 11.5.3, 11.5.4, 13.3.8, 13.4.3, 13.4.6, 13.5.1, and 13.5.3.

variables:	full name:	restriction set:
PC	previous conjunct proposition number	integer
PCV	previous conjunct verb	core value of verb
NCV	next conjunct verb	core value of verb

C.3.4 AGREEMENT CONDITIONS

Cf. 11.2.3 and 13.2.3.

if AUX′ = do′, then AUX = n-s3′
if AUX′ = hv′, then AUX ϵ {hv, n′}
if AUX′ = be′, then AUX = be

if $N' = nn'$, then $N \epsilon \{nn, sn, pn\}$
if $N'= sn'$, then $N \epsilon \{nn, sn\}$
if $N'= pn'$, then $N \epsilon \{nn, pn\}$

if $NP \epsilon \{nm, snp\}$, then $NP' \epsilon \{n', ns3', ns13', d', a'\}$
if $NP = ns1$, then $NP' \epsilon \{n', n\text{-}s3', ns1', ns13'\}$
if $NP = ns3$, then $NP' \epsilon \{ns3', ns13'\}$
if $NP = np\text{-}2$, then $NP' \epsilon \{n', n\text{-}s3'\}$
if $NP = np$, then $NP' \epsilon \{n', ns3', n\text{-}s3', n\text{-}s13', d', a'\}$
if $NP = obq$, then $NP' \epsilon \{d', a'\}$
if $NP = pnp$, then $NP' \epsilon \{n', n\text{-}s3', n\text{-}s13', d', a'\}$
if $NP = pro2$, then $NP' \epsilon \{n', n\text{-}s3', n\text{-}s13', d', a'\}$

C.4 Abstract Surfaces

Cf. 3.5.3, 6.2.2, 6.3.2, 6.3.4, 6.4.2, etc.

surface: full name:

an	adnominal adjective
av	adverbial adjective
ax	auxiliary
cc	coordinating conjunction
d	determiner
fv	finite verb
n	proper name
nn	noun
nv	nonfinite verb
sc	subordinating conjunction
wh	relative pronoun
p	punctuation sign
pp	preposition

C.5 Rule Names

C.5.1 **LA-hear**, cf. 11.4.1, 13.2.4, and 15.6.2.

rule name: *paraphrase:*

AUX+NFV	auxiliary plus nonfinite verb
ADV+NOM	adverbial adjective plus nominative
ADVNOM+FV	adverbial–nominative combination plus finite verb
DET+ADN	determiner plus adnominal adjective

rule name:	paraphrase:
DET+INT	determiner plus intensifier
DET+NN	determiner plus noun
FV+NP	finite verb plus noun phrase
INT+ADJ	intensifier plus adjective
IP + START	interpunctuation sign plus start of next sentence
NOM+ADV	nominative plus adverbial adjective
NOM+FV	nominative plus finite verb
NP+PREP	noun phrase plus preposition
PREP+ADN	preposition plus adnominal adjective
PREP+INT	preposition plus intensifier
PREP+NN	preposition plus noun
PREP+NP	preposition plus noun phrase
PREPP+PREP	prepositional phrase plus preposition
S+IP	sentence plus interpunctuation sign
V+ADV	verb plus adverbial adjective
V+INT	verb plus intensifier

C.5.2 **LA-think**, cf. 12.1.1 and 14.1.1.

rule name:	paraphrase:
N_A_N	noun_adnominal_noun navigation
N_A_V	noun_adnominal_verb navigation
V_N_N	verb_noun_noun navigation
V_N_V	verb_noun_verb navigation
V_V_V	verb_verb_verb navigation

C.5.3 **LA-speak**, cf. 12.4.1 and 14.2.1.

rule name:	paraphrase:	lexicalization function
-ADN	realizing an adnominal adjective	lex-an
-AUX	realizing an auxiliary	lex-ax
-DET	realizing a determiner	lex-d
-FVERB	realizing a finite verb	lex-fv
-NoP	realizing a name or a pronoun	lex-n
-NOUN	realizing a noun	lex-nn
-NVERB	realizing a nonfinite verb	lex-nv
-STOP	realizing a full-stop	lex-p

C.6 List of Analyzed Examples

C.6.1 INTRAPROPOSITIONAL FUNCTOR–ARGUMENT STRUCTURE

1. Julia knows John. (3.4.2; 3.5.3)
2. The man gave the child an apple. (6.2.1; 6.2.2)
3. Every man loves a woman. (6.2.7)
4. The little black dog barked. (6.3.1; 6.3.2)
5. Fido barked loudly. (6.3.3; 6.3.4)
6. Fido has been barking. (6.4.1; 6.4.2)
7. The book was read by John. (6.5.1; 6.5.2)
8. Julia ate the apple on the table. (6.6.2; 6.6.4)

C.6.2 EXTRAPROPOSITIONAL FUNCTOR–ARGUMENT STRUCTURE

9. That Fido barked amused Mary. (7.2.1; 7.2.2)
10. John heard that Fido barked. (7.3.1; 7.3.2)
11. The dog which saw Mary quickly barked. (7.4.1; 7.4.2; 7.4.3)
12. The little dog which Mary saw barked. (7.5.1; 7.5.2)
13. When Fido barked Mary smiled. (7.6.1; 7.6.2)

C.6.3 INTRAPROPOSITIONAL COORDINATION

14. The man, the woman, and the child slept. (8.2.1; 8.2.2)
15. John bought an apple, a pear, and a peach. (8.2.4; 8.2.5)
16. John bought, cooked, and ate the pizza. (8.3.2; 8.3.3)
17. John loves a smart, pretty, and rich girl. (8.3.4)
18. John talked slowly, gently, and seriously. (8.3.5)
19. Bob ate an apple, walked his dog, and read a paper. (8.4.1; 8.4.5)
20. Bob bought, peeled, and ate an apple, a pear, and a peach (8.4.4)
21. Bob ate an apple, Jim a pear, and Bill a peach. (8.5.1; 8.5.4)
22. Bob, Jim, and Bill ate an apple, a pear, and a peach. (8.5.3)
23. Bob bought, Jim peeled, and Bill ate the peach. (8.6.1; 8.6.4)
24. Bob, Jim, and Bill bought, peeled, and ate the peach. (8.6.3)

C.6.4 EXTRAPROPOSITIONAL COORDINATION

25. Julia sang. Then Sue slept. John read. (9.1.1)
26. Sue slept. John bought, cooked, and ate a pizza. Julia sang. (9.1.2)
27. Julia slept. John sang. (9.2.1; 9.2.2)
28. That the man, the woman, and the child slept surprised Mary. (9.3.1, 1)
29. That the man bought, cooked, and ate the pizza surprised Mary. (9.3.1, 2)
30. That Bob ate an apple, a pear, and a peach, surprised Mary. (9.3.1, 3)

31. Mary saw that the man, the woman and the child slept. (9.3.2, 1)
32. Mary saw that the man bought, cooked, and ate the pizza. (9.3.2, 2)
33. Mary saw that Bob bought an apple, a pear, and a peach. (9.3.2, 3)
34. Mary saw the man who bought, cooked, and ate the pizza. (9.3.3, 2)
35. Mary saw the man who bought an apple, a pear, and a peach. (9.3.3, 3)
36. Mary saw the pizza which Bob, Jim, and Bill ate. (9.3.4, 1)
37. Mary saw the pizza which the man bought, cooked, and ate. (9.3.4, 2)
38. Mary arrived after Bob, Jim, and Bill had eaten a pizza. (9.3.5, 1)
39. After Bob had bought, cooked, and eaten the pizza, Mary arrived. (9.3.5, 2)
40. Mary arrived after Bob had eaten an apple, a pear, and a peach. (9.3.5, 3)
41. That Bob ate an apple, walked his dog, and read a paper, amused Mary. (9.4.1, 1)
42. That Bob ate an apple, Jim a pear, and Bill a peach, amused Mary. (9.4.1, 2)
43. That Bob bought, Jim peeled, and Bill ate the peach, amused Mary. (9.4.1, 3)
44. Mary saw that Bob ate an apple, walked his dog, and read a paper. (9.4.2, 1)
45. Mary saw that Bob ate an apple, Jim a pear, and Bill a peach. (9.4.2, 2)
46. Mary saw that Bob bought, Jim peeled, and Bill ate the peach . (9.4.2, 3)
47. The man who ate an apple, walked his dog, and read a paper loves Mary. (9.4.3, 1)
48. Mary saw the peach which Bob bought, Jim peeled, and Bill ate. (9.4.4, 3)
49. Mary arrived after Bob had eaten an apple, walked his dog, and read a paper. (9.4.5, 1)
50. After Bob had eaten an apple, Jim a pear, and Bill a peach, Mary arrived. (9.4.5, 2)
51. Mary arrived after Bob had bought, Jim had peeled, and Bill had eaten the peach. (9.4.5, 3)
52. Julia is singing.^{STAR} Susanne is dreaming.$^{\text{(STAR)}}$ (9.5.2, 1)
53. Julia is singing.^{STAR} Susanne is dreaming.$^{\text{STA}'\text{R}'}$ (9.5.2, 2)
54. Who is singing? ^{STAR} Julia.$^{\text{STA}'\text{R}'}$ (9.5.2, 3; 9.5.3)
55. Who did John say that Bill believes that Mary loves? (9.5.6)
56. Peter left the house. Then Peter crossed the street. (9.6.1, 1)
57. Peter crossed the street. Before that Peter left the house. (9.6.1, 2)
58. Peter, who had left the house, crossed the street. (9.6.2, 1)
59. After Peter had left the house, he crossed the street. (9.6.2, 2)

C.6.5 INTRA- AND EXTRAPROPOSITIONAL COREFERENCE

60. Julia ate an apple. Then Julia took a nap. (10.1.2, 1)
61. Julia ate an apple. Then she took a nap. (10.1.2, 2)
62. %John shaved John. (10.1.2, 3)
63. John shaved himself. (10.1.2, 4; 10.2.3)
64. The man washed his hands, clipped his nails, and shaved himself. (10.1.2, 5)
65. That *Mary* had found the answer pleased *her*. (10.3.2)

66. *%She* knew that *Mary* had found the answer. (10.3.3)
67. That *she* had found the answer pleased *Mary*. (10.3.4)
68. *Mary* knew that *she* had found the answer. (10.3.5)
69. Every farmer who owns *a donkey* beats *it*. (10.4.2)
70. *%She* was kissed by the man who loves *the woman*. (10.4.3)
71. The man who loves *her* kissed *the woman*. (10.4.4)
72. *The woman* was kissed by the man who loves *her*. (10.4.5)
73. When *Mary* returned *she* kissed John. (10.5.2)
74. *%She* kissed John when *Mary* returned. (10.5.3)
75. When *she* returned *Mary* kissed John. (10.5.4)
76. *Mary* kissed John when *she* returned. (10.5.5)
77. When *Mary* returned John kissed *her*. (10.5.8)
78. %John kissed *her* when *Mary* returned. (10.5.9)
79. When *she* returned John kissed *Mary*. (10.5.10)
80. John kissed *Mary* when *she* returned. (10.5.11)
81. The man who deserves it will get the prize he wants. (10.6.2)

C.6.6 EXTRAPROPOSITIONAL COORDINATION

82. Julia sleeps. John sings. Susanne dreams. (11.5.1–11.5.4; 12.2.1–12.2.4; 12.5.1–12.5.4)

C.6.7 INTRAPROPOSITIONAL FUNCTOR–ARGUMENT STRUCTURE

83. The heavy old car hit a beautiful tree. The car had been speeding. A farmer gave the driver a lift. (13.3.1–13.5.8; 14.1.4; 14.4.1–14.6.9)

C.6.8 ADNOMINAL AND ADVERBIAL MODIFIERS

84. Julia ate the apple on the table behind the tree in the garden. (15.1.14; 15.2.1–15.2.8; 15.3.1; 15.3.2)
85. Julia ate the apple fast. (15.3.3; 15.3.4)
86. Julia ate the apple quickly on the table. (15.3.6)
87. Quickly Julia ate the apple. (15.3.7; 15.3.10)
88. On the table Julia ate the apple. (15.3.8)
89. Julia quickly ate the apple. (15.3.9)
90. On the table Julia quickly ate the apple. (15.3.11)
91. The very big table (15.4.4–15.4.6)
92. On the big table (15.4.7–15.4.9)
93. On the very big table (15.4.10–15.4.13)
94. Very quickly Julia ate the apple. (15.5.1–15.5.2)
95. Julia very quickly ate the apple. (15.5.3–15.5.4)
96. Julia ate the apple very quickly. (15.5.5–15.5.6)

C.6.9 REALIZING BASIC WORD ORDERS FROM TWO-PLACE PROPOSITIONS

97. The girl could have eaten an apple. (A.2.4)
98. Could the girl have eaten an apple? (A.4.2)
99. Aß das Mädchen den Apfel? (A.4.3)
100. Könnte das Mädchen einen Apfel gegessen haben? (A.4.4)
101. Could the apple have been eaten by the girl? (A.5.2)

Concluding Remark

According to Brooks (2002, p. 5), robots with human capabilities will be a reality by 2022. This raises the question of whether the computational reconstruction of natural language communication will be achieved (i) nonsymbolically on the basis of statistics alone or (ii) by a symbolic, rule-based, functional framework like Database Semantics (DBS), supplemented by statistics.

That statistics alone is not enough is shown by the following analogy:[1] "Imagine that the Martians came to Earth and modeled cars statistically: they would never run!" In other words, frequency-based correlations are not sufficient for building a working automobile. Instead, a detailed functional model of the combustion engine, the brakes, the steering mechanism, the transmission, the differential, etc., is required – and similarly for the computational reconstruction of natural language communication.

DBS has been designed to provide such a functional model by integrating

1. a traditional grammar approach based on the morpho-syntactic classification of word forms and the analysis of valency, agreement, and word order,
2. a traditional logic approach based on the notions of reference, functor–argument structure, coordination, coreference, and inference,
3. a modern database consisting of external interfaces, a data structure, and an algorithm, and
4. the methodological principles of interface equivalence, input/output equivalence, functional equivalence, and the incremental upscaling of an efficient (real-time) implementation for verifying the declarative specification of the overall system.

These components have been combined here in the systematic reconstruction of the robot's auto-channel (cf. 1.4.3). The resulting system is only a beginning, however. The many places in need of additional work are pointed out throughout the text.

---

[1] Borrowed from FoCL'99[2], p. 40.

Bibliography

Abney, S. (1991) "Parsing by chunks," in R. Berwick, S. Abney, and C. Tenny (eds.) *Principle-Based Parsing*. Dordrecht: Kluwer Academic

Ágel, V. (2000) *Valenztheorie*. Tübingen: Gunter Narr

AIJ'01 = Hausser, R. (2001) "Database Semantics for natural language," *Artificial Intelligence*, 130.1:27–74

Ajdukiewicz, K. (1935) "Die syntaktische Konnexität," *Studia Philosophica* 1:1–27

Anderson, J.R., and C. Lebiere (1998) *The Atomic Components of Thought*. Mahwah, NJ: Lawrence Erlbaum

Austin, J.L. (1962) *How to Do Things with Words*. Oxford, England: Clarendon Press

Barsalou, L. (1999) "Perceptual symbol systems," *Behavioral and Brain Sciences* 22:577–660

Bar-Hillel, Y. (1964) *Language and Information. Selected Essays on Their Theory and Application*. Reading, MA: Addison-Wesley

Barwise, J., and J. Perry (1983) *Situations and Attitudes*. Cambridge, MA: MIT Press

Beaugrande, R.-A., and W.U. Dressler (1981) *Einführung in die Textlinguistik*. Tübingen: Niemeyer

Berners-Lee, T., J. Hendler, and O. Lassila (2001) "The Semantic Web," *Scientific American*, May 17, 2001

Bertossi, L., G. Katona, K.-D. Schewe, and B. Thalheim (eds.) (2003) *Semantics in Databases*. Berlin Heidelberg New York: Springer

Biederman, I. (1987) "Recognition-by-components: a theory of human image understanding," *Psychological Review* 94:115–147

Bloomfield, L. (1933) *Language*, New York: Holt, Rinehart, and Winston

Bochenski, I. (1961) *A History of Formal Logic*. Notre Dame, Indiana: Univ. of Notre Dame Press

Bransford, J.D., and Franks, J.J. (1971) "The abstraction of linguistic ideas," *Cognitive Psychology* 2:331–350

Bresnan, J. (ed.) (1982) *The Mental Representation of Grammatical Relation.* Cambridge, MA: MIT Press

Bresnan, J. (2001) *Lexical-Functional Syntax.* Malden, MA: Blackwell

Brill, F. (1993) "Automatic grammar induction and parsing free text: a transformation-based approach," in *Proceedings of the 1993 European ACL*, The Netherlands: Utrecht

Brill, F. (1994) "Some advances in rule-based part of speech tagging," AAAI 1994

Brooks, R.A. (2002) *Flesh and Machines: How Robots Will Change Us.* New York, NY: Pantheon

Chang, Suk-Jin (1996) *Korean.* Philadelphia: John Benjamins

Carbonell, J.G., and R. Joseph (1986) *"FrameKit+: a knowledge representation system,"* Carnegie Mellon Univ., Department of Computer Science

Charniak, E. (2001) "Immediate-Head parsing for language models," Proceedings of the 39th Annual Meeting of the Association for Computational Linguistics

Carpenter, B. (1992) *The Logic of Typed Feature Structures*, Cambrigde: Cambridge Univ. Press

Choe, Jay-Woong, and R. Hausser (2006) "Handling quantifiers in database semantics," in Y. Kiyoki, H. Kangassalo, and M. Duží (eds.), *Information Modelling and Knowledge Bases XVII.* Amsterdam: IOS Press Ohmsha

Choi, Key-Sun, and Gil Chang Kim (1986) "Parsing Korean: a free word-order language," *Literary and Linguistic Computing* 1.3:123–128

Chomsky, N. (1957) *Syntactic Structures.* The Hague: Mouton

Chomsky, N. (1995) *The Minimalist Program.* Cambridge, MA: MIT Press

Clark, H. H. (1996) *Using Language.* Cambridge, UK: Cambridge Univ. Press

CoL'89 = Hausser, R. (1989) *Computation of Language, An Essay on Syntax, Semantics, and Pragmatics in Natural Man-Machine Communication*, Symbolic Computation: Artificial Intelligence, pp. 425, Berlin Heidelberg New York: Springer

Collins, M. J. (1999) *Head-driven Statistical Models for Natural Language Parsing.* Univ. of Pennsylvania, Ph.D. Dissertation

Copestake, A., D. Flickinger, C. Pollard, and I. Sag (2006) "Minimal Recursion Semantics: an introduction," *Research on Language and Computation* 3.4:281–332

Croft, W. (1995) "Modern syntactic typology," in M. Shibatani and T. Bynon (eds.) *Approaches to Language Typology*, Oxford: Clarendon Press

Dauses, A. (1997) *Einführung in die allgemeine Sprachwissenschaft: Sprachtypen, sprachliche Kategorien und Funktionen*. Stuttgart: Steiner

Déjean, H. (1998) *Concepts et algorithmes pour la découverte des structures formelles des langues*. Thèse pour l'obtention du Doctorat de l'université de Caen

Dorr, B. (1993) *Machine Translation: A View from the Lexicon*. Cambridge, MA: MIT Press

Earley, J. (1970) "An efficient context-free parsing algorithm," *Commun. ACM* 13.2:94–102, reprinted in B. Grosz, K. Sparck Jones, and B.L. Webber (eds.) *Readings in Natural Language Processing* (1986), Los Altos, CA: Morgan Kaufmann

Eberhard, K.M., M.J. Spivey-Knowlton, J.C. Sedivy, and M.K. Tanenhaus (1995) "Eye movements as a window into real-time spoken language comprehension in natural contexts," *Journal of Psycholinguistic Research* 24.6:409–437

Elmasri, R., and S.B. Navathe (1989) *Fundamentals of Database Systems*. Redwood City, CA: Benjamin-Cummings

Engel, U. (1991) *Deutsche Grammatik. 2nd ed.*, Heidelberg: Julius Groos

Fillmore, C., P. Kay, L. Michaelis, and Ivan A. Sag (forthcoming) *Construction Grammar*. Stanford: CSLI

Fischer, W. (2004) *Implementing Database Semantics as an RDMS*. Diplom Thesis, Department of Computer Science, Universität Erlangen–Nürnberg

FoCL'99 = Hausser, R. (1999/2001) *Foundations of Computational Linguistics, Human–Computer Communication in Natural Language, 2nd ed.*, pp. 578, Berlin Heidelberg New York: Springer

Frederking, R., T. Mitamura, E. Nyberg, and J. Carbonell (1997) "Translingual information access," presented at the AAAI Spring Symposium on Cross-Language Text and Speech Retrieval

Frege, G. (1967) *Kleine Schriften*. I. Angelelli (ed.), Darmstadt: Wissenschaftliche Buchgesellschaft

Gazdar, G., E. Klein, G. Pullum, and I. Sag (1985) *Generalized Phrase Structure Grammar*. Cambridge, MA: Harvard Univ. Press

Geach, P.T. (1969) "Quine's syntactical insights," in D. Davidson and J. Hintikka (eds.), *Words and Objections, Essays on the Work of W. v. Quine*. Dordrecht: Reidel

Geurts, B. (2002) "Donkey business," *Linguistics and Philosophy* 25:129–156

Gibson, E. J. (1969) *Principles of Perceptual Learning and Development*. Englewood Cliffs, NJ: Prentice Hall

Givòn, T. (1997) *Grammatical Relations: A Functionalist Perspective*. Amsterdam: John Benjamins

Greenbaum, S., and R. Quirk (1990) *A Student's Grammar of English*. London: Longman

Greenberg, J. (1963) "Some universals of grammar with particular reference to the order of meaningful elements," in J. Greenberg (ed.) *Universals of Language*. Cambridge, MA: MIT Press

Grice, P. (1957) "Meaning," *Philosophical Review* 66:377–388

Grice, P. (1965) "Utterer's meaning, sentence meaning, and word meaning," *Foundations of Language* 4:1–18

Grosz, B., and C. Sidner (1986) "Attention, intentions, and the structure of discourse," *Computational Linguistics* 12.3:175–204

Halliday, M.A.K., and R. Hasan (1976) *Cohesion in English*. London: Longman

Hanrieder, G. (1996) *Incremental Parsing of Spoken Language Using a Left-Associative Unification Grammar*. Inaugural Dissertation, CLUE, Universität Erlangen–Nürnberg [in German]

Hauser, M. D. (1996) *The Evolution of Communication*. Cambridge, MA: MIT Press

Hausser, R.: for references cited as SCG'84, NEWCAT'86, CoL'89, TCS'92, FoCL'1999, AIJ'01, and L&I'05, see p. VIII above. For online papers and a list of publications, see http://www.linguistik.uni-erlangen.de/de_contents/publications.php

Hausser, R. (2002a) "Autonomous control structure for artificial cognitive agents," in H. Kangassalo, H. Jaakkola, E. Kawaguchi, and T. Welzer (eds.) *Information Modeling and Knowledge Bases XIII*, Amsterdam: IOS Press Ohmsha

Hausser, R. (2005b) "What if Chomsky were right?" Comments on the paper "Multiple solutions to the logical problem of language acquisition" by Brian MacWhinney, *Journal of Child Language* 31:919–922

Helfenbein, D. (2005) *The Handling of Pronominal Coreference in Database Semantics*. MA-thesis, CLUE, Universität Erlangen–Nürnberg [in German]

Hellwig, P. (2003) "Dependency unification grammar," in V. Ágel, L.M. Eichinger, H.-W. Eroms, P. Hellwig, H.-J. Heringer, and H. Lobin (eds.) *Dependency and Valency. An International Handbook of Contemporary Research*, Berlin: Mouton de Gruyter

Herbst, T. (1999) "English valency structures – a first sketch," *Erfurt Electronic Studies in English* (EESE) 6/99

Herbst T., D. Heath, I. F. Roe, and D. Götz (2004) *A Valency Dictionary of English: A Corpus-Based Anaysis of the Complementation Patterns of English Verbs, Nouns, and Adjectives*. Berlin: Mouton de Gruyter

Heß, K., J. Brustkern, and W. Lenders (1983) *Maschinenlesbare Deutsche Lexika. Dokumentation – Vergleich – Integration.* Tübingen: Niemeyer

Hubel, D.H., and T.N. Wiesel (1962) "Receptive fields, binocular interaction, and functional architecture in the cat's visual cortex," *Journal of Physiology* 160:106–154

Hudson, R. A. (1976) "Conjunction reduction, gapping and right-node-raising," *Language* 52.3:535–562

Hudson, R. A. (1991) *English Word Grammar.* Oxford: Blackwell.

Hurford, J., M. Studdert-Kennedy, and C. Knight (1998) *Approaches to the Evolution of Language.* Cambridge, England: Cambridge Univ. Press

Ickler, T. (1994) "Zur Bedeutung der sogenannten 'Modalpartikeln'," in *Sprachwissenschaft* 19.3-4:374–404

Jackendoff, R. S. (1972) "Gapping and related rules," *Linguistic Inquiry* 2:21–35

Jacobson, P. (2000) "Paycheck pronouns, Bach–Peters sentences, and variable-free semantics," in *Natural Language Semantics* 8.2:77–155

Jezzard, P., P.M. Matthews, and S. Smith (2001) *Functional Magnetic Resonance Imaging: An Introduction to Methods.* Oxford: Oxford Univ. Press

Kamp, J.A.W., and U. Reyle (1993) *From Discourse to Logic.* Dordrecht: Kluwer

Kasami. T. (1965) "An efficient recognition and syntax algorithm for context-free languages," Technical Report AFCLR-65-758

Kay, M. (1980) "Algorithm schemata and data structures in syntactic processing," reprinted in B.J. Grosz, K. Sparck Jones, and B. Lynn Webber (eds.) *Readings in Natural Language Processing* (1986). San Mateo, CA: Morgan Kaufmann, 35–70

Kempson, R., and Cormack, A. (1981) "Ambiguity and quantification," *Linguistics and Philosophy* 4:259–309

Kirkpatrick, K. (2001) "Object recognition," Chapter 4 of G. Cook (ed.) *Avian Visual Cognition.* Cyberbook in cooperation with Comparative Cognitive Press, http://www.pigeon.psy.tufts.edu/avc/toc.htm

Kučera, H., and W.N. Francis (1967) *Computational Analysis of Present-Day English.* Providence, Rhode Island: Brown Univ. Press

Kycia, A. (2004) *An Implementation of Database Semantics in Java.* MA-thesis, CLUE, Universität Erlangen–Nürnberg [in German]

L&I'05 = Hausser, R. (2005) "Memory-Based pattern completion in Database Semantics," *Language and Information*, 9.1:69–92, Seoul: Korean Society for Language and Information

Lakoff, G., and M. Johnson (1980) *Metaphors We Live By*. Chicago: The Univ. of Chicago Press

Lakoff, G., and S. Peters (1969) "Phrasal conjunction and symmetric predicates," in D.A. Reibel and S. Schane (eds.), 113–142

Langacker, R. (1969) "Pronominalization and the chain of command," in D.A. Reibel and S. A. Schane (eds.), 160–186

Lee, Kiyong (2002) "A simple syntax for complex semantics," in *Language, Information, and Computation,* Proceedings of the 16th Pacific Asia Conference, 2–27

Lee, Kiyong (2004) "A computational treatment of some case-related problems in Korean," *Perspectives on Korean Case and Case Marking*, 21–56, Seoul: Taehaksa

Lees, R.B., and E.S. Klima (1963) "Rules for English pronominalization," *Language* 39:17–28

Lenders, W. (1990) "Semantische Relationen in Wörterbuch-Einträgen – Eine Computeranalyse des DUDEN-Universalwörterbuchs," *Proceedings of the GLDV-Jahrestagung 1990*, 92–105

Lenders, W. (1993) "Tagging – Formen und Tools," *Proceedings of the GLDV-Jahrestagung 1993*, 369–401

Leśniewski, S. (1929) "Grundzüge eines neuen Systems der Grundlagen der Mathematik," Warsaw: *Fundamenta Mathematicae* 14:1–81

LIMAS-Korpus (1973) Mannheim: Institut für Deutsche Sprache.

Liu, Haitao (2001) "Some ideas on natural language processing," in *Terminology Standardization and Information Technology* 1:23–27

Lobin, H. (1993a) "Linguistic perception and syntactic structure," in E. Hajicova (ed.) *Functional Description of Language,* Charles Univ., Prague

Lobin, H. (1993b) *Koordinations-Syntax als prozedurales Phänomen*. Tübingen: Gunter Narr

MacWhinney, B. (1987) "The Competition Model," in B. MacWhinney (ed.) *Mechanisms of Language Acquisition,* 249–308, Hillsdale, NJ: Lawrence Erlbaum

MacWhinney, B. (ed.) (1999) *The Emergence of Language from Embodiment*. Hillsdale, NJ: Lawrence Erlbaum

MacWhinney, B. (2004) "A multiple process solution to the logical problem of language acquisition," *Journal of Child Language* 31:883–914

MacWhinney, B. (2005a) "Item-based constructions and the logical problem," *ACL 2005*, 46–54

MacWhinney, B. (2005b) "The emergence of grammar from perspective," in D. Pecher and R. A. Zwaan (eds.), *The Grounding of Cognition: The Role of Perception and Action in Memory, Language, and Thinking*, 198-223, Mahwah, NJ: Lawrence Erlbaum

März, B. (2005) *The Handling of Coordination in Database Semantics*. MA-thesis, CLUE, Universität Erlangen–Nürnberg [in German]

Mann, W.C., and S. A. Thompson (eds.) 1993 *Discourse Description: Diverse Linguistic Analyses of a Fund-Raising Text*. Amsterdam: John Benjamins

Matthews, P.M., J. Adcock, Y. Chen, S. Fu, J. T. Devlin, M. F. S. Rushworth, S. Smith, C. Beckmann, and S. Iversen (2003) "Towards understanding language organisation in the brain using fMRI" in *Human Brain Mapping* 18.3: 239–247

Mel'čuk, I. A. (1988) *Dependency Syntax: Theory and Practice*. New York: State Univ. of New York Press

Mel'čuk, I. A., and A. Polguère (1987) "A formal lexicon in the meaning-text theory," in *Computational Linguistics* 13.3-4:13–54

Meyer-Wegener, K. (2003) *Multimediale Datenbanken: Einsatz von Datenbanktechnik in Multimedia-Systemen. 2nd ed.*, Wiesbaden: Teubner

Montague, R. (1974) *Formal Philosophy*. New Haven: Yale Univ. Press

Neisser, U. (1964). "Visual search," *Scientific American* 210.6:94–102

NEWCAT'86 = Hausser, R. (1986) *NEWCAT: Parsing Natural Language Using Left-Associative Grammar*, Lecture Notes in Computer Science 231, pp. 540, Berlin Heidelberg New York: Springer

Newton, I. (1687/1999) *The Principia: Mathematical Principles of Natural Philosophy*. I.B. Cohen and A. Whitman (Translators), Berkeley: Univ. of California Press.

Nichols, J. (1992) *Linguistic Diversity in Space and Time*. Chicago: The University of Chicago Press

Nyberg, E.H., and T. Mitamura (2002) "Evaluating QA systems on multiple dimensions," paper presented at the LREC Workshop on Resources and Evaluation for Question Answering Systems, Las Palmas, Canary Island, Spain, May 28, 2002

Nyberg, E. (1988) *"The FrameKit User's Guide, Version 2.0,"* CMU-CMT-MEMO

Östman, J.-O., and M. Fried (eds.) (2004) *Construction Grammars: Cognitive Grounding and Theoretical Extensions*. Amsterdam: John Benjamins

van Oirsouw, R. R. (1987) *The Syntax of Coordination*. London: Croom Helm

Peirce, C.S. *Collected Papers*. C. Hartshorne and P. Weiss (eds.), Cambridge, MA: Harvard Univ. Press. 1931–1935

Pereira, F., and S. Shieber (1987) *Prolog and Natural-Language Analysis*. Stanford: CSLI

Peters, S., and Ritchie, R. (1973) "On the generative power of transformational grammar," *Information and Control* 18:483–501

Piaget, J. (1926) *The Language and Thought of the Child*. London: Routledge

Pollard, C., and I. Sag (1987) *Information-Based Syntax and Semantics. Vol. I, Fundamentals*. Stanford: CSLI

Pollard, C., and I. Sag (1994) *Head-Driven Phrase Structure Grammar*. Stanford: CSLI

Portner, P. (2005) "The semantics of imperatives within a theory of clause types," in Kazuha Watanabe and R.B. Young (eds.), *Proceedings of Semantics and Linguistic Theory 14*. Ithaca, NY: CLC Publications

Post, E. (1936) "Finite combinatory processes – formulation I," *Journal of Symbolic Logic* I:103–105

Quillian, M. (1968) "Semantic memory," in M. Minsky (ed.), *Semantic Information Processing*, 227–270, Cambridge, MA: MIT Press

Quine, W. v. O. (1960) *Word and Object*. Cambridge, MA: MIT Press

Quirk, R., J. Svartvik, G. Leech, and S. Greenbaum (1985) *A Comprehensive Grammar of the English Language*. New York: Longman

Reibel, D.A., and S. A. Schane (eds.) (1969) *Modern Studies of English*. Englewood Cliffs, NJ: Prentice Hall

Reiter, E., and R. Dale (1997) "Building applied natural-language generation systems," *Journal of Natural-Language Engineering* 3:57–87

Rosch, E. (1975) "Cognitive representations of semantic categories," *Journal of Experimental Psychology*, General 104:192–253

Ross, J.R. (1969) *On the cyclic nature of English pronominalization*, in D.A. Reibel and S. A. Schane (eds.), 187–200

Ross, J. R. (1970) "Gapping and the order of constituents," in Bierwisch, M., and K. E. Heidolph (eds.) *Progress in Linguistics*. The Hague: Mouton

Roy, D. (2003) "Grounded spoken language acquisition: experiments in word learning," *IEEE Transactions on Multimedia* 5.2:197–209

Russell, B. (1905) "On denoting," *Mind* 14:479–493

Sag, I., G. Gazdar, T. Wasow, and S. Weisler (1985) "Coordination and how to distinguish categories," *Natural Language and Linguistic Theory* 3:117–171

Schank, R., and R. Abelson (1977) *Scripts, Plans, Goals, and Understanding: An Inquiry into Human Knowledge Structures*. Hillsdale, NJ: Lawrence Erlbaum

Saussure, F. de (1972) *Cours de linguistique générale*. Édition critique préparée par Tullio de Mauro, Paris: Éditions Payot

SCG'84 = Hausser, R. (1984) *Surface Compositional Grammar*, pp. 274, München: Wilhelm Fink Verlag

Searle, J.R. (1969) *Speech Acts*. Cambridge, England: Cambridge Univ. Press

Sedivy, J.C., M.K. Tanenhaus, C.G. Chambers, and G.N. Carlson (1999) "Achieving incremental semantic interpretation through contextual representation," *Cognition* 71:109–147

Shieber, S. (ed.) (2004) *The Turing Test. Verbal Behavior as the Hallmark of Intelligence*. Cambridge, MA: MIT Press

Sowa, J.F. (1984) *Conceptual Structures*. Reading, MA: Addison-Wesley

Sowa, J. F. (2000) *Conceptual Graph Standard*. Revised version of December 6, 2000. http://www.bestweb.net/ sowa/cg/cgstand.htm

Spivey, M.J., M.K. Tanenhaus, K.M. Eberhard, and J.C. Sedivy (2002) "Eye movements and spoken language comprehension: effects of visual context on syntactic ambiguity resolution," *Cognitive Psychology* 45: 447–481

Stassen, L. (1985) *Comparison and Universal Grammar*, Oxford: Basil Blackwell

Steedman, M. (2005) "Surface-Compositional scope-alternation without existential quantifiers," Draft 5.1, Sept 2005

Steels, L. (1999) *The Talking Heads Experiment*. Antwerp: limited pre-edition for the Laboratorium exhibition

Stein, N. L., and Trabasso, T. (1982). "What's in a story? An approach to comprehension," in R. Glaser (ed.), *Advances in the Psychology of Instruction. Vol. 2*, 213–268. Hillsdale, NJ: Lawrence Erlbaum

Tarski, A. (1935) "Der Wahrheitsbegriff in den Formalisierten Sprachen," *Studia Philosophica* I:262–405

Tarski, A. (1944) "The semantic concept of truth," in *Philosophy and Phenomenological Research* 4:341–375

TCS'92 = Hausser, R. (1992) "Complexity in Left-Associative Grammar," *Theoretical Computer Science*, 106.2:283-308

Tesnière, L. (1959) *Éléments de syntaxe structurale*. Paris: Editions Klincksieck

Thórisson, K. (2002) "Natural turn-taking needs no manual: computational theory and model, from perception to action," in B. Granström, D. House, and I. Karlsson (eds.) *Multimodality in Language and Speech System*, 173–207, Dordrecht: Kluwer

Tomasello, M. (1999) *The Cultural Origin of Human Cognition*. Cambridge, MA: Harvard Univ. Press

Tomita, M. (1986) *Efficient Parsing for Natural Language*. Boston: Kluwer Academic

Tugwell, D. (1998) *Dynamic Syntax*. Ph.D. Thesis, Univ. of Edinburgh

Twiggs, M. (2005) *The Handling of Passive in Database Semantics*. MA-thesis, CLUE, Universität Erlangen–Nürnberg [in German]

Vergne, J., and E. Giguet (1998) "Regards théoriques sur le 'tagging'," in proceedings of the fifth annual conference *Le Traitement Automatique des Langues Naturelles* (TALN)

Weydt, H. (1969) *Abtönungspartikel. Die deutschen Modalwörter und ihre französischen Entsprechungen*. Bad Homburg: Gehlen

Wittgenstein, L. (1921) "Logisch-philosophische Abhandlung," *Annalen der Naturphilosophie* 14:185–262

Winograd T. (1983) *Language as a Cognitive Process*. London: Addison-Wesley

Wierzbicka, A. (1991) *Cross-Cultural Pragmatics: The Semantics of Human Interaction*. Berlin: Mouton de Gruyter

Younger, D. (1967) "Recognition and parsing of context-free languages in time n 3," *Information and Control* 10.2:189–208

Name Index

Subject Index